BEYOND THE NORTHLANDS

BEYOND THE NORTHLANDS

VIKING VOYAGES AND THE
OLD NORSE SAGAS

Eleanor Rosamund
Barraclough

OXFORD
UNIVERSITY PRESS

UNIVERSITY PRESS

Great Clarendon Street, Oxford, OX2 6DP,
United Kingdom

Oxford University Press is a department of the University of Oxford.
It furthers the University's objective of excellence in research, scholarship,
and education by publishing worldwide. Oxford is a registered trade mark of
Oxford University Press in the UK and in certain other countries

First Edition published in 2016

Impression: 1

Published in the United States of America by Oxford University Press
198 Madison Avenue, New York, NY 10016, United States of America

British Library Cataloguing in Publication Data
Data available

Library of Congress Control Number: 2016931924

ISBN 978-0-19-870124-8

Printed in Great Britain by
Bell & Bain Ltd., Glasgow

For Lindsey, Richard, Imogen, Christian, Rowena,
and Benjamin, my own viking warband.

ACKNOWLEDGEMENTS

There's a word in Old Norse—*heimr*—that means both 'world' and 'home'. This says a lot about how the Norse viewed things. Over the course of researching and writing this book, I've explored many worlds and found many homes, thanks to the kindness of those I met on the way. In fact, I've met so many people that someone is bound to have slipped off these pages, in which case apologies and thanks to you too. Mistakes, typos, oversights, bloopers, inaccuracies, clangers—all are of course my own.

I found my first home as an undergraduate at Cambridge, in the Department of Anglo-Saxon, Norse and Celtic (ASNC). Many thanks to Judy Quinn, for introducing me to the joys of Old Norse, whetting my appetite for adventures in far-flung northern climes, and good-naturedly refusing to accept my panic-stricken letter of resignation during the first term of my Ph.D. Heartfelt thanks also to Elizabeth Ashman Rowe, for her boundless generosity in reading and commenting on anything and everything I sent her, including a full draft of this book. Thanks also to Jonny Grove for setting me on the right research track several times, first with trolls, then with landscapes, both of which fed into this book one way or another. For their masochistic insistence on reading tortuous early draft chapters that no one should have been subjected to, I am eternally grateful to Rosie Bonté and Denis Casey. Warmest thanks also to Pamela Welsh and Dan Carr, who were unfortunate enough to befriend an ASNCer, kind enough to read the whole book, and now know more about vikings than they ever wanted to. Finally, there's no way I could ever thank Paul Russell enough, so I'm not going to try. Hopefully he knows.

Moving onto Oxford I found another home. To Heather O'Donoghue, who supported me throughout my time there, thank you. I am deeply grateful to Carolyne Larrington for countless reasons, not least for reading an entire draft of this book. From her comments I have learnt many useful things, not least that 'hoards' and 'hordes' are not interchangeable entities, there is no travel-guide series called *Lonely Plant*, private parts are not covered in public hair, vikings do not sail in hips, and the adjective 'weird' should be used sparingly. I found another extraordinary home and extraordinary friends as an

Extraordinary Junior Research Fellow at The Queen's College, thanks to Rebecca Beasley, Paul Madden, and many other fellows and staff. Becky, you helped me in so many wonderful ways with this project. To John Blair, thank you for your guidance, support, and friendship. To Chris Salamone, who walked me around the Botanic Garden when my brain needed unknotting and acted as my partner in crime when there were chocolate biscuits to liberate from the tea cupboard, thank you. To Alison Madden, thank you for giving me a place to lay my head and for your stirring performance as Byrhtnoth in our 'Battle of Maldon' re-enactment. Sorry for choosing the coldest day of the year for that road-trip. And to those at the Leverhulme Trust who took a punt on me and offered me the Early Career Fellowship to write this book, thank you from the bottom of my heart.

I'm very grateful to Durham University for giving me my next home, and to Elizabeth Archibald most of all for her unwavering support and friendship. Like Halley's Comet, people like Elizabeth only appear once or twice in a lifetime, and I'm very lucky to have caught her mid-orbit. Through Elizabeth, I also found myself part of another family, St Cuthbert's Society: thank you to JCR and SCR members alike for enduring, even encouraging, so many viking-themed conversations. I am extraordinarily lucky to have found such good friends at Durham, many of whom fuelled my writing with tea and cake, read chapter drafts and even provided photographs for this book. Thank you particularly to Helen Foxhall Forbes, Megan Cavell, James Brown, Mandy Green, Phil Bolton, and Frances Leviston. Thank you also to Daniel Newman for his help with Arabic translations, and to Giles Gasper for the elephant tip-off.

Beyond Cambridge, Oxford, and Durham, I am grateful to be part of an extraordinary network of Norse scholars. First and foremost, thank you to Judith Jesch at Nottingham, who is always on hand to impart wisdom, however daft my questions. Thank you to Matthew James Driscoll at the Arnamagnæan Institute in Copenhagen, who has also endured more than his fair share of my daft questions over the years. *Takk fyrir* to Svanhildur Óskarsdóttir and Haukur Þorgeirsson at the Árni Magnússon Institute for Icelandic Studies in Reykjavík, and to everyone in both institutes who helped me out with manuscripts. Thank you to Dale Kedwards and Tom Birkett for not pretending my multiple emails had got lost in the post. Thank you to John Shafer, for directing me to his Ph.D. thesis (available online for all interested readers). Thank you to Turi King, who helped explain viking DNA to a bear of very little brain.

And thank you to my 'Supernatural North' partners in crime, Stefan Donecker and Danielle Cudmore, whose ideas helped to shape my own.

Unexpectedly, I also found myself another home in which to finish this book, over the ocean at the University of Wisconsin–Madison (which is even further than Leif the Lucky got). Deepest thanks to the Department of Scandinavian Studies for welcoming me with open arms, and to Kirsten Wolf and Peggy Hager in particular. Thank you also to the Institute for Research in the Humanities, especially Ann Harris, who looked after me so well that at one point I had *two* offices. As I'm sure the vikings also knew, ports in storms can come from unexpected directions.

Researching this book has taken me on all sorts of far-flung adventures of my own, thanks to the generosity of many funding bodies: the Leverhulme Trust, the Department of Anglo-Saxon, Norse and Celtic in Cambridge, The Queen's College and Faculty of English Language and Literature in Oxford, and the Department of English Studies, the Faculty of Arts and Humanities, and the Institute for Medieval and Early Modern Studies in Durham. Thanks to all of these sources of funding, I have been knighted by a walrus penis bone in the Royal and Ancient Polar Bear Society and terrified out of my wits in a deserted Arctic lighthouse. I have skinny-dipped in a Greenlandic fjord, developed saddle-sores from too many weeks on the back of an Icelandic horse, and been rescued by a Greenlandic farm dog who sensed that a hungry polar bear had come ashore. I have been proposed to by a spice merchant in Istanbul's Grand Bazaar, and danced all night in Rome at a party to honour a transvestite prostitute called Renata. I've also done a fair amount of research on the way. All these adventures mean that I have quite a few more people to thank.

In Greenland, little did I know that the man I sat next to when cadging a ride with a boatful of archaeologists would become such a good friend and guide to Norse Greenland. Georg Nyegaard has already told me off for saying thank you too many times, but I have a thousand reasons to thank him so I'll get round it with a simple *tusind tak*. Thank you also to everyone at Grönlandsresor for their many kindnesses and for keeping me alive in Greenland that first summer: Monika Larsson, Silke Gersdorf, and of course Jytte Christensen, one of the toughest and most capable individuals I have ever encountered. Talking of tough and capable individuals, thank you to also to Michael Rosing—caribou hunter, politician, sailor, and reindeer cookbook author—and Miilla Lennert, both of whom kept me alive the second summer with such panache. Heartfelt thanks also to Henrik Skydsbjerg at Tupilak Travel in Nuuk, and to his daughter Arnajaraq. In Ilulissat, thank you to Silver—perhaps the only Italian living in Arctic Greenland—at Ilulissat Tourist Nature, who together with his wife looked after me with such kindness. Closer to home, I'm grateful to Kevin Edwards at Aberdeen, who was always ready to answer emails that popped up in his inbox with subject lines such as 'More Bloody Polar Bears', and to Hanne Thirup Fahl for the Danish lessons that got me round Greenland in one piece. Finally, warmest thanks to Stephen and Pauline Moorbath for afternoon teas in the conservatory and tales of Arctic adventures past.

In Istanbul, many thanks to Abdil and Ozkan Bircer at Turkey Tours by Local Guides. In Rome, love, thanks, and a million *baci* to Antonia Silvaggi, and to Enrico Cava, Monica Zorzan, Antonio David Fiore, Giorgio Cacioppo, Emilia De Cola, Stefano Repoli, and little Leonardo. Never again will any research trip be complete without a toddler in tow. In Tromsø, hearty thanks to Richard Holt and Rune Blix Hagen for being such brilliant sports every time I pointed a microphone at them, to the rest of the 'Creating the New North' research group for their feedback, and to Reidar Bertelsen for the photographs. A little further down the coast, thank you to Runar Storeide for his quiet generosity. Enormous thanks also to the BBC's Philippa Ritchie, fellow arctic explorer and friend, and to everyone at the BBC who was interested enough in this research project to sign me up as a New Generation Thinker and kept letting me back into Broadcasting House afterwards, particularly Matthew Dodd, Fiona McLean, Robyn Read, Melvin Rickarby, and Jacqueline Smith.

Deepest thanks to Peter Robinson, my agent at *RCW*, who was there from that first crackly phone conversation from Greenland and didn't give up on me even when I started sending emails with 'Dooooooooom' in the subject line. Thank you also to his then-assistant Alex Goodwin, who got me back onto the right track during the longest coffee meeting in history (the caffeine will have probably left my bloodstream by the end of the decade), and to Federica Leonardis. I am incredibly lucky to have found such a marvellous commissioning editor in Matthew Cotton at Oxford University Press, who made the whole thing so much fun and discovered my weakness for millionaire's shortbread. Thank you also to Matthew Humphrys, Luciana O'Flaherty, Kizzy Taylor-Richelieu and Emma Slaughter who saw the project through to the end, to picture researcher Rosanna van den Bogaerde, to copy-editor Jeff New and proofreader Andrew Hawkey, and to mapmaker Tom Coulson.

Finally, it's an old cliché but *heimr* is most definitely where the heart is, and I reserve my biggest thanks for my family. To my mum Lindsey, my first reader and my fellow far traveller on so many adventures (sorry about the occasional broken bones and for making you walk up that volcano). To my dad Richard for his uncanny belief that I was destined to follow the Norsemen even when I had an enormous teenage strop, threw a book from the Jorvik Viking Centre down the stairs after him, and said I never wanted to study ASNC (apologies are more than a decade overdue). To Imogen, Christian, and Benjamin, for listening to my feverish viking ramblings on so many long walks and car drives (and double thanks to Imo, not only for reading my work but also for writing that 'My Loverly Little Storee of Vikings in the Eest By Eli Barracluff' chapter for me). To Rowena, for giving me the confidence to go out into the world, even if I got pretty wet and muddy in the process. And to John Clay, who read every damn page until he went cross-eyed, communicated his professional criticism in the form of cartoon marginalia, and listened patiently to my 'never writing a book again' rants before taking me out for head-clearing hikes. For this and so much more, there aren't enough thanks in the world. Bring on the next adventure.

CONTENTS

LIST OF ILLUSTRATIONS

LIST OF MAPS

BASIC PRONUNCIATION GUIDE
TO TRICKY LETTERS

For the most part, I have given Old Norse personal and place-names in their Anglicized forms (for example, *Gudrid* and *Thorstein* rather than *Guðríðr* and *Þórsteinn*). Modern Nordic personal and place-names are in the original. Occasionally words and names have been quoted in Old Norse, in italics. In these cases the following rough pronunciation guide might be useful. Since most literature written in Old Norse comes from Iceland, and, relatively speaking, there haven't been many pronunciation changes in the intervening centuries—far fewer than, say, the pronunciation changes between Chaucer's English and Modern English—it is common to pronounce Old Norse according to Modern Icelandic pronunciation. This is what is described below, although there are plenty of online guides available for those who want to know more about the intricacies of the subject.

Á / á = as in 'h<u>ow</u>'
É / é = as in '<u>ye</u>ll'
Í / í = as in 'sw<u>ee</u>t'
Ó / ó = as in 'sl<u>ow</u>'
Ú / ú = as in 't<u>oo</u>'

Ð / ð = as in '<u>th</u>is' (voiced 'th')
Þ / þ = as in '<u>th</u>in' (unvoiced 'th')
J / j = as in '<u>y</u>es'
ll / rl = '<u>tl</u>'
r = short rolled 'rr' (barely one trill)

Æ / æ = as in 'w<u>i</u>ne'
Œ / œ = as in 'w<u>i</u>ne'
Ǫ / ǫ = as in 'f<u>u</u>r'

Useful Modern Scandinavian letters:

Æ / æ = as in 'p<u>a</u>t' or 'b<u>a</u>d'
Å / å = as in '<u>a</u>we' or 'l<u>a</u>w'
Ø / ø = as in 'f<u>u</u>r' or 's<u>i</u>r'

· Vikings ·

A longboat full of Vikings, promoting the new British Museum exhibition, was seen sailing past the Palace of Westminster yesterday. Famously uncivilised, destructive and rapacious, with an almost insatiable appetite for rough sex and heavy drinking, the MPs nonetheless looked up for a bit to admire the vessel.

The Times, 16 April 2014

CHAPTER 1

Inroads from the Sea

Dragons over Northumbria

The vikings have always had a reputation as the bad boys of the medieval world: axe-wielding village pillagers and bloodthirsty monk-murderers with names such as Ivar the Boneless, Erik Bloodaxe, and Ragnar Hairy-Breeches. They could hardly complain about the bad press. After all, their first major attack in England was a brutal raid on the island monastery of Lindisfarne, in the summer of AD 793. According to the *Anglo-Saxon Chronicle*,* their arrival was foreshadowed by omens that seared the Northumbrian sky:

In this year came dreadful portents over the land of the Northumbrians, and the people were terrified most pitifully. There were immeasurable whirlwinds and sheets of lightning, and fiery dragons were seen flying through the air. These signs were soon followed by a great famine, and a little after that…the despicable ravaging of the heathen men annihilated God's church on Lindisfarne with plundering and slaughter.[1]

Lindisfarne—also known as Holy Island—is a tidal island two miles off the Northumbrian coastline. At the time of the attack, it lay in the political heartlands

---

* The *Anglo-Saxon Chronicle* is made up of seven main manuscripts. It began to be written down nearly a century after this raid, during the reign of King Alfred (r. 871–99). By the late ninth century things had got decidedly sticky for the Anglo-Saxons, and the invaders were in charge of a large part of England. With the benefit of ninth-century hindsight, it was clear that the events that had taken place in the dying years of the eighth century had heralded a terrible sea-change for the Anglo-Saxon world.

of the Anglo-Saxon north; a fabulously wealthy ecclesiastical powerhouse. To give some idea of the monastery's clout, it was here that the Lindisfarne Gospels were created in around AD 700. This beautiful manuscript is one of the finest treasures of the Anglo-Saxon world, crawling with densely knotted interlace patterns and thickly textured with coloured inks and gold leaf. Originally it was bound in a priceless leather cover studded with jewels and metals—a 'treasure binding'—made by a hermit and goldsmith named Billfrith. The manuscript was made to honour St Cuthbert (c.634–87), who had led the community at Lindisfarne and is patron saint of northern England. When St Cuthbert's coffin was opened in the nineteenth century, eye-wateringly expensive items from seventh-century Lindisfarne were discovered inside, including a comb made of elephant ivory, an embossed silver altar cloth, and a golden cross studded with garnets.

Books, saints, and prayers were no defence against axes and swords wielded by heathens from across the North Sea. Lindisfarne was unprotected and conveniently cut off at high tide, with low sandy bays perfect for landing shallow-bottomed longboats. As far as the vikings were concerned, Lindisfarne was a plump sitting duck. Two weeks before midsummer, when the long days

FIGURE 1.1 Lindisfarne, overlooking the bay by the monastery

stretched out as far as the wide horizon, dark blurs appeared on the skyline. Gradually, the blurs grew into longboats, slicing through the sea towards the Northumbrian coast. Their square sails swollen with summer wind, the boats bore down on the island.

It would have been no comfort to the monks of Lindisfarne, but these vessels were at the cutting edge of ship technology: powerful oak vessels with stable keels and thin, flexible frame timbers. They were capable of battling the heavy gales and high waves that the sailors would have encountered as they left the relative safety of their coastlines and voyaged further afield across the wide ocean. From a Scandinavian point of view, this well-tuned little nautical orchestra was a thing of beauty: a testament to technological accomplishment and fine craftsmanship. From an Anglo-Saxon point of view, it was an instrument of God's divine retribution.

Perhaps the monks were at prayer, or at their chores, or tucking into lunch, when news came that unknown vessels were nearing the shore. Perhaps they hurried out to see what the fuss was about, or barricaded themselves inside and prayed for deliverance. Whatever their reaction, the events that followed were more brutal than anyone could have imagined. Weapons gripped in their gnarled, sea-weathered hands, the vikings fell upon Lindisfarne 'like stinging hornets' and 'fearful wolves', as the twelfth-century writer Symeon of Durham described it. They plundered the monastery, dug up the altars, and seized any valuables they could find. The monks were cut down where they stood, or taken to the sea to be drowned. The luckier ones were driven away, 'naked and loaded with insults', while others were trussed up, presumably destined for the slave market.[2]

No eyewitness accounts survive of the bloody strike. The only testimony from the monastery itself is a memorial stone made in the following century, perhaps commissioned by the monks to remember their butchered brothers. The stone bears witness to the terrible events that took place on that day in early June. On one side, seven warriors stand ready to attack, swords and axes raised above their heads. On the other side, little figures kneel before the cross, the sun and moon hang in the sky, and two hands reach out to encircle the world: Judgement Day has arrived.

As news of the attack spread, shockwaves reverberated through the country and across the water into Europe. Word reached the ears of Alcuin, an

Anglo-Saxon monk and scholar who was living at the court of Charlemagne. Horrified, he wrote to the Northumbrian king Aethelred:

Never before has such terror appeared in Britain as we have now suffered from a pagan race, nor was it thought that such an inroad from the sea could be made. Behold, the church of St Cuthbert, splattered with the blood of the priests of God, despoiled of all its ornaments.[3]

Alcuin came from York and was well acquainted with the local monastic communities in Northumbria; perhaps he even knew some of the victims. Certainly he knew Higbald, who was bishop of Lindisfarne at the time of the attack. Alcuin's letter to his friend moves swiftly through a gamut

FIGURE 1.2a One side of the Lindisfarne memorial stone depicting seven armed figures

FIGURE 1.2b The other side of the Lindisfarne memorial stone depicting Judgement Day

of emotions: anguish for what his brothers had endured, distress at the pagan violations, forebodings of further disasters, an uneasy suspicion that sins must have been committed to merit this divine punishment, and a determined call for the brothers to defend themselves:

The calamity of your tribulation saddens me greatly every day, though I am absent; when the pagans desecrated the sanctuaries of God, and poured out the blood of saints around the altar, laid waste to the house of our hope, trampled on the bodies of saints in the temple of God like dung on the streets.... Either this is the beginning of greater tribulation, or else the sins of the inhabitants have called it upon them. Truly it has not happened by chance, but is a sign that it was well merited by someone. But now, you who are left, stand manfully, fight bravely, defend the camp of God.[4]

Unhappily, Alcuin's fears of hardships still to come were not unfounded. He could not have known it, but as he listened to grave reports from the north, what he was hearing was the first rattling pebbles of a landslide that would rumble and thunder down the centuries, shaking the coastlines and waterways of Western Europe. Ever since, AD 793 has been emblazoned on the parchments of medieval chronicles and the pages of history books: the ominous year in which the curtain rose on the Viking Age.

Danelaw

Of course, history is rarely so cut-and-dried. The attack on Lindisfarne wasn't even the first time that Scandinavians had spilt blood on Anglo-Saxon shores. According to the *Anglo-Saxon Chronicle*, a smaller scuffle took place four or five years earlier, at the other end of the country, on the Isle of Portland in Dorset. On this occasion, it was a royal official who got it in the neck:

In these days there first came three ships of the Northmen, and the royal official rode down to meet them. He wanted to take them to the king's town because he didn't know who they were, but there they killed him. These were the first ships of the Danish men that sought out the land of the English.[5]

Shocking as these events were—not least for the unfortunate royal official in question—the episode is hardly on a par with descriptions of the Lindisfarne raid, with dragons in the sky and blood on the altars. It isn't even clear what three boatloads of Scandinavians were doing in Dorset. The description in the *Anglo-Saxon Chronicle* hardly sounds like a planned attack, and certainly not the sort of let's-pillage-this-village type of raid that battered the shores of Lindisfarne.

Nevertheless, an unpleasant sea-change was blowing in from chilly northern waters. Rumours of unidentified pagan pirates loitering around the coastal waters of Britain and Western Europe buzz nervously at the edges of texts from this period. For example, the *Royal Frankish Annals* describe how in 800 Charlemagne organized a defensive fleet in the coastal region adjoining the Gallic sea, 'which was then infested with pirates'.[6] After a flurry of raids—the plundering of Lindisfarne was followed by attacks on monasteries such as Monkwearmouth-Jarrow in north-east England and Iona in Scotland—things went quiet for a time. But by the mid-ninth century a new wave of Nordic invaders had returned to trouble the country, and this time they intended to stay.

In 865 the Great Heathen Army landed on England's south coast. They brought East Anglia to its knees, and then sliced their way up the country, led by two brothers called Ivar and Halfdan. Several centuries later, Ivar was furnished with an unusual nickname—'boneless'—which has spawned several interesting theories regarding his character and physical attributes: perhaps a not-very-subtle reference to his deficiencies in the bedroom, or an indication that he suffered from *osteogenesis imperfecta* ('brittle-bone disease'). More likely, the explanation is less colourful: a misreading of the Latin word *exosus* ('detestable') as *exos* ('boneless').*[7] As the Anglo-Saxons and their Scandinavian aggressors battled for control, kingdoms began to topple. Over the years, territorial boundaries were drawn and redrawn, first in blood, then on the parchment pages of peace treaties. But the struggles continued.

The tenth century dawned on an England ripped in half, with much of eastern and central England under Scandinavian control. In time, this area became known as the Danelaw. By the middle of the century, the shadowy figure of Erik Bloodaxe was ruling Northumbria from the viking stronghold of York—*Jórvík*—before being driven out and killed in 954. With Erik's death, viking rule came to an end, at least for the time being. But towards

---

* According to the Norse legends that grew up around Ivar, he and his brothers (who by now had acquired imaginative names such as Bjorn Ironside and Sigurd Snake-in-the-Eye) were spurred on by the death of their father, who had been murdered by the king of Northumbria. The sons exacted the nastiest form of revenge on their father's killer: the Blood Eagle. The victim was placed face down while his ribs were cut from his spine and pulled outwards. Then his lungs were drawn out through his back, so that the ribs and lungs were exposed like bloody wings. This all sounds very unpleasant, but whether or not this practice ever took place is a matter of considerable debate. (See R. Frank, 'Viking Atrocity and Skaldic Verse: The Rite of the Blood-Eagle', *English Historical Review* 99 (1984), 332–43.)

the end of that century a new wave of raids started up again, and the Anglo-Saxons began paying the raiders off with tribute. This was why the unfortunate Anglo-Saxon king Aethelred gained the nickname 'the Unready', which has nothing to do with him always being last out of the house in the morning or late for meetings, but instead is linked to his poor handling of the viking crisis. This nickname only came about in the twelfth century, as an ironic play on his name: the Old English word *æthel* means 'noble' and *ræd* means 'counsel', so his name basically meant 'noble-counsel, bad-counsel'.*

The renewed raids led to escalating ethnic tension, culminating in the St Brice's Day massacre of 1002, which came about after King Aethelred ordered all Danes living in England to be killed. Nor was this the only instance of brutal violence against the Scandinavian immigrant community. In 2008, during building work at St John's College in Oxford, the skeletons of over thirty young men were discovered, many with horrible slashes and puncture wounds from blades. Chemical analysis of the bones suggests that they were Scandinavians who died around this time, although they are unlikely to have been St Brice's Day victims themselves.

Unfortunately for Aethelred, his problems were set to multiply. The Anglo-Saxons continued to beat back and buy off viking invaders for the next decade, until, in 1013, King Svein Forkbeard of Denmark mounted a large-scale invasion. Soon enough, Aethelred had been exiled to France, and Svein was crowned king on Christmas Day. But this was a short-lived victory, quite literally, for Svein was one of England's shortest reigning monarchs, dead only five weeks later. His son, Knut—better known as King Canute— did much better; as ruler of England, Denmark, and Norway, he managed to juggle the interests of the Anglo-Saxons and Scandinavians for twenty years.

Even the cataclysmic events of 1066 didn't rid the country of Norse rulers. 'Norman' is simply a contraction of 'Northman'. Several generations earlier, around the time when the Danelaw was being established in England, the king of France offered a chunk of northern France to a group of vikings if they would

---

* Or, as one Anglo-Saxon historian translates it, 'noble counsel, my foot!' (S. Keynes, 'A Tale of Two Kings: Alfred the Great and Æthelred the Unready', *Transactions of the Royal Historical Society* 36 (1986), 195–217, at 195.)

protect the land from other vikings. In time they settled down, married local women, and adopted their language, but their veins ran with Nordic blood.

Eggs and dregs

The same is true of the British Isles. Although it might seem as though the vikings have long since vanished, there are traces of them everywhere—clues buried in our culture for us to remember them by. Down to the present day, echoes of our Nordic past remain in our modern place-names, in our language, and, in many cases, even in our blood. Do you like a boiled *egg* for breakfast as you slurp the *dregs* of your tea? Do you go *berserk* if your *husband* steals the *cake* you were saving for your *guest*? These are all Old Norse words that have made their way into the English language. The same is true of place-names. What is probably the rudest place-name in the British Isles (and there are some strong contenders) comes from the Norse settlers. In both Orkney and Shetland there are places that rejoice in the name of Twatt, which comes from the Old Norse word *þveit*, meaning a clearing or piece of land. Happily, Twatt tea-towels, mugs, and coasters are available from all good tourist shops in the region. Spot the Norse Place-Name is an excellent game to play next time you're on a long car journey. Every time you see a place-name ending in '-by' you score three points, because '-by' comes from the Old Norse word for 'settlement' or 'farm'. '-holme', meaning 'small island' or 'marshy place', gets you two points, while a place-name ending in '-thorpe' scores you one point, because '-thorpe' comes from the Old Norse word for a smaller settlement.* If you're travelling through Yorkshire, the East Midlands, or East Anglia you'll be rolling in points by the end of the journey, because this was the heart of the Danelaw, and these parts of the country are peppered with Norse place-names.

As for viking blood running in the veins of modern Britons, certainly there are many who would like to believe that. When a 2014 YouGov poll asked people: 'Do you think you have any Viking ancestry?', 31 per cent of respondents were 'definitely' or 'probably' sure that they did.[8] On the one hand, these

---

* Probably. '-thorpe' is the most problematic of these place-names, which is why you only get one point for this one.

FIGURE 1.3 Twatt, Orkney

statistics may tell us rather a lot about the very human capacity for romantic wishful thinking. On the other hand, it's likely that a good proportion of this 31 per cent were absolutely right. Logically, it would make sense that anyone of British descent could have 'viking ancestry': we all have two biological parents, four grandparents, eight great-grandparents, and so on. If we traced these lines back to the time of the vikings, we would end up with more possible ancestors than the actual population of the world at the time. In this case, it's pretty likely that many have a 'viking' in their family tree. The difficulty is that, because our soup of DNA is such a complex mix, it is hard to pinpoint which bit, if any, came from which distant ancestor.

What *can* be measured, however, is the proportion of different types of chromosome in different parts of the country, which can tell us something about who lived there in the past. Researchers based at the University of Leicester have been working on 'The Viking DNA Project', sampling the types of Y-chromosome present in male populations from Britain and Norway. It turns out that the proportions of a Y-chromosome common in Norwegian men is also high in areas of the British Isles that were heavily settled by the Norse during the Middle Ages. In Shetland the percentage was 41 per cent, in Orkney 50 per cent, in the Isle of Man 39 per cent, in the Wirral 38 per cent, and in West Lancashire 38 per cent. This is in stark contrast to the proportion of this Y-chromosome in areas where there was little Norse settlement (10 per cent in Llangefni and 21 per cent in Mid-Cheshire).[9] In other words, the vikings may seem like a faint, bloody stain on our collective past, but in many ways they never really left.

Today's viking stereotype is of Scandinavian scoundrels who nipped across the North Sea on their longboats to indulge in a spot of pillage and murder, and later decided they liked the land enough to stay. Horrible hairy heathens who—long after Western Europe had converted to Christianity—still believed in bawdy myths about gods, giants, and dwarves, spawned and snuffed out in a bloody tide of sweat, spew, and spittle. Violent men from a violent time when life was cheap and short, who were happy to make it a bit cheaper and shorter if it suited them. In a politically correct, digitized, sanitized age, the vikings continue to cast a powerful shadow. Their fearlessness, their love of adventure, even their bloody brutality, attracts and repels in not-quite-equal measure.

Of course, this stereotype has created a counter-stereotype insisting that the vikings weren't that bad after all. For instance, the promotional material for the 2014 British Museum exhibition *Vikings: Life and Legend* emphasized their skills in seafaring and their creation of international cultural networks that extended across four continents. Still, the star of the exhibition was a viking warship 37 metres in length, which stretched across the main exhibition room. Violence sells. This was the most-discussed exhibit in newspaper reviews; an article in the *Guardian* described it as cutting through the air 'like a sword through flesh, relentless'. The same reviewer was less impressed by the exhibition as a whole, summing it up as a 'bloodless collection of bowls and brooches', and declaring mournfully: 'I felt like crying. Where were the swords?'[10]

Slaughter-wolves

So who, or what, were the vikings? The answer depends very much on who is being asked, where they lived, and when. The word 'viking' is like an onion: as we travel further back in time, we peel back layers of meaning and interpretation. The English word can be traced to at least the eighth century, where it appears in Latin–English glossaries equating the Latin word *piraticum* ('piracy') with the English word *wicingsceaðan* (*sceaða* meaning 'crime' or 'theft').[11] So the Old English word *wicing*, at least to begin with, meant 'pirate' or 'raider'. At this point in time the word had no particular connection to seaborne Scandinavian marauders, who were yet to shake the coastlines of the British Isles.

By the late tenth century the word had clearly taken on that resonance, in light of the events of the preceding 200 years. An Old English poem known as the *Battle of Maldon* describes a bloody fight between Scandinavians and Anglo-Saxons on the Essex coastline, which took place in August 991. Things ended badly for the Anglo-Saxons, many of whom fell with their leader on the saltmarshes. Several Anglo-Saxons are identified by name—the poem was probably composed soon after the battle, for an audience who knew many of those who had died—but the attackers are nameless and faceless, identified only as 'seamen' (*sæmenn*), 'slaughter-wolves' (*wælwulfas*), and 'vikings' (*wicingas*).

A couple of decades later, and several hundred miles further north, Archbishop Wulfstan of York had a very clear idea of who the vikings were, and he didn't like them very much. At some time between 1010 and 1016 he composed his punningly titled *Sermo Lupi* ('The Sermon of the Wolf', an Anglo-Saxon in-joke because Wulfstan means 'Wolf-Stone' in Old English). In it, he berated his congregation for bringing God's wrath—and therefore the viking raiders—down upon the nation. The end of the world was approaching, Wulfstan declaimed from his pulpit, and the English had been led astray by the devil. His assessment of society was not altogether encouraging; one can almost see the spittle fly from Wulfstan's lips as he listed those 'sorely injured through sin':

Here are man-murderers and kin-killers and priest-slayers and haters of monasteries; and here are perjurers and murderers; and here are harlots and child-killers and many foul adulterous fornicators; and here are sorcerers and valkyries; and here are plunderers and robbers and spoilers of the world's goods; and, to speak briefly, countless crimes and misdeeds.[12]

The Scandinavians were clearly uppermost in Wulfstan's mind as he spoke. He referred to the 'heathen people', 'heathen lands', and 'false gods', and gave the example of a slave who escaped his master and abandoned Christendom 'to become a viking' (*to wicinge weorþe*).

Around the same time, there was also a Scandinavian version of the word in circulation: *víkingr*.* Broadly speaking, a *víkingr* sailed abroad to seek adventure and loot. A related word—*víking*—described the expedition itself, as in, 'he went on a *víking* in the summer and got lots of booty'. The words *víkingr* and *víking* start to appear on Scandinavian runestones from around the mid-tenth century, although this later date doesn't necessarily mean that the words emerged later in Scandinavia than in the British Isles (literacy was a far later development in Scandinavia, so written evidence only survives here from later on). Raids abroad could be dangerous for the marauders as well as their victims: certain runic inscriptions commemorate men killed while on a *víking*. On at least fifteen runestones the word even appears as a personal name.[13]

In Norse prose and poetic texts—which only started to be written down in the late twelfth century—the word is used fairly frequently, with the more definite meaning of 'freebooter, rover, pirate', as one dictionary translates it.[14] Tough men are said to have been great *víkings* in their youth, and young men are said to go on *víkings* in the summer months before returning home. Often they are rowdy lads looking to burn off excess energy, have an adventure, and make some money. Occasionally they are older, in which case they tend to be violent, disruptive figures who find it hard to fit into society. The term *vestr-víking* is also used, meaning 'west-raid/expedition', and referring specifically to raids on the coastlines of the British Isles and Western Europe. The poor monks of Lindisfarne had been the first to experience a *vestr-víking*, but they wouldn't be the last.

In short, not all inhabitants of early medieval Scandinavia were vikings. Not even vikings were vikings all the time. The only people who were vikings all the time were men whose parents had named them 'Viking'. The word doesn't refer

---

* It isn't clear whether the word 'viking' originated in Scandinavia or England. Possibly there is a common form of the word that pre-dates the Viking Age, but the etymology of the original word is not easily established. In the Old Norse version—*víkingr*—the *vík* element may be related to the Old Norse word for 'bay', perhaps connected to the seafarers' habit of navigating (or rather prowling) bays, creeks, and fjords in their boats. In the Old English version—*wicing*—there may be a relationship with the word *wic*, meaning a temporary encampment of the kind built by raiders on the coastline.

to an ethnic or cultural group in its entirety, but to an activity and its participants. The Anglo-Saxons knew this too: more generally they referred to Scandinavians as *þa Deniscan* (the Danes) or *Norþmen* (Northmen/Norwegians). The two terms were relatively interchangeable; a 'Dane' could be used to describe any Scandinavian, as we see in the *Anglo-Saxon Chronicle* entry about the murder of the king's official, where both *Norþmen* and *Deniscan* are used.

Those living in the medieval Nordic world were never under any illusion that they were all vikings. But they were part of a common cultural sphere, in which they referred to themselves with terms such as *Norrænn*, *Norskr*, and *Norðmenn*. Today we often use the rather imprecise, catch-all equivalent: 'Norse', or 'Old Norse'. The basic meaning of all these words—both medieval and modern—is 'northern'. More generally it is used to refer to the cultures, literatures, and inhabitants of the medieval Nordic diaspora as a whole, which stretched out from mainland Scandinavia—predominantly Norway, but also Denmark and Sweden—across the islands of the North Atlantic.* They were also connected by a common language, which they called the *dönsk tunga* ('Danish tongue'). As in Old English, 'Danish' in this respect does not refer to the Danish nation specifically, but to Nordic people more generally. Later, when Danish influence waned and the Norwegians became more powerful, the language became known as *Norænna* ('Norse' or 'Norwegian'). There were dialectal differences between the types of Old Norse spoken in different parts of Scandinavia and its overseas settlements. Most of what we will be looking at is technically Old West Norse, because this is what was spoken in Norway, Iceland, and the other settlements west of Scandinavia, and it was this corner of the world that the sagas come from. Today we generally call this language Old Norse.

Gradually the word 'viking' dropped out of the English language. It reappeared at the beginning of the nineteenth century, heralding a renewed enthusiasm for all things northern and medieval. The first modern use of the word was recorded in 1807, three decades before Queen Victoria's coronation. But for the Victorians in particular, the word wasn't only reserved for Scandinavian raiders and adventurers. It swallowed up the whole Norse world.

---

* Unlike the word 'viking', 'Norse' is not a term that was used by the Anglo-Saxons or Scandinavians during the Middle Ages. The word first appears in the sixteenth century, where it referred to the Norwegians and the language they spoke. Versions of the word appear in Dutch (*noors*), Norwegian, Danish, and Swedish (*norsk*).

Northland of old

Many of the most famous writers, composers and artists of the nineteenth century had an interest in vikings that now has been almost forgotten. Sir Walter Scott, perhaps best remembered for his services to the Scottish tourist board, was equally inspired by the Nordic past of the British Isles. His 1822 novel *The Pirate* was particularly instrumental in shaping the way that the vikings were perceived in the era. As Andrew Wawn notes in his book *The Vikings and the Victorians*:

By day he toiled at the 'tartaning' of Scotland; but by night he mused on the residual Viking spirit of the Orkneys and Shetlands....*The Pirate* became one of the definitive texts in the construction of the old north in nineteenth-century Britain.[15]

Similarly, today William Morris is best known for the intricate designs that adorn the wallpapers and textiles of countless tasteful homes; his thieves steal strawberries, they do not raid monasteries. But he was captivated by the 'Northland of old', and translated several Old Norse texts into English with his Icelandic friend Eiríkur Magnússon. In 1871 he even made the long pilgrimage to Iceland, hitching a ride on a Danish mailboat from Edinburgh. In his poem 'Iceland First Seen' (1891), he captures the bleak northern landscape in typical Victorian romantic style:

Why do we long to wend forth through the length and breadth of a land,
Dreadful with grinding of ice, and record of scarce hidden fire,
But that there 'mid the grey grassy dales sore scarred by the ruining streams
Lives the tale of the Northland of old and the undying glory of dreams?[16]

Twenty-five years after Morris's northern voyage, a little-known violin teacher from Worcester was putting the finishing touches to a Norse-themed choral work that would catapult him to national celebrity. Sir Edward Elgar is celebrated as the most British of composers; every year at the Last Night of the Proms, the Royal Albert Hall rocks to lusty strains of his 'Land of Hope and Glory'. First performed in 1896, his *Scenes from the Saga of King Olaf* is a very different beast, packed with pagan gods, carousing feasts, and a boisterous sea-battle against Danish invaders. In the notes written at the beginning of the full score, Elgar remarks: 'In the following Scenes it is intended that the performers should be looked upon as a gathering of skalds (bards); all in turn take part in the narration of the Saga.'[17]

Beyond Britain's shores, others were similarly inspired by this mysterious northern world. Written in France in 1864, Jules Verne's *Journey to the Centre of the Earth* features a runic manuscript written by the medieval Icelandic saga-writer Snorri Sturluson, which holds the key to the adventure. Over in Germany, the most famous composer to be inspired by these northern impulses was Richard Wagner. He reawoke the dragon-slaying heroes and gods of Norse legend to give them new voices and songs, his greatest hits including the blood-pumping 'Ride of the Valkyries'. Wagner was also indirectly responsible for the eternal confusion over the viking horned helmet. No viking ever wore such an item, but in 1876, for the first performance of Wagner's *Ring Cycle* at Bayreuth, the costume designer Carl Doepler decided that horned helmets would be just the thing to complete the outfits.[18]

The viking myth continued to be built upon throughout the twentieth century. World War I signalled an end to the upbeat, nationalistic mood that had characterized much of the nineteenth century. In the shell-shocked societies of inter-war Europe, the fascination with the north and its mysteries became a dangerous breeding ground for national and political radicalism, particularly in Germany. Scientific racial theories were combined with Classical and Norse mythology to create the idea of Hyperborea, home of the Aryan race. Nazi leaders such as Heinrich Himmler were particularly interested in Nordic mysticism and runic symbols, while Hitler himself was notoriously fond of Wagner's music. Briefly spooling forward in time, a number of recent films have also taken as their starting point the Nazi interest in the mysticism and mythologies of the 'ancient north'. Not all of these are of the highest quality, but they include *Blood Creek* (2009), featuring a Nazi scholar on a quest for viking runes and immortality, *Frostbite* (2006), about an elderly Swedish Nazi trying to create a master race from a vampire girl, and *Hellboy* (2004), in which Nazis—including members of the Thule Society—build a portal off the coast of Scotland and inadvertently summon an infant demon.

Taking inspiration from his day job as professor of medieval literature at Oxford, J. R. R. Tolkien based his tales of hobbits, dwarves, and rings on many of the same Old Norse texts so beloved by the Nazis. He was furious about Hitler's misappropriation, as he explained in a letter to his son Michael:

FIGURE 1.4 Horned helmets at Bayreuth: illustration of Hunding by costume designer Carl Doepler (1876)

C. E. Doepler.

FIGURE 1.5 *The Funeral of a Viking* by Sir Frank Dicksee (1893) (subsequently used by Swedish Viking Metal band Bathory for the cover of their 1990 album, *Hammerheart*)

I have in this War a burning private grudge—which would probably make me a better soldier at 49 than I was at 22: against that ruddy little ignoramus Adolf Hitler... Ruining, perverting, misapplying, and making for ever accursed, that noble northern spirit, a supreme contribution to Europe, which I have ever loved, and tried to present in its true light.[19]

Happily for Tolkien, the northern spirit prevailed. Today, we may have first encountered the vikings and their world through swashbuckling films such as *The Vikings* (1958), where the vikings wear hot pants and furry leg-warmers, and one man is sentenced to death by wolf pit while another meets his end by man-eating crab. Possibly we have read *Asterix and the Normans,* in which the vikings come from the frozen north to learn the meaning of fear (fearlessness being a terrible disadvantage when one needs to be shocked out of an attack of the hiccups). If we are of a certain age, we may have grown up with Noggin the Nog, gentle king of the Northmen in the British animated cult classic. If we have youth on our side, we may be more familiar with modern incarnations of Norsedom such as Hiccup Horrendous Haddock the Third, young hero of the book and film series *How to Train Your Dragon,* or the shaven-headed, tattooed Ragnar Lothbrok, badass (anti-)hero of the historical television drama *Vikings.*

Even so, what lies at the heart of all these interpretations and images is a culture far more fascinating and complex than anything that we can take from the popular media, from our imaginations, or from half-remembered history lessons.

So far, we have seen what the world thought—and still thinks—of the vikings, or more accurately, the Norse. We have seen them through the eyes of their Anglo-Saxon victims, their Victorian devotees, and from writers, artists, musicians, and academics who all wanted a piece of them for themselves. All we have looked at so far is a geographical sliver of their world, where they were known—and continue to be known—as vikings. But Western Europe was only the tip of the iceberg. In the centuries that followed the sacking of Lindisfarne, Norse ships of oak and iron transported these northern voyagers to all corners of the medieval world and beyond, where they not only raided but also traded with locals, explored and colonized new lands, and embarked on pilgrimages and crusades. They expanded westwards across the North Atlantic, settling Greenland for several centuries and attempting to settle the fringes of the North American continent. North beyond the Arctic Circle they traded and allied themselves with nomadic tribes, collecting tribute from them and marrying their women. In the east, they navigated the great waterways of Russia, trading furs, slaves, and amber all the way down to the shores of the Caspian Sea and beyond to Baghdad. In the balmy south, they embarked on pilgrimages and crusades to Rome and Jerusalem, and became members of the emperor's elite personal bodyguard in far-away Constantinople. Some of these enterprises were predominantly Icelandic affairs, others Norwegian, Swedish, or Danish. But they were all—in their different ways—part of the same medieval Norse diaspora; a remarkable, diverse, far-travelling culture that made its mark on many of the great civilizations of the age.

The Norse appear in written accounts from across the medieval world, just as they do in texts from Anglo-Saxon England. They feature in Greek sources from Constantinople, Russian sources from Kiev and Novgorod, and Arabic sources from Baghdad and Spain. They go by different names—Northmen, Rus, Varangians—but they are still there. Sometimes they are bloodthirsty raiders, said by holy men to be a punishment sent from God. Sometimes they are revered warriors, cutting a swathe through a common enemy. Sometimes they are wily traders, getting the best price from local merchants by whatever means necessary. Sometimes they are northern kings visiting their distant royal cousins, seeking gainful employment in far-off cities, or pursuing wild adventures far from home.

The common denominator is that all these voices come from the outside. But what about the Norse themselves? What did *they* think of the world and the people and civilizations they encountered? What stories did they bring back home when they returned from their adventures? What happened to these stories over the years, as they were retold in front of winter fires and passed down from generation to generation? Who was forgotten, and who was remembered? Which details fell out of the tales, which were added, and where did they come from?

To try and answer these questions, we need to zoom in on a little island of ice and fire, battered by waves out in the middle of the North Atlantic and hanging just below the Arctic Circle—Iceland.

CHAPTER 2

Fire and Ice

Terra nova

Iceland is a country in the first flush of youth, in more ways than one. It steamed and spluttered its way into the world a mere 16–18 million years ago or thereabouts, riding on the back of the North Atlantic Ridge. Even now it fizzes with youthful energy, prone to erratic volcanic explosions and covered in a pimply profusion of geysers and bubbling mud-holes. Not for nothing is it called the Land of Fire and Ice.

This is also a land born of the Viking Age. As ice ages and empires came and went, Iceland remained splendid in its fiery northern isolation. It was only at the end of the ninth century that Norwegian ships reached its shores and disgorged their cargo of livestock, furniture, and settlers, who came with the intention of making Iceland their home. Today most Icelanders can still trace their ancestry back through the generations, all the way to these first settlers.

However, as far as we can tell, the first people to set foot on Iceland were not Norse, but Irish. Writing from the Frankish kingdom, a man called Dicuil described an intrepid band of Irish holy men who set off in their coracles, braving the stormy Atlantic waters in search of contemplative solitude. It was the winter of 794, little more than a year after the glint of sharpened metal had appeared off the coast of Lindisfarne. They reached an island north of Britain where they stayed for a few months, isolated from everyone except each other and—so Dicuil tells us—the itchy stowaway lice that they picked from their clothes by the light of the midnight sun.

Several North Atlantic islands fit Dicuil's description, and it isn't certain whether it was Iceland they had reached on this occasion. But a similar group of

FIGURE 2.1 Land of Fire: a steaming geothermal pool in Iceland

holy men is mentioned in the *Book of Icelanders* (*Íslendingabók*), written in the early twelfth century by an Icelander called Ari the Wise. According to this account, the men beat a hasty retreat when the pagan Scandinavians began to arrive:

Christians were here then, whom the Northmen call *papar*, but they later left because they did not want to stay here among heathen people, and left behind Irish books, bells, and croziers.[1]

No archaeological evidence has been found in Iceland to support Ari's reference to the *papar*, and in any case almost a century separates Ari's holy men from Dicuil's. However, material finds from elsewhere, including Orkney and Shetland, prove that there were hardcore holy men who sailed the trackless northern seas in search of remote islands where they could become hermits. Perhaps some of them did indeed reach Iceland, as Ari suggests. Maybe one day an archaeologist will strike it lucky, and the truth will surface.

With the Norse settlement of Iceland, we are on rather firmer ground. We can be fairly certain that in the second half of the ninth century, ships began

FIGURE 2.2 Land of Ice: Snæfellsjökull, one of Iceland's many glaciers (and the gateway to subterranean adventure in Jules Verne's *Journey to the Centre of the Earth*)

to leave Norway bound for Iceland, their keels ploughing salty furrows through the sea.[2] Beards flecked with spume, many of the voyagers decided to take the long way round via the British Isles to stock up on women and slaves, or at least this is the traditional story. Studies of the genetic make-up of modern Icelanders have shown that 80 per cent of the Icelandic men sampled carried a Y-chromosome of Norwegian origin while 20 per cent had the Irish or Scottish equivalent, which suggests that a similar proportion of the first male settlers came from Norway and the British Isles. Yet strikingly, the mitochondrial DNA samples taken from a selection of Icelandic women showed that only 37 per cent of their maternal ancestors set out from Norway, while as much as 63 per cent of the female settlement population came from the British Isles.[3]

Whatever their origins, these proto-Icelanders found themselves the new occupants of one of the last unpopulated—but habitable—large landmasses in the world. This was a highly unusual situation, for by this time, only

New Zealand was still to be settled by the Polynesians at the end of the thirteenth century. To all intents and purposes, therefore, Iceland was a *terra nova*, save perhaps for the aforementioned handful of holy men (who under any circumstances would have struggled to create the next generation of settlers between them).

Incredibly, we know the precise date—plus or minus two years—that the Norse began to settle the island, thanks to the same writer who described how the holy men fled. Ari dates the settlement to the time when the Great Heathen Army was devastating England, and takes pains to name his sources:

…according to the reckoning and tallying of Teit my foster-father, whom I consider the wisest of all men, the son of Bishop Isleif, and my uncle Thorkel the son of Gellir, who had a long memory, and Thurid the daughter of Snorri the Chieftain, who was both very wise and not unreliable—when Ivar the son of Ragnar Hairy-Breeches had Saint Edmund, king of the English, killed. That was 870 winters after the birth of Christ.[4]

Ari's dating of the settlement—to the time of the murder of King Edmund of East Anglia at the hands of Ivar the Boneless—may seem improbably precise to a modern reader, considering he was writing 250 years after the event itself and relying on the testimony of his friends and family.* But extraordinarily, Ari's statement is backed up by evidence from the most fitting of Icelandic sources: a volcanic ash cloud.

Across the country, the very earliest settlement layer sits directly above a layer of volcanic ash: shadows and stumps of turf-walled buildings, tools fashioned from whalebones, shards of birch and willow charcoal, slag-splattered sites of iron production, beloved bones of horses and dogs buried as grave-offerings, forgotten fragments of cows, walruses, and birds scattered in the middens, even remains of earthworms that hitched a ride tucked up in

---

* Ivar is first credited with the death of King Edmund in Abbo of Fleury's Latin *Passion of King Edmund* and the Old English adaptation of this work, both written in the tenth century. According to these accounts, Edmund refuses to recant his Christian faith and is tied to a tree by the vikings, where he is first whipped and then shot at until he is 'all covered with their missiles like the bristles of a hedgehog'. The heathens cut off his head and throw it into a forest, where it is later found by his followers, clasped between the paws of a protective wolf and shouting 'Here! Here! Here!' to alert the holy head-hunters.

the ballast of the settlers' ships.[5] Traces of debris from this same volcanic explosion have also been found in the ice-cores taken from the Greenlandic ice-cap, where patterns of seasonal freezing and thawing produce layers of ice that can be counted up and dated like tree rings. These Greenlandic ice-core rings show that the ash cloud came from a volcano in southern Iceland, and fell in around AD 871.[6] In other words, a date that tallies almost exactly with what Ari says.

The soon-to-be Icelanders arrived as pagans. They brought their old gods with them, and are said to have continued as before: eating horses, exposing babies, seeking favours from local guardian spirits, and conducting midwinter sacrifices. Yet gradually, the tendrils of religious change began to wind their way north. At the turn of the new millennium the Icelanders adopted Christianity as their official religion. With Christianity came the tools of writing and the dubious honour of occupying the northernmost, westernmost outpost of European Christendom.

The Icelanders' first major writing project was to record the laws: the unshakeable bedrock of Icelandic society. Previously, the laws had been recited every year by the Law Speaker at the national assembly (called the Alþingi, even down to the present day). Over the long, dark winter of 1117–18, as stars and northern lights painted the night sky, the laws were written down in the farmhouse of Haflidi Masson, a chieftain from the far north of Iceland. Soon, the Icelanders' repertoire expanded. They gained a reputation as the history-keepers of the north, writing down not only their own history but also that of other nations. As the medieval Danish historian Saxo Grammaticus explained in his *History of the Danes* (*Gesta Danorum, c.*1185):

The diligence of the men of Iceland must not be shrouded in silence; since the barrenness of their native soil offers no support for self-indulgence, they practise a steady routine of temperance and devote all their time to improving our knowledge of others' deeds, compensating for poverty by their intelligence. They regard it a real pleasure to discover and commemorate the achievements of every nation.[7]

Over the following centuries, parchments were filled with histories and grammatical treatises, fabulous poems of Norse myths and legends, biblical translations, saints' lives and homilies, cosmographical texts about the earth and heavens, encyclopedic lists of marvellous races and exotic lands. They were also filled with the sagas.

Saga stories

Today we might use the word 'saga' to describe a drawn out, convoluted series of events: perhaps a bad commute to work or an ongoing family feud. In literary works, 'saga' tends to be used for a series of novels spanning several generations of the same family, for instance, John Galsworthy's *Forsyte Saga* (1922) or more recently the vampirlicious *Twilight Saga* (starring a centenarian vampire who hangs around an American high-school mooning after a teenage girl). Such usages tell us little about what the sagas actually are.

The sagas are medieval Iceland's unparalleled storytelling legacy to the world. Their diversity and range is stunning, encompassing a wide range of geography, history, and people. The pared-back intensity of saga narratives is enough to rival any Greek tragedy, Shakespearean comedy, or Hollywood epic. Thwarted love affairs tangle themselves into bloody knots of family feuds and revenge killings. Strong men crack jokes even at the point of death, as they gaze upon the weapon thrust into their guts. Lusty young men jump into bed with farmers' daughters, queens, and even troll-women. Weapons gleam, lawyers scheme, heroes travel, plots unravel, trolls huff, dragons puff, longboats glide, outlaws hide, and so the saga world turns under the northern sky. Some of the best-known stories include the tragic *Saga of Burnt-Njal*, with a final body-count of nearly 100, and the *Saga of Egil Skallagrimsson*, with a brawling drunkard of a protagonist who also happens to be an emotionally delicate, brilliant poet. Elsewhere we meet the tragic outlaw Grettir, who wrestles monsters and the undead out in the wilderness yet has a fatal flaw: a childish terror of the dark. Beyond Iceland's familiar horizons, the narrative threads whorl out into the wider world, with tales of men and women who sailed over the seas and across the inland waterways to all corners of the medieval world and beyond. Here we meet far travellers such as Gudrid, a formidable woman who journeys to North America and gives birth to a child, or Erik the Red, a hot-tempered serial killer who founds a Norse colony out in Greenland.

All these examples come from the best-known group of sagas today: the Sagas of Icelanders (*Íslendingasögur*). Their focus is early Iceland during the Settlement Era, from around 870—when Iceland was settled—up to the early decades of the eleventh century. The Sagas of Icelanders engage with many robust and authentic social themes, such as the settlement itself, genealogical details, legal wranglings, corrupt leadership, religious conversion, and foreign

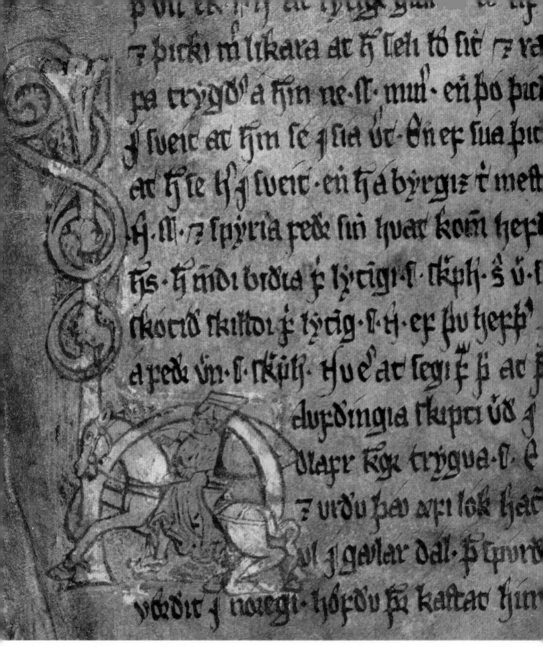

FIGURE 2.3 Illuminated manuscript letter from the *Saga of Burnt-Njal* (Kálfalækjarbók, *c.*1350)

kings who need taking down a peg or two. Yet it is equally possible for the narratives to modulate into eerier keys to tell uncanny tales of murdered men who sing in their burial mounds, witches who bring about deaths by carving bloody runes into driftwood, curses made by dead men who return to plague the living, and ill-fated weapons that cast long shadows over several generations.

Not all sagas are interested in early Iceland and its inhabitants. Another type of saga, called the Kings' Sagas (*Konungasögur*), describes the colourful lives and grisly deaths of early Scandinavian kings, mostly from Norway. Their geographical span is wide-ranging; we follow these kings as they journey beyond the Nordic world into Europe, Russia, and the Middle East. These are some of the earliest sagas, and are often preserved as compilations in manuscripts with visually evocative names, such as *Morkinskinna* ('Rotten Parchment'), *Fagrskinna* ('Beautiful Parchment'), and *Hrokkinskinna* ('Wrinkled Parchment').

The Sagas of Icelanders and Kings' Sagas concern themselves with the historical past, although this does not mean that they are historical documents. Other types of saga are more like fairytales, blending stories of mythical heroes and romance-tinged legends with folktales, supernatural adventures, and bawdy comic episodes. These saga categories are a ragbag of medieval and modern terminologies. It has been suggested that, very broadly speaking, the most important markers of a saga genre are its chronological and geographical settings; literally, there is a time and place for every saga genre.[8]

For instance, the Legendary Sagas (*Fornaldarsögur*) weave a narrative world beyond Iceland, predominantly in Scandinavia. Unlike the Kings' Sagas, they are set in a quasi-mythical, unfixed time long before the settlement of Iceland. But we must remember that these sagas were only brought together as a genre in the nineteenth century, when they were collected into three volumes and given the title *Fornaldarsögur Norðurlanda*, literally, 'sagas of ancient times from northern lands'. Certainly, we cannot be sure that the original medieval saga writers and their audiences would have grouped these sagas together in the same way.

Other sagas are more exotic in their origins. The Chivalric Sagas (*Riddarasögur*) describe the adventures of highborn knights and heroes, usually in a European setting but venturing further afield into more exotic climes. This most European of saga genres began life not in Iceland but in Norway, at the royal court of King Hakon Hakonarson (r. 1217–63). The first Chivalric Sagas were translations and adaptations of Arthurian stories of courtly romance and questing knights. Eventually the Icelanders decided they could do a better job, and started to write their own, original Chivalric Sagas, the saga equivalent of today's online fan fiction. As a result, there are two categories of Chivalric Sagas: translations and original compositions.[9]

Mouths and manuscripts

The sagas were born in a cultural ferment where laws, genealogies, navigational details, historical events, origin myths, family stories, folktales, and poems were transmitted by word of mouth. They began life as oral stories, reshaped and retold as they were passed down the generations, moulded by many mouths, elaborated to incorporate new details, and embellished to make better winter tales to tell around the fireside. This is reflected in the word *saga* itself, which is connected to the Old Norse verb *segja*, meaning 'to say' or 'to tell'. It is also reflected in the phrase used to describe how the sagas were eventually set down in writing; what the medieval Icelanders called *setja saman* ('piece together'). Although in their written forms the sagas were written down by a single—almost always anonymous—author, the narrative effect can be rather like a Greek Chorus, with those who shaped and recorded the sagas like chorus leaders, directing a cluster of voices that span both the later period of saga composition and the earlier period in which the stories are set. As a result, many of the best-known sagas are neither wholly fictional stories nor straightforward historical records. They inhabit the hazy borderlines between fact and fabrication, orality and literacy, past and present. They contain indigenous knowledge about the world and learned material transmitted from continental Europe.

The sagas that survive are preserved in several large manuscript collections, predominantly in Reykjavík and Copenhagen. Reading an Old Norse manuscript can feel rather like trying to crack a wartime code, its dense script peppered with a mystifying array of dots, dashes, and little letters hovering above the lines. Some of these manuscripts are even harder to decipher than they should be, because early scholars came up with the clever idea of pouring water over them in order to magnify the words. Jón Helgason, one of the great Norse manuscript experts of the mid-twentieth century, also had a habit of smoking his pipe over the manuscripts in the Arnamagnæan Institute in Copenhagen. As the medievalist Christine Fell later reminisced,

I seem to recall that at the British Museum (now Library) we were asked not to breathe on the manuscripts and at the Bodleian we had to swear not to introduce fire into the library, though neither of those proscriptions obtained here in the Arnamagnæan, where the fire in Professor Jón Helgason's pipe rarely went out on the smoking-sofa at the top of the staircase.[10]

Some medieval Icelandic manuscripts include elegant illuminations and quirky illustrations, particularly those containing high-status law codes and religious texts. For instance, in one manuscript a passage on driftage rights opens with an illuminated letter containing a beached whale being flensed (de-blubbered) by four little men. Tests on this manuscript have revealed the presence of rich pigments imported from Europe: a chemical rainbow of scarlet vermilion, yellow orpiment, ruby realgar, blue azurite, red ochre, and bone white.[11]

However, for the most part, the medieval parchments that preserve these Norse–Icelandic writings may seem rather plain in comparison to the most famous and flamboyant illuminated manuscripts that lit up medieval Europe. Even so, the medieval Icelanders took no less care over the production of their prized texts. The process of writing was lengthy and physically demanding, as medieval Icelandic scribal scribbles reveal. In the margins of one manuscript a scribe observes—probably from bitter personal experience—that 'it's bad to write in a northwester'. Elsewhere, a forlorn figure in the throes of existential ennui breaks off from his work to scrawl at the bottom of the page, 'I feel I have been a long time alone in the scriptorium'. In another manuscript, a scribe bluntly declares that 'writing bores me', while yet another has a bone to pick with a man named Dori, presumably his employer: 'you do me wrong, Dori, you never give me enough fish.'[12]

Very unusually for the medieval world, it wasn't just monkish scribes who wrote sagas, but also wealthy farmers and chieftains. Little wonder, then, that so many of the saga manuscripts are the least adorned—and often grubbiest—of the surviving medieval parchments. These muddy-brown, rather lacklustre pages are very appropriate vehicles to have carried the sagas down the centuries. These were not showy, fussily high-status stories that demanded gold-leafed embellishments and jewel-encrusted covers. They were written for the entertainment of man, not to the glory of God. The majority of the saga manuscripts were practical cultural artefacts, housed in turf farmhouses across the country and containing stories to be read out loud to the household after the day's work was over. Well handled and well thumbed almost to the point of disintegration, bound between wooden boards or sewn between sealskin leather covers, these sagas were written *by* Icelanders, *for* Icelanders. The understated appearance of these manuscripts with their inky-black lettering also chimes with the sagas' narrative style: supremely laconic, emotionally undemonstrative, darkly comical, factually restrained, coolly intelligent, and above all very *Nordic*.

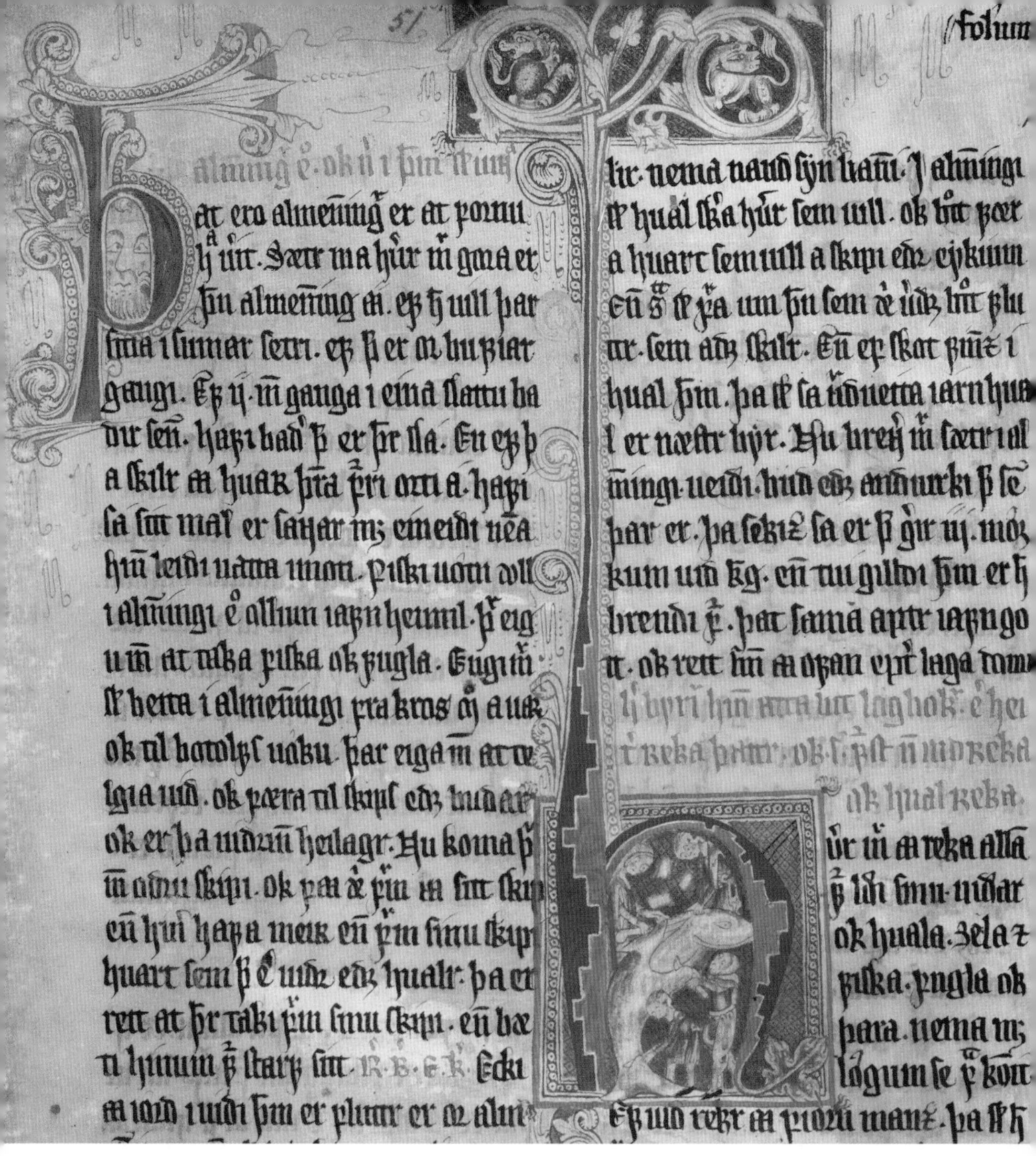

FIGURE 2.4 Four men de-blubbering a whale in an illuminated manuscript letter (Skarðsbók, 1363)

Trials by water and fire

The sagas were written down between the twelfth and the fifteenth centuries, although they continued to be copied up to the twentieth century. Once there were many more sagas than those surviving today. Partly this is because not all sagas were written down, but even if the sagas were committed to parchment, there was no guarantee that the manuscripts themselves would make it through the centuries unscathed. For instance, in the autumn of 1682 a ship sailing from Iceland to Denmark sank off the coast of north-east Iceland, with no survivors. The vessel was also carrying a summer's worth of collected Icelandic manuscripts and books that were being taken to Copenhagen by the king's Keeper of Antiquities. There was no record of what had been gathered in Iceland and then consigned to the briny depths, and when the great manuscript collector Árni Magnússon tried to establish what had been on board, the answer came back: 'a load of parchment book rubbish.'[13]

Even if the manuscripts survived the sea voyage without becoming terminally soggy, they were far from home and dry. Dusty, crackling parchments make fine tinder, as Árni Magnússon discovered to his cost during the Great Fire of Copenhagen in October 1728. As the city burned, Árni and his men turned their attention to the library, and as a rather bungled fire-fighting mission unfolded in the panicked streets, three or four carriage-loads of Norse manuscripts and other ancient documents were rattled to safety across the hot cobbles.*

Blurred lines

Like the medieval Norse themselves, the sagas are far travellers. Taken all together, the saga world is broad and multidimensional. It extends from Arctic Scandinavia in the far north to Byzantium and the Holy Land in the south, from Russian kingdoms and rivers of the east to Greenland and the fringes of North America in the west. It also has chronological depth, stretching from

---

* Relatively speaking, Árni was fortunate; other academics lost their entire collections in the blaze. The Great Fire of Copenhagen was not the only eighteenth-century conflagration to have such a devastating effect: a mere three years and three days later, many ancient manuscripts were destroyed or badly damaged in the Ashburnham House fire close to Westminster Palace in London. Famously, the librarian Dr Bentley was seen fleeing the building with the *Codex Alexandrinus* tucked heroically under his arm (a fifth-century manuscript containing the Bible written in Greek). It was during this fire that the only surviving copy of the Old English poem *Beowulf* had its closest shave, its charred edges testifying to what must have been the squeakiest period of its millennium-long lifespan.

the vague, legendary Scandinavian past all the way to the political machinations of thirteenth-century Iceland. What emerges from this saga world is a
mixture of realism and fantasy, quasi-historical adventures and exotic won-
der-tales that rocket far beyond the horizon of reality. A protagonist might
travel north for the sober extraction of taxes and goods from the Sámi of northern Scandinavia. Equally, he might find himself embroiled in a magic-tinged love
affair, or spirited away to a kingdom of trolls and giants. Descriptions of
stormy western voyages to Greenland might include extremely accurate sailing information about the times and directions taken to sail from one landmass to the next. Yet, once in Greenland, newcomers could find themselves
welcomed by Erik the Red in the Eastern Settlement, or threatened by uncanny
troll sisters in the wildernesses. A different type of saga hero might set out to
seek political sanctuary or learn foreign languages in the exotic kingdoms of
the east. But beyond these kingdoms lie wastelands stretching to the edge of
the Earthly Paradise itself, crawling with dragons, bird-faced men, and
man-eating giants. Saga characters heading south towards the centre of medieval Christendom might have their spiritual hearts set on pious pilgrimages
or bloody crusades in Rome and Jerusalem. However, if they were of a more
mercenary disposition a more likely goal might be service in the Varangian
Guard, the Byzantine emperor's elite gang of personal bodyguards. And if
they travel far enough, they might find themselves falling off the map altogether, surrounded by the marvellous and monstrous races that caper at the
edges of medieval maps and manuscripts.

Despite this plurality, the result is not a random hotchpotch of disconnected images. Rather, what emerges is a fluid, fragmented, multidimensional picture of the world. Through the saga lens, some parts of the world
come into sharp focus, some are blurred and abstract, and some are entirely
absent. There is no all-encompassing worldview, no definitive mental map,
no precise literary atlas. There are no neat lines drawn between one region of
the world and the next, no absolute boundaries that separate cultures.
Although this book is structured according to the four main compass points,
north naturally bleeds into east, east bleeds into south, south bleeds into
west, and west bleeds into north. Or, as the author of one saga put it: 'There
might be people who hear such sagas and not believe them to be truthfully
compiled, because he who is ignorant of the location of countries may call
that east which is west, and that south which is north.'[14] But the ragged lines,
overlaps, grey areas, and inconsistencies are as important as the precisely

measured distances, comprehensive explanations, and broad-brushstroke caricatures of other races. This is how humans perceive and interpret the world.

It is this world, as it was perceived by the medieval Norse across the centuries, that we will be exploring in the following chapters. Taking each of the compass points in turn, we will look at the furthest-flung regions visited by Norse travellers: the outlandish peripheries, the little-known edges, and the exotic kingdoms.[15] We will explore what Norse men and women got up to in these far-off places, sometimes discovering new lands and peoples, at other times playing parts in some of the greatest civilizations of all time. We will encounter the voices of people from across the medieval world who met these northern foreigners in a variety of guises, and read words spoken and written in terror, anger, indifference, bemusement, amusement, fascination. Equally, we will try to discover what the Norse themselves made of the world and its inhabitants, not only at the time itself but also many generations later, when these tales were finally written down. By that time much of the information had been reshaped, reinterpreted, added to, misremembered, or forgotten entirely. Even so, the sagas endured.

FIGURE 2.5 *Ottar*, a reconstruction of *Skuldelev 1*, a Norse cargo ship of the type that would have been used for long-distance voyages

· North ·

Cold crown of the world. Boreas exhales
the breath that's preserved him all these years,
kept the wolverine alive, and the spruce-blue stars
keen as crystals of virgin ice
clipping the pines on their northern slopes.

'The Taiga', Frances Leviston

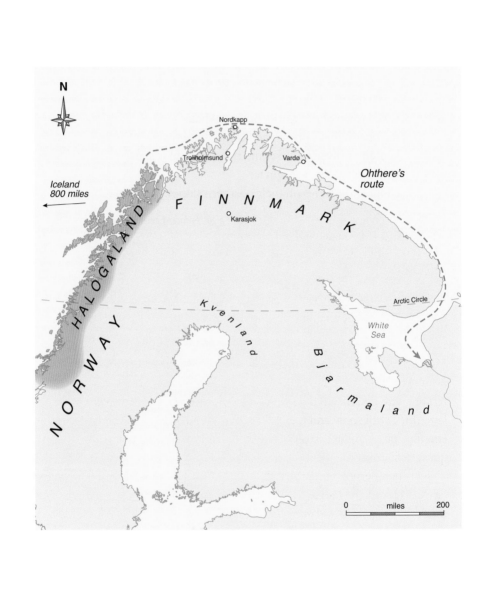

N

Nordkapp

Trollholmsund

Vardø

Ohthere's
route

Iceland
800 miles

F I N N M A R K

Karasjok

H
A
L
O
G
A
L
A
N
D

N
O
R
W
A
Y

K
v
e
n
l
a
n
d

Arctic Circle

White
Sea

B
j
a
r
m
a
l
a
n
d

0   miles   200

CHAPTER 3

In the Lands of the North

Out of space, out of time

Think of the Norse and we think of the north. As the mournful bassoon pipes over the opening credits of *Noggin the Nog*, a voice intones solemnly:

In the lands of the North, where the Black Rocks stand guard against the cold sea, in the dark night that is very long, the Men of the Northlands sit by their great log fires and they tell a tale.

The same is true of another iconic cartoon, *Asterix and the Normans*, which despite the title guest-stars vikings who hail from 'northern lands where winters are hard and the night lasts for months on end'.* Theirs is a wintry homeland thick with snow and ice, where they quaff liquor from the skulls of their enemies and conduct 'scientific experiments' with clubs and axes in their quest to discover the meaning of fear.

Such northern associations also existed in the Middle Ages. The Anglo-Saxons named the Norse for the cardinal direction they came from, calling them 'Northmen' (*Norþmen*). Over on the Continent, writers of Frankish annals overwhelmingly referred to them as *Nortmanni*, usually in the context of violent and bloody raids.[1] This strongly northern identity was also reflected in the names the Norse used for themselves, their language, and their lands: they used words such as *Norðmann* ('Northman'), *Norðrlönd* ('Northern Lands'),

---

* We won't dwell on the chronological implausibility of the vikings visiting Roman-occupied Gaul.

FIGURE 3.1 Asterix and the Normans (aka vikings)

Norræna (the Norse language), *Norrænn* ('Norse'), and *Norskr* ('Norse'). Norway was *Noregr* (a contraction of *Norðvegr* meaning 'North Way'), while Iceland—*Ísland*—was named after that most northern and chilly of substances, ice.

Unfortunately for the Norse, the north was a culturally loaded, not always positive cardinal direction with which to be connected. From the earliest times it had been associated with the wild, unfamiliar margins of the earth, populated by all sorts of uncanny and outlandish beings.[2] For the Ancient Greeks, secure in the temperate and bountiful centre of their Mediterranean world, it was inconceivable that humans could inhabit the frozen north. So they filled it with the mythical Hyperboreans, a happy, long-lived people who dwelled beyond the north wind itself (literally so, since this is the meaning of the word *hyperborea*). Writing in around 450 BC, the Greek historian Herodotus located Hyperborea somewhere north of a belligerent, one-eyed race called the Arimaspi, who lived in the foothills of the snowy Riphean Mountains and fought with their griffin neighbours. It was here that Apollo, the god of sun and light, was said to go for his winter holidays.*

* Ancient writers and modern scholars variously located the Riphean Mountains in the Alps, the Arctic Circle, and the Ural Mountains. In the twentieth century a mountain range on the moon was named *Montes Riphaeus* after its legendary antecedent. This is particularly appropriate because for most of the ancient world the far north was as remote and inaccessible as the moon is for us today.

FIGURE 3.2 Noggin the Nog illustration by series creator Peter Firmin, who was inspired by the Lewis Chessmen in the British Museum

Another far-off, semi-mythical northern land that can be traced back to Ancient Greece is 'Ultima Thule', which was thought to be the most northerly landmass on earth. In the fourth century BC a Greek explorer-geographer called Pytheas wrote that he had sailed six days north of the British Isles, to a land bathed by perpetual daylight at midsummer, where the sea was clogged with sheets of ice that looked like jellyfish. Pytheas wrote an account of his travels—called *Things about the Ocean*—that no longer survives, but there are several references to his work by other Classical writers, most of whom thought he was a liar who had made the whole thing up. The island of Thule became a geographical metaphor for the idea of ultimate, remote northernness; a reputation that was carried across the centuries and down to the present day. To give just one example, Edgar Allan Poe's poem 'Dream-Land' (1844) includes the lines:

> I have reached these lands but newly
> From an ultimate dim Thule—
> From a wild weird clime that lieth, sublime,
> Out of SPACE—out of TIME.

As antiquity gave way to the Middle Ages, the notion of a mysterious, even monstrous north persisted. The ninth-century German missionary Rimbert of Hamburg-Bremen had no doubt that the north was a wild weird clime. In fact, he was of the opinion that dog-headed men roamed the lands north of the German border in Denmark. As we know from correspondence between Rimbert and a theologian called Ratramnus of Corbie, the chief concern occupying this intrepid holy man's mind was whether these dog-heads had souls, and if so, whether he should attempt to convert them to Christianity. Rimbert's letter to Ratramnus no longer survives, but Ratramnus' reply gives us an idea of what was troubling Rimbert:

You asked what you ought to believe about the dog-headed ones, namely, whether they arose from the line of Adam or possess the souls of animals.[3]

Perhaps Rimbert should have worried about what other diabolical creatures he might meet on his travels. When we think of devils and demons, we are probably inclined to think of heat, red-hot pokers, and the fiery pits of hell. But there was an alternative, chillier tradition circulating in the Middle Ages that placed Satan himself in the far north. Such an association between demonic forces and the cold, icy north can be traced back to early Christian theologians and their interpretation of biblical passages such as this one from the Book of Isaiah:

> How you are fallen from heaven,
> O Lucifer, son of the morning!
> How you are cut down to the ground,
> You who weakened the nations!
> For you have said in your heart:
>   'I will ascend into heaven,
>   I will exalt my throne above the stars of God;
>   I will also sit on the mount of the congregation
>   On the farthest sides of the north'.

The idea of the devilish north had lost none of its potency by the early decades of the fourteenth century, when Dante Alighieri wrote his *Divine Comedy*. Here, Satan is depicted as a slobbering, slavering demon with three mouths, frozen up to his chest in ice. Likewise, Geoffrey Chaucer made the connection between demonic beings and the north in the *Canterbury Tales*, written several decades later; in *The Friar's Tale*, we meet a sinister, softly spoken devil-yeoman who dwells 'fer in the north contree'. By the time John Milton came to write *Paradise Lost* in the seventeenth century, these associations were firmly established, and Milton has Lucifer setting himself up at the 'quarters of the north'.

Spooling back again a few centuries, for the Anglo-Saxons, cowed by Viking raids, the link between the north and pagan evil must have been painfully appropriate. Disappointingly, the famously melodramatic prayer, 'from the fury of the Northmen deliver us, O Lord', is almost certainly apocryphal; there is nothing to suggest that the monks squealed anything of the sort as they fled from the advancing longboats. Even so, for Alcuin—the Anglo-Saxon monk with the busy pen whom we met in Part I—it was only to be expected that malevolence and destruction should come from the north. Soon after the raid on Lindisfarne, a letter from Alcuin arrived at the monastery at Jarrow, a few miles down the road. Its content was not encouraging:

You live near the sea from which this danger first came. In us is fulfilled what once the prophet foretold: 'From the North evil breaks forth, and a terrible glory will come from the Lord.'[4]

As the Anglo-Saxons were only too well aware, a real north, populated by real people and animals, had started to emerge from northern mists. Writing at the beginning of the twentieth century, the Norwegian over-achiever Fridtjof Nansen—polar explorer, scientist, diplomat, humanitarian, and Nobel laureate*—had the following to say about this moment in time:

Thus at the close of antiquity the lands and seas of the North still lie in the mists of the unknown. Many indications point to constant communication with the North, and now and again vague pieces of information have reached the learned world.

---

* Nansen was a true renaissance man of many talents and interests. Behind a glass case in Tromsø's Polar Museum, north of the Arctic Circle, there is a copy of his doctoral thesis on 'The Structure and Combination of the Histological Elements of the Central Nervous System'. Nansen was particularly interested in the neurological workings of the hagfish: an eel-like, slime-secreting fish with a face only a mother could love.

Occasionally, indeed, the clouds lift a little, and we get a glimpse of great countries, a whole new world in the North, but then they sink again and the vision fades like a dream of fairyland.[5]

This northern fairyland retreated as the Middle Ages advanced. Ideas about the earth and its inhabitants—inherited from the Bible and from Classical and Late Antique writers—began to be reconsidered and reshaped as traders, raiders, merchants, colonizers, and missionaries began to push back the northern boundaries of the world. And, as might be expected, the people pushing back hardest of all were the northerners themselves.

Wonders of the north

Those who lived in Nordic lands were aware of how marginal their northern homelands were in relation to the rest of medieval Europe. The *King's Mirror* (*Konungs skuggsjá*) is a Norwegian text written in around 1250. Ruminating on 'the wonders that are here with us in the north', the author ponders how marvellous certain northern skills must seem to those living in the south, even if they are not so remarkable for northerners themselves.[6] He singles out skiing as an extraordinary northern talent that would baffle southerners:

It would seem to them a greater wonder if they heard about men who knew how to tame wood and boards so that, as soon as he has tied planks eight or nine ells long to his feet, a man who is no more nimble than other men when he only has his ordinary shoes on can beat a bird in flight or the swiftest greyhound in a race or a reindeer that leaps twice as fast as the hart.[7]

The text goes on to describe the wonders of other northern lands such as Iceland and Greenland, with their vivid northern lights, great frosts, boundless ice, fiery displays, strange bodies of water, and monsters that dash about the ocean. Even for a text such as the *King's Mirror*, written in a consciously northern cultural milieu, the strangest phenomena occur in other, more distant northern lands.

Out in the North Atlantic, the Icelanders may or may not have had to wrestle with ocean monsters as the *King's Mirror* suggested, but theirs was an island inextricably linked to the north. Early on, Iceland had become associated with Ultima Thule, the semi-legendary island of Classical writings, not least in the imagination of the medieval Icelanders themselves. In the bowels of the Norse manuscript collection in Reykjavík there is an Icelandic manuscript (GKS 1812 4to) that was put together in several stages between 1182 and 1400. The manuscript contains a *mappa mundi* ('world map') with the written names of countries positioned for the most part according to where the Icelanders thought they were located in the world. We will return to this map later on. For now, the important thing to note is that Iceland is squashed right at the edge of the map, up against the northern rim of the world. The only country on this map that is further north than Iceland is marked as *Tile* (i.e. 'Thule'), which sits directly on top of Iceland. Possibly the mapmaker was equating the two lands directly with each other, or perhaps he wanted to show that Iceland was just south of Thule: the last habitable, civilized land before the utmost north.[8]

All cardinal directions are relative. Unless you happen to find yourself at the North Pole, there is always somewhere and often someone—or at least something—more northerly than you. The question is: who lived north of the Northmen?

When we think of the medieval Norse setting out from their homelands, we're most likely to imagine them coming *from* the north and travelling *to* the south. But they also travelled north, up into the Arctic territories of northern Scandinavia and across into Russia. These lands were an important source of wealth and power throughout the Viking Age, particularly for the Norwegians. They traded with their Arctic neighbours, especially the people known today as the Sámi (in the past called Laplanders), who lived immediately to their north as well as in territories further south in Norway and Sweden. In medieval Norse texts—including the sagas—the Sámi are most often called the *Finnar*, not to be confused with the modern Finns of Finland.[9] There were other Arctic peoples whom the Norse had dealings with, such as the Bjarmians (whom they called the *Bjarmar*) and the Kvens (known to the Norse as the *Kvenir*), who lived further east, towards the White Sea.

Throughout the Middle Ages, the northern fur trade was big business in Europe. The Sámi were predominantly nomadic hunters and fishermen with easy access to prestigious Arctic resources such as animal skins and furs. Such

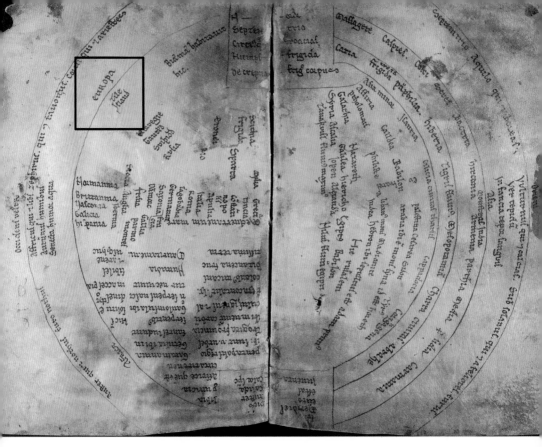

FIGURE 3.3 The utmost north: Iceland and Thule on a medieval Icelandic *mappa mundi* (c.1182–1400)

goods were highly valued by Europeans, and Norse traders could sell them on further south for a hefty profit.

In return, the Norse supplied the Sámi with goods that could only be produced by settled farming societies. Dairy products were much sought after as trading goods, along with metals and grains.[10] Both the Norse and the Sámi benefited from this arrangement, but it was not necessarily a straightforward, equal relationship of trade and exchange. The Norse southerners also extracted taxes and tribute from their northern neighbours, a practice described by one academic as a 'coercion-and-extortion racket'.[11]

Broadly speaking, this was 'North' for the Norse: the northernmost part of Scandinavia beyond the Arctic Circle, and the lands stretching east to the White Sea in Russia. Of course, this wasn't technically 'North' for the Icelanders, which is important for when we come to look at the sagas. If you sail directly north from Iceland, you will eventually hit an unpleasantly icy, potentially polar-bear-infested stretch of the East Greenlandic coastline. Yet the Icelanders had close links to Norway, historically, culturally, and politically. Much of the first generation of Icelanders had emigrated from Norway, travel and trade between Norway and Iceland was frequent, and by the time the sagas were being written down, Iceland was under the control of the Norwegian crown. Consequently, many sagas are either set in Norway or have Norwegian preludes or episodes, some featuring the far north and its inhabitants.

This was a north of blurred territories and borderlands; neither Norse lands nor wholly foreign. (See Map 1.) Such a liminal identity is reflected in the Norse word for the northernmost part of Scandinavia: Finnmark (or *Finnmǫrk* in Old Norse). The *Finn* element refers to the *Finnar* (Sámi) who occupied it, while *mǫrk* comes from the Proto-Indo-European root **mereg-*, meaning 'edge' or 'boundary'. The word found its way into many languages across the world, such as the Classical Latin margo from which we get the English word 'margin'. But in medieval Scandinavia, dense forests often formed the boundaries between two territories. As a result, 'mark' also came to mean 'forest' in Old Norse (even in Iceland, where there were no trees).

In these borderlands, and beyond, there was considerable cultural contact and interaction between the Norse and the Sámi. Excavations of eleventh- and twelfth-century Sámi graves from central Scandinavia have uncovered bodies that were prepared for burial with a mixture of Norse and Sámi burial customs. The bodies were wrapped in shrouds made of birch bark, a feature typical of Sámi graves from the period. At the same time there were also Norse items, including wool and linen textiles, brooches, rings, and coins. Female graves excavated from both Norse and Sámi burial sites suggest that high-status marriages took place between Norse and Sámi elites.

Stranger finds have also come to light, including a Sámi man buried with typical male Sámi items, such as an ornate belt. He was also the proud owner of Norse items usually associated with females, including a silver brooch and finger ring, crystal beads, and a linen dress. Even more strangely, his body had been pushed up against the side of the grave, as if making room for someone or something else. It has been suggested that this man was a Sámi *noaidi* or shaman, buried with the tools of his trade and enough room in his grave for the spirits to squeeze in next to him.[12]

The cross-dressing shaman in his grave may hold a clue to understanding the reputation that grew up around the Sámi. They were known as magic-makers, with particular talents for calling up storms, prophesying the future, and shape-shifting. This reputation followed them down the centuries to the present day. It may well have started with the Norse, their closest southern neighbours.

Deep magic

Texts from medieval Scandinavia reveal not only how the Norse cooperated with the Sámi, but also how they perceived them culturally. One of the most dramatic and memorable descriptions of the Norse and the Sámi interacting in the far north comes from the *History of Norway* (*Historia Norwegiae*), a Latin text probably written in the second half of the twelfth century. The account begins with a straightforward description of the Sámi themselves: they wear skins, travel on skis, hunt wild animals, and live in moveable hide huts. It also explains how the Sámi pay the kings of Norway an annual tribute of many animal furs: mostly squirrels and ermines, but curiously also 'a certain servile class of beaver which fetches a very small price and on account of frequent use for work is not furry but smooth-skinned'.[13] But swiftly the passage changes tone, describing the 'intolerable ungodliness' of these strange northerners and the 'devilish superstition they exercise in the art of magic'.[14] The evidence for this is a disturbing magical ritual, as seen through the bewildered eyes of a group of Norsemen who were staying with Sámi hosts during a trading expedition. The traders came from Halogaland (*Hálogaland* in Old Norse), the northernmost province in medieval Norway, and the last Norse territory before Finnmark. One day, during dinner, their hostess collapsed and dropped dead. The shocked Norsemen watched as a *magus* ('wizard') was summoned to bring her back from the spirit world with his magical rituals. But things didn't go to plan:

Then a wizard spread out a cloth under which he made himself ready for unholy magic incantations and with hands extended lifted up a small vessel like a sieve, which was covered with images of whales and reindeer with harness and little skis, even a little boat with oars. The devilish *gandus* [spirit] would use these means of transport over heights of snow, across slopes of mountains and through depths of lakes. After dancing there for a very long time to endow this equipment with magic power, he at last fell to the ground, as black as an Ethiopian and foaming at the mouth like a madman, then his belly burst and finally with a great cry he gave up the ghost.[15]

At this point another *magus* was summoned, and explained to the visiting guests how his unfortunate colleague had died. While in his trance he had travelled to the spirit world, where he transformed himself into a whale. As he was gliding through a lake, he ran into the spirit of one of his enemies, which had taken the form of sharpened wooden stakes. He swam straight into the stakes, which skewered his belly so that it burst open, killing him. Having explained this to the visitors, the second *magus* then went down into the spirit world himself, where he found the spirit of the dead woman and brought her back to the land of the living. Finally, the author concludes by telling his readers that he has 'selected these piecemeal from among the innumerable deceptions of the Lapps [Sámi] and offered them as illustrations of such a godless group for the benefit of people who live at a greater distance from them'.[16] Once again, everything seems stranger and more foreign from further away.

In all likelihood, this so-called *magus* was actually a Sámi shaman, and the Norse traders had witnessed a shamanistic ritual.[17] If so, this is the earliest known description of such an event, as seen through the interpretive lenses of both the bemused Norse traders and whoever wrote the *History of Norway*. From the Norse point of view, this is a ritual peppered with images of the Arctic: whales, harnessed reindeer, little skis, snowy heights, mountain slopes, and deep lakes. These people and their magical abilities are inextricably linked to the landscape of their northern homeland. Yet this is also proof of their ungodly devilishness, at a time when the rest of Scandinavia had become firmly Christian. This state of affairs would continue for several more centuries; it was only in the eighteenth century that the Sámi were converted officially to Christianity, and even today they retain their reputation for magic.

If the Norse had witnessed dramatic shamanistic rituals of the kind described in the *History of Norway*, then it is easy to see how cultural associations formed concerning the Sámi and their strange magical talents. Worse, they were pagans, and pagans living in the far north at that. No wonder that the Sámi were thought to have more than a touch of the diabolical about them.

Over the centuries, the link between the Sámi and the uncanny continued to grow in the Norse imagination. Such associations went very deep, and can

Tab. XC.

be seen in the law codes, the very foundation stones of medieval Nordic cultures. Several passages from medieval Norwegian law codes explicitly prohibit 'believing in the Sámi', or visiting the Sámi to learn one's future.[18] There is also a report of a legal case from the late fifteenth century concerning Anna *finszka* ('the Sámi'), who was accused of teaching *trolldom* ('magic') to a woman named Margrit.[19]

Darkness will give way

As the Middle Ages gave way to the early modern period, the unsettling reputation of the Sámi as a people with unnatural and dangerous pagan powers was to have grim consequences. The spate of Finnmark witch trials that happened in the seventeenth century is one of the most extreme cases. What unfolded across the coastal villages and tiny towns of Finnmark was just one cluster of tragedies in that dark era of witch-hunts that gripped Europe and its American colonies from the fifteenth to the eighteenth centuries. Finnmark was a prime target. After all, everyone knew that evil came from the north, and this region was home to not only Scandinavians but also the pagan Sámi with their magical skills. Not all the accused were Sámi: as a matter of fact it was Scandinavian women in the small fishing villages along the coast who suffered the most. But in at least one, deeply disturbing case, an old man called Anders Poulsen was accused and convicted of witchcraft specifically because he was a Sámi shaman. His tragic story is a reminder of the dark side of the north and its supernatural associations.

The Norwegian port of Vardø is the easternmost town in Scandinavia, further east than Istanbul, Kiev, or St Petersburg. Its coat of arms depicts the rays of the sun breaking over the sea, with the motto, *cedant tenebræ soli*, 'darkness will give way to the sun'. Tucked away behind the town, down on the seashore, stands a monument that memorializes one of the blackest, bloodiest periods in the town's history: a darkness that even the Arctic midsummer sun would struggle to overcome. This is the Steilneset Memorial. One part, called 'The Damned, The Possessed, and the Beloved', is a cube made entirely of smoked

FIGURE 3.4 A Sámi shaman with his drum. Copper engraving by O. H. von Lode (1767)

glass. Inside the cube is a chair, placed on a wooden pyre. From the seat of the chair hot orange flames flare into the air, hissing and fizzing loudly. High up, seven oval mirrors encircle the room, each bigger than a man, representing the judges who sentenced these so-called witches to be burnt. The flames dance back in the mirrors, mingling with the reflection of whoever stands beneath.

The other part of the memorial is a white fabric cocoon over 100 metres long, suspended from wooden frames, reached by a long wooden gangplank. Inside is almost total blackness, except for a series of tiny square windows running down the walkway. A bare lightbulb in front of each window represents one of the ninety-one men and women of Finnmark condemned to death during a series of witch trials at the end of the seventeenth century. Hanging by every window, a black banner lists the names and crimes of the accused. The word *trolldom*—'magic'—appears frequently. Almost all of the banners end with the same chilling sentence: *dømt til ild og bål* ('condemned to be burnt at the stake'). At the very end of the wooden walkway the final banner is for Anders Poulsen, who was almost 100 years old at the time. He took his shaman's drum to the trial, where he showed the judges how he used it, trying to persuade them that there was nothing un-Christian or devilish about what he did. Even so, he was convicted, but before he could be executed he was hacked to death in his cell by a fellow prisoner.

Remarkably, the drum Anders used to demonstrate his shamanic skills still survives. It was spirited away by Danish missionaries after his death, and is now kept in the basement of the National Sámi Museum at Karasjok. Not unlike the sort described many centuries earlier in the *History of Norway*, the drum is decorated with little picture symbols—dark brown, possibly drawn in the shaman's own blood—the great reindeer at the top of the world, the sun and the moon, men and women holding hands in the middle, and what seem to be capering demonic figures at the bottom. A desiccated bear's paw dangles impotently from the side of the drum, claws intact, shrivelled to the size of a small child's hand.

Traditions about the magical talents of the Sámi continued as the centuries went on: this is a theme that runs through Nordic folklore and fairytales. In one story, a Sámi bursts into tears when he sees hunters flaying a bear that

FIGURE 3.5 Steilneset Memorial: art installation by Louise Bourgeois, Vardø

they have just killed: they have murdered his grandfather. In another, a sailor worried about his pregnant wife is helped out by his Sámi shipmate, who puts himself into a magical trance to find out that the woman has just given birth to a bouncing baby boy. Related stories about the magical 'Finns' also sprang up on the Northern Isles of Shetland and Orkney, which were ruled by the Norse until the fifteenth century and remained closely connected to Scandinavia long after. The 'Finn Folk' are said to be supernatural, shape-shifting sea-dwellers (rather like the 'selkies' of Scottish and Irish folklore), while Finns themselves had a reputation for practising the dark arts. Into the twentieth century, as the folklorist Andrew Jennings notes, the adjective 'Finnie' was still applied to 'peculiar old women'.[20] And even today in Finnmark, the Sámi have a reputation for being able to stem the flow of a bleeding wound.

On occasions, the word *Finnr* simply became synonymous with 'magic'. In a nineteenth-century collection of Icelandic folktales there is a reference to 'Finn Breeches' (*finnbrækr*).[21] A grisly replica set of these fetching trousers hangs in the Museum of Icelandic Sorcery and Witchcraft, where they are called 'necropants' (*nábrok*). The museum website describes the process by which one obtains and uses these 'Finn Breeches', which begins with getting permission from a living man to use his skin after his death:

After he has been buried you must dig up his body and flay the skin of the corpse in one piece from the waist down. As soon as you step into the pants they will stick to your own skin. A coin must be stolen from a poor widow and placed in the scrotum along with the magical sign, nábrókarstafur, written on a piece of paper. Consequently the coin will draw money into the scrotum so it will never be empty, as long as the original coin is not removed. To ensure salvation the owner has to convince someone else to overtake [*sic*] the pants and step into each leg as soon as he gets out of it. The necropants will thus keep the money-gathering nature for generations.[22]

Whether there was any historical link between the Sámi and this form of magic is rather unlikely, but in this instance the words 'magic' and 'Finn' seem to have become interchangeable.

'Much knowing'

Over in medieval Iceland, perceptions and memories of the Sámi lost none of their potency as the sagas began to be written down in the thirteenth century.

As the name suggests, most sagas categorized as Sagas of Icelanders anchor themselves in Iceland and focus on the exploits of Icelanders. Yet many open with a prelude set in Norway, tracing family lines back to their Norwegian origins. During these preludes, Sámi characters may pop up from time to time, with more than a touch of the uncanny about them.[23]

Strange Sámi characters drift through the opening chapters of the *Saga of the People of Vatnsdal* (*Vatnsdæla saga*), which opens in Norway. A soothsaying Sámi woman is invited to a feast held by the Norse. The saga describes her as *fjǫlkunnig*, which means 'much knowing', but with the implication that what she knows is of a magical nature. She sits in the place of honour decked out in her party clothes, and men go to her to hear what the future holds for them. One refuses, Ingimund, the hero of the saga. Against his will, the seeress predicts that he will leave Norway and settle in Iceland. He is furious, but a chain of events has already been set in motion that will eventually lead him out to Iceland.

Determined to fight fire with fire and circumvent the prophecy, Ingimund summons three magical Sámi men, who, the saga tells us, 'came from the north'.[24] He tells them: 'I'll give you butter and tin if you go on a mission for me to Iceland.'[25] This is no ordinary errand, but a dangerous magical journey in which the Sámi will send their spirits to Iceland over the course of three nights to scope out the region of the country that Ingimund is destined to settle. When they return, they tell him:

We Sámi-boys are exhausted and we've had lots of trouble…the Sámi woman's spell was so strong that we put ourselves in great danger.[26]

This is a saga narrative tinged with Sámi magic, capable of helping or hindering the Norse depending on who wields it. At the same time, historical undercurrents run deep. The episode reflects exactly the sort of magical beliefs that grew up around the Sámi: their abilities to see the future and go on out-of-body journeys. What the saga describes is exactly the sort of practice banned by later Norwegian law codes. The legal prohibition against 'believing' in the Sámi suggests something more akin to superstition, but in the sagas these powers are portrayed as genuine. Ingimund even offers to pay the Sámi in butter and tin; in other words, just the kind of goods that the historical Sámi would have been keen to acquire from the visiting Norse traders such as those who featured in the *History of Norway*.

In the *Saga of the People of Vatnsdal*, the Sámi themselves are simply narrative catalysts, invited briefly into the Norse world and faded out of the saga once they have served their purpose. Even so, when the Sámi enter the sagas an immediate tension arises from the fact that they are alien beings within the Norse world. Located on the peripheries, they are at the same time culturally familiar and unfamiliar. The closer the Sámi get to the Norsemen in the sagas, the more dangerous they can be, and the most dangerous creature of all is a Sámi wife.

Snow queens

For Hans Christian Andersen the north was home to the Snow Queen in her empty, endless palace of snowdrifts, frozen lakes, and northern lights. C. S. Lewis created a White Witch to rule over a Narnia gripped by an eternal winter (but never Christmas). Philip Pullman's Arctic skies were filled with Finnish witches riding cloud-pine branches, listening to the music of the aurora. Yet many centuries before these writers dreamt up their creatures of ice and enchantment, the saga writers had populated the north with their own uncanny, magic-making women.

As we have already seen, archaeological evidence tells us that marriages took place between the Norse and the Sámi. At the same time, it is true that the Norse were concerned about the magical talents of their neighbours, as revealed in laws and other texts from medieval Norway. In the sagas the two traditions intersect, and taking a Sámi wife becomes a risky business.

Norse–Sámi marriages are often presented as narrative set-pieces in which Norwegian kings marry Sámi brides. The most famous of these is the marriage between King Harald Fairhair and a Sámi woman named Snaefrid, whose name means 'Snow Fair', conjuring up an immediate association with the far north despite the fact that she actually comes from a more southerly part of Norway. The following story comes from the *Saga of Harald Fairhair* (*Haralds saga ins hárfagra*) which is part of a compilation of Kings' Sagas called *Heimskringla* ('circle of the world'), written in around 1230 by the Icelandic politician and poet Snorri Sturluson.* We take up the story at the point where King Harald has been persuaded to enter a tent belonging to a Sámi man. The saga calls this tent a *gammi*, which is one of the few loanwords in Old Norse taken

---

* Snorri came to a rather sticky end, having incurred the wrath of the Norwegian king. On the king's orders he was murdered with an axe in his own cellar, having uttered his final, futile words: 'Don't strike!'

from the Sámi language. Inside the tent the king meets the beautiful Snaefrid. She offers him a cup of mead, and as he takes it he is instantly bewitched:

He took the cup and her hand together, and at once it was as though fiery heat ran through his skin. Straight away, he wanted to have her that night.[27]

The enchanted king marries Snaefrid and abandons his kingdom, bewitched by her beauty. Eventually she dies, but the magic remains and her body doesn't decay. The mournful king sits by her for three winters, hoping that she will wake up. Eventually, he is persuaded to change her bedding, and at that moment the spell is broken. A ghastly smell rises from her corpse, which turns *blá* or 'blue-black'; in the sagas the colour of bruises, murderers' cloaks, corpses, and the undead. Worse, she is riddled with more than the usual maggots and flies that inhabit dead bodies:

As soon as she was moved from the bed, every kind of rottenness and foul smell and stench came from the corpse. It was hurried to the pyre, and she was burned. Before this was done, the corpse turned blue-black and from it swarmed snakes and adders, frogs and toads, and all sorts of vermin.[28]

In this episode, the association between the Sámi and their spells assumes fairytale proportions. But in this Norse version of Snow White, it is the witch herself who is suspended in sleeping death. Nor is she the only Sámi to be named after a cold northern homeland, real or imagined: her compatriots in other sagas are given names such as *Mjöll* ('Fresh-Snow'), *Snær* ('Snow'), *Drífa* ('Snow-Drift'), *Gísl* ('Ski-Pole'), and *Öndur* ('Ski').[29] In reality, the Sámi occupation area extended much further south than is often assumed, and there was a large degree of overlap between Norse and Sámi cultural areas.[30] Yet many medieval sources situate the Sámi in a frozen northern wilderness, strapping skis on their feet and bows on their backs. The same is true in the occasional references to the far north made by writers from beyond the Norse world. For instance, in his geographical description of northern climes, the eleventh-century writer Adam of Bremen referred to Sámi women who live in the perpetually snowy mountains. He described how these women, in order to insulate themselves from the cold, 'grow beards in the extremely rough alps of that region'.[31]

Later in the same *Saga of Harald Fairhair*, a Norwegian king finds himself a bride in Finnmark. He is Erik Bloodaxe, perhaps the same historically insubstantial ruler of Northumbria in the mid-tenth century, but a far more corporeal, colourful figure in the Norse sagas. She is Gunnhild, not a Sámi but a Norse woman, with a father who comes from the northernmost Norwegian province of Halogaland. Gunnhild has come north to learn dark arts from two of the most powerful Sámi magicians in the land. In her vivid description of the pair, ordinary northern activities such as hunting and skiing are puffed up to prodigious proportions and combined with murderous magical talents:

Both of them are so knowing that they can follow tracks like hounds, both on thawed ground and on hard frozen snow. They are so good at skiing that nothing can escape them, neither man nor beast, and whatever they shoot they hit, which is why they have killed every man who has come near here. If they get angry, then the earth itself flinches from their glare, and if they catch sight of any living creature then it falls down dead.[32]

Gunnhild is a stock character in the sagas. She appears in several tales, most often as a woman of magic and malice. On one occasion she transforms herself into a bird and sits twittering by a poet's window all night, trying to distract him so that he will be unable to compose the poem that will prevent him being executed in the morning. In another particularly memorable episode, the jealous Gunnhild causes her lover's private parts to inflate so monstrously that he is unable to sleep with his new bride, who quickly uses this as a reason to divorce him.[33] Gunnhild was a genuine historical person, although there is no evidence that she had anything to do with the far north. In reality, she is more likely to have come from Denmark. However, as has been noted, for saga storytellers the link between the Sámi and their magical abilities was probably a neat explanation for her reputed skills in this area.[34]

Unless your member has been inconveniently and impractically enlarged by an angry northern witch, sex can lead to babies. Sex with a Sámi woman— Norse women rarely, if ever, sleep with Sámi men in the sagas—is no different. It seems that a mixed lineage was nothing to be ashamed of, and children of Norse–Sámi parentage are occasionally mentioned in Norse texts other than the sagas. For instance, the thirteenth-century Book of Settlements (Landnámabók) is an account of the first generations to settle Iceland, detailing which part of the country they settled and who their ancestors were. One line at least is said to be descended from a Sámi ruler:

Hrosskel was the son of Thorstein and Lopthoena. He married Joreid the daughter of Olvir, who was the son of Mottul, king of the Sámi.[35]

Such mixed-heritage children occasionally appear in the sagas too. King Harald and Snaefrid were said to have four sons, whom the king briefly banished from the kingdom when released from his dead wife's enchantment. Some of their descendants seem to have inherited her magical tendencies: one great-grandson crops up later in *Heimskringla* to plague the king with his troublesome weather-magic talents. On the other hand, at least one Norwegian king declared himself to be descended from one of Snaefrid and Harald's offspring, and it was through this line that he claimed the throne; clearly in this case his Sámi heritage was no barrier to Norwegian kingship.[36] On the other hand, in sagas located at the more fantastical end of the spectrum, children with Norse–Sámi blood are rather mysterious, otherworldly characters, tinged with the magic of the north. We will return to children such as these later on.

In most of these cases—apart from Gunnhild—it is the Sámi themselves who enter the Norse world. But other sorts of tension develop when the sagas take us north, into the unstable borderlands of the Norse world and beyond into Finnmark itself. In this liminal space, identities, loyalties, and even realities are all mutable. The two worlds begin to bleed into each other, until men struggle to remember where they started. This is a volatile world where trade, politics, religion, love, and magic are all potential flash-points. When the smoke clears, the Norsemen may be facing the Sámi with trading goods or weapons in their hands. They may even be standing shoulder to shoulder with them, staring down their fellow countrymen from the other side.

CHAPTER 4

North of all Northmen

As far north as whale hunters go

In the last decades of the ninth century, a trading ship glided out of the icy waters of northern Scandinavia. It was a magnificent high-prowed merchant ship of oak planks and iron rivets, loaded with luxurious Arctic wares: soft snow-white furs, rough hairy hides, and smooth walrus ivory.[1] Riding low in the water, it set off down the Norwegian coastline, bound for business in the major trading ports of southern Norway and Denmark. From there a new course was set to the west, and the ship set off again, prow pointing towards the waters of Anglo-Saxon England.[2]

The owner of this ship was a trader and explorer whom we know as Ohthere. He was a wealthy man from Halogaland, close to the borders between Norway and Finnmark. Now he found himself many hundreds of miles from home, in a land ripped apart by his fellow Norsemen. Ohthere was a rare bloom in this part of the world: a Scandinavian who came bearing gifts, not arms. Weighed down by precious walrus ivory for the king, Ohthere and his band of sea-hardened sailors made their way to the court of King Alfred.

In south-west England Alfred stood centre stage, ruler of the kingdom of Wessex. He had come to power six years after the Great Heathen Army had crossed the North Sea in 865. Within a few years, vast swathes of England had fallen to the Northmen. All Anglo-Saxon England was occupied. All except

FIGURE 4.1 *Lofotr*, a reconstruction of the Gokstad ship and similar to the sort that would have been used by Ohthere

Wessex, the only kingdom of indomitable Anglo-Saxons that still held out against the invaders.

As war raged, the backdrop flickered from besieged royal strongholds to the desolate Somerset marshes, from stormy battlefields to bloody seascapes. Finally a treaty was signed that established the boundaries between Anglo-Saxon and Scandinavian territories. With that, the scene was reset to Alfred's royal court, and onto this stage stepped Ohthere. After many cold, wet weeks at sea, he now stood in halls and chambers 'marvellously constructed of stone and wood', as Alfred's contemporary biographer, Asser, described them.[3] Candlelight danced around the walls, illuminating rich, heavy textiles hung to keep out draughts that came whistling through the cracks. It was impressive, but Ohthere had probably seen many remarkable sights in his life, and he had a tale of his own for Alfred and his battle-scarred men.

As the traveller from the far north spoke, the backdrop was transformed from scenes of war-ravaged England to the Arctic regions, far further than even the cosmopolitan Alfred had ventured. Ohthere conjured up an alien landscape peopled by whale hunters, fur trappers, fishermen, and walrus-ivory traders. The account begins:

Ohthere said to his lord, King Alfred, that he lived furthest north of all the Northmen. He said that he lived in the land that lies northward along the Western Sea. He said that the land stretches very far north from there, but it is all wasteland, except in a few places where the *Finnas* camp—hunting in the winter and fishing in the summer by the sea. He said that on one occasion, he wanted to discover how far north the land extended, or whether anyone lived to the north of that wasteland. Then he travelled northwards along the land.[4]

These wastelands were not deserted, nor were they populated by the dog-headed creatures and diabolical fiends of medieval imagination (bear in mind that Ohthere lived in the same century as Rimbert, the missionary who was worried about what he should do if he met dog-headed men in Scandinavia). *Finnas* is the Old English equivalent of *Finnar*: the Sámi. These weren't the only inhabitants of the far north that Ohthere met on his travels. He also came across a people called *Beormas* in the Old English account; settled farmers who cultivated the lands east of the White Sea. These are the Bjarmians—*Bjarmar* in Old Norse—who also feature in the sagas and other medieval Norse texts, usually as wild, vicious pagans. Saga encounters between the Bjarmians and the Norse often read like Indiana Jones adventures, with wild and murderous tribes, mysterious religious idols, pagan temples guarded by gruesome priestesses, and piles of treasure waiting to be stolen. Perhaps unsurprisingly, Ohthere says nothing of the sort, only that he didn't dare to sail across the river and land there 'because of hostilities' between the *Beormas* and the Norse.[5]

The intrepid Ohthere kept journeying north until he was 'as far north as the whale hunters ever go'.[6] When he came to the Arctic Ocean he turned eastwards, and sailed across the top of Scandinavia, keeping the coastline to his right and the open sea to his left. Finally, he came to a 'great river';[7] probably the Northern Dvina in what is now the north-west corner of Russia, which flows into the White Sea. (See Map 1.)

Ohthere hadn't travelled north simply to sightsee. He was also a prosperous trader, made wealthy by the Arctic riches on his doorstep. The northern coastline of Finnmark may have been physically challenging, but it was also rich in marine resources with rivers, sheltered harbours, and grassy valleys. As he told King Alfred, his journey north was for business as well as pleasure:

In addition to exploring the land, he went there mainly for the walruses, because they have very fine bones in their teeth—they brought some of these teeth to the king— and their hide is very good for ships' ropes.[8]

As we will see in later chapters on Greenland, the walrus was the ultimate 'nose to tail' commodity of the medieval north. Their tusks were prized as ivory, their hides made excellent rope, and their dense penis bones were used for tools such as knife handles. (Traditionally, Inuit hunters in Greenland also used these penis bones as the legs for three-legged stools suitable for sitting on the ice and fishing.) One of these 'fine bones'—walrus ivory—would have been a gift truly fit for a king.*

Perhaps this wasn't the only Arctic treasure that Ohthere brought with him. Another passage tells us that, when Ohthere visited King Alfred, 'he had six hundred tame reindeer still unsold'.[9] As Ohthere seems to have gone on to explain, 'they call these wild animals reindeer; there were six "decoy reindeer": those are very valuable to the *Finnas*, because they trap wild reindeer with them'.[10] It isn't clear from this whether Ohthere had brought these reindeer

---

* Today, the Royal and Ancient Polar Bear Society in Hammerfest, Norway, uses a walrus penis bone to knight new members of their organization. During the induction ceremony the neophyte kneels on an uncomfortable stool made of rope, and the walrus penis bone is tapped on both shoulders in turn. Unless the inductee is made of very stern stuff, they may be slightly put off by the stuffed walrus head mounted on the opposite wall, staring down mournfully throughout the proceedings.

with him on his voyage or whether they were still back home in northern Norway. The fact that they are described as 'unsold' might indicate they had been brought along in order to be sold, but the practicalities of transporting 600 seasick reindeer from northern Norway to south-west England makes the whole thing seem rather doubtful. More likely, they were an index of Ohthere's wealth; the Norwegian equivalent of cattle. Whether or not the Anglo-Saxons understood this is unclear. From the ambiguous wording, perhaps something of the sense of what Ohthere meant was lost in translation.*

Any man who owned a seagoing ship—perhaps several—capable of sailing from northern Norway to western England was not doing badly for himself. Ohthere must have been a rich and powerful man. The reason he knew so much about these Arctic tribes was because he traded with and collected tribute from them. Most likely, Ohthere came to Anglo-Saxon England also to trade, although this isn't specified in the account, which simply notes that he visited important market towns in Norway and Denmark on the way.

Ohthere's account suggests he enjoyed close relationships with the northern tribes he did business with. He was aware that the *Finnas* and the *Beormas* spoke similar languages, which indicates that he could communicate directly to them or had an interpreter with him. If it were the latter, then Ohthere wouldn't be the last Norseman to take interpreters with him to the far north. An Icelandic manuscript from the fourteenth century also tells a story about a Norwegian priest travelling to Finnmark, who had to talk to the Sámi through *túlkar* ('interpreters').[11]

Although Ohthere didn't want to land in the territory occupied by the *Beormas* on that occasion, relations between this group and the Norse traders couldn't have been exclusively hostile. Ohthere also says that they told him stories of neighbouring lands and peoples there, not all of which he believed:

The *Beormas* told him many stories, both about their own land and the lands that surrounded them. But he didn't know what was true, because he didn't see them for himself. It seemed to him that the *Finnas* and the *Beormas* spoke nearly the same language.[12]

---

* Even if Ohthere left his reindeer at home, someone at some point in the Middle Ages *did* bring reindeer—or at least bits of them—to medieval England. In the church of Abbots Bromley in Staffordshire six pairs of reindeer antlers are mounted onto the walls, which have been radiocarbon dated to the eleventh century. There were no native reindeer in England at the time, so they may well have been imported from Scandinavia. The whole thing is rather mysterious, but in any case, for centuries, the good folk of Abbots Bromley have danced an annual 'horn dance', complete with antler headdresses. A photograph from around 1900 shows a row of solemn, hirsute gentlemen, all sporting magnificent antlers on their heads and luxuriant beards on their chins.

FIGURE 4.2　The icy coastline of Finnmark

Ohthere's attitude to wild tales of the north is remarkably empirical, almost journalistic in tone. As far as we can tell, his own account seems to be based on experience and fact. What Ohthere did not see for himself, he did not believe. This is even more remarkable because it was written down at a time when the far north lay on the hazy boundaries between reality, hearsay, and imagination, although of course not for Ohthere. The description only survives because it was inserted into the Old English translation and reworking of the *Seven Books of History against the Pagans* (*Historiarum adversum paganos libri septem*), an influential historical and geographical work written in the early fifth century by a Spanish theologian and historian called Paulus Orosius. That Ohthere's description was thought fit for inclusion in one of the most influential textbooks of the medieval world suggests that it was considered an accurate account of the trade routes, tribes, and resources of the Arctic. Certainly, there is nothing remotely strange or supernatural in Ohthere's account of the north: the authentic voice of a fearless, self-reliant trader and explorer who navigated some of the toughest waters in the known world, grew wealthy on the bounty of the Arctic, and believed only what he could see with his own eyes.

This is our first glimpse of the historical north in which the saga stories are rooted, coming not from the north itself but from the war-ravaged lands of Anglo-Saxon England. The account is written in Old English, not Old Norse, with Ohthere's words probably recorded by a court scribe. This is why we know him as Ohthere—the Old English version of his name—rather than Ottar, which is probably closer to what he was called at home. It isn't clear how Ohthere communicated with Alfred and his court. Perhaps he was able to speak some form of English—fluent or pidgin—after all, he was an international trader, and the languages would have been, to some extent, mutually understandable (with a few grunts and hand gestures thrown in). Alternatively, his words may have been translated by a fellow Norseman now living in England at Alfred's court, which was a bustling hub of international activity. There were several prominent families of ex-vikings who had made their peace and come over to King Alfred's side; maybe Ohthere's translator was from among them. In any case, there is a sense of immediacy in this process, which might also explain some of the hazier parts of the account (not least the six hundred reindeer) and the fact that there are certain words and phrases that, despite being written in Old English, echo Ohthere's Norwegian mother tongue. This is particularly true of the animals, tribes, and topography of the north, unfamiliar to an Anglo-Saxon audience and so without the equivalent vocabulary. The Old English word *hranas* ('reindeer') comes from the Old Norse word *hreinar*. Likewise, *horshwæl* ('walrus') comes from the Old Norse *hrosshvalr*.[13] Reading this passage, it is as if we are hearing Ohthere's own voice, describing his voyage and having to improvise the appropriate vocabulary for his Anglo-Saxon audience. Through this sole surviving text Ohthere speaks to us, just as he spoke to King Alfred and his retinue more than a millennium ago.

After Ohthere the trail goes cold for a time. As the centuries advanced, the world that Ohthere described started to fade. By the thirteenth century, when the sagas started to be written down, Norse activities in Finnmark and around the White Sea had slowed considerably. The climate was changing, so that ships were often blocked in by Arctic sea-ice. There was increasing competition from the Russian merchants of Novgorod, who also wanted a slice of this lucrative trade. There may also have been growing tensions between the Norse and those they were trading with. This is what is described in a contemporary Kings' Saga from the thirteenth century called the *Saga of Hakon Hakonarson*

(*Hákonar saga Hákonarsonar*), which describes how Norse traders quarrelled with the king of the Bjarmians. After this, a Norse ship was lost on the coast of Finnmark. According to the saga, this was the last ship that made the voyage there.[14] But out in Iceland the memory of the far north endured, and eventually worked its way into the sagas, as a world of shifting borderlands, political tensions, and ambiguous identities, which intersect with magic, marvels, and even monsters.

King of the north

In his own homeland, Ohthere was a creature of the borderlands. As he told King Alfred, he lived 'furthest north of all the Northmen'. To his north lay the wild wastelands of Finnmark, inhabited by tribes well known to him and his men. To his south lived his fellow Norwegians and an ambitious king— King Harald Fairhair—who wanted to bring all of Norway under his control. Still, if Ohthere had anything to say about his dealings with his southern countrymen, or King Harald Fairhair, it was not included in the Old English account. His only interaction with a king is as an independent agent in a foreign country.

In the sagas, however, the northern borderlands are the stage upon which fiery political dramas are played out. Often, the main actors are powerful chieftains from the north and ambitious kings from further south. Recalcitrant leaders from the borderlands are potentially problematic elements within Norse society, with valuable assets to protect and uncanny foreign allies to call on. As a result, the north can quickly become a troubling, destabilizing region for Norwegian kings with big plans. It can also be a dangerous place for the Norse traders who operate in it: a remote frontier territory where the king's authority seems a long way off, and ambitious young men have room to grow and prosper. Or so they think. But as the following story illustrates, vaulting ambition can overleap itself in a heartbeat, with fatal consequences.

Meet Thorolf, the Richard Branson of the saga world: a charismatic, blond, energetic man with a lucrative business empire in the far north. Thorolf features in the opening chapters of the *Saga of Egil Skallagrimsson* (*Egils saga Skallagrímssonar*). Composed in the thirteenth century, this is one of the most famous and dramatic of the Sagas of Icelanders. In this Norwegian prologue to the main action out in Iceland, we witness Thorolf's spectacular rise and fall as he inadvertently becomes entangled in a power-struggle with a jealous king.

More than any other saga episode set in the far north, this is the one that adds narrative flesh to the historical bones of Ohthere's account. The two texts represent an intriguing intersection between historical record and saga narrative, although they were written down several centuries apart. Thorolf's saga life shares some extraordinary parallels with the historical figure of Ohthere, and the opening chapters of the saga are set at the same time that our real-life Arctic adventurer lived. In this saga too, connections to Finnmark are very profitable, and initially Thorolf is able to exploit them to his heart's content. However, unlike Ohthere, who is presented (or at least presents himself) as an autonomous trader with full control over his own destiny, Thorolf's ties to Norwegian society are tighter and more problematic. The thrust of the narrative concerns how other Norsemen—and the king in particular—react to the wealth and power accumulated by one man. With the promise of money and power comes jealousy, political skulduggery, and murder.

Thorolf's story unfolds against a politically turbulent backdrop. It is the mid-ninth century, and King Harald Fairhair is trying to bring the whole of Norway under his control. Northern Norway and the chieftains of Halogaland are the king's biggest political headache. Halogaland is a vast region, located far from the king's secure power-base further south. It is the home of powerful men who—like Ohthere—have been made wealthy by their connections to Finnmark, and don't necessarily want to share.

Thorolf is in charge of trade and tax-collecting in Finnmark, on the understanding that the king gets a hefty cut of the profit. He is an affable man, but ruthlessly protective of his assets. Rival groups of traders and plunderers are dealt with swiftly and brutally. Like Ohthere, Thorolf enjoys a close working relationship with the Sámi. Yet, rather ominously, their professional cordiality is maintained at a price. As they trade and collect taxes from their northern neighbours, the saga states that 'everything progressed with relaxed chat and friendship, but also with some degree of fear'.[15]

Today, rich Norwegians make their money from their country's most valuable natural resource: oil. In the ninth century, the natural resources most in demand were ermine, beaver, squirrel, and sable furs, dried cod, and animal hides. The saga describes how Thorolf grows wealthy on his profits from Finnmark and commissions a magnificent dragonheaded longship:

In the spring he had a big longship with a dragon's head built, furnished with the best of everything, and brought it with him from the north. Thorolf completely monopolized the fishing in Halogaland and had his men fishing for herring and cod. There were plenty of seals and eggs, and he arranged it that everything was brought to him. He never had fewer than a hundred freedmen at his home. He was a generous, liberal man, very good friends with important men and everyone who lived in the neighbourhood. He became a powerful man and took great care over equipping his ship and weapons.[16]

In this description, Thorolf's longship replete with dragonhead is the Norse equivalent of a billionaire's super-yacht, which may or may not be a saga exaggeration. Even so, the saga makes an important point about how Thorolf is setting himself up against the king, perhaps unintentionally so. Today, we are so used to the stereotype of Norse ships with dragonheads mounted on the front that we might skim through this saga description without giving it much thought.* As a matter of fact, material evidence for such dragonheads is limited, certainly if we rely on the remains of Norse ships discovered underwater or buried in the ground. We know that they existed, not least because carvings of Norse ships with dragonheads have been found scratched into wood and stone from locations as diverse as Bergen and Istanbul (although in the case of the Bergen carving, a casual observer might be forgiven for assuming that the Norse fixed carved rabbit heads to their vessels). Moreover, in the case of a ship burial from c.925 found at Ladby in Denmark, the ship's prow was decorated with a 'dragon's mane' of iron curls to go with a mounted dragonhead on top, although only the iron curls survive. But it

---

* The Norse might be best known for their dragonhead ships, but they were certainly not the only ones to fix images of monstrous creatures to the front of their vessels. In fact, the best example of such a dragonhead was found in the river Scheldt (Belgium), which has been dated with carbon-14 analysis to somewhere between the fourth to sixth century AD. Prior to this it was assumed to be from a viking ship. Kenneth Clarke's seminal television series *Civilisation* (1969) opens with him standing by the river Seine, describing how, 'to the mother of a family trying to settle down in her little hut', a viking prow would have seemed 'as menacing to her civilization as the periscope of a nuclear submarine'. As ominous organ music crashes away in the background, the artefact chosen to illustrate this point is the aforementioned late-Roman dragonhead.

seems that such ships were not everyday vessels, just like not every car has a Rolls Royce 'silver lady' figurine on the bonnet. Later written texts give us more information. We know that superstitions were attached to these dragon-heads in Norse tradition, designed to frighten both malevolent sea spirits and enemies. Such a powerful tool had to be used carefully: the thirteenth-century Icelandic *Book of Settlements* mentions a law prohibiting sailors from approaching land without removing the dragonheads from their ships, lest they frighten away the land spirits. But for the most part when sagas and poems make references to dragonheads mounted on ships, it is in the context of famous vessels belonging to rulers.[17] Therefore, to return to the saga, by commissioning a magnificent ship resplendent with dragonhead mounted on the prow, Thorolf may be subtly—even inadvertently—setting himself up as the king's rival in terms of wealth and political power in the region. And as we will see later on, Thorolf is not the only Halogalander to build himself a splendid ship with a dragonhead, nor is he the only Halogalander to suffer the king's wrath.

Dragonheads aside, in many respects Thorolf's trading career mirrors that of his historical counterpart Ohthere. According to the saga, one of Thorolf's magnificent ships is sent on a trading expedition to England, just like the one Ohthere undertook. Blue-and-red striped sail hoisted, it leaves Norway loaded with Arctic goods to be traded for wheat, honey, wine, and cloth: 'he loaded it with dried fish and hides and ermine, then added grey furs and other pelts that he had got from the mountains. It was a huge amount of wealth.'[18]

From this description, it's easy to see why a king looking to consolidate his own power might start to get a bit twitchy. Thorolf is popular with all the right people, he has exclusive access to an Arctic cornucopia of herring, seals, and eggs, and he has more than 100 men working for him. Worse, he not only has ships, but also weapons. But Thorolf's good fortune is a double-edged sword. The king becomes nervy at Thorolf's snowballing power and wealth, and when Thorolf throws a lavish feast for him, he sulks from start to finish. Eventually, Thorolf's luck runs out when his jealous rivals persuade the crotchety king that he is being double-crossed. They tell him:

He bought everything: the Sámi paid him tribute, and he promised that your stewards wouldn't enter Finnmark. He intends to make himself king over the north, both Finnmark and Halogaland.[19]

No man should proclaim himself king of the north. With this lie, Thorolf's fate is sealed, and the king orders his men to burn his former friend alive in his house. As the flames flicker around the door, Thorolf runs outside, only to be dispatched with a deadly blow struck by the king himself.

Thorolf's enemies may have lied, but like all the best lies, theirs had a deeper vein of truth. Even as we read the saga, it might be that we are not *quite* sure whom to believe. Thorolf seemed to be playing by the rules, but he was *very* rich, his foreign friends were *very* friendly, and his ship was *very* big. Perhaps the king's paranoia was understandable.

Pagans and politics

As we have seen in the story of Thorolf and King Harald Fairhair, the north was a politically vulnerable region for Norwegian kings, at the very edge of—or beyond—their control. The chieftains of the north occupied a cultural middle ground; their interests and priorities were not necessarily the same as those of other Norwegians, likewise the nature of their interactions with the tribes of Finnmark. This was still true over a century later, when Norwegian kings tried to extend the frontiers of Christianity. In sagas set at the time of the conversion in Norway, kings have even more to fear from the men of the borderlands: stroppy pagans whose religious faith is intrinsically bound up with their political autonomy.

The conversion of Norway is a tale of two Olafs, the name of the two kings who had the biggest roles to play in the Christianization of the country. King Olaf Tryggvason ruled from 995 to 1000 before vanishing mysteriously (according to the sagas) during a sea battle. King Olaf Haraldsson—later St Olaf, patron saint of Norway—ruled from 1015 to 1028 before being driven into exile in Russia. Returning to Norway two years later, he was killed at the Battle of Stiklestad. Several sagas were written starring these popular kings, parts of which describe their attempts to convert Norway to Christianity and strengthen their control over the country. Northern Norway proves particularly problematic: a pagan stronghold controlled by northern chieftains who are staunch protectors of their faith, autonomy, and wealth. Even worse, these chieftains have powerful foreign support in the shape of their Sámi neighbours: dangerous allies with a reputation for magic.

The first Olaf, King Olaf Tryggvason, has been described as 'Christ's best hatchet-man', which gives us some idea of his conversion methods.[20] This

FIGURE 4.3 Manuscript page from *Heimskringla's Saga of Olaf Tryggvason* (c.1300–1324)

certainly applies to his treatment of two northern chieftains in the *Saga of Olaf Tryggvason* (*Óláfs saga Tryggvasonar*), which is part of the *Heimskringla* compilation of Kings' Sagas. The first thorn in Olaf's side is a man called Raud the Strong. Raud is a powerful Halogalander from a group of islands located around sixty miles north of the Arctic Circle. The islands are called *Goðeyjar*—'the islands of the gods'—the gods in question being pagan Norse ones. Historically, these islands comprised a major heathen stronghold throughout the conversion era (and even today several large heathen burial mounds can be seen on them).[21]

According to the saga, Raud's proudest possession is a huge ship with a golden dragonhead mounted on the front, a tail curving up from the back, and sails that look like dragon's wings propelling the vessel over the sea. It is said to be the most beautiful craft in Norway: part of a big, bold political statement that challenges the king's power and authority in the region, much more so than in the case of Thorolf. Raud also has many supporters from the far north, and he himself is skilled in weather-magic: 'He was a powerful man. A great number of Sámi followed him, when he needed them. Raud was a heathen worshipper and very skilled in magic.'[22] Just like the magical Sámi seeress we met in the previous chapter, Raud is described as 'much knowing' (*fjǫlkunnigr*), and as he sails in his magnificent ship, he conjures up a fair wind to speed him on his way. At the same time, he uses his talents to call up terrible storms against his enemies. When King Olaf sails north to confront Raud in a final showdown, he and his men can only battle through the magical storms by arming themselves with the weapons of the new religion:

Bishop Sigurd took all his vestments and went to the prow of the king's ship. He had candles lit and incense brought out, and set up a crucifix on the prow. There he read the gospel aloud and said many other prayers, and sprinkled holy water all around the ship.[23]

Bristling with lit tapers, doused with holy water, and wreathed in a fog of incense, the king's ship sails into the fjord like a damp, smoked hedgehog. Eventually the royal hatchet-man catches up with the pagan, and takes a terrible vengeance on him. When Raud refuses to convert to Christianity, the king's men force an adder down his throat, which chews its way out and kills him. Finally, to add insult to injury, Olaf confiscates the dragon-head ship.

Raud is not the only northerner who meets with a grisly end because of his refusal to convert. In the same saga we are introduced to another chieftain, Eyvind Split-Cheek, who is part of a northern warband assembled to defend Halogaland against the king. Eyvind's entire being is so utterly bound up with the north, Sámi magic, and paganism that he couldn't convert to Christianity if he tried. When neither promises of lands nor threats of torture can persuade Eyvind, a basin of red-hot embers is placed on his belly until it bursts. The dying man tells the king:

I can't be baptized. I'm a spirit brought to life in the shape of a man by Sámi magic, because my father and mother couldn't conceive a child.[24]

The idea of a childless couple asking supernatural entities for help is common throughout many folklore traditions. In this case, the Sámi themselves take on the role of such otherworldly beings. Theirs is a kind of magic so intrinsically bound to paganism that Eyvind—the literal embodiment of this Sámi enchantment—must die rather than reject his faith and convert to Christianity.

A few decades later, and also on a campaign to take control over the whole of Norway, King Olaf Haraldsson—the second Olaf—finds himself plagued by pagan enemies from the north. The worst of them is a man

FIGURE 4.4 Protected by his magical reindeer skins, Thorir kills King Olaf. Illustration by Halfdan Egedius for a Norwegian translation of *Heimskringla* (1899)

named Thorir the Hound. He too collects tribute from the tribes of the north, competing directly with the king's men for grey furs, beaver skins, and sable pelts.

Olaf Haraldsson was killed in battle in 1030, fighting against the Norwegian chieftains who opposed him. In the saga description of this final battle, Thorir the Hound is among the ranks of the king's enemies. He advances into the fray suffused with magic of the north. Around his shoulders is a cloak of reindeer skin, fashioned for him by the Sámi. This is no ordinary garment, but rather one of twelve skins, 'with so much magic that no weapon could catch on them'.[25] Sure enough, when Olaf slashes at Thorir's shoulder, 'the sword wouldn't bite, and it seemed as though dust flew up from the reindeer skin'.[26] When the fighting ends, King Olaf lies dead on the battlefield. Thorir and his reindeer cloak are unscathed, protected by the powerful magic of his friends in the north. A verse, apparently composed by the king's poet Sigvat, describes the moment when Olaf—here described as the 'fire-sender of the mast-tops', a kenning for a generous man—tries to strike Thorir down:*

> The munificent king himself discovered most fully
> how the mightily strong witchcraft
> of the magic-talented Sámi
> saved the very powerful Thorir,
> when the fire-sender of the mast-tops
> struck the Hound's shoulders
> with the gold-covered sword:
> the blunt one bit least.[27]

For Raud the Strong, Eyvind Split-Cheek, and Thorir the Hound, their political autonomy, pagan beliefs, Sámi links, and magical powers all come together to shape their northern identity on the borderlands of Norway and Finnmark. The two Olafs look forward to a unified, Christian Norway. The obstreperous Halogalanders cling to a past in which they are proud, powerful, and pagan. Ohthere—whom we know to have inhabited these same lands over a century earlier when the country was still firmly pagan—may well have felt the same. He was certainly not a spirit brought to life by Sámi spells, nor did he magically whip up the wind as he approached the English coastline. Even so, perhaps to the Christian Anglo-Saxons there was also something rather otherworldly about this traveller who had come so far from the north.

Sailing by

Today, the far-northern landscapes that Ohthere conjured so vividly for King Alfred over a millennium ago—landscapes that would later become the stage for saga stories of bloody rebellion and dangerous enchantment—have changed little. It is still possible to follow the route described in Ohthere's account, all the way from the city of Tromsø (close to where Ohthere probably came from) up and around the northern coastline of Norway until you reach

---

* Kennings are word compounds used in Old Norse poetry to describe something without naming it directly (the Norse equivalent of a cryptic crossword clue). For instance, a sword might be described as the 'icicle of blood' or 'leek of war', while the sea might be the 'blood of the earth' or 'realm of lobsters'.

the Russian border. The landscape has a bleak, bare beauty: jagged, looming mountains, deep fjords that sparkle in the summer sunshine and freeze as the winter darkness closes in, and endless rocky wastelands around the coast, just as Ohthere described. A little further inland are swathes of spindly forests, where autumn arrives overnight to transform fragile green leaves into slivers of orange flame. The sun hardly touches some of the deeper valleys; here, the stunted trees are nothing more than sprays of dead, blackened twigs where the weight of the snow has suffocated them over the slow winter. Out on the long, empty roads, a driver is more likely to meet a herd of thick-pelted, shaggy rein-deer than another car. Teetering on the edge of the ocean and surrounded by sparse wilderness, most of Finnmark's tiny coastal towns—Hammerfest, Honningsvåg, Vadsø, Vardø, Kirkenes—are incongruously, almost jarringly, modern. This is the legacy of Finnmark's darker recent history and the scorched-earth policy—known as Operation Nordlicht ('Northern Light')—employed by the occupying Nazis as the tide of war turned against them and they fled before the Soviet advance. Today, in these little frontier towns, Oht-here's spirit lives on, in industries based on natural resources, trade, and inter-national transport, such as offshore oil drilling, fishing, and container shipping.

Following the coastline, all the major landmarks by which Ohthere would have navigated are still there. After many days sailing he would have sighted the brooding, towering cliffs of Nordkapp, now marketed to tourists as the northernmost point in Europe. Technically, this isn't true: the nearby penin-sula of Knivskjellodden (pronounced *k-neev-shell-oh-den*) sticks out a little fur-ther north into the sea, but it's a wretched five-mile scramble to the end point, during which you will be observed from a distance by dispassionate herds of reindeer as you stumble over jagged rocks, fall into muddy bogs, all the time shrouded in a dreich, drizzling mist. Today, a visitors' centre is perched on top of Nordkapp, containing, amongst other things, the utterly incongruous Royal Thai Museum, a kitsch riot of bright colours and exotic flowers com-memorating a visit by the king of Siam in 1907. But in Ohthere's day Nord-kapp would have been a bleak but vital navigational aid, just as it has been to generations of sailors ever since.

Following the coast east towards Russia, by land or by sea, will eventually bring a traveller to Vardø, the little port with the enormous witch-trial me-morial. A short boat-ride out of the harbour is the tiny island of Hornøya, the northeasternmost fragment of Norway, pitted with puffin burrows and crowned with thick tangles of cloudberries (a Scandinavian delicacy rather like raspberries but the colour of copper and honey). Almost certainly Ohthere would have sailed past this island on his way east. Perhaps he even stopped there to rest, mend his sea-battered ship, and gather supplies. Today the island is uninhabited, but visitors can stay the night in the working light-house. This is all very well—and feels rather romantic—on a fine sunny day, when one can sit outside on a little patch of grass, looking out over the sea to the hazy Russian mountains beyond. As dusk approaches, this sense of con-tented cosiness only intensifies, as little fishing boats, smaller than Ohthere's ship would have been, glide past on their way east, lights twinkling in the dusk. But as dusk melts into night, the sounds of the moaning wind, the mournful cry of the seabirds, and the sombre scraping and grinding of the lighthouse mechanism are magnified. There is no escape from the island, and as the light circles the ocean, illuminating the churning waves below, an over-active imagination can start to play tricks on the unwary mind. All through the long night, a traveller may feel as though they have followed Ohthere into a barren northern land of supernatural terrors, all of their own making.

Monsters are easily conjured up in the dark northern night. There is some-thing about the dramatic, barren landscapes of the north that the imagination easily fills with the magical, the monstrous, and the supernatural. The Sámi are a case in point. But the ultimate monstrous, supernatural creatures of the Nordic world are trolls and giants, many of whom lurk in the far north. To understand this world, we have to leave Ohthere and his fellow Norse traders in the sagas, and turn to different sorts of tales. Tales about where the wild things are.

CHAPTER 5

Where the Wild Things Are

Fighting with monsters

The philosopher Friedrich Nietzsche wrote: 'He who fights with monsters should look to it that he himself does not become a monster.' This is a piece of advice that certain northbound saga heroes could have benefited from, though in their case, the danger comes not only from fighting monsters, but also from fraternizing, feasting, and even fornicating with them.

Welcome to the far north of the Legendary Sagas, a north populated not only by magically predisposed humans such as the Sámi, but also more dangerous and terrible beings. In this Norse version of the 'wild weird clime' imagined by armchair—and actual—travellers across the millennia, a colourful cast of trolls, ogres, and giants traipse across the Arctic stage: some with a taste for man-flesh, others with snot dripping down their faces, others sex-crazed and skinless. The art of understatement—so famous in many of the Sagas of Icelanders—is not much in evidence here. Often these tales are parodies with their tongues set firmly in their cheeks. Pagan priestesses slip on pools of vulture blood in their holy temples, lusty young heroes roam the north humping every farmer's daughter they can persuade into bed, and Arctic kings transform themselves into whales and dragons, crushing enemies with their body weight or ripping open bellies with their talons. In the eccentric world of the Legendary Sagas, heroes bound for the far north are rarely more than a remote fjord or craggy mountain pass away from the shock of their lives.*

This vision of the north owes more to the powers of the human imagination than to historical reality. Even so, strong historical currents still flow beneath the surface. The north is still characterized by enchantment, paganism, trading resources, political tensions with the south, and love affairs between Norse men and northern women. The main difference between these sagas and the sagas that were the focus of the previous chapters is that, in the ones we are about to explore, these themes are as likely to surface in tales about trolls and giants as they are in stories featuring the human inhabitants of Finnmark.

A hairy situation

Meet Ketil Trout, son of Hallbjorn Half-Troll. The family comes from Hrafnista, an island off the coast of Halogaland. Like many of the Halogalanders we have met thus far—the wealthy traders and troublemaking pagan chieftains of the Kings' Sagas and Sagas of Icelanders—Ketil's eyes are fixed firmly on the northern lands beyond his borderland home. But in Ketil's story the strangest, most outlandish characteristics of the region are magnified, creating even more distance between the real north described by Ohthere and the saga north presented here. Take the following episode from the *Saga of Ketil Trout* (*Ketils saga hœngs*), the first of four so-called *Hrafnista sagas* about successive generations of men from this family.

One autumn, young Ketil sails north on a fishing expedition, but his ship is caught in a ferocious storm that sweeps him away to Finnmark. Ketil wakes to find his ship being shaken to pieces by a malevolent troll-woman, and escapes by jumping into his rowing-boat with a cask full of butter. All seems lost, but Ketil is saved from briny oblivion by a Sámi man named Bruni, who magically transforms himself into a whale and protects Ketil from the waves. That night, Bruni invites his friends round to feast on Ketil's butter—'This butter is a feast

---

* Legendary Sagas set in this giant-infested far north are a rather mixed bag in terms of their readability. It all sounds rather exciting, but one dramatic event shunts into the next, until they pile up in a confused heap. Sometimes reading these sagas can feel like someone telling you the dream they had last night: unfocused, unsubtle, and a bit boring.

for us!' the hungry guests cheer—while under a blanket in the far corner of the room, Ketil gets intimately acquainted with Bruni's daughter, Hrafnhild.[1] The son they conceive that night is born with hair all over his cheek, and so they call him Grim Hairy-Cheek. According to one version of the story, this was caused by Hrafnhild peeping out from under the blanket at the moment Grim was conceived, and catching sight of one of her father's friends who also had a hairy cheek (saga genetics being a law unto itself). Later on, when Ketil has returned to Hrafnista, Hrafnhild comes to visit with their little son. Ketil's furious father Hallbjorn explodes at his son: 'Why did you ask that troll to come here?'[2] Crushed, Hrafnhild leaves for Finnmark, while the unrepentant Hallbjorn snorts: 'It's bad for you to love that troll!'[3] Ketil journeys north many more times, and meets far stranger beings than shape-shifting, butter-guzzling Sámi: in his lifetime he encounters troll-women black as pitch and tall as mountains, man-eating ogres, and a dragon that sears the dark night sky with flames. But of Hrafnhild there is no trace, and he never sees her again.

If we came to this story cold, as it were, it might not make much sense as anything other than a wild fantasy. But distant notes of historical reality, cultural perceptions, and narrative traditions still chime in this tale. Many of the same motifs are here that we have seen before, just in an exaggerated, more fantastical form. Once again, the inhabitants of the far north are the Sámi, a people with magical talents, capable of shape-shifting. The young lovers are another example of a Norse–Sámi sexual union, just as, for example, King Harald and the beautiful but dangerous Snaefrid. Likewise, the butter feast may seem odd if taken in isolation, until we remember that dairy products— along with metal and certain types of meat—were prized by the nomadic Sámi. In some ways we are in familiar territory, but the boundaries have started to shift.

Moreover, a new player has entered the stage: the brooding, shadowy figure of the troll. It is there in the troll-woman who shakes Ketil's boat to pieces. It is there in the furious words of Ketil's father, who dismisses Hrafnhild as a 'troll'. It is even there—rather hypocritically—in the nickname of Ketil's father: Half-Troll (*hálftröll*). If 'troll' is simply used in a derogatory sense for the Sámi, then the nickname may be a hint that Hallbjorn too has non-Norse blood running in his veins. Alternatively, there may be a more menacing explanation, for despite his disgust at Hrafnhild and his repeated warnings to his son not to venture north, we discover that he too has fraternized with the more unsavoury inhabitants of the lands beyond his home. During one particularly unpleasant adventure in the north, Ketil stumbles across a pit full of carcasses: whales, polar bears, seals, walruses, and—most grisly of all—salted man's flesh. The owner of this Arctic larder is an enormous, horrible-looking giant who refers to Ketil's father as 'Hallbjorn my friend'.[4] By consorting with monsters, Hallbjorn becomes half-monstrous himself, at least in name.

In this particular episode, trolls lurk only at the edges of the story. In subsequent generations of the Hrafnista clan, northern trolls, giants, and their kind play more prominent roles in affairs of the heart. The second of the *Hrafnista sagas* is the *Saga of Grim Hairy-Cheek* (*Gríms saga loðinkinna*). Here too, Grim, the furry-faced son of Ketil and Hrafnhild, sails to Finnmark, where he becomes the object of this hideous creature's affections:

She was no taller than a seven-year-old girl, but so fat that Grim doubted he could even get his arms around her. She was long-faced and hard-faced, hook-nosed and shoulder-hunched, dark-faced and pinch-cheeked, filthy-faced and bald at the front. Her hair and skin were black. She wore a shrivelled skin smock, which didn't come down below her buttocks. She's not exactly kissable, thought Grim, as snot dripped down her cheek.[5]

Admittedly, this comically horrible creature is actually Grim's (human) fiancée, who was spirited away before her wedding and transformed into a monster by a jealous Finnmark troll. However, he doesn't find that out until he has been forced to kiss her and share a bed with her, thus breaking the spell in traditional fairytale style.

Another generation on, in the *Saga of Arrow-Odd* (*Örvar-Odds saga*)—the third *Hrafnista saga*—Ketil's grandson Arrow-Odd also enjoys a holiday romance in the far north. This time it isn't with a Sámi, but a giant girl. The tone of the episode is light-hearted: when she sees him for the first time, she assumes that he is a baby because he is so tiny compared to her, so she puts him in a cradle and sings him lullabies. But Arrow-Odd has other ideas:

…when it seemed to her that he was getting restless in the cradle, she laid him in the bed next to her and wrapped herself around him. And so it happened that Odd played all the games he wanted and they got on very well with each other.[6]

One thing leads to another, and when the giant girl discovers she is pregnant, her first response is incredulity. She tells Arrow-Odd: 'it might seem unlikely that you had something to do with this, since you're so little and puny to look at. But still there's no doubt that you're the only one who could be the father of this child.[7] In the space of two generations, the men of Hrafnista have gone from coupling with their Sámi neighbours to sleeping with giantesses. The female inhabitants of the far north may grow ever more supernatural, but they have lost none of their allure.

In the Kings' Sagas, the Sámi brides of Norse husbands trail a dangerous magic with them into the marital bed. But by bringing them into the Norse world they can be neutralized, up to a point at least, for their husbands themselves remain fundamentally unchanged. Even in the case of King Harald Fairhair, once Snaefrid's body is moved, the enchantment is lifted from him and he is himself again. By contrast, the men of Hrafnista are invested bodily in the north. In the case of Ketil and Arrow-Odd, they not only conduct love affairs there, but also father children. Such total immersion has far-reaching consequences. Ketil's father picks up the nickname 'Half-Troll', while the child Ketil conceives with Hrafnhild sports a furry cheek his whole life; a mark of otherness that he shares with an unnamed, butter-loving Sámi man. In the next generation, Arrow-Odd has enough problems of his own to contend with, cursed with a lifespan of 300 years. Even so, Arrow-Odd's earliest adventures are in the Arctic lands beyond his home, where a massacre sets off a chain of events that will dog him throughout his preternaturally long life. His mortal enemy is a monstrous half-human, half-ogre, conjured up by the Arctic tribes of the north in revenge for the massacre. Both the Sámi and their equally uncanny neighbours, the Bjarmians, are complicit in the creation of this terrible being, which involves persuading the Bjarmian king into bed with a damp, waterfall-dwelling ogress:

…they took an ogress from under a great waterfall, full of magic and sorcery, and laid her in bed next to King Harek, and he had a son with her. He was sprinkled with water and called Ogmund. He was unlike most living men even at a young age, as would be expected because of his mother, but also because his father was a mighty pagan sacrificer. As soon as Ogmund was three years old he was sent to Finnmark, and there he learnt all kinds of spells and witchcraft. Then, when he was fully trained, he went back home to Bjarmaland. He was then seven years old and as large as a fully grown man, powerful in strength and evil to deal with. His stay with the Sámi hadn't helped his appearance, because he was then both black and blue, while his hair was black and hung down matted over his eyes where his fringe should be.[8]

Unfortunately, this isn't the last time we'll meet Ogmund in this book.

By the time we reach the last saga in the quartet—the *Saga of An-Bowbender* (*Áns saga bogsveigis*)—the power seems to have gone out of the north. Arrow-Odd's own son is the star of this saga, but it opens with the information that 'people didn't think he was in any way like his ancestors, who were Ketil Trout and the other men of Hrafnista, except in his size'.[9] Most of An-Bowbender's adventures take place in the south, and it is only in the final lines of the saga that he returns to Hrafnista. Even then, he cannot escape his destiny as a man of the northern borderlands, and ends his days fighting gangs of trolls and ogresses.

Giantland geography

In other Legendary Sagas the human population of Finnmark is forgotten entirely, and ever-more monstrous inhabitants of the Arctic north blow in on the icy wind: human–ogre hybrids, malevolent pagan gods, obese half-naked women with vulture claws, and gruel-eating nymphomaniacs. As one scholar has noted, 'when the exploration of the Scandinavians was brought to a halt by the wastes of the Arctic pack-ice, flights of fancy took the saga-authors to even wider horizons'.[10]

In some texts we find entire societies of trolls and giants hidden high in the frozen wastelands, frolicking, feasting, fighting, and fornicating in their far-northern kingdoms. For the most part, the geography of these kingdoms is vague. All we really know is that the saga heroes find themselves in wild, troll- and giant-infested realms located either north of Scandinavia or further east in Russia. But occasionally, the saga authors have a stab at creating a compre-hensive geographical model of this region, incorporating both the real and fantastical lands of the north. One such description opens the *Saga of Hervor and Heidrek* (*Hervarar saga ok Heiðreks*).[11] Fans of J. R. R. Tolkien's work may find themselves experiencing a distinct sense of déjà vu; just as in *The Lord of the Rings*, this saga features a feisty shield-maiden who rides to battle, dwarves called Durin and Dvalinn, a forest named Mirkwood, an enchanted sword taken from a haunted barrow, and magical chain-mail that can't be pierced by weapons. In fact, the standard edition and translation of the saga was pro-duced by Christopher Tolkien, youngest son of the above and a scholar of medieval literature, like his father.[12]

The saga survives in several, slightly different, versions. The beginning of one version opens with a geographical description of the far north, including two giant kingdoms, Jotunheimar (literally 'the home of giants') and Ymisland (named after Ymir, the gigantic primeval being of Norse mythology from whose corpse the world was shaped). These two 'giantlands' are incorporated into a realistic, more recognizable far-northern geography that includes Halogaland and Gandvik, the Norse name for the White Sea:*

It is found written in ancient books that north of Gandvik was Jotunheimar, while to the south between there and Halogaland was Ymisland....giants and some half-giants lived in those northern parts. In those days there was a great blending of races.[13]

In another version of the same saga this propensity is even more marked. Here, Finnmark too is incorporated into this mythical geography, and Jotunheimar is said specifically to be 'in Finnmark'.[14] A semi-mythical land of giants has been overlaid onto the real-life geographical places—Halogaland, Finnmark, the White Sea—once described so matter-of-factly by Ohthere to King Alfred. But while for Ohthere the region was home to fishermen and hunters, for the Legendary Sagas it is where the wild things are.

Glittering plains

Even when the Sámi and their neighbours have been ousted from their homelands and replaced by the stuff of fairytales and nightmares, the historical past still casts a faint shadow. Take, for instance, the mysterious Gudmund, ruler of the realm of *Glæsisvellir* or 'Glittering Plains'. The location of this place is explained later in the same geographical description that opens the *Saga of Hervor and Heidrek*:

Gudmund was the name of a chieftain in Jotunheimar; his home was at Grund, in the region of Glaesisvellir. He was a powerful and wise man, and he and his people were so old that they lived the lifespans of many men's lives.[15]

---

* Even real-life geographical locations such as these may have a touch of the uncanny about them. *Gand* refers to something enchanted, an object used by magicians, or something fiendish and monstrous, so Gandvik can be translated as 'Magic Bay'. Incidentally, the name of Tolkien's wizard Gandalf is a compound of the Old Norse words *gandr* (magic) and *álfr* (elf). Tolkien took the name from an Old Norse mythological poem, where it appears in a list of dwarf names (most of which Tolkien also made use of in *The Hobbit*).

Gudmund is a frequent visitor to the saga world, putting in guest appearances in several Legendary Sagas. He is a multifaceted figure whose true identity is difficult to pin down, and his character and age shift dramatically depending on the story in question. In one tale he is a green youth struggling to make his mark in the world of giant politics.[16] In another—unspeakably filthy and innuendo-ridden—saga, he is an established and somewhat boisterous king who toasts each of the pagan gods in turn and capers drunkenly to bawdy harp-tunes.[17]

His role is more complex—verging on the diabolical—in the dark *Tale of Helgi Thorisson* (*Helga þáttr Þórissonar*). This story combines many of the themes that characterize stories about the far north: trade, paganism, magic, politics, and love affairs. In this tale Gudmund never appears in person, but lurks behind the scenes, a mysterious and malevolent presence. Decidedly pagan, Gudmund takes on shades of a northern devil, tussling with King Olaf Tryggvason for possession of a man's very soul. As the king says of his unseen adversary: 'I've heard it said about Gudmund of Glaesisvellir that he is very skilled in magic and dangerous to deal with, and bad things happen to men who end up in his power.'[18]

Bad things certainly happen to Helgi, one of King Olaf Tryggvason's men, who ends up inadvertently embroiled with Gudmund. The trouble starts when Helgi sets off on a trading expedition to Finnmark with his brother. Within the first few lines of the tale we may already recognize some patterns familiar to stories set in the north, not least in the goods that the Norsemen take to sell: 'It happened one summer that the brothers went north on a trading expedition to Finnmark, taking butter and bacon to sell to the Sámi.'[19] But despite this deceptively familiar opening, this is not a tale about Norse–Sámi trade, nor trouble between King Olaf and the chieftains of Halogaland. Instead, it morphs into a love story between a Norseman and a woman from the far north, not a Sámi, but Gudmund's beautiful, dangerous daughter Ingibjorg. This is no holiday romance, but an encounter that will leave Helgi physically and mentally changed forever.

On their way back from the trading expedition, Helgi meets Ingibjorg in a forest swirling with fog, and spends three blissful nights in her bed. The following Yule, Helgi is spirited away from King Olaf's court during a storm, and taken to Glaesisvellir to be Ingibjorg's lover. What follows is a battle of wills between the Christian Olaf and the pagan Gudmund, as each seeks to bring Helgi over to his side. In sagas describing King Olaf's tussles with the powerful inhabitants of the north—men such as Raud the Strong and Eyvind Split-Cheek—the struggle for power is framed as a conflict between Christianity and paganism. Here, too, the clash is between a wilful ruler from the south and an obstreperous chieftain from the north, but the framework is entirely different. Moreover, the two men never meet. Like two old Jedi knights, they fight in a non-physical dimension, through the power of Christian prayer and pagan magic.*

King Olaf eventually compels King Gudmund to return Helgi to the royal court, but Gudmund has the last, gruesome laugh. Helgi is bundled back home with his eyes gouged out, and tells the king: 'because of your prayers he let me go free, so that you might see what had happened to me.'[20] Once again, Christianity has proved toxic to the inhabitants of the north, though this time not for the native pagans who live and rule there. This time the victim is a Norse visitor from further south. It transpires that Olaf's pious prayers had disastrous consequences for Helgi's charmed love-life, for the more Olaf prayed, the more Ingibjorg's ardour cooled, until: 'It seemed to her that she couldn't sleep with me without feeling pain, if she touched me naked, and it was mostly because of this that I left.'[21] Unluckily for Helgi, his mysterious lover was unwilling to let him go in one piece, and clawed both his eyes out first so that other women wouldn't be able to enjoy him either. Helgi's father is delighted to see him released 'from the hands of trolls', echoing how Hallbjorn Half-Troll referred to his son's Sámi girlfriend.[22] However, Helgi's own response is more ambivalent. When the king asks him how he found Glaesisvellir:

'Excellent,' he said, 'and nowhere has seemed better to me.' Then the king asked about King Gudmund's customs, followers, and deeds. Helgi gushed approvingly about it all and said that it was even better than he could put into words.[23]

In this tale, the themes typical of sagas set in the far north seem to have cross-pollinated. Helgi's lover is a woman from the far north. Initially, their affair may seem typical of a Norse man/northern woman attachment, but the gulf between them is too great. Christianity is a complete passion-killer for Ingibjorg. Just as the pagan Eyvind Split-Cheek had to die rather than convert to Christianity, so Gudmund's daughter literally can't bear to touch her lover, protected as he is by King Olaf's prayers.

* But no lightsabers.

Perhaps the catch is that Helgi wanted to stay in the north. If he had just sowed his wild oats in the permafrost and returned south, or even brought his lover with him, perhaps the outcome would have been happier. But since he wanted to cross over fully into a realm of trollish magic, paganism, and free love, he had to pay the price. Blurred boundaries are all well and good, but when magic, trolls, and giants are involved, there are grave consequences to going native. Helgi may have been kidnapped by a sinister pagan king and blinded by his lover, yet he would like nothing more than to return to this strange and supernatural northern kingdom and leave his own world behind him. By compulsion or design, he has given himself completely to the far north. Far from being rescued 'from the hands of trolls', as his father believes, Helgi wants nothing more than to fall back into their loving embrace.

Butter and bacon

Finally, the past casts different shadows in other sagas, not all as dark and bloody as in the case of Helgi. The magnificent Queen Eagle-Beak—skinless nymphomaniac and former lover of both Thor and Odin—is a fine example. This unconventional queen of Jotunheimar puts in an appearance in the *Saga of One-Handed Egil and Asmund the Berserker-Slayer* (*Egils saga einhenda ok Ásmundar berserkjabana*).

The two heroes of the tale, Egil and Asmund, travel north to Jotunheimar on the hunt for two kidnapped Russian princesses. Wandering out in the wilderness, they are taken in by Queen Eagle-Beak, who lives in a cave and rules over the land. As she cooks up a vat of gruel for their dinner, they all tell each other stories of their pasts: of berserkers and zombies in burial mounds, of kidnapped dwarf babies, and of eighteen giant daughters who all sleep with the pagan god Thor. The youngest of these daughters was Queen Eagle-Beak herself, but 'I'm now plagued by such ravenous lustfulness,' she tells her visitors, 'that I seem unable to live without a man'.[24] It turns out that Thor isn't the only pagan god the queen has bedded: on a quest to procure a magical cloak she ended up in the underworld getting intimate with the great Odin himself. As the gruel bubbles and thickens, she tells her dinner-guests: 'First I lay with Odin, then I leaped over the fire and got the cloak, but ever since I've been skinless all over my body.'[25] Perceptive readers might suspect that this saga has its tongue pressed firmly into its cheek. But suddenly, in the middle of these tall tales of porridge, passion, and paganism, echoes of an authentic Arctic past begin to sound.

Queen Eagle-Beak is enlisted to help rescue the princesses from the clutches of their evil giant kidnappers. She comes south with the rescue party on their journey back to the human world to join in the celebrations. As a reward for her help, she is given 'a butter-trough so big she could barely pick it up, and she said that such a gift would be considered rare in Jotunheimar'.[26] She is also given two flanks of bacon weighing a ton and, as the saga tells us, 'the old woman thought these were more valuable than if she had been given a load of gold'.[27] Remember that the nomadic Sámi were interested in goods that their settled, agrarian neighbours could provide: butter, metals, and meat from farmed livestock. Even as Queen Eagle-Beak leaves for the north again, skin-less, man-hungry, and staggering under the weight of salted pig, the real-life inhabitants of the far north still cast a shadow over the tale, from a distance of several centuries.

Trolls and giants don't only inhabit far-northern Arctic kingdoms in the sagas. Plenty more of their kind lurk at the edges of sagas set in Iceland itself, even if they don't always take centre-stage. Even in the most socially realistic sagas, trolls and giants are part of the day-to-day vocabulary of the protagonists: the curse 'may the trolls take you' is uttered by more than one angry character, while in one saga we find the proverb: 'One should warn even an ogre if he sits naked by the fire.'[28] Elsewhere, a particularly incendiary slanging-match between two men ends with an insult involving the trollish guardian spirit of the region: 'you are the bride of the guardian spirit of Svinafell, and it's said that every ninth night he uses you as a woman.'[29] Likewise, in the so-called Legendary Sagas supernatural creatures are well represented all over the place, not least giants and trolls. They tend to be a fairly unruly, dangerous, comical lot: vicious man-eaters, hard drinkers, and exhibitionists who wear clothes that leave very little to the imagination.

Yet more often than not, trolls and giants are found out on the wild margins of the world, lurking in rocky mountain caves or striding over barren expanses of wilderness. In particular, the bleak, dangerous beauty of the far north leaves plenty of space to fill in the gaps. This is true not just of the sagas. Take the northern coast of Finnmark, once described with such precision by Ohthere.

FIGURE 5.1 Interview with a troll-woman for a radio documentary, Trollholmsund

Out here too, where there is often nothing for miles but boulders, scrubland, and the ocean beyond, there are places where the human imagination has brought the landscape to life. As soon as the mist comes down or dusk descends on Knivskjellodden—the jagged spit of land sticking out just a little further north into the sea than nearby Nordkapp—the larger stones and boulders scattered on hillsides can play tricks on the mind very easily, taking the shape of animals, humans, or worse. Sometimes walkers have given them a helping hand: from a certain distance, one pile of rocks looks exactly like an old troll-woman with a hat pulled low over her eyes, a long beaky nose, and a pipe protruding from her lips. Likewise, the clue to what can be seen at Trollholmsund, 75 miles down the coast from Nordkapp, is there in the name. Out on a promontory facing into the sea, a group of looming limestone stacks stand huddled together around a smaller, chunkier piece of stone. Some of them are uncannily anthropomorphic, and so it is easy to see how the following Sámi legend sprang up around them. The stacks were once a group of trolls who were travelling over the moors of Finnmark with a great chest filled with gold and silver. When they reached the sea they couldn't go any further, and with sunrise fast approaching, they started looking for holes big enough to hide in. But the sun rose before they could find anywhere to shelter, and they turned to stone, together with their treasure chest.

It is easy to see why humans have always populated the unknowable places of the world with strange, otherworldly beings. The further north you go—bodily or imaginatively—the more extreme the conditions become and the harder it is to survive. So, by extension, what *can* survive there must be somehow 'other', supernatural, or even inhuman, in possession of remarkable powers or extraordinary physical traits: from Hyperboreans to dog-headed men and demons, from the Sámi themselves to giants and trolls. In many ways, then, the Legendary Sagas bring us full circle. The northern fairyland once imagined by the Norwegian explorer Fridtjof Nansen may have retreated during the Middle Ages, but the idea of a mysterious, even monstrous, north never lost its appeal. At the northernmost edge of the world, trolls and giants spring from the Norse imagination to populate the cold wilderness. At times they may bear striking similarities to some of the real-life inhabitants of Arctic Scandinavia, at least in terms of how the sagas present them: a taste for butter and bacon, a penchant for Norse male lovers, magical talents, an aversion to Christianity. But when the sunlight returns to the sky, trolls turn to stone and melt back into the landscape, leaving nothing but wilderness and stories.

· West ·

'How did you find America?'
'Turn left at Greenland.'

John Lennon, A Hard Day's Night

CHAPTER 6

Westward Ho!

The last homely house

Hannibal had his elephants. Genghis Khan had his horses. Churchill had his bomber-planes. And the Norse had their ships. Salty wind rippling through their hair, we imagine them ploughing the ocean, fearlessly seeking territories and treasures beyond the horizon. But how many of these voyagers never made it to the other side? How many were swamped by sudden walls of water that came crashing onto the deck, or died of sickness out on the cold, open sea? How many Norse men and women ended their own little sagas at the bottom of the ocean, far from their farms and families?

One of the most formidable, dangerous voyages of the medieval Norse world was the one that took the Norse west to Greenland, over the vast, turbulent waters of the North Atlantic. It wasn't a trip to be undertaken lightly. The thirteenth-century *Book of Settlements* notes that on the first big expedition that set out from Iceland to Greenland in AD 985, only fourteen of the twenty-five ships made it to the other side.

Norwegian sources take a similarly dim view of sailing conditions in the region. Returning to the *King's Mirror*, we find descriptions of the walls of water, harsh winds, frost, and snow that plagued Greenland's coastline, as well as seas infested by monsters (though the author hastily adds that he doesn't think they are seen very often). According to this text, one of the greatest dangers for sailors was the thick ice that clogs the coastline of east Greenland, for: 'As soon as the deepest part of the ocean has been crossed, then there are such great volumes of ice in the sea that I know of no other place like it in all the world.'[1] Woe betide those who try to make land too soon and become trapped in the icy margins between land and water:

Some of those who become trapped there have lost their lives but others have managed to escape, and we have met some of them and heard their reports and stories. But all those who have got stuck in these ice drifts have adopted the same strategy: they have taken their small boats and dragged them up onto the ice with themselves and in this way have tried to reach land, but the ship and all other valuable possessions had to be abandoned and lost.[2]

Despite the dangers, for around 450 years—a span of time that takes us back from the present day to the reign of Queen Elizabeth I—the coastal fjords of south-west Greenland were home to generations of Norse families. They built farmsteads of stone, wood, and turf, constructed irrigation systems to water their fields, and grazed their livestock on the green, grassy slopes below the mountains. They hunted seal, reindeer, arctic hare and fox, ptarmigan, whale, and walrus. They established laws and churches, and even built a little cathedral, nestled between steep mountain slopes at the head of a sheltered fjord. They fell in and out of love, fought and feuded, told tales and sang songs, got injured, fell sick, and mourned their dead. Norse Greenland was the Last Homely House west of the sea; the last bastion of medieval Europe.* But while it lay on the outermost fringes of the known world, it was no primitive outpost.

The Norse began to settle Greenland from Iceland at the end of the tenth century, led by the formidable Erik the Red. By 1500 their farms and fields lay empty and abandoned. But at its height, the total population of Norse Greenland numbered a few thousand inhabitants. They lived in two main areas, both on the west coast of Greenland. (See Map 2.) The larger of the two they called (somewhat confusingly) the Eastern Settlement, which was scattered around the fjords of south-west Greenland. At most, there were probably around 250 inhabited farmsteads in the region. The smaller, known as the Western Settlement, was located in fjords several hundred miles to the north-west. This was about a third of the size; only around eighty farmsteads have been found in this area.[3]

---

* For those not of a sufficiently nerdy disposition, the original 'Last Homely House' is Rivendell, an elven outpost in Tolkien's *The Hobbit* and *The Lord of the Rings*. As the wizard Gandalf tells his travelling companions: 'You are come to the very edge of the Wild, as some of you may know. Hidden somewhere ahead of us is the fair valley of Rivendell where Elrond lives in the Last Homely House' (*The Hobbit*, ch. 3).

As the map shows, the two areas where the Norse lived would have been better named the 'Southern Settlement' and the 'Northern Settlement', or so it would seem. But geographical perceptions are highly subjective and context-specific. The Norse did not view the country from above, as we do on modern-day maps. As they sailed up the Greenlandic coastline, they would have been travelling in a westward direction for much of the time. Unsurprisingly, these names have caused some confusion over the centuries. The Danish-Norwegian missionary Hans Egede came in search of the Norse Greenlanders in the 1720s, hoping to bring his long-lost Nordic brethren into the Lutheran fold. What no one knew is that they had died out a couple of hundred years earlier. Quite reasonably, Egede assumed that the Eastern Settlement was on the east coast of Greenland and the Western Settlement was on the west coast, not realizing that east Greenland is horribly icy and barely habitable. So when Egede came across ruined buildings in south-west Greenland, he assumed he had found the Western rather than the Eastern Settlement.[4] The ruins of the Western Settlement were waiting in the fjords close to Nuuk—now the capital of Greenland—founded by Egede himself as a base from which to conduct his missionary work amongst the Inuit Greenlanders. When Egede failed to locate the Norse, he turned his attention to harvesting Inuit souls on the chilly coastal islands where the natives hunted seal and fish. It was during this mission that the Lord's Prayer was translated for the first time into Greenlandic, including the line: 'give us this day our daily seal meat.'[5]

Certainly, there was plenty of seal-eating going on amongst the Norse Greenlanders too, especially as the centuries wore on, living conditions got worse, and the population became more dependent on marine animals as a food source. This blubbery beast was of fundamental importance to the Norse Greenlandic diet, but it wasn't everyone's favourite dinner. Far more reindeer remains have been found in the middens of high-status farms and especially the bishop's residence at Gardar (now Igaliku). Since the bishops were foreigners brought over from Scandinavia to minister to a remote Greenlandic flock, they may not have developed a taste for seal meat, preferring more familiar delicacies such as reindeer.

The animals once hunted by the Norse are still present in the Greenlandic landscape. Reindeer migration routes sometimes pass by the remains of Norse farmsteads on their way down to the seashore. A muddle of still-wet hoofprints will tell any ruin-hunter that they are not the first visitors of the day and a herd of reindeer have ventured down from the mountainside an hour or two earlier. At other times the prints may be the insubstantial, wispy tracks of an arctic fox. Perched high up on the slopes of a fjord, one tiny Norse farmstead has become home to a family of these creatures. Get too close to the stones, and an ethereal, high-pitched screaming rises up from the ground, answered by a louder, angrier scream from the cliffs behind the farmstead. If a fuzzy mass of tiny white heads and snouty pink noses pops up from a hole in the foundations, you can be sure you have disturbed a den of baby arctic foxes, now calling indignantly to their mother. Of course, this is the point where you beat a hasty retreat back to your boat and leave the fox family to get on with their lives, but if you had been a Norseman you'd probably have been rubbing your hands together with glee. Animal pelts, particularly exquisitely soft, blue-grey furs such as those of the arctic fox, would have fetched a high price when the traders arrived from the east.

Hunting—both for subsistence and trade—was an essential part of the Norse Greenlandic economy, but first and foremost the Norse Greenlanders were farmers. Even in good times, they were locked into a delicately balanced cycle of hunting and farming. The precariousness of farming in Greenland is evident even today. In the summer, many Norse farm ruins become swamped by lush green grass, and flooded with the heady scent of camomile and juniper. Searching for some of the more obscure Norse ruined farmsteads becomes a risky business; at any moment you may lose a member of your party, only to discover that the unfortunate individual has plunged several feet down the side of an invisible farm wall. The soil around these farms is particularly fertile because of the organic waste material left by the Norse farmers. On the steep slopes of one fjord in the Western Settlement, an enterprising local man has taken to growing vegetables on top of what was once a Norse waste-dump and selling them to top restaurants in Nuuk.

So a summer visitor to Greenland can see exactly why the Norse would have settled here. In the months when the light barely leaves the sky, the weather is often dry and balmy. In the sheltered fjords that snake inland from the coast it can get so warm that the sparkling blue-green waters become the perfect place for a sneaky skinny-dip. But come September, when the northern lights begin to ripple across the sky, the days grow short and the fjords freeze. The long, brutal winter is on its way. A few bad farming years in a row, a hunting disaster that wiped out all the local men, or merchants' ships that failed to arrive from the east, and life in Norse Greenland would have begun to unravel rapidly.

The Eastern Settlement was the larger of the two settlements, with higher-quality land for farming, longer summers, and better connections to

Iceland and Norway back east. No wonder that this was where the bishopric was established. The Western Settlement was more vulnerable, perched on the very margins of farmable land. Located several hundred miles further up the coast, it had shorter summers and longer, harsher winters. More fodder was needed to keep the animals alive over the winter, and more farmland was needed to get the same yield of crops and grass. This is obvious just from walking or riding from one farm to the next: the farmsteads of the Western Settlement are built at twice the distance from each other than those in the Eastern Settlement, so that each farmstead in the Western Settlement had twice the amount of (poorer-quality, lower-yield) land at its disposal. But the Western Settlement had its own advantages, not least excellent hunting and mountains full of soapstone for making lamps and bowls. More importantly, it was a natural springboard for hunters heading north. Hundreds of miles further up the coast lay the snow-encrusted, iceberg-infested region that the Norse called *Norðrseta* (literally the 'Northern Seat', but usually translated as the 'Northern Hunting Grounds'). Today, this region can be equated broadly with Disko Bay, an area including the vast Ilulissat Icefjord, a UNESCO World Heritage Site located 150 miles north of the Arctic Circle.

Today, tourists flock to Ilulissat to take midnight boat trips through the ice fields in the summer, or glide across the snow on husky-drawn sledges during the winter. When the Norse occupied Greenland, packs of hunters braved the long, treacherous journey to the frozen wilderness beyond the Arctic Circle. They battled the elements and ferocious animals in their quest for natural resources much prized by medieval Europeans: walrus ivory and hides, furs, gyrfalcons, and even live polar bears. At its height, Norse Greenland was a vibrant, hardy society that drew much of its lifeblood from the lucrative natural resources of the Arctic. A live polar bear was a gift fit for a king, walrus ivory could be fashioned into exquisite works of art, while walrus hide made the best ships' ropes in the world. Thirteenth-century Norwegian church records note the tithes paid by the Greenlanders to the Norwegian crown: walrus-ivory tusks, walrus-hide ropes, ox hides, and sealskins, all of which could be converted into gold and silver.[6] The walrus-ivory tusks were particularly valuable: in 1327, around 520 Greenlandic walrus tusks were sold in Bergen as a crusade tax to fund the Norwegian king's campaign against Novgorod. It has been estimated that this was the equivalent of around 780 cows: more than the annual tax given to Norway by almost four thousand Icelandic farmers.[7]

Yet despite these exotic resources, the Norse Greenlanders were dependent on Iceland and Norway for many of the basic building-blocks of their society: metal for tools and weapons, wood for building houses, grain, and the accoutrements of Christianity. As long as ships from the east continued to arrive in their fjords, the Norse Greenlanders could survive: their furs and ivory were in demand, and could be exchanged for the fundamental trappings of the Norse world. What happened when the ships failed to materialize is another matter, as we shall see. Eventually—but not inevitably—the settlements began to decline and fade away. The question of what happened to the last of the Norse Greenlanders is still up for debate: in some ways the Norse equivalent of the mystery of the *Marie Celeste*.

Frozen in time

Even today, the ghosts of Greenland's medieval inhabitants feel present in the landscape. The nomadic hunter-gatherers who occupied the country after the Norse—the ancestors of today's Greenlanders—trod lightly upon the land. As a result, Norse ruins are still scattered across the grassy slopes above the fjords and below the glaciers. This is particularly the case in the Eastern Settlement, where a remarkable number of buildings survive: an entire church with six-foot-thick walls, a banqueting hall lined with stone benches, shepherds' bothies built into the rocky mountainside, storehouses and horse pens teetering by fjords thickly packed with ice. Other than in the small towns, Greenland has practically no roads, and a traveller in search of Norse ruins has to resort to more unusual methods of transportation: boats, horses, and helicopters, to name three. On horseback, it is possible to explore the fjords of the Eastern Settlement, riding between the stone-walled farmsteads that stand empty on the hillsides, so complete that one almost expects a Norse man or woman to step from the front door clothed in a thick woollen kirtle and soft leather shoes.*

---

* One year I explored the fjords of the Eastern Settlement on the back of an Icelandic horse, a beast with eyes so bright blue that he had been given a Greenlandic name that translates roughly as 'he-whose-eyes-pop-out-of-his-head-when-he-sees-a-beautiful-woman-walking-past'. Icelandic horses were the steeds of choice for the medieval Norse, but they are not particularly romantic in appearance: they are hardy, stoic beasts, built like saggy old sofas, capable of trudging up treacherous, almost-vertical mountainsides while the rider closes their eyes, prays for deliverance, and tries not to imagine the sheer drop to the pounding sea below.

FIGURE 6.1 Horse (named 'he-whose-eyes-pop-out-of-his-head-when-he-sees-a-beautiful-woman-walking-past') at the end of a valley filled with Norse ruins in the Eastern Settlement

In the Western Settlement, the Norse remains are often more elusive than in the Eastern Settlement, but in many ways preservation conditions are even better because of the permafrost. One site, known as 'The Farm Below the Sand', is the only example of an almost-complete medieval Nordic farm. Here, some extraordinary animal remains have been discovered, such as a goat crushed under a farm wall, its skin and hair preserved in the icy ground. More remarkably, as the archaeologists dug down into the byres, they were hit by the acrid, pungent smell of animal dung and hay, released for the first time since the last occupants abandoned the farm.

North-west of 'The Farm Below the Sand', on the shoreline of the most important farm in the Western Settlement—Sandnes—once stood a church next to the chieftain's hall. Over the centuries, the glacier that sits above the

FIGURE 6.2 Snow-capped mountains at the entrance to the fjords of the Western Settlement

site deposited so much silt in the fjord that the waters rose by several metres and covered the church. Now nothing remains of the church but the foundation-stones and grave-slabs, which are only visible at low tide: a ghostly outline glimmering in the wet sand. This being Greenland, even if low tide falls close to midnight during the summer, it is still possible to row ashore to see the ruins illuminated by sunlight nearly bright as day.*

Below the ruined farms and churches, the cold Greenland soil preserves a vibrant picture of life and death in this Norse colony. Entire dresses, hoods, and hats were found in the Norse graveyard at Herjolfsnes, on the coastline at the southernmost tip of the Eastern Settlement. This time, it was not permafrost that was responsible for the freezing preservation conditions, but the polar ice that packed the nearby sea. The items of clothing included some fashionable pieces that would not have looked out of place

---

* Sandnes is situated at the head of the Ameralik Fjord, just south of Nuuk. When Fridtjof Nansen and his five companions completed the first crossing of Greenland's interior in 1888—a hellish six weeks on sledges and skis over the inland ice—it was this fjord that they came out at, skiing down to the shoreline from the glacier above. They fashioned a boat using their tents, sledges, and wood from the willows growing on the hillsides, and sailed down the fjord towards Nuuk (then called Godthåb).

in medieval France or England. A little further up the coastline at the bishop's residence, the skeleton of one of the bishops himself was discovered complete with his official ring and crozier. The bishop is missing one of his feet; it has been suggested that he lost it in an attack of frostbite, but it is more likely to be a crime committed by an early archaeologist's spade. Other burials point to more violent ends: a knife was embedded so deeply in one unfortunate man that he had to be buried with it still stuck between his ribs. There are also several bodies from a mass grave that seem to have been killed by sharp axe or sword-blows to the head, perhaps during the course of a bloody feud. Another woman had a fractured hyoid (throat) bone that had healed before her death, suggesting that someone had tried to strangle her. In legal cases today, such an injury is an indication of domestic violence.[8]

Items found at farms across the Eastern and Western Settlements paint a cheerier picture, and many of them are on display at the Greenland National Museum down by the old harbour in Nuuk. At one site was found a tiny carved wooden boat, at another some little wooden horses: perhaps toys to amuse small children. Elsewhere, a woven ringlet of blond hair had been tucked away and hidden in a nook in the wall of the women's weaving room: perhaps a forgotten or abandoned love-token for a boy from the next farm. Even unwanted items chucked onto a rubbish heap prick the imagination; one midden contained a misshapen carving of a polar bear, with a beautifully realistic head but a body completely out of proportion. In the same heap lay a faulty die with only half the numbers carved onto the six faces. Everything was going well until the die-maker lost concentration and inscribed the wrong number onto the wrong face. It's almost possible to hear the hisses of frustration as the carvers realize their mistakes, chuck their half-finished pieces onto the rubbish heap, and stomp off in a huff.

From these remains, we can piece together a unique picture of a lost medieval world: a Nordic Pompeii literally frozen in time. In other respects, Norse Greenland is a mysterious place, and we know almost nothing about those who lived in this harsh but beautiful land. In comparison to medieval Iceland, where the impulse to write things down seems to have been embedded in the inhabitants' cultural DNA, there is an almost total lack of written evidence from Norse Greenland. This does not mean that nothing was written, only that no parchments have yet been found. Greenland had its own religious

FIGURE 6.3a Polar bear carved from walrus ivory, found in the midden of an Eastern Settlement farm

FIGURE 6.3b Carved wooden horses found in the ruins of an Eastern Settlement farm

centres, however small, and it's very possible that written material would have been produced in one of these. Here and there we stumble upon possible clues to the Greenlanders' storytelling culture, such as a poem from a medieval Icelandic manuscript where the scribe has given it the title the *Greenlandic Lay of Atli* (*Atlamál in grœnlenzco*). This bloodthirsty tale is part of the same set of legends on which Wagner drew for his *Ring* Cycle, and ends with a vengeful woman slaughtering her children and serving them up as dinner to her murderous husband. What link—if any—there may have been between this poem and the Greenlanders is unclear, apart from the fact that one character dreams uneasily of a savage, man-eating polar bear (literally a *hvítabjörn*, 'white bear').

The only writing that survives from Greenland is runic inscriptions. There are around two hundred in all, some mundane, others moving. These runes might be as simple as a woman's name carved on a box lid—'Bjorg'—while others are echoes of long-forgotten tragedies. In one coffin, a rune-stick was found bearing the words: 'This woman, named Gudveig, was laid overboard in the Greenland Sea.' The coffin was empty apart from a little bit of fatty material, possibly indicating that it had once contained a body. Perhaps this was Gudveig's husband who still wanted to be buried beside her—in whatever way possible—when his own time came. Such inscriptions offer tantalizing clues to tales of vanished lives, but archaeology can only take us so far. For more complete, colourful tales of life and death in Norse Greenland, we have to turn to the sagas.

Tempers and tourism

The best known, most detailed sagas about Greenland are a remarkable pair called the *Saga of Erik the Red* (*Eiríks saga rauða*) and the *Saga of the Greenlanders* (*Grœnlendinga saga*). Together, they are known as the Vinland sagas. This is because they also describe Norse expeditions to the edge of the North American continent, which the Norse called *Vínland* after the wild grapes that grew there (*vín* means 'wine' in Old Norse, and *vínber* are 'grapes'). The sagas may date from the first decades of the thirteenth century, which would make them fairly early in terms of saga chronology. However, no written version of either saga survives from that time. The *Saga of Erik the Red* is preserved in two manuscripts, one from the early fourteenth century and one from the fifteenth century. The *Saga of the Greenlanders* is only found in one manuscript, which was compiled in the last few years of the fourteenth century. This means that more than two centuries separate these sagas from the events they describe, and a further two centuries separate the events from the surviving manuscripts preserving the sagas. Despite this gap, the two share many details about voyages, characters, and events. This is all the more remarkable given that they seem to have been drawn from a shared pool of oral traditions rather than one being copied directly from the other.[9] These are not the only sagas with episodes set in Greenland. Some are early, such as the *Tale of Einar Sokkason* (*Einars þáttr Sokkasonar*), also known as the *Tale of the Greenlanders*, a thirteenth-century short story about how the Greenlanders secured a bishop of their own. Other sagas concerning Greenland seem to date from a good deal later, and these will be returned to below.[10]

Both the *Saga of Erik the Red* and the *Saga of the Greenlanders* describe the settlement of Greenland, which begins, in typical saga style, with feuds, brawls, and murders. When the dust clears, the man in the middle is a hot-tempered, belligerent character called Erik the Red. Like a naughty schoolboy scrapping in the playground, Erik couldn't keep his axe to himself. He had already been forced out of Norway 'because of killings', as one of the sagas tells us bluntly.[11] Once in Iceland, Erik got in with another bad crowd and started another murderous feud. Eventually he was outlawed for three years and forced to leave the country.

Of such fiery tempers are adventurers made. Undaunted, Erik set off in search of new lands. He had heard about a new country to the west, sighted by a storm-tossed sailor who had been blown off course a few years earlier. Erik spent the next three summers exploring the coastline and fjords of west Greenland. He identified the best bits of land and quickly stamped his name on them: 'Erik's Island', 'Erik's Fjord', and 'Erik's Holm'. The years and months whizz by in a few sentences:

The first winter he stayed on Eiriksey, which lies near the middle of the Eastern Settlement. The spring after that he went to Eiriksfjord, where he made himself a home. That summer he travelled to the western wilderness and gave place-names far and wide.[12]

This typically understated saga description makes Erik's adventure sound pretty straightforward, even pedestrian. Of course, it was nothing of the sort; the time-scale and distances involved were enormous. If we're to believe the sagas, he spent three years alone, sailing up and down a treacherous, uninhabited coastline of deep fjords, pockets of pastures, barren wastelands, towering mountains, and vast glaciers. He covered the areas that would later be settled and named the Eastern and Western Settlements, travelling further and further up the coast of this unknown, empty country each summer when the thick snows had melted and the sun had returned to the sky. Perhaps he also reached the Northern Hunting Grounds, their fjords clogged with ice even at the height of summer.[13]

Looking at Greenland on a map or even flying over it in a plane, it's hard to get a sense of its true scale.* Even today, the massive ice-breaker ferry that sails up and down the west coast—run by the *Arctic Umiaq Line*, named after the boats traditionally used by Inuit women and children—takes two days to travel from Narsaq (the town nearest to the Eastern Settlement) to Nuuk (Greenland's capital, close to the Western Settlement). Continuing on across the Arctic Circle to Disko Bay (once part of the Northern Hunting Grounds) takes another three days, and this is only a very small stretch of Greenland's coastline. Erik's ship could have fitted many times over into a modern ice-breaker ferry, and unlike the ferry he wasn't even sailing in a straight line. He was looking for deep, sheltered fjords that cut into the land, suitable for farming and settling. In a modern motorized boat, the fjords that Erik discovered still take days to explore. Even in the balmiest of conditions, many afternoons bring warm, strong winds that rush down from the mountains and into the fjords. Trying to sail the wrong way across the choppy waters is an

---

* I only realized how enormous Greenland was when I started trying to plan my first visit. I'd organized plenty of research trips in the past: how difficult could it be this time? So I would approach Greenlandic travel companies and helpful archaeologists with sunny optimism and carefully plotted maps, showing them how I was going to jump from *this* little fjord over here to *that* little mountain over there, doubtless leaving after a leisurely breakfast and pottering up to the next site in time for tea. Every time, I'd be let down gently but firmly: this tiny stretch of water alone would take three days to sail down. Did I realize that that particular fjord was entirely blocked by ice all the year round? Had I considered the fact that I'd have to charter a helicopter to get to that out-of-the-way farm? Did I know that there were no roads outside the settlements? No buses? No trains? No hire-cars? Had I thought this through *at all*?

exercise in trying to keep your lunch down, as the boat bangs and thumps across the waves. In a medieval sailing-boat, lunch would be the least of a sailor's problems. Erik would have spent much of his time battling winds and navigating a coastline riddled with twists and turns, exploring many disappointingly treacherous, potentially ice-packed stretches of water before he hit upon the few 'goldilocks' fjords that could sustain a European-style Norse society.

After three years Erik returned to Iceland, promptly got into yet another fight, and left again to settle Greenland properly. He was joined by friends, family, and followers, all looking for new lives in a new land. If anyone knows anything about the Norse settlement of Greenland, they probably know that Erik named the country 'Greenland' (*Grænland* in Old Norse), apparently as an act of early tourist-board marketing. The sagas note this was 'because he said that men would be very keen to go there, if the land was well named'.[14] This may be true, but it doesn't mean that Erik was lying. In comparison to Iceland, summers in the fjords of West Greenland are warm and dry. At Narsarsuaq airport, across the fjord from where Erik established his farm Brattahlid (now Qassiarsuk) in the Eastern Settlement, tourists can be observed striding manfully out of the little red planes, clad in Nordic-patterned woolly jumpers and furry boots. Within ten minutes or so the woolly jumpers have been knotted around their waists and everyone is sitting outside the little wooden café down the road with ice-creams and cold cans of Coke. But equally, the weather can change very quickly, and when the thick mists arrive from the mountains, planes can neither land nor take off. You can find yourself unexpectedly stranded alone in the little youth hostel for days, stumbling ineptly through Danish translations of *Harry Potter* and surviving on jars of pickled gherkins left by Scandinavian backpackers.

The climate was even warmer and drier during the first centuries of the settlement, which coincided with what is known as the Medieval Warm Period. Today—and probably then too—during the summer yellow camomile flowers creep along the ground, tangling together with harebells and berries in a profusion of ceramic pink, and inky black and blue. The grass is lush, and the hillsides are covered in straggling bushes of scrubby willow and pungent juniper. In the areas settled by the Norsemen, the country was well named.

Outside over there

From the point of view of the saga writers in Iceland, Greenland was very much Outside Over There: a Norse colony across the ocean, at the edge of the known world. A sense of remoteness and cultural instability trickles through the saga stories. The country had been founded by the socially unstable, disruptive figure of Erik the Red, and in other sagas outlaws and other unruly characters sail west across the ocean to escape bloody feuds and legal disputes, the saga equivalent of running off to join the Foreign Legion.[15] In reality, Greenland was no lawless Wild West. No written law-codes survive from the country, unlike *Grágás* ('Grey Goose'), medieval Iceland's collection of laws. But there is no reason to think that law was any less important in Greenland than anywhere else in the Norse world, which rang with the words 'with law shall the land be built'.*[16] Two possible legal assembly sites have been identified in the Eastern Settlement, one close to Erik's farm at Brattahlid and one near the bishop's residence at Gardar.[17] There are records of at least one legal execution that took place in Greenland, which we'll return to later. There are also occasional references to the country's legal processes in the sagas. In the *Tale of Einar Sokkason*, legal processes are carried out 'according to Greenlandic law',[18] and during a feud with visiting Norwegians the locals protest, 'we want to follow the laws that operate here'.[19]

Even so, the Greenland of the sagas is an outpost of Norse society. Frequently, it is characterized as a country of wintry isolation, meagre resources, lingering paganism, and ferocious storms that batter little ships as they bob across the ocean. Some of these impressions are rooted in reality. The route west to Greenland was particularly long and difficult, with strong winds, turbulent, foggy patches, and frequent cyclones. Norse men and women in their open boats would have faced a rough journey. We already know from the *Book of Settlements* that only fourteen ships out of twenty-five made it to Greenland on the first expedition. Other sources speak of disorienting winds and currents, darkness, icebergs, and snowstorms on the way out to Greenland. In the sagas, memories of these difficult voyages are intertwined with a sense that—from an Icelandic point of view, at least—a voyage to Greenland is a voyage

---

* Even today, these words are the motto of both the Icelandic police force and Shetland, which was itself ruled by the Norse for many centuries.

towards the furthest reaches of the Norse world.[20] At the beginning of the *Saga of the Greenlanders*, a man sets off to visit his father in Greenland. As Iceland dips below the horizon, it almost seems to be swallowed up by the ocean: 'the land became water.'[21] Soon the wind drops and the unfamiliar seascape becomes threatening and difficult to navigate: 'northern winds and fog descended, and they couldn't tell where they were going.'[22] Other sagas describe fogs, mists, fatal sicknesses, shipwrecks, and even a sea of flesh-eating worms. In the *Tale of Einar Sokkason*, two ships are sent to escort a bishop from Norway to Greenland. One is lost in fierce storms, and is only found several years later by hunters, washed up in the wilderness. They discover men lying dead by their axes and half-chopped wood, exhausted by lack of food. Opening the door of a makeshift hut, the hunters are hit by the stench of decomposing human flesh.

Worse things can await those who reach Greenland safely. The *Saga of Erik the Red* describes how, after a typical voyage of swollen seas and fatal sick-nesses, a shipload of new settlers arrives in the Eastern Settlement. Almost as soon as they arrive, famine and death strike, revealing the fragile dividing-line between life and death. According to the saga: 'At that time there was a great famine in Greenland; very little was caught by those who had gone hunting, and some never returned.'[23]

Onto this dark, desperate stage steps Thorbjorg the pagan seeress, the last of ten sisters gifted with foresight. The description of her eerily outlandish appearance is one of the longest afforded to any character in the sagas:

She wore about herself a blue-black mantle, which was covered in precious stones all the way down the hem. Around her neck she wore glass beads, and on her head a black lambskin lined inside with white catskin. In her hand she carried a staff with a knob on the top, coated in brass and set with precious stones. She wore a belt around her waist with a large skin purse attached, in which she kept the charms that she needed for her prophecies. On her feet she wore furry calfskin boots, tied with long laces that had big pewter knobs on the ends. On her hands she wore catskin gloves, which were white and furry.[24]

Thorbjorg is no scruffy witch of the blasted heath. She is an honoured—if rather creepy—guest, wearing a mantle of the same *blá* ('blue-black') colour that was used to describe the colour of King Harald's dead Sámi bride, Snae-frid. Her clothing not only sets her apart from the other guests at the feast, but also emphasizes her high status: the mantle is of an expensive foreign cut, and she glitters with precious stones and metals. In a society where most metal had to be imported, her cutlery is every bit as impressive, and she eats her dinner of animal hearts and kids'-milk porridge with a brass spoon and a knife of brass and ivory. Her role in the saga is even more important: she has come to perform the magical pagan chants that will bring the famine to an end.

In the Greenland of the sagas, the looming shadow of paganism is never far away. The settlement of Greenland took place in the years leading up to the turn of the millennium, when the North Atlantic was on the cusp of conversion. The *Saga of the Greenlanders* notes that, in the early years of the settlement: 'The people of Greenland were heathen at that time.'[25] When the first shoots of Christianity appear in the country, the clash between the old and new religions can be comical. When Erik's wife converts to Christianity, a disgruntled Erik refuses to give up his pagan faith. Subsequently he becomes even more disgruntled, because 'Thjodhild didn't want to sleep with Erik once she had converted, which was very much against his wishes'.[26]

FIGURE 6.4 Reconstruction of 'Thjodhild's Church', built beside the ruins of Erik the Red's farm at Brattahlid in the Eastern Settlement

Whether or not Thjodhild actually subjected poor Erik to a sex strike we will never know. But when the Norse site thought to be Erik's farm at Brattahlid was excavated, the remains of a very early chapel were discovered. To celebrate the new millennium, a replica of this so-called Thjodhild's Church was built overlooking the fjord, complete with low stone-and-turf walls encircling the site, wooden walls, and a grassy turf roof.*

Generally speaking, the sagas have a robust, rational approach to paganism. Conversion narratives often feature angst-ridden characters unwilling to abandon the heathen gods worshipped by their ancestors. The saga writers often treat them sympathetically, and without the shades of neuroticism that other medieval Christian authors reserve for their pagan forebears. But in the Greenland of the sagas there is still an uneasy sense that such practices have lingered longer than they should have. There may be some truth in this. During excavations at the bishop's residence in the Eastern Settlement, the skulls and skull fragments of twenty to thirty walruses, their teeth neatly extracted, were found uniformly buried in and around the church. This strange find could be added to the four or five narwhal skulls that had been discovered in the east end of the chancel many decades earlier. Presumably the skulls came from the Northern Hunting Grounds. The archaeologists who discovered them were puzzled, suggesting that there seemed to be 'something remarkable, something mystic' in this arrangement. They continued: 'It is perhaps not impossible that religious or demoniacal ideas have been attached to these strange animals which were hunted so far away from the settlement, and which were of such great value to the population.'[27] This may or may not have been true, but in an unstable, marginal land where hunger and starvation were often little more than a few unlucky weeks away, such hunting rituals and superstitions could have been a way of maintaining a measure of psychological control over this unpredictable environment.

---

* When I visited Brattahlid, the church was being mended by a group of Icelanders who had been brought over especially for the job. They were led by a blond, heavily bearded man built like a bull. He complained long and loudly about being given the wrong sort of turf to work with—this stuff would erode away in no time—and then ushered us inside the church for an impromptu performance of Icelandic storytelling and singing. His teenage son looked like he wanted the ground to swallow him up: 'He's always showing off like this', he hissed, as his dad launched himself heartily into another long round of traditional verses.

Winter of discontent

Further up the coast in the Western Settlement, even darker deeds await. Both Vinland sagas tell variations of a story featuring paganism, plague, hauntings, and even a horny zombie. According to the story as it appears in the *Saga of the Greenlanders*, Thorstein (one of Erik the Red's sons) and Gudrid (his wife) are lost at sea all summer and driven by storms to the Western Settlement. They are invited to stay the winter with a lugubrious pagan farmer, whose gloomy name—Thorstein the Black—matches the gloomy surroundings. He dampens the mood immediately when he tells the shipwrecked couple, 'It will be very lonely to stay with me, because it's only the two of us here and I'm very self-sufficient'.[28]

Thorstein the Black takes them to his farmstead where he lives with his wife, but as winter starts to bite the mood becomes dark, isolated, and claustrophobic. Sickness strikes the farm and its inhabitants begin to drop like flies. In the version of the story told in the *Saga of Erik the Red*, one evening Gudrid accompanies the farmer's dying wife to the outdoor privy. The sick woman looks towards the doorway and cries out:

I won't go outside like this. There's a host of all those who are dead standing in front of the door, and amongst them I recognize your husband Thorstein and myself. What a horrible thing to see![29]

By the morning the farmer's wife is dead, but like the ghosts she saw lurking in the doorway, she doesn't go quietly. In a scene that is both comic and dreadful, the mortally sick Thorstein Eriksson is horrified to find her reanimated corpse showing him unwanted attention. Thorstein manages to get word to his host, 'that there was hardly any peace because his wife wanted to rise to her feet and get under the bed-covers with him'.[30] When the farmer races back to the farmhouse to put an end to his wife's unearthly shenanigans, he finds her tottering towards their guest's sickbed. The only way of stopping her is to take hold of her hands and drive an axe deep into her breast.

In the sagas, the living dead do not drift around in white sheets groaning and rattling their chains. They can ride house-roofs on winter nights, rip animals apart, break men's spines, and, in this case, try to seduce visitors. Shrouded in the gloom of Greenland's perpetual winter twilight, sickness and spectres stalk the Western Settlement, and help is very far away.

Bred on frost

From an Icelandic-saga point of view, Greenland is a country of meagre resources. When merchants visit Erik the Red's farm for the winter, he becomes more and more melancholy at the thought of the poor Yule feast he has to offer the men. Undaunted, the Icelandic merchants unload malt, flour, and grain from their ship, and the saga tells us, 'preparations for a Yule feast began, and it was so impressive that it seemed to everyone that such splendour had scarcely been seen in such a poor land'.[31]

Historically, while Greenland was a poor land in some ways, it was very wealthy in others. Today the full extent of Greenland's mineral wealth is only just being realized. In the medieval period the great discovery was the Arctic riches found in the Northern Hunting Grounds. Today the Ilulissat ice fjord, part of what was once the Northern Hunting Grounds, is one of the most popular tourist spots in Greenland. Out in the fjord, jagged shards and bulky chunks of ice—white, dirty grey, turquoise, cobalt blue—drift towards the open sea, some taller than houses. Sometimes they fizz gently, cracking and popping like ice-cubes in a cold drink. Sometimes they rumble and thunder distantly from across the water, like a thousand glass bottles being emptied into a skip. In photographs the ice seems serene and still, but in reality it can be fierce, swift, and deadly.

The iceberg that sank the *Titanic* in 1912 probably calved from the west coast of Greenland, most likely from Ilulissat itself. It was also in a cave just north of Ilulissat that the mummified bodies of six women, a four-year-old boy, and a six-month-old baby were discovered in 1972, literally freeze-dried by the cold. They had been dead for around 500 years. All were exquisitely dressed in seal and reindeer skins, and five of the six women had tattoos on their faces, made with reindeer sinews blackened with soot. The little baby is the best-preserved of the mummies; were it not for the fact that his eyes are missing, he could almost be asleep. The young boy may have had Down's Syndrome, and his shoes seem to have been put on the wrong feet. It isn't clear how these women and children died or even whether they died at the same time, though recent DNA analysis has revealed that they were all related. When the grave was first discovered, it was thought that they might have drowned when their *umiaq* capsized (the boats traditionally used by women and children). Perhaps, it has been suggested, an iceberg flipped over in the fjord, making a giant wave that sunk the boat.³² Certainly, such accidents were possible in this dangerous terrain, as the Norse hunters would have known only too well.

Little is known about Norse activities in this beautiful, dangerous part of Greenland, other than what can be pieced together from tiny fragments of evidence. In 1824, three lines of runes carved onto smooth black stone were found on the windswept, rocky island of Kingittorsuaq (pronounced *kin-git-or-soo-ack*) in the region of the Northern Hunting Grounds. The stone was found tucked into one of three triangular cairns on a mountaintop. It bears the names of the three Norsemen who built the cairns, perhaps during a hunting expedition early in the year. Incredibly, the runes tell us the month—April—and even the approximate date—25th—on which they built the cairn: 'Erling Sighvatsson and Bjarni Thordarson and Eindridi Oddsson on the Saturday before the minor Rogation Day piled these cairns and...' Here, the inscription becomes uninterpretable, and our three Arctic adventurers fade from sight, left to battle the bitter cold.³³ What happened to them will never be known. Fridtjof Nansen—the aforementioned Norwegian superhuman—knew Greenland intimately, having led the first crossing across its inhospitable

FIGURE 6.5   Ilulissat ice fjord under the midnight sun

interior.* He had first-hand experience of the treacherous, deadly terrain that the three men had battled, and wrote:

The most remarkable thing is that the cairns are stated to have been set up in April, when the sea in that locality is covered in ice. The three men must either have wintered there in the north, which seems the more probable alternative; they may have then been starving, and the object of the cairns was to call the attention of possible future travellers to their bodies—or they may have come the same spring over the ice from the south, and in that case they most probably travelled with Eskimo dog-sledges, and were on a hunting expedition, perhaps for bears.[34]

It's comforting to imagine that whoever Erling, Bjarni, and Eindridi were, they made it back home safely. But not everyone did. Scattered over several Icelandic manuscripts are scraps of a grisly story concerning a man called Lika-Lodin, a Greenlander from the mid-eleventh century.[35] The clue to his occupation is in his nickname—*Lík*—which means 'corpse'. Lodin used to spend his summers sailing north of the settlements, collecting the bodies of hunters and sailors who had died icy deaths far from home. Often—according to fragments of the story that survive—he would find carved runes close to the corpses, detailing the horrible ways in which they had died. Elsewhere there are descriptions of the terrible fate of sailors whose ship was wrecked off the east coast of Greenland in 1189. Here too, runes were said to have been found beside the bodies, also describing how they met their end. As we have already seen, ice mummies preserved in the frozen conditions are not unheard of in Greenland, but here there is a hagiographical twist to the tale, for only the body of the holy man has been preserved:

Their ship was wrecked by the Greenlandic wilderness, and everyone perished. This was known because fourteen winters later their ship was found, and the corpses of seven men were discovered in a cave. One of them was Ingimund the priest, whose body was whole and undecayed, likewise his clothes. Beside him lay the bones of six men, and also wax and runes that related the story of their fate.[36]

---

* Nansen's life and extraordinary accomplishments are chronicled on a website called 'Badass of the Week', where he is described as a 'vicious strip of solidified testosterone' with an 'unstoppable desire to constantly freeze his balls off and risk his life in the name of science and kickassery'. On Nansen crossing Greenland: 'To this point, nobody had ever attempted an exploration of the interior of Greenland, and the closest anybody had come to reaching the North Pole was writing a letter to Santa Claus, but Nansen didn't give a crap about any of that shit. Nothing would stand in the way of him kicking one of Saint Nick's reindeer in the antlers. He landed a ship on the East coast of Greenland, unpacked his skis, and got ready to freeze his junk off.'

None of this bodes well for the three men who piled the three cairns that cold April day. Nor do the other pieces of information that add more to our picture of the Northern Hunting Grounds. A few lines of a poem called the *Poem of the Northern Hunting Grounds* (*Norðrsetudrápa*) survive as quotations from two medieval Icelandic texts written in the thirteenth century.[37] Through this fragmented lens we glimpse a harsh and desolate landscape: 'When fierce gusts of wind from the snow-white mountains teased apart and wove together the storm-happy daughters of Ægir, bred on frost.'[38] In Old Norse mythology, Aegir is the giant-god of the sea and his nine daughters are the waves. The poet uses them to conjure up the stormy, frost-encrusted waters of Arctic Greenland, churned up by icy blizzards from the glacial mountains. The chances that he actually knew the Northern Hunting Grounds is very remote. After all, in his novel *Northern Lights* Philip Pullman was able to conjure up an Arctic realm of armoured polar bears and Finnish witches without ever having visited the far north himself. Even so, if this is what the rune-carvers were up against high in the Arctic and early in the year, it's extraordinary that they were able to unbend their frozen hands long enough to pile the cairns and carve the runes on that icy April day.

Other than the runestone from Kingittorsuaq, Norse hunters left few traces of their presence in the far north, except what they brought home with them. In the Western Settlement a handful of carved ivory figurines have been found: creatures that the hunters would have met on their expeditions. Despite their diminutive size—each as tiny as a small child's finger—these exquisite pieces perfectly capture the memory of a polar bear's bent back, a walrus' thick tusks, and a falcon's folded feathers. The Northern Hunting Grounds may have been a tough working environment, but for some at least, the call of the wild was hard to forget.

The sagas make little mention of the Northern Hunting Grounds. The *Saga of Erik the Red* contains several references to hunting trips in the 'uninhabited wilderness' (*óbyggðir*), which may or may not refer to the far north. But those who have travelled or lived in Greenland are often identified by the riches specific to the country: the flash of an ivory knife-handle, a belt of walrus hide, even a live polar bear trotting behind them. We have already met the pagan seeress of the *Saga of Erik the Red*, with her brass-mounted ivory knife. Later in the same saga Erik's son, Leif the Lucky, is blown off course to the Hebrides and wastes no time in getting cosy with a mysterious local woman. When he leaves her (pregnant with Leif Jr.), he gives her a 'gold finger ring, a Greenlandic woollen cloak, and an ivory belt'.[39] Elsewhere, in the *Tale of Einar Sokkason*, a

FIGURE 6.6 Gyrfalcon carved from walrus ivory, found in the ruins of the farm at Sandnes in the Western Settlement

Greenlander sails to Norway to request a bishop for the country, taking ivory and walrus-hide ropes 'to get on side with the chieftains'.[40] He also has a bear—presumably of the polar variety—amongst his retinue; a present for the king of Norway.

In other sagas, these natural resources play a central role in the action. In the *Saga of Crooked Ref* (*Króka-Refs saga*), the chief protagonist settles down in Greenland only to ignite a—very Greenlandic—feud over the killing of a polar bear in the snow. The saga is stuffed with lucrative natural resources: belts and ropes made from walrus skin, walrus ivory, furs, polar bears, and falcons. It features a Norwegian royal trader who arrives to secure precious gifts for his king:

One was a polar bear, fully grown and very well trained. The second gift was an ivory chess set made with very skillful workmanship. The third gift was a walrus skull with its ivory intact; it was engraved all over and covered in gold.[41]

118

There is plenty of evidence for items such as these beyond the saga stories. Starting with the last item, a golden walrus skull with its ivory intact, similar artefacts—minus the gold coating—have been discovered at several Norse Greenlandic sites. Walrus ivory was one of Norse Greenland's major exports. Most frequently, only walrus-bone fragments are found at farms, but occasionally upper jawbones have been discovered, bluntly removed from the rest of the skull. Since walrus tusks are embedded in the upper jawbone, Norse hunters used to separate this part of the skull using a sharp weapon like an axe, and take it home where they could remove the precious ivory. From a hunting point of view this makes sense for transport purposes, particularly when the walruses were killed in the far north. Walruses are heavy creatures, and it would have been much more convenient to butcher them up in the Northern Hunting Grounds and return with the most valuable parts, particularly tusks for ivory and skin for ships' ropes, rather than transport a heap of blubbery dead animals hundreds of tough miles down the coast. The most valuable parts included tusks for ivory, tough penis bones, molar teeth to be fashioned into amulets, and skin for ships' ropes; all but the last of these survive in the archaeological record.[42]

Walrus ivory was a major component of Norse Greenland's economy throughout the lifetime of the colony. From this raw material were fashioned many expensive, intricately carved artefacts that were highly valued in medieval Europe, such as the chess pieces described in the above saga. Most of the famous Lewis Chessmen—discovered in the Outer Hebrides in 1831 and carved in perhaps Norway or Iceland in the second half of the twelfth century—are made of walrus ivory (the rest are made of whalebone). This may be Greenlandic ivory, also 'made with very skilful workmanship', just like the set described in the saga.

The *Saga of Crooked Ref* isn't the only story to feature a live Greenlandic polar bear brought as a present for a king. Such a creature also plays a starring role in the *Tale of Audun from the West Fjords* (*Auðunar þáttr vestfirzka*). This is a singular story preserved in several different manuscripts. It takes the form of a biography of a plucky young Icelander abroad, but has been described by one scholar as 'a folktale in a historic setting'.[43] Having traded everything he owns in exchange for the bear while in Greenland, the poverty-stricken Audun travels to Norway then Denmark with his furry friend in tow. This bear becomes his passport through war-torn kingdoms and into the courts of mighty kings, who are keen to get their hands on this 'great treasure'.[44]

Unfortunately for Audun, his more pressing, practical concern is how to feed this voracious eating-machine. The king's steward cautions him: 'You should bear in mind that this creature might die on you, because it needs lots of food and your money seems to be drying up.'[45]

For advice on how to feed his bear, Audun might have consulted another medieval polar-bear owner: King Henry III of England. In 1252 Henry was given a 'white bear' as a present from King Hakon of Norway, to add to the menagerie of exotic animals that he kept in the Tower of London. It was tied up, but allowed to swim and fish in the river Thames. Where the bear originally came from isn't specified, but it may well have been Greenland. Regarding the upkeep of the bear, Henry sent the following orders out to his sheriffs from Windsor Castle:

The king sends greetings to the sheriffs of London. We command that you have made for the keeper of our white bear, which recently was sent to us from Norway and is in our Tower of London, one muzzle and one iron chain to hold the bear when he is out of the water and one long, strong cord to hold the same bear when he is catching fish in the river Thames.[46]

Most Londoners confronted with the incongruous image of a polar bear fishing for its dinner on the banks of the Thames wouldn't have imagined just how far this exotic creature may have come from, or just how dangerous his journey first to Norway and then to England might have been. But the Norse appetite for adventure, exploration, and discovery didn't stop at the Northern Hunting Grounds. New lands waited west beyond the ocean horizon. Little more than a decade after Erik the Red settled Greenland, Norse expeditions began to strike out for these new lands, many led by Erik's own children. What they discovered there was rather more than they bargained for.

CHAPTER 7

New World

Snorri's story

On a grey, damp day at the end of September, a Norse ship called *Snorri* reached its final destination: North America. It had been out at sea for over two months, propelled through more than a thousand miles of chilly northern waters by nothing other than a square sail and oars. There had been little shelter for the sailors on board ever since they had set sail west from Greenland, with their bellies full of whale skin, seal blubber, smoked reindeer, and dried halibut. On board, rations were less exotic; their most prized source of energy was an oat-based biscuit they simply called 'gold'.

On the way, they had sighted reindeer roaming the mountainsides and polar bears snoozing on the rocky outcrops. Interested walruses cruised past to get a look at the strange creatures that had entered their waters. A pod of pilot whales tracked the ship for hours as it crossed the grey polar seas north of the Arctic Circle.

Weeks passed. When the sea breezes blew, *Snorri* slipped easily over the waves, guided at night by stars and northern lights that lit up the inky sky. When the wind dropped, the sailors drifted helplessly where the currents took them. At such times, those who knew the old faith turned to the pagan gods for help, clambering naked onto the deck, lifting their arms to the heavens, and hollering to the god Frey for a good wind.

Day by day the ship moved up the Greenland coastline and crossed the chilly, choppy waters of the Davis Strait. Turning south, it skirted the icy, rocky edges of Baffin Island, and continued down the impossibly long Labrador coastline. Finally, it had reached its destination: L'Anse aux Meadows on the northernmost tip of Newfoundland. Incredibly, this tiny ship had brought its crew safely all the way to the North American continent.

A few dozen yards from the shore, *Snorri* ground to a halt in the shallows. Undaunted, the plucky sailors weighed anchor and flung themselves over-board, jubilantly splashing their way to land. A motley welcome party had come to greet them, some snug under coloured woollen shawls and luxurious beards to keep out the wind and wet. Mothers welcomed home their far-travelling sons and friends were reunited, before the happy, hungry adventur-ers sat down to a banquet of squid, char, mussels, moose, reindeer, and partridge berry jam.

Remarkably, we know the exact year that this voyage took place. We even know the precise date when the sailors reached their destination.

It was Tuesday, 22 September 1998.

Snorri was a reconstructed Norse cargo ship—a *knarr*—designed, built, and crewed by an intrepid team of Americans and Danes. Their aim was to retrace the route taken by Erik the Red's son, Leif the Lucky, when he sailed from Greenland to Newfoundland around AD 1000.

This was no easy task. A year earlier, their first expedition had come to a premature and watery end when the ship's rudder failed in the middle of the Davis Strait. For a Norse crew sailing this dangerous stretch of water one thousand years earlier, it is likely that such an event would have ended not only their voyage but also their lives. For the modern-day crew it was a disap-pointment, and a chance to go back to the drawing-board.

The following summer they set off again from Nuuk. The Greenlanders threw them an official farewell party, featuring traditional food and dancing. Less than a week into the voyage, an American member of the crew was delighted to discover the existence of the fine British biscuit, the Hob Nob. He wrote in the online journal:

A word about the cookies called Hob Nobs: they are 'gold'. I mean that statement to be heard as if spoken in a low, measured, reverential tone, with a Danish accent, if pos-sible. Erik [his Danish shipmate] occasionally says that about things he really approves of, like hot chocolate or his sleeping bag.[1]

In total, the voyage took a lengthy eighty-seven days. The right wind was cru-cial, and its presence or absence was totally beyond the sailors' control. That is, until one day, moored off the Labrador coastline, when the leader of the expedition sat in his sleeping bag. He was reading about the pagan god Frey, who was said to own the fastest ship in the world, which was always followed by the wind:

I knew then what I had to do. I jumped out of my bag and ran from beneath our tarp. I was quite naked. I lifted up my arms and called out, 'Hey, Frey! Listen! We need some help…please give us some following winds!' Luckily, all the guys except Terry and Doug were in Nain, and Terry was on shore, I think.* I was still a little hesitant, though, and ended it there. I felt he knew I meant it, although it was quite a lousy calling-out-to-a-god thing. It's just not something one gets much practice at.…We did, however, get a good wind the next day. So ever since, I have been having a running dialog with Frey—not all the time, but whenever it seems appropriate.[2]

Whether with or without Frey's help, *Snorri* finally reached L'Anse aux Meadows, on the tip of Newfoundland. The location was enormously significant: the first confirmed Norse outpost found in North America. This UNESCO World Heritage Site is also home to a reconstructed Norse longhouse, and a troop of viking re-enactors. They were there to greet the soggy arrivals in their traditional costumes, together with friends, family, and locals who had gathered for the occasion. A suitably Norse feast was devoured in the reconstructed longhouse, before the triumphant speeches began. A millennium after the first Norse men and women crossed west from Greenland, a Norse ship had returned.

Sailing the saga seas

When Erik set off for Greenland under the shadow of outlawry, it would have been of little interest to anyone other than his friends and family. As far as most locals were concerned, Erik was an unruly handful: he had clobbered one man too many and left the country to cool off. As far as the rest of the world was concerned, a weather-beaten outlaw navigating the distant fjords of a glacial landscape was not even a speck of dust on the radar.

---

* Nain is the northernmost permanent settlement in Newfoundland and Labrador, nearly a thousand miles north of L'Anse aux Meadows.

Even so, this little-noticed event was of enormous significance. Erik's voyage west was the first fine thread of a watery web that would span the entire North Atlantic. From Greenland, groups of Norse explorers—led by Erik's own children and in-laws, if we are to believe the sagas—would sail further west, all the way to the fringes of the North American continent. As they edged along this unfamiliar coastline, they had no idea they were making world history.

Unlike the intrepid modern crew who sailed across the ocean in *Snorri*, medieval Norse sailors did not set off on their voyages with journals tucked under their arms. Even so, despite the lack of first-hand written accounts, these expeditions didn't go unrecorded. When the voyagers returned from weeks, months, or even years away from home, they brought tales of where they had been and what they had seen. As the stories were passed down the generations, they were repeated and reshaped by the mouths that told them.

Until a few decades ago, when additional evidence began to emerge (more of that later), the Vinland sagas—the *Saga of Erik the Red* and the *Saga of the Greenlanders*—were the only real indication that the Norse had really reached the North American continent. Other than that, there are only occasional passing references to 'Vinland' in a handful of other texts. The earliest is in the work of the eleventh-century German chronicler Adam of Bremen. In his *History of the Bishops of Hamburg* (*Gesta Hammaburgensis ecclesiae pontificum*), written in the 1070s, he alluded to reports of a far-off ocean, told to him by King Svein of Denmark: 'He spoke also of yet another island of the many found in that ocean. It is called Vinland because vines producing excellent wine grow wild there.'[3] Yet such shadowy allusions would mean nothing without the more detailed descriptions in the sagas.

The sagas were the first 'Letters from America', written down in Iceland but rooted in the oral tales of those who had sailed all the way across the ocean. This is indicated in the last line of the *Saga of the Greenlanders*, which refers to Karlsefni, the leader of one of the expeditions: 'It was Karlsefni who recounted most fully of all men the events that took place on all these voyages, some of which have now been written down.'[4] But even the sagas are not watertight proof of any such voyages. Fact and fiction are tricky beasts to separate in the sagas at the best of times, particularly when accounts of epic sea voyages sit next to tales of plague-ridden corpses rising from the dead. By the time these events came to be recorded, different versions of the stories had developed and certain details had become hazy, with differing accounts of who had done what, when they had done it, and why. The *Saga of the Greenlanders* describes six voyages west of Greenland, and the *Saga of Erik the Red* only three. The third is a big beast of an expedition that amalgamates many of the events that the *Saga of the Greenlanders* spreads over several voyages. These differences are to be expected. What is more remarkable is how many similarities remained between the two sagas.

Today, cruise-ships churn the waters between Greenland and Canada, bristling with camera-wielding tourists keen to capture these dramatic landscapes. When these same waters were crossed by the Norse a millennium earlier, they had more practical concerns: resources and navigational aids. These priorities are embedded in the Vinland sagas; remnants of oral information passed down the generations.[5] During the first expedition in the *Saga of Erik the Red*, three ships leave the Western Settlement. Led by Karlsefni, they loop up and around the Davis Strait, between Greenland and Canada. From there, they head south down the coast:

They sailed south for two days. Then they saw land, and launched their boats so they could explore it. There they found large stone slabs, many twelve ells wide. There were many arctic foxes there. They named the land and called it Helluland [Stone Slab Land]. From there they sailed south for two more days, and turning south-east they found a land overgrown with trees and with many animals. An island lay offshore to the south-east; there they killed a bear and afterwards called the island Bjarney [Bear Island] and the land Markland [Forest Land]. From there they sailed south along the coast for long time and came to a peninsula. Land lay on the starboard side, with long stretches of strands and sands....They called the strands Furdustrandir [Wonder Strands] because they were long to sail along. Then the land became indented with bays. They sailed their ship into one of them.[6]

In the *Saga of the Greenlanders* the first part of the route is almost identical. This time it isn't Karlsefni who leads the voyage, but Erik's son, Leif the Lucky. As he explores, he gives the lands geographically descriptive names, making them a useful navigational tool for future expeditions. At the same time, this naming process allows Leif to stamp a Norse identity upon these lands and incorporate them into his own world. In the history of modern polar exploration, the same practice can be seen in many of the place-names assigned to chilly Arctic wastelands. Some echo the hardships of the expeditions themselves: Dismal Island, Cape Disappointment, Exasperation Inlet, and so on. Others describe the conditions in a particular location, most rather dreary, including Echo Mountain, Gale Ridge, and Nothing Passage. Still others commemorate the names of Arctic explorers and scientists, such as Mount Amundsen, Mount Scott, and Mount Shackleton.

Once again in the *Saga of the Greenlanders* Helluland is the first land they reach. But the description in this text is slightly different from that of its saga twin: the land is a sterile, rocky slab with vast glaciers covering the uplands. Next they come to Markland, which is flat and covered in trees. This time there are no wild animals roaming the forest and no unlucky bear to be bashed. In their place we find new details, such as white sandy beaches and sloping sea-shores. After the ships leave Markland they sail for two days with a north-easterly wind behind them, until they sight land:

There were lots of shallows near the shore and their ship ran aground. The sea seemed to be a long way from the ship, but they were so curious about getting to the land that they didn't want to wait for the tide to return, so waded to the land via a river that flowed to the sea from a lake. As soon as the water was back under their ship, they took their boat and rowed back to the ship, sailed it up the river to the lake, then cast anchor. They carried their hammocks from the ship and built booths on land. Later they decided to stay there over the winter, so they built large houses there.[7]

By this point, the parallel tracks on which the two sagas are running have diverged a little. While the sailors of the *Saga of the Greenlanders* are making camp and built overwintering houses, their counterparts in the *Saga of Erik the Red* have gone off in a different, vaguer direction somewhere further down the coast. But in both accounts the voyagers begin to discover the fine resources that the land has to offer: wild vines, grapes, and wheat. In the *Saga of the Greenlanders* the discoverer is Tyrkir, a wizened, wrinkled German who has lived amongst the Norse for many years. He disappears, and when he returns he is very excited about something:

First he talked for a long time in German, his eyes shot in many directions and he scrunched up his face. They didn't understand what he was saying. Then after some time he spoke in Norse: 'I wasn't gone much longer than you but I've got some news to report: I've found grapevines and grapes!'[8]

FIGURE 7.1 Rocky Helluland (now Baffin Island)

126

FIGURE 7.2   Forested Markland (now Labrador)

FIGURE 7.3   Reconstruction of a Norse building at L'Anse aux Meadows, Newfoundland

In the *Saga of Erik the Red* two Scottish slaves are put ashore to explore the land, a feral pair who can run faster than animals. Like Tyrkir, they return clutching grapes and wild wheat. The Norse have reached the region they name Vinland, after the wild grapes they find growing there.

L'Anse aux Meadows

Over the years, the question of where the Norse actually went has been much debated.[9] Helluland is almost certainly Baffin Island, with its rocky terrain, inhospitable mountains, and towering glaciers. Markland is probably a forested part of the Labrador coastline. Further south, things get a little hazier, but Vinland seems to be the area around the Gulf of St Lawrence, New Brunswick, and Nova Scotia. But there is one place that we know for sure that the Norse visited: L'Anse aux Meadows. (See Map 2.)

In 1961, just outside a little fishing village on a northern peninsula of Newfoundland, the Norwegian archaeologists Helge Ingstad and Anne Stine Ingstad began an extraordinary excavation. On a wide, grassy bay at L'Anse aux Meadows, looking out onto the distant coastline of Labrador, they found the remains of eight Norse buildings with thickly turfed walls and wooden-framed roofs. Some were large halls, seemingly built for living in. Others were workshops, used to repair boats and ships. This site doesn't appear to have been built to be a permanent settlement. No land had been farmed and no buildings erected to hold animals and supplies. Rather, given that the Norse sailors would have journeyed more than a thousand miles across the sea from Greenland, this was a site where leaky holes could be plugged, rusty nails replaced, and sea-battered planks and weathered sails mended.[10]

The site wasn't occupied for long. No burials have been found, and the middens are fairly empty. The abandonment of L'Anse aux Meadows seems to have been a deliberate, orderly affair, because when the last occupants left, they took all their tools and valuables with them. Two of the buildings were even set on fire, perhaps by the Norse as they set off for the final time with no intention of returning. The buildings have been dated to around AD 1000, which is around fifteen years after Erik first settled Greenland. This date fits neatly with the timeline recorded in the Vinland sagas, and it seems highly likely that these are the houses said to have been built by Leif in the *Saga of the Greenlanders*.[11]

If the site at L'Anse aux Meadows was a stepping-stone to the south, its swift desertion may suggest that this was not a long-lived venture. But even if no further adventures are recorded in the sagas and no archaeological evidence has been found to suggest that there were later expeditions, there are also tantalizing little details that don't fit into this neat picture, reminding us how little we actually know. The Icelandic annals record that in 1347 a Greenlandic ship ended up drifting to Iceland on its way back from Markland, perhaps on an expedition to collect wood: 'Then a ship came from Greenland, smaller in size than little Icelandic boats.... It was anchorless. There were seventeen men on board, and they had sailed to Markland but were later shipwrecked here.'[12] L'Anse aux Meadows is the only Norse site on the North American continent about which we can be completely certain. But doubtless there are other secrets still waiting to be uncovered. In 2012, archaeologists announced that they had identified a possible Norse site on Baffin Island (or Helluland, to give it its Norse name). They had discovered fragments of pelts made from the fur of European black rats, a whalebone shovel used to cut turf, tiny pieces of yarn spun in the Norse style, and the ruins of buildings rather like those from Norse sites in Greenland.[13] Even when this book was in the final stages of production, reports started to appear in newspapers concerning another possible Norse site at Point Rosee on the south-west tip of Newfoundland, discovered with satellite images taken from space.[14] The Norse voyagers have many more secrets still to yield up. Until then, the sagas remain our main source of information about what the Norse may have got up to in Vinland.

A taste of paradise

The Vinland of the sagas is a land of unimaginable bounty, where the explorers are faced with an embarrassment of riches:

They found wild wheat on the low-lying land, and vines wherever there was woodland. Every brook was full of fish. They dug pits where the land and water met at high tide, and when the tide went out there were halibut in the pits. There were very many animals of all kinds in the forest.[15]

In the face of this infinite abundance, thoughts naturally turn to long-term settlement. In the *Saga of the Greenlanders*, the information that 'they intended to settle the land if they could' is coupled with descriptions of abundant fish, grapes, and timber.[16] One of Erik the Red's sons even picks out a suitable spot to build his farm. But though the explorers are keen to embrace the land as their own, they find themselves always on the peripheries. It is the foreign elements within their party—the German in the *Saga of the Greenlanders* and the Scottish slaves in the *Saga of Erik the Red*—who are able to go further into the land itself and discover wild wheat and grapes. A sense of unease and insecurity grows as events unfold. In the *Saga of Greenlanders* Karlsefni's voyage ends with them packing up hastily and returning to Greenland with a shipload of produce: 'Then Karlsefni stated that he didn't want to stay there any longer, and wanted to get back to Greenland. Now they prepared for their voyage and took many profitable things from there, grapevines and berries and skins.'[17] For even as the Norsemen explorers enjoy this taste of paradise, they find a worm lurking in the apple. They are not alone.

Trouble with the natives

In 1930 archaeologists excavated a major Norse farm in Greenland's Western Settlement. This was the aforementioned Sandnes, with the underwater church foundations that only appear at low tide. These foundations were hiding a crucial piece of evidence. In a wet, sand-muddy corner of the churchyard, a pointy piece of stone was found. The excavation leader was Aage Roussell (a remarkable figure who would later become a member of the Resistance during the Nazi occupation of Denmark). This is how he described the item:

There is no reason for attributing this handsomely executed little specimen with its winged tang to the Norsemen, but curiously enough the form has not been met with in the Greenland Eskimo finds, whereas exactly similar heads occur in northern Canada. I shall not embark upon a discussion of this peculiar circumstance.[18]

Let's delve a little further into this 'peculiar circumstance' that Aage was reluctant to discuss, for this tiny stone arrowhead is the only piece of evidence from Greenland that confirms that the Norse sailed west to the ends of the ocean. No one knows exactly how it made its way to Greenland. Perhaps it was brought back as a souvenir; an exotic memento of encounters with a strange native race. Alternatively, the arrow's final resting-place in a graveyard might suggest its involvement in someone's unpleasant end. In the sagas there is at least one account of death by Native American arrowhead, so perhaps the arrow came back embedded in the flesh of a fallen Norseman:

The Skraelings shot at them for a while, then ran away as quickly as they could. Then Thorvald asked his men whether they were wounded at all; they said that they weren't hurt. 'I've got a wound under my arm,' he said, 'because an arrow flew between the edge of the ship and my shield, and under my arm. Here is the arrow, which will be my death.'[19]

Without the Vinland sagas, the origins of the little stone arrow would have remained mysterious. But thanks to these two texts, we know it was probably made by the people known in the sagas as Skraelings (*Skrælingar*). Other than the arrowhead pulled from the churchyard in the Western Settlement, little evidence survives of direct interaction between the Norse and natives. Occasionally, Norse artefacts are uncovered in Native American sites from this time. However, it is more likely that most of them rattled up and down the coastline without Norse involvement, passed on through the far-reaching trading networks of the native tribes. The most famous of these is the so-called 'Maine Penny', a little silver coin pulled from an archaeological site on the Maine coastline in 1957. It came from the reign of King Olaf the Peaceful, who ruled Norway from 1067 to 1093. At this time the site was an important centre for trade between native tribes, linking networks that spidered up and down the coastline. Some of the items uncovered at the site come all the way from Labrador and Newfoundland. The Norse coin probably travelled south in a similar fashion, traded down the coast through these networks. Other tiny traces hint at direct contact: a native-style lamp found at the Norse site at L'Anse aux Meadows, and metal fragments from native sites that seem to use Norse smelting methods. On Baffin Island at an abandoned site used by indigenous hunters around 700 years ago, soft strands of arctic hare fur woven into cord were also found. Since at this time the native inhabitants of the region had no spinning or weaving traditions, it has been suggested that the hunters may have picked up this skill from Norse visitors to the island. Sparse evidence of this kind tallies with the basic picture painted by the Vinland sagas: sporadic voyages, patchy attempts to make contact and trade, followed by breakdowns in communication and cordiality. Most likely, the full picture will never be known.[20]

'Skraeling' is a catch-all term used to describe anyone the Norse encountered on these far-western voyages. In reality, the Norse travellers would have come into contact with several distinct groups who occupied Canada's coastal regions at this time. Furthest north, around the area the Norse called 'Helluland', lived the Dorset people. Further south, in the region of 'Markland', lived the ancestors of the Innu of Labrador and the Beothuk of Newfoundland. Still further south, in bountiful 'Vinland' there would have been many settlements scattered around the bays and rivers around the Gulf of St Lawrence. These various lands and waterways were home to various tribes, including the Iroquois and the Algonquins.[21] The word 'skraeling' is an unflattering one, although exactly where it comes from and what it means is unclear. It may possibly be linked to the verb *skrælna*, which means 'to become shrivelled', and so carry the sense of feebleness, scrawniness, and general physical inferiority.[22] The saga descriptions of these tribes reinforce this sense of physical and cultural otherness: 'They were black, hideous men with horrible hair on their heads, big-eyed and broad-cheeked.'[23]

Almost all Norse–Skraeling interactions in the Vinland sagas can be filed under 'T', for 'trade', 'trouble', and usually both. There is a twitchiness that underlies all the encounters, exacerbated by the fact that, as the *Saga of the Greenlanders* notes, 'neither understood the other's language'.[24] Under such circumstances, interpreting the mood becomes tricky. In the *Saga of Erik the Red*, the solution is signs and symbols:

Early one morning, when they looked about, they saw a great number of skin kayaks. Wooden poles that looked like flails were being waved in the boats, and they were being swung in a clockwise direction. Then Karlsefni asked, 'What might this signify?' Snorri Thorbrandsson answered him, 'It's possible that it's a sign of peace—we should pick up our white shields and lift them in return.'[25]

The Skraelings are keen to trade with these strange newcomers to their land. What they want more than anything else is red cloth, which they trade for expensive pelts and grey furs:

The Skraelings took a long strip of red cloth for each skin and tied it around their heads. This bartering carried on for a while. When there wasn't much of the cloth left that they were trading with Karlsefni, they cut it into such small pieces that none were broader than the width of a finger, but the Skraelings gave just as much for them as before, or even more.[26]

Ever the ones to take full advantage of a commercial opportunity, the Norse are unexpectedly propelled into a nascent trading network. To modern readers, expensive pelts in exchange for little strips of red cloth may smack of the sort of exploitation and colonialism usually associated with visitors who came to

America several centuries later. In a similar episode from the *Saga of the Green-landers*, the Skraelings' pelts and furs are exchanged for milk products. Here, the implication is that this is a rather one-sided deal, because 'they carried their goods away in their bellies, but Karlsefni and his fellow travellers kept their bundles and pelts'.[27] But it's possible—if any of this actually happened—that the Skraelings weren't getting such a raw deal. As far as can be established, these particular tribes had no spinning or weaving traditions, which would have made cloth very valuable.[28] Perhaps, if furs and pelts were very easy to come by, then the Skraelings thought *they* were ripping off these strange newcomers. After all, it has been pointed out that when the European settlers and Algonquin tribes came to trade in the Great Lakes region several centuries later, the Native Americans were amazed to find that the newcomers were so obsessed by greasy old beaver skins, since they were used to singeing them off in the fire while cooking the beaver for dinner or using them as baby nappies.[29]

On occasions the Skraelings also ask for swords and spears, although the Norse refuse. As with the red cloth, then, their interest may have been in the metal the weapons were made of, rather than their more obvious uses. After all, metal was 'a scarce and necessary raw material for the cutting tools and weapons of Inuit technology', as the archaeologist Patricia Sutherland has noted.[30] On the rare occasions when the Skraelings do get hold of weaponry, they have no idea what to do with it. In the *Saga of Erik the Red* a native finds an axe lying beside a fallen Norseman. To him, this treasure is useless because it breaks against stone, so he chucks it away. Of course, if we are going to buy the argument that the Skraelings wanted weapons because they were made of metal, then it doesn't follow that he would have thrown the weapon away. This is an important reminder that speculation can only take us so far, and it doesn't do us much good to take the sagas too literally, even when—or particularly when—they are our main source.

Through the looking glass

Saga descriptions of the first encounters with the Skraelings read like a somewhat jumbled, second-hand anthropological report, detailing their appearance and early attempts at trade. But once they appear on the scene, Vinland has changed forever for the Norse. It may be as full of fine resources and fertile land as before, but it is no conveniently uninhabited *terra nova*. With each new interaction with the Skraelings, Vinland moves further away from the Norse grasp. In this increasingly unfamiliar, unknowable world, Norse cultural norms cannot be assumed. With no common understanding of the world—other than the desire to trade—and no way of speaking to each other, miscommunication can be deadly. In the *Saga of Erik the Red* a bellowing bull brought by the Norse terrifies the natives so badly that they return to attack the incomers. Before, both groups had signalled their peaceful intentions with poles waved clockwise and white shields. This time the Skraelings signal war, waving their poles anticlockwise and howling at the tops of their voices. The Norsemen lift red shields in response. The Skraeling weapon of choice is something never seen before by the explorers from across the sea: 'a very large ball on a pole, about as big as a sheep's belly and blue-black in colour, and they launched it from the pole up onto the land, over Karlsefni and his men, and it made a hideous sound when it came down.'[31] It's hard to know what this weapon would have been, since all we have is an account (many times removed) from the point of view of the Norse, who clearly didn't know what it was. Comparisons are sometimes made with the so-called 'ballista' or 'demon's head' of Algonquin tradition, described by the nineteenth-century geographer, geologist, explorer, and ethnologist Henry Rowe Schoolcraft.*[32] The Norse, however, have no frame of reference within which to interpret this dangerous object. With the Skraelings seeming to press in on all sides, they can do nothing but flee up the river in terror. Suddenly, the vast horde disappears as quickly as it arrived: a development interpreted by the Norse as a magical illusion. But this isn't the logical magic of the Sámi of northern Scandinavia, which fits into the rational order of the saga world. Instead, it is part of a strange, contradictory place increasingly full of illusions and uncertainties, where nothing is quite as it seems.

One of the oddest episodes of all comes from the *Saga of the Greenlanders*. It concerns Gudrid, whom we last met in the Western Settlement surrounded by

---

* Although an outsider by birth, Schoolcraft was well placed to explain Algonquin traditions through his marriage to the Native American writer Jane Johnston (or to give her native name, Bamewawagezhikaquay, which means 'Woman of the Sound that the Stars Make Rushing through the Sky'). Jane was of mixed Ojibwe and Scots-Irish heritage, and met Schoolcraft when he was appointed as the first US 'Indian Agent' for the Michigan Territory. After their marriage she taught Schoolcraft the Ojibwe language and customs, and through him, her knowledge of Native American stories became an important source of information, not least for Henry Wadsworth Longfellow's *Song of Hiawatha*.

the undead. She goes on to marry Karlsefni and travels with him to Vinland, where she becomes the first known European to give birth on the North American continent. In many ways, Gudrid is the real hero of the Vinland sagas. A modern sculpture by the Icelandic artist Ásmundur Sveinsson was erected at Laugarbrekka in Western Iceland, where she was born. She stands in a ship, one hand resting on the square, toothy dragon's head that forms the bow. Her other hand balances her little son Snorri, who stands on her shoulder. His face is tilted upwards, little arm raised to the sky, but Gudrid's eyes are fixed firmly ahead, on the long sea road before her.

Events in Vinland unfold at a time when relations between the Norse and the Skraelings are deteriorating. A palisade has been built around the Norse farmstead, and Gudrid sits inside, next to her baby son's cradle. Suddenly, she realizes they are not alone:

Then a shadow fell across the doorway, and in came a rather short woman wearing a black kirtle and a ribbon around her head. She had light chestnut-coloured hair, pale skin, and huge eyes, the like of which had never been seen in another person's head. She went over to where Gudrid sat and spoke; 'What's your name?' she said. 'My name is Gudrid and what's your name?' 'My name is Gudrid,' she said. Then Gudrid (the mistress of the house) held out her hand for the woman to sit beside her, but at that moment Gudrid heard an enormous crash and the woman disappeared. The crash was because one of Karlsefni's men had killed a Skraeling because he had tried to take their weapons. Now the Skraelings fled as quickly as possible, leaving their cloth and wares behind them. No one had seen the woman apart from Gudrid.[33]

The saga gives no more information about this curious incident. Who is this woman? Why can she speak to Gudrid in her own language? Why does she say that her name is Gudrid too? Her disappearance is even more mysterious. Has she vanished by magic, or has she simply taken fright at the noise and fled? Is she a native who has entered the camp and parrots Gudrid's words? Perhaps a hallucination conjured up by this increasingly strange land and those who inhabit it? Or simply an error by a tired scribe who felt he had been in the scriptorium too long?[34]

In any case, even before Gudrid meets her unexplained doppelgänger the palisades have been erected and the Norse defences are up. The land that the Norse approached with such high hopes reveals itself as one step too far across the sea; the first land that cannot be claimed and colonized in the thus-far inexorable Norse march over the North Atlantic.

Paradise lost

Despite the difficulties posed by the native Skraelings of Vinland, there are blacker, bloodier deeds to be played out on this far-flung stage, and these involve the Norse alone. In the final western voyage of the *Saga of the Greenlanders* bad blood wells up and spills over into slaughter. The expedition is led by Erik the Red's illegitimate daughter Freydis ('an extremely haughty woman', as the saga describes her) and her husband ('a petty little man').[35] With them is a second ship led by two brothers. They head for the houses built by Leif, Freydis' brother, but trouble is brewing from the start. Over a miserable, jittery winter, a frosty atmosphere descends between Freydis and the brothers. At her instigation, Freydis' menfolk march over to the house where the brothers and their followers are staying, and murder them. But Freydis isn't content to stop at the brothers: 'Now all the men there were killed, but the women were left because no one wanted to kill them. Then Freydis said: "Put an axe in my hand." So it was done. Then she attacked the five women who were there, and left them dead.'[36] From here, the survivors set sail from Vinland for the last time, leaving the soil reddened by the blood of their countrymen. Freydis has sworn everyone to secrecy, on pain of death. It is only back in Greenland that the gory tale comes to light, extracted from Freydis' shipmates under torture. In this saga version of *Lord of the Flies*, a land without established laws and codes of behaviour exposes what horrors may lurk behind an individual's socialized exterior. For the *Saga of the Greenlanders* at least, this final image of Vinland is as a dark, nightmarish world of the explorers' own making: a paradise lost.

Those of a more imaginative disposition might be tempted to connect this horrible episode with the archaeological evidence for the abandonment of the site at L'Anse aux Meadows, and the burning of the two buildings. Was this perhaps an attempt to cover up real-life bloody murders? Most likely, we will never know. If a version of the same episode also featured in the *Saga of Erik the Red*, we might be on (slightly) firmer ground, but it doesn't. Freydis also appears in this text, but as a more admirable character. During a Skraeling attack she alone is able to scare the natives away, by uncovering her chest and slapping her naked breast with a sword. The act is all the more impressive because she is heavily pregnant at the time, although why exactly such an action would have terrified the Skraelings is never explained. Here, as with the 'double-Gudrid' episode, perhaps the original saga audience had more information than we do, and knew how to interpret this scene. Alternatively, possibly it was always meant to be confusing, and they would have been as mystified as a modern reader. Despite the apparent beauty of Vinland and the natural resources it contains, this will always be an unstable, alien land, lying on the margins between the familiar Norse world and an exotic, unknowable sphere beyond.

Off the map

In the *Saga of Erik the Red*, an even stranger being hovers in the explorers' peripheral vision: a one-legged creature of murderous intent:

One morning, Karlsefni and his men saw something glittering above a forest clearing, which made them cry out. When it moved, they saw it was a uniped, which shot off down to the riverbank where they were anchored. Erik the Red's son Thorvald was seated at the ship's helm, and the uniped shot an arrow into his guts. Thorvald pulled out the arrow and said: 'There's fat around my belly. We've found a land of great opportunities, but we'll hardly benefit from them.' Thorvald died from these wounds a little later.[37]

We are being brought to the very edge of the world in true medieval European style. Those familiar with the famous Hereford *mappa mundi* (made in around 1290 and now on display in Hereford Cathedral) might remember a little, one-footed man somewhere in the vicinity of India, grinning impishly from under his tiny beard.[38] Similar images exist from other parts of medieval Europe, engraved on the stones of church towers, carved into the ends of wooden church pews, and frolicking on the margins of illuminated manuscripts. It is as if this creature has jumped straight out of an illustrated *mappa mundi*, or one of the encyclopedic lists of the marvellous and monstrous races that lurk at the unknown, unseen edges of the earth. The difference, of course, is that Norse travellers *had* once visited this far-flung region of the world, long before the sagas were committed to writing. In the *Saga of Erik the Red*, knowledge originating with those who had once visited these lands—albeit centuries before the tales were set down in writing—is combined with bookish

FIGURE 7.4 Pole-carrying uniped on a pockmarked page of the Icelandic *Physiologus* (*c.*1190–1210)

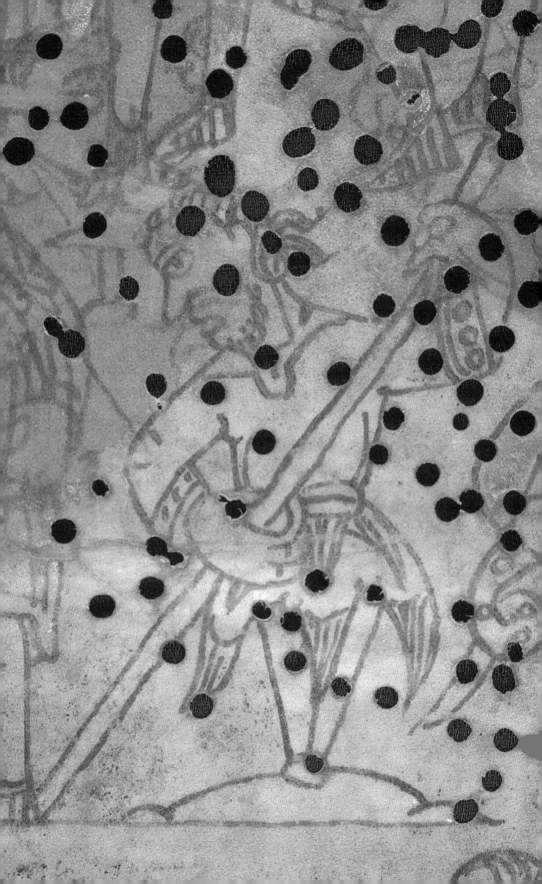

information derived from medieval Continental sources and, ultimately, texts from Classical Antiquity.*

Learned ideas about the marvellous races that populated the hidden places in the world were certainly circulating in medieval Iceland. Take the *Physiologus,* one of the most influential texts of the Middle Ages, originally composed in Greek in the second century AD. It contains descriptions of plants, animals—both real and fabulous—and marvellous races, and was widely translated and adapted throughout the Middle Ages into languages including Latin, Ethiopic, Armenian, Syriac, Arabic, Old Slavonic, Old High German, Old English, and Old Norse. Only two scraps of *Physiologus* material survive from medieval Iceland, written in around 1200. One of these ragged fragments contains a little illustration of an angry-looking uniped holding a pole of some kind. He is only just visible behind the liberal peppering of holes, not made by the jaws of a hungry bookworm but by an enterprising individual who punched holes in the parchment so he could use it to sift flour.

Lists of marvellous races are also included in two encyclopedic manuscripts from medieval Iceland. One is in a manuscript called *Hauksbók,* which was compiled at the beginning of the fourteenth century. This vellum has close connections to the Norse expeditions to Greenland and Vinland: not only does it contain one of the two surviving versions of the *Saga of Erik the Red,* but it was also compiled by a man called Hauk Erlendsson, who claimed direct descent from Gudrid and Karlsefni. The description of the uniped in *Hauksbók*'s list of marvellous and monstrous races also mentions a pole like the one carried by the pockmarked uniped in the manuscript illustration: 'Unipeds have such an enormous foot on the ground that they use it to shelter themselves from the sun while they sleep. They are as swift as animals and run with a pole.'[39] Perhaps inspiration for the marvellous uniped in the *Saga of Erik the Red* came from his one-legged cousin elsewhere in the *Hauksbók* manuscript, literary influences seeping through the parchment from one page to another. In typical saga style, we have moved from realistic details of sea navigation

---

* The mythical uniped can be traced far back into the Classical world. Most commonly it was known as a *sciapod* ('shadow-foot'), due to its habit of lying on its back and shading itself from the sun with its enormous foot, like a giant golf umbrella. This one-legged creature hopped out of Antiquity and into the Middle Ages, together with other fantastical beings such as dog-headed men (Cynocephali), tiny creatures at constant war with crop-stealing cranes (Pygmies), and beings that can wrap themselves up in their own enormous ears as though they were sleeping bags (Panotii).

and nascent trading to outlandish one-legged creatures who have developed a novel alternative to sun-cream.

At the time of the Vinland voyages, Norse Greenland was in its infancy, barely a couple of decades old. Leif, Gudrid, Karlsefni, and Freydis were amongst the first tough, hardy shoots of a society that would spring up from the icy soil and thrive for several hundred years. But eventually, the end would come, and later generations of Norse Greenlanders would live to see the decline and destruction of the colony they called home.

CHAPTER 8

The Way the World Ends

A frosty reception

In the autumn of 2011, the *Times Comprehensive Atlas of the World* became an unlikely headline hitter. Its publishers had just released the thirteenth edition of the atlas, an event that should have made little more than a ripple on the pond of the publishing world. Instead, it set off a tsunami of scientific outrage. For readers who might be interested in locating evocative Greenlandic place-names such as Qaanaaq ('eroded ice den'), Tuttulissuaq ('large place with reindeer'), Nanortalik ('the place with polar bear'), Alluitsup Paa ('the place without blowholes for seals'), and Semersooq ('location of many big glaciers'), there was a shock waiting for them on Plate 94.* Greenland had shrunk. Fifteen per cent of the country's permanent ice cover had been erased. Around the coastline, what had once been white ice was now brown rock and scrub. According to the glossy press release that accompanied the publication, Greenland's shrinking ice was 'concrete evidence of how climate change is altering the face of the planet forever—and doing so at an alarming and accelerating rate'.[1]

---

* There are many other places that these same readers would *not* have discovered in the *Times Atlas*, as I learnt to my disappointment when I tried to find them in the Map Room in Cambridge's University Library. These include Ammassaataasaq ('the place that looks like a bag of dried capelin fish'), Pukuluffik ('there where one snacks on berries'), Quajaqqisaarsuaq ('place infested with slippery algae'), Anarsivik ('there where you encounter bird droppings'), and Iviangernat ('those that remind one of women's breasts'). They can be found at the website <http://gst.dk/media/2915900/den-groenlandske-lods-forklaringer-til-stednavne_2015.pdf>.

This claim was met with a frosty reception by scientists from across the world, who pointed out that there was no supporting scientific evidence. The whistle was blown by members of the Scott Polar Research Institute in Cambridge, who described themselves as 'puzzled' and the situation as 'regrettable' (a damning verdict, barely one step away from 'disappointing' in the biting lexicon of British academia).[2] Eventually, HarperCollins retracted both the claims and the map itself.[3] Today there are two maps of Greenland in the edition, the second on a loose sheet inserted between the pages, sporting a whiter, icier coastline. More than likely, in future editions of the atlas, the shape and size of Greenland's ice sheet will have to be altered once again.

This was an uproar that could have only arisen in an age characterized by debates about global warming and climate change. As one commentator on this unfortunate incident noted: 'While, at one level, this dispute was about the accuracy of cartographic representation, it was also a political battlefield between climate scientists, mapmakers, and skeptics of global warming.'[4] The state of Greenland's ice sheets and glaciers has become something of a political hot potato, a dramatic symbol of a world population that may be sleepwalking its way to oblivion.

Ice Age

Over half a millennium earlier, the Norse Greenlanders seem to have found themselves facing the opposite problem. Little more than two centuries after Erik the Red settled Greenland, a serious cold snap was on its way. We tend to associate the Little Ice Age with a slightly later period of time: it was during the Little Ice Age that the Thames began to freeze over regularly, leading to the famous Frost Fairs of London that were held on the ice from the 1600s to the 1800s. It was also during the Little Ice Age that many great artists began to paint famous wintry scenes, such as the *Hunters in the Snow* by the Flemish artist Pieter Bruegel the Elder and the *Skating Minister* by the Scottish painter Sir Henry Raeburn.[5] But in Greenland—and the North Atlantic more generally— this climatic downturn hit much harder and much earlier.

The first centuries of the Norse Greenlandic colony coincided with a warm phase in the North Atlantic and further afield, known today as the Medieval Warm Period. But in the first decades of the 1200s the climate started to deteriorate. Norse Greenlanders living and working in the Western Settlement and the Northern Hunting Grounds would have been the first to feel the effects. Over time storms became more frequent, the temperatures dropped, and the fjords and coastal waters became blocked with sea ice. This would have been a particular problem for the acquisition of valuable Arctic resources such as walruses, so vital to the Norse Greenlandic economy. Further south, the Eastern Settlement wasn't seriously affected until the following century. At that point, ships trying to get into the fjords would have found their way blocked by thick sea ice, particularly in the summer. All this would have had a catastrophic effect on farming, hunting, and trading.[6]

The voyage to Greenland had always been long and tricky, but as the conditions worsened and the Atlantic pack ice began to grow, the old sea routes became blocked. This is described in a mid-fourteenth-century Norwegian source, based on an account of Greenland by a priest called Ivar Bardarson. Ivar came from Bergen in Norway, but he lived in Greenland for twenty years. The description begins:

It is said by knowledgeable men who are born out in Greenland and later travel abroad, that north from Stad in Norway to Horn, which lies on the east coast of Iceland, it is seven days sailing due west. From Snæfellsnes in Iceland, which is the closest point to Greenland, it is two days and two nights sailing due west to Gunnbjorn's skerries, which lie exactly between Greenland and Iceland. That was the old sailing route, but now ice comes down from the north of the ocean, so near to the aforementioned skerries that no one can sail the old route without putting their life in danger.[7]

This doesn't mean that the Norse Greenlanders woke up one morning to find their country had been transformed into a wintry Narnia. There had been cycles of better and worse weather during the Medieval Warm Period, and there were similar cycles during the Little Ice Age. But gradually, over time, conditions got worse. The Norse Greenlanders had always lived in a marginal, seasonally vulnerable land, where they had to combine farming and hunting in order to survive and there was little surplus to fall back on. They were already reliant on trade from the east, and imports such as grain and metal to maintain their European lifestyle. For those farming the pockets of land between Greenland's deep fjords and steep mountain slopes, a run of bad summers and worse winters could prove disastrous. Unfortunately for the Norse Greenlanders, this was far from the only problem they were facing.

Silent death

Today, ruined farmsteads litter the fjords once inhabited by generations of medieval Norse men and women. But the question of what happened to the colony is a tricky one to answer. There is no evidence for a single traumatic event that could have wiped them out: no tsunamis, no mass genocides, no packs of bloodthirsty polar bears roaming the hills. The question of what happened and why has been hotly debated ever since the ruins were discovered in the eighteenth century by Hans Egede the missionary. Suggestions have ranged from plagues of caterpillars to warfare with the nomadic hunters that had started to make their way down the coastline from Arctic Canada.

As is often the way with historians, the explanation *du jour* may reflect as much about current events as past realities. In the 1920s the biological anthropologist F. C. C. Hansen turned his attention to the recent excavation of a Norse graveyard in the Eastern Settlement (the aforementioned Herjolfsnes, where the beautifully preserved clothes were discovered). His goal was to prove that there had been biological degeneration in the last generations of Norse men and women to live in Greenland. The skeletons, he suggested, were evidence of 'a race of small people, with little strength, physically weakened and with many defects and pathological conditions'.[8] These findings have been largely disproved; most recently the archaeologist Niels Lynnerup argued that Hansen's thesis reflected rather more about dominant scientific theories of the 1920s and 1930s concerning racial purity and degeneration.[9] Today, in a period dominated by climate-change discourse, changing climatic conditions have been brought to the forefront of the debate, just as in the first pages of this chapter. But increasingly it has been recognized that there is no single explanation for the demise. Although we may never know exactly how it happened, the silent death of Norse Greenland was probably due to a combination of factors: a localized series of short, sharp shocks combined with gradual, insidious changes that crept up on the population over the years, decades, and even centuries.

Several general patterns can be seen. One problem seems to have been overgrazing and soil erosion, the medieval equivalent of running out of petrol. Year after year, the fields suitable for producing winter fodder and grazing livestock had been used and reused, and slowly they were becoming worn out. Without the means to feed their cows, sheep, and other domestic animals, the Norse Greenlanders could not function as a European-style farming society.

Another difficulty may have been competition from newcomers to the fjords occupied by the Norse. When Erik the Red first settled Greenland, he found an apparently uninhabited country. This had not always been the case; for thousands of years waves of migrating hunters had settled Greenland from Arctic Canada, and over the millennia different groups had come and gone. The Norse settlers were well aware of this. According to the *Book of Icelanders* when Erik the Red and his followers arrived, they found fragments of skin boats and stone tools in both the east and west of the country. By around AD 1200 a new group of Arctic hunters—the ancestors of today's Greenlandic Inuit—had crossed into the country. Like the natives of North America, the Norse texts call them *Skrælingar*. The first encounters between the Norse Greenlanders and this new group of people were in the Northern Hunting Grounds. The *History of Norway* reports ominously:

Beyond the Greenlanders some manikins have been found by hunters, who call them Skrælings. Weapon-wounds inflicted on them from which they will survive grow white without bleeding, but if they are mortal the blood hardly ceases flowing. But they lack iron completely: they use whales' teeth for missiles, sharp stones for knives.[10]

It doesn't require a particularly fertile imagination to guess how the hunters discovered the bleeding habits of the Skraelings. On the other hand, an entry in the Icelandic annals for the year 1379 suggests that these newcomers gave as good as they got (or, at least, that was the impression given by the Icelanders, safe on their own little island where they were the only inhabitants): 'The Skraelings attacked the Greenlanders, killed eighteen of their men and took two boys into slavery.'[11]

This new group began to make its way down the west coast of Greenland, probably helped by the changing climatic conditions of the thirteenth century. By the fourteenth century it seems they had reached the outer fjords of the Western Settlement.[12] The incidents reported in the two texts quoted above suggest that interactions could be fractious, and in the past it was believed that the Norse Greenlanders had been wiped out by the aggressive newcomers. However, no evidence has ever been found to support this theory. In fact, the evidence for Norse–Inuit interactions is extremely patchy. A handful of Norse artefacts have been found in Inuit settlement sites: bronze bell fragments, chainmail, iron blades, wooden spoons, even a little Norse ivory chess-piece—a rook—intact apart from one missing turret. Perhaps these were picked up by curious Inuit exploring Norse farms after their inhabitants had left. Alternatively, they may be the remains of occasional trading between the two groups. If habit was anything to go by, the Norse would have wanted natural resources such as furs or ivory, which would have been traded on to merchants from the east leaving no trace in the Norse archaeological record. This might explain why very few Inuit artefacts have been found in Norse occupation layers.[13]

One final piece of evidence regarding Norse–Inuit interactions comes from Inuit folktales, although this is a particularly unreliable sort of evidence, and a gap of several centuries separates the period of Norse–Inuit contact from the time when these stories were written down. In 1875 a Danish glaciologist called Hinrich Rink published *Tales and Traditions of the Eskimo*, a collection of oral stories gathered from the West Greenlanders. Some of the 150 stories in this volume have the sort of lurid titles that would grace Victorian penny dreadfuls: 'The Bloody Rock', 'The Widow's Vengeance', and 'The Woman who was Mated with a Dog'. Four stories describe interactions between the Inuit and a mysterious people they call *Kavdlunait*, meaning 'foreigners'. These *may* preserve Inuit oral memories about the Norse Greenlanders, and if so, the stories hint at a complex relationship between the two groups. In 'Ungortok, the Chief of the Kakortok', a bloody feud ends with an Inuit chopping off the arm of a dead Norseman. The illustration that accompanies the story has the Inuit standing above the corpse, severed arm raised aloft (complete with gory blood dripping onto the snow). Another story tells of a brutal raid by the *Kavdlunait* on a group called the Kaladlit:

It is said that the Kaladlit of the south country at times were attacked in the autumn season, when the lakes were frozen over, and the sea-shore was all bordered with ice. It once happened that a man had been out hunting, and came home with two white whales. In the evening a couple of girls came running into the house crying, 'The enemy is coming upon us!'[14]

What happens next is horrible, even if it's just a story with no historical truth behind it. The master of the house is forced to watch his mother being dragged across the frozen lake by her hair, the two terrified girls are told to throw themselves into the sea if the attackers get too close, and almost all those living in the house are slaughtered. On the other hand, there are stories that describe more cordial relations between the two groups: 'The First Meeting of the Kaladlit with the Ancient Kavdlunait in Greenland' is a tale of fast friendships, friendly competitions, and even mutual language-learning.

FIGURE 8.1 Ungortok, Chief of the Kakortok, in an illustration from Rink's *Tales and Traditions of the Eskimo* (1875)

Who knows what historical fractions can be distilled from these nineteenth-century tales? Perhaps none. After all, the Norse and the Inuit had very different lifestyles and needs. The Norse lived by sedentary dairy agriculture supplemented by hunting and trade, while the Inuit were migratory hunters who hunted some animals that the Norse did not. Perhaps there were tensions and clashes, but it is hard to find evidence to support this.

While new arrivals from the north may have created a few difficulties for the Norse Greenlanders, an even more serious problem concerned arrivals from the east, or rather the lack of them. Greenland had always been the last firm link in a cultural chain that stretched all the way across the North Atlantic from mainland Europe. Over time, the link started to weaken. Europe was moving on, and Greenland was not moving with it. Greenland's natural resources, once so exotic and valuable, were becoming less in demand. Alternative sources of ivory—elephants—were made available as trading routes opened up in the east. Worse, in the thirteenth century new merchants—the Hanseatic League—had started to dominate trade in the North Sea area. The Hanseatic League was a confederation of merchant guilds that had originated in north Germany in the mid-twelfth century. Soon it grew into a powerful trading network that stretched from London in the west to Novgorod in the east. The League had a presence in many of the Scandinavian cities that had previously looked west to Greenland, particularly Bergen in Norway. They were interested in fine silks, woollen and linen fabrics, fish, timber, honey, grains, and metals, *not* polar bears and walruses.

At the same time, Europe was experiencing problems of its own. The eastern trading routes and growth of the Hanseatic League may have been profitable, but microbes, fleas, and rats were as easily transported as silks, wood, and cloth. In the middle of the fourteenth century the Black Death hit Europe. The Norwegians were struck down in around 1349, wiping out perhaps 30–50 per cent of the population.[15] The Icelanders were luckier, at least to start with. In the chaos that ensued, shipping between Norway and Iceland ground to a halt, and the plague didn't make it over the sea. However, an outbreak of something extremely unpleasant—whether it was the Black Death or another disease—finally reached them in 1402, and when it arrived it did so with a vengeance: somewhere between one-third and two-thirds of the population was lost.[16]

There is no evidence that these plagues ever reached Greenland, but so many dead meant that there were fewer ships on the move. The last record of a ship coming to Greenland is an entry in the Icelandic annals from 1406, only a few years after plague hit Iceland. Even then, the voyage was apparently accidental: 'In that year Thorstein Helmingsson, Snorri Torfason, and Thorgrim Solfason sailed to Greenland in one ship; they had travelled from Norway and intended to go to Iceland. They were in Greenland for four winters.'[17] Of course, just because there are no further records of voyages to Greenland doesn't mean that there weren't any after this date. Even so, the numbers of reported voyages had started to tail off during the previous few decades, which probably reflects a general decline in sea traffic.

The Norse Greenlanders have been criticized for their cultural conservatism, and their inability—or unwillingness—to adapt to their changing surroundings. Perhaps there is some truth in this. Certainly, this was the argument put forward by Jared Diamond in his influential bestseller, *Collapse: How Societies Choose to Fail or Survive* (2005). In his discussion of the Norse Greenlanders' adoption of European styles of clothing and architecture, Diamond argues:

The adoptions carry the unconscious message, 'We are Europeans, we are Christians, God forbid that anyone could confuse us with the Inuit.'…To us in our secular modern society, the predicament in which the Greenlanders found themselves is difficult to fathom. To them, however, concerned with their social survival as much as with their biological survival, it was out of the question to invest less in churches, to imitate or intermarry with the Inuit, and thereby to face an eternity in Hell just in order to survive another winter on Earth.[18]

The assumption here is that the Norse should have seen the writing on the wall and adopted the nomadic hunter-gatherer lifestyle of their new fellow countrymen. But in many ways, this is an unfair and unrealistic assumption to make. For a start, the Norse settlers of Greenland *had* adapted. Early on, they had realized that the domestic livestock they had brought with them from Iceland (sheep, horses, cattle, pigs, and goats) weren't going to be enough to keep them going in their new homeland. Consequently they started to hunt marine mammals, such as migrating seals, which made their way along the coast of West Greenland every spring. On land they hunted the reindeer that trekked along the mountains close to the Norse farmsteads. These were communal activities that needed everyone's cooperation, as were the annual walrus hunts that took place in the Northern Hunting Grounds. This is clear from the archaeological record: in the early centuries of the settlement the diet of Norse Greenlanders was dominated by domestic livestock, supplemented by wild animals such as reindeer. In later centuries seals became an ever more important source of food, particularly on the poorer farms. Seal oil also became an important source of fuel for heat and light; at least one lamp has been found containing charred traces.[19]

It is probably more accurate to say that, as one recent study has argued, 'Their failure was an inability to anticipate an unknowable future'.[20] Humans can only adapt so far to new circumstances, particularly if these creep up on a society slowly. For instance, if the United Kingdom ran out of energy next week but Europe and America continued to power on as usual, Britons wouldn't become fur-clad hunter-gatherers overnight. They would be far more likely to up sticks and travel the few miles across the sea to the Continent, or get on the next plane heading to the States. Likewise, the Norse Greenlanders were neither the first nor last culture to live beyond their means. Their intensive farming of the little fertile land they had may have caused soil erosion and deforestation—which, incidentally, was exactly what happened in Iceland too—but this is nothing compared to the rate at which we guzzle resources and pump out noxious chemicals into the atmosphere today. Faced with the choice between a cosily heated, well-lit house tonight versus the vague threat of floods and melted icecaps at some distant point in the unknowable future, most people will crank up the thermostat, switch on the lights, and settle down for the evening. Culture is a habit that is hard to break. In the end, there were too many cards stacked against the Norse Greenlanders: climate change, soil damage, isolation from Europe, and perhaps out-competition by—even conflict with—the hunter-gatherers that had moved into the area.

Not with a bang

The Western Settlement was the first to disappear down the icy plughole, probably at some point in the middle of the fourteenth century. There is only one written account that has anything to say about the end of the settlement, the remarkable text concerning the same Ivar Bardarson who described ice on the old shipping routes to Greenland. Ivar had been sent to Greenland from Norway during the summer of 1341, travelling on church business 'over the wide and stormy sea' (as the Bishop of Bergen wrote in his letter of recommendation).[21] Ivar lived in the Eastern Settlement for twenty years, managing the bishop's estate at Gardar. At some point during this time he became one of several men chosen to go on an expedition to the Western Settlement. But when they finally reached its steep-sided fjords, they were in for a shock. There was no one there.

The account that describes this unsettling incident only survives as a confusing paper-trail of manuscripts, transmitting Ivar's story like a game of

Chinese Whispers. The original description of Greenland was probably written down after Ivar returned to Norway, dictated by Ivar to a scribe (perhaps
like Ohthere at the court of King Alfred). He starts with a detailed description of the farms of the Eastern Settlement, which seem to be thriving. But
things are less rosy in the more vulnerable, marginal Western Settlement, the
canary in the Norse Greenlandic mine:

Now the Skraelings have destroyed all the Western Settlement. There are still horses,
goats, cows, and sheep there, all running wild, and no people, neither Christian nor
heathen. Everything that is described here was told to us by Ivar Bardarson the Greenlander, who was in charge of the bishop's estate at Gardar in Greenland for many
years. He saw all of this because he was one of those chosen by the Lawman to go to
the Western Settlement and drive the Skraelings out of there. But when they arrived
they found no people, neither Christian nor heathen, only some wild cows and sheep,
so they slaughtered the wild cows and took as many as could fit on board the ship and
sailed home, and the aforementioned Ivar was with them.[22]

It is hard to establish exactly what was going on here, even if we accept the
accuracy of the report, which is quite an assumption to make in itself. The
Skraelings are held entirely responsible for the destruction of the settlement,
although this doesn't explain the complete absence of human life and the livestock running wild. Perhaps the Western Settlement hadn't entirely collapsed
at this point; after all, the farmsteads extended over several long fjords, and it
isn't clear whether Ivar and his party visited them all.

If Ivar really did find domestic animals running wild in the hillsides, it
seems likely that the locals had simply upped sticks and left, rather than
stay put and starve to death. But this isn't the full picture. On at least one
farm in the area habitation seems to have come to an end abruptly and trau-
matically at around this time. Archaeologists found the bones of young
lambs, calves, and hunting-dogs, all with cut-marks suggesting the carcasses had been butchered for food. On the same farm there were also the
bones of wild arctic hare and ptarmigan, which are rarely found in farms
from the Western Settlement because they provide so little energy that the
Norse rarely bothered to catch them.* This was a farm on starvation rations.

---

* The ptarmigan is a type of grouse kitted out for inhospitable northern climes, with white
winter plumage that camouflages it in the snow and foot-feathers that act like snowshoes. In
America it is known as the 'snow chicken' and in Japan as the 'thunder bird' (raichō), not to be
confused with the British sci-fi puppet show first broadcast in the 1960s.

Over the freezing, dark winter, they had become desperate to eat anything they could find: first scrawny hares and ptarmigan, then the young livestock, without which they had no farming future. Finally, they turned to the hunting-dogs.[23]

The evidence for the end of the Western Settlement isn't all as gloomy as this: there are no mass graves and no signs of widespread trauma on the farmsteads. When things reached the point of no return—perhaps partly because of worsening weather conditions making northern hunting difficult, partly because of poor harvests, and partly because of competition and threats from the incoming Skraeling hunter-gatherers—those living in the Western Settlement beat a hasty retreat to their neighbours living further south in the Eastern Settlement, taking what valuables they could.[24] It is quite possible that they arrived with reports of Skraelings coming into the district, which would explain why Ivar was sent north together with other men to drive them away. Perhaps they were not expecting to find the once-thriving fjords so completely and eerily deserted: the doors of the farmhouses staring emptily back at them from the hillsides as grass and weeds began to sprout on the middens.

Over the next few decades the Eastern Settlement continued to thrive. But at some point in the 1400s, and certainly by 1500, it too had collapsed. What happened during the final decades is shrouded in mystery. The latest surviving reports to come out of the Eastern Settlement concern events that took place in 1407 and 1408. Both were written down in Iceland, apparently transmitted by members of the last known voyage from Iceland to Greenland. The two episodes couldn't be more different in tone. The first, which took place in 1407, was the burning of a man for witchcraft. The Icelandic annals relate the tragic story:

A man called Kolgrim was burnt to death in Greenland for sleeping with another man's wife, called Steinun, the daughter of Hrafn the Lawman ... Kolgrim seduced her with black magic and was sentenced to be burnt; the woman was never the same afterwards, and died there a little later.[25]

We will never know whether Kolgrim seduced Steinun against her will, or whether the accusation of witchcraft was simply a way for Steinun's husband and prominent father to save face. Did she die of shock, or a broken heart, or was her death soon after simply a coincidence?

The report gives no indication of any nascent deterioration in the settlement. Even so, there is evidence to suggest that accusations of witchcraft rise at times of social stress and unrest. In fact, as the economist Emily Oster has pointed out, the most feverish period of witchcraft trials in Europe coincided with the Little Ice Age itself and the resulting economic downturn. As we have already seen in earlier chapters, witches—particularly Sámi witches— were believed to control the weather and bring down storms. Likewise, the infamous treatise on witches, the *Malleus Maleficarum* ('Hammer of Witches') published in 1486, included a chapter entitled 'How they Raise and Stir up Hailstorms and Tempests, and Cause Lightning to Blast both Men and Beasts'.[26] At times when the world seemed even less controllable than usual, witchcraft was a neat explanation for events that couldn't be explained or managed. Witches were also convenient scapegoats when a society needed someone to blame. A single report of a Greenlandic witch-burning is hardly a statistic, let alone a pattern, but it is still worth thinking about. By the time Kolgrim and Steinun met, the Western Settlement had already disappeared. Now conditions were starting to deteriorate in the Eastern Settlement as well, and fewer ships were arriving from the east. They didn't know it, but only a few decades after their own tragedy the Eastern Settlement would also be deserted.

The second, and very last, record of life in Norse Greenland is a cheerier event: the marriage of Thorstein Olafsson and Sigrid Bjornsdottir in the church at Hvalsey in 1408. Three separate testaments to the marriage survive, verified by witnesses after they had returned to Iceland. One is from a relative of the bride, written in north-west Iceland on 15 August 1424: 'I, Saemund Oddson, testify that I was in Hvalsey in Greenland, and I saw and heard my kinswoman Sigrid Bjornsdottir marry Thorstein Olafsson according to my advice and consent.'[27]

The church and ruined buildings at Hvalsey still stand today. In fact, they are among the best-preserved in Greenland, and include two enormous stone halls and fourteen houses. The beautiful stone church in which the marriage was held is still complete, apart from the missing roof and the floor, now a thick grassy carpet. Once, the thick stone walls could be seen from miles around, painted a brilliant white with lime mortar. In past centuries the church was called 'Qaqortoq' (pronounced *kah-kor-tock*) in Greenlandic, which means 'white'.[28] This is now the name of the nearby town, which is the biggest in southern Greenland, with a population of 3,000 people. Even though they are long gone, echoes of the Norse remain, not only in the landscape but also occasionally in place-names.

FIGURE 8.2 Church ruins at Hvalsey in the Eastern Settlement

The broad fjord waters and high mountains surrounding Hvalsey are unchanged since the days of Sigrid and Thorstein. Once one has got over the shock of disturbing an entire flock of sheep that have made camp inside the church (causing them to thunder from the doorway, peppering everything in sight with panicky black pellets), it takes very little imagination to picture the wedding taking place inside the bright, gleaming walls, as the September ice drifted past in the fjord below. Quite likely, it was also at Hvalsey that Kolgrim was burnt to death. Even on a sunny, blue-skied day sitting by the chilly fjord waters munching a squashed, elderly bar of chocolate, it is hard to forget that these may be exactly the same fjords and hillsides that Kolgrim looked out on as he was taken by the flames.

There are no suggestions in the texts that things were wrong in the Eastern Settlement at this point. But perhaps the story of the newlyweds Sigrid and Thorstein reflects the larger reality of what was happening in the Eastern Settlement. Both husband and wife were actually Icelandic rather than

Greenlandic (although Sigrid had already been in Greenland for a decade).[29] A few years after the wedding they returned home to Iceland and took over the land that Sigrid had inherited from her family. Maybe they weren't the only young couple to do so. The plague had wiped out much of the Icelandic population, and suddenly there were empty farms and opportunities available back east. Perhaps gradually—as is often the way—the young people began to leave their families in the Eastern Settlement. Even at its peak, the population of Greenland had never been large, and without the young to continue farming and hunting, these crucial communal activities would have dwindled. Half-a-millennium after Erik the Red had sighted Greenland for the first time, the last lights were starting to go out. For the Norse Greenlanders, this was the way the world would end: not with a bang but with a phut.

Dark and dangerous land

Although the sagas are a major—if problematic—source of information for the early years of the Norse Greenlandic colony and the voyages further west, they don't throw much direct light on its demise. This is only to be expected; after all, a major difficulty for the Norse Greenlanders was the gradual decline in communication and contact with the wider Norse world. Moreover, while Greenland had been settled initially from Iceland, its connections to Norway—the dominant political power in the North Atlantic—became far more important over time. But even though the lines of communication between Greenland and Iceland were becoming increasingly fragile, Greenland didn't disappear from the sagas. How the later sagas depict Greenland can help us to understand the changing perception of the country in the wider Norse world, and Iceland in particular.

The sort of sagas that featured in the last two chapters—particularly the Vinland sagas—were written down relatively early, during the twelfth and thirteenth centuries when Norse Greenland was still thriving and its connections to the east were still healthy.[30] In these sagas, Greenland is the last link in a chain of Norse-occupied lands stretching across the North Atlantic. Since it is the last link in this chain, we detect a sense of cultural instability at the edge of the world, characterized by plagues, sea storms, and famines. But these sagas also include details of Erik the Red's exploration and settlement of the country, life in the Eastern and Western Settlements, the political and religious machinations that unfold in the community, and expeditions launched to explore lands further west.

In later sagas, a realistic if unstable Greenland is replaced by a darker, more unsettling world of storms and shipwrecks, sea ice, uninhabited wildernesses, and even monsters. The Western Settlement disappears entirely from these later narratives, and the Eastern Settlement becomes increasingly vague and sketchy. Eventually, the human community disappears altogether, and visitors to Greenland's shores are confronted by an eerie world inhabited by grisly fur-clad trolls who stalk the desolate coastlines and empty fjords of the Greenlandic wilderness.[31]

Take the *Saga of the People of Floi* (*Flóamanna saga*), probably written in the early fourteenth century. It is a rather bizarre saga in general, featuring hideous dead men who leave their burial mounds to terrify the living, and a trip to Ireland where people live underground in little houses. The Greenlandic episode is no different. Before the ship has even set sail for Greenland, Thorgils, the leader of the expedition, runs into difficulties. The disgruntled pagan god Thor appears in his dreams, threatening to wreck the ship:

Now Thorgils waited for good winds, and he dreamt that a man came to him, large and red-bearded. He said: 'You have chosen a tricky journey for yourself.' The dream man seemed rather ugly to him. 'It will go badly for you,' he said, 'unless you turn back to me and believe again; then I'll watch over you.'...Then it seemed to Thorgils that Thor led him to a certain cliff, where waves crashed on the rocks—'You'll find yourself in waves like these and never escape, unless you turn back to me.' 'No,' said Thorgils, 'go away, you horrible fiend!'[32]

Once at sea, the winds drop, the ship is blown off course, and supplies quickly run low. A week before winter, the ship is wrecked under the vast glaciers of East Greenland, far from the Norse settlements. Remember the description of East Greenland from the *King's Mirror*, where sailors abandon their ships and scramble up onto the ice to escape a frozen death in the water. Here this horrible fate is dramatized: the company find themselves trapped in a claustrophobic, glacial wilderness, plagued by sickness, madness, and death. Since this is a saga, a handful of malevolent zombies are thrown in for good measure, all of whom have it in for poor Thorgils. After Yule, the saga tells us, the dead men walk again: 'There were now very many ghosts and most of them went straight for Thorgils.'[33]

As supplies run low, tensions run high, and soon enough, being chased by zombies is the least of Thorgils' problems. After a day exploring the glacier above, he comes back to the hut where he left his wife and baby son. A pathetic little sucking sound is coming from the bed, and when he goes to investigate, he finds his baby boy trying to suckle from the corpse of his wife, who has been stabbed to death. 'Everything was very bloody,' the saga says, and 'all the provisions had been carried off'.[34]

In this frozen wilderness, it is not only shipwrecked humans who are desperate for food. Greenland has a supernatural population, which is also in competition for the scarce resources of the icy coastline:

One morning when Thorgils was alone outside, he saw a big beached whale in the ice. Next to it were two troll women, tying up big sacks. Thorgils leapt at them with his sword 'Earthhouse-Gift' and struck at one of them just as she lifted up the load, so that it was knocked out of her hand. The sack fell down, and she ran away. Then Thorgils and his men took the beached whale, and there was plenty of food.[35]

Eventually, when the ice begins to break up, the much-diminished company begins to make its way round the coastline, up to the Eastern Settlement. But this is no longer the welcoming Eastern Settlement of the Vinland sagas, where Erik the Red greets new arrivals with open arms and gets mournful when he can't provide visitors with a proper Yule feast. The relationship between Erik and Thorgils is decidedly frosty, and Thorgils' little boy is attacked by what he thinks is a 'big, beautiful doggie' but turns out to be a polar bear.[36] On the islands dotted around the fjord outlaws have holed themselves up, plundering the farms and bringing misery to the district. Worse, in the Western Settlement robbers lurk offshore and try to abduct young women. This is the latest saga that features the Western Settlement in any way, but only as a brief window onto a dark and dangerous place. There is no sense of connection to real-life events in Greenland, nor oral traditions brought back by travellers from the west. Rather, in this saga Greenland has developed an independent life as a setting within the storytelling tradition, with cartoonish storms, glaciers, polar bears, and trolls writ large in the saga writer's imagination.

Elsewhere these trends are even more pronounced. The strange, troll-populated *Saga of Bard, the God of Snæfellsnes* (*Bárðar saga Snæfellsáss*) dates from the fourteenth century. It is one of the zaniest sagas of the lot, starring a half-troll, half-giant called Bard who becomes the guardian spirit of Snæfellsnes (a peninsula in Western Iceland and one that plays a starring role in Jules Verne's *Journey to the Centre of the Earth*). Helga, Bard's eldest daughter, is accidentally pushed out to sea on an ice floe, and drifts from Iceland to Greenland in seven days. As soon as she arrives, the three major inhabitants of Greenland are invoked: 'Then Erik the Red lived in Brattahlid…Erik was married to Thjodhild…Their son was Leif the Lucky. Erik had settled Greenland one year earlier. Helga stayed with Erik over the winter.'[37]

Chronologically speaking, whoever wrote this saga dropped a clanger. Earlier, the saga described how Helga left Norway with her family when King Harald Fairhair assumed control of the country. Historically, Harald rose to power in the 870s. Conversely, Erik settled Greenland in the 980s. Rational individuals might consider it petty-minded to quibble about a missing century when we're dealing with a saga where the daughter of a troll-giant drifts from Iceland to Greenland in seven days on an iceberg. And they would probably be right. But the point is that, as far as this saga is concerned, Erik the Red has become the literal embodiment of Norse Greenland. Just as a Hollywood film about London or Paris might open with a shot of Big Ben or the Eiffel Tower, so this saga feels the need to include Erik and his family, regardless of whether it makes chronological sense. In any case, the more disconnected the story from its setting and the less that the audience would have actually known about the location, the less such inconsistencies would have mattered.

In the *Saga of Bard*, the Eastern Settlement isn't the fully populated colony of earlier sagas. Other than Erik, his wife, and son, the only other person mentioned is an Icelander called Skeggi, who becomes Helga's lover. This is a small, threatened group, open to monstrous attacks from beyond the settlement. The cold and dark are bad enough, but the winter brings worse creatures from the wilderness, for: 'Over winter, trolls and monsters came down into Eiriksfjord and did the greatest harm to everyone, smashing ships and breaking men's bones.'[38]

In this case, Greenland has been stripped back to one location—Erik's farm—and four named inhabitants, all of them vulnerable to the sinister forces that lurk beyond the fjord.[39] But in another, later tale, Greenland is utterly transformed into an icy wilderness, populated almost exclusively by aggressive supernatural creatures. Erik, his wife and son are nowhere to be seen, and the Eastern Settlement doesn't get a mention.

The *Tale of Jokul Buason* (*Jökuls þáttr Búasonar*) stars a man on the run. His name is Jokul—which, appropriately, means 'Glacier'—and he ends up on a ship bound for Greenland, having accidentally killed his father. Typically for a voyage to Greenland, the ship is lost at sea and shrouded in fog for much of the summer. Come autumn, snowstorms descend, 'with heavy hails and frosts, so that every raindrop froze as it landed'.[40] Jokul finds himself washed up in the wilderness below Greenland's icy mountains, his clothes frozen solid. During the night he wakes to find two filthy creatures rifling through the shipwreck. According to their chatter, they intend to give him a choice: either he must marry one of them, or they'll eat him. But the two are hardly tempting marriage prospects, and as they stride towards Jokul, their pantomime grotesqueness is revealed:

They were frowning and long-nosed, and their lips hung down on their chests. They were wearing skin tunics, which were so long at the front that they kept treading on them, but at the back the tunics only came up to the top of their bums. They slapped their thighs and behaved in a very unladylike way.[41]

This is a country devoid of human inhabitants and overrun by giants. They are ruled by the terrible Skram, 'king of all the wilderness', who kidnaps humans with magic spells and even terrifies the giants he commands.[42] The Norse settlements have disappeared entirely, to be replaced by stormy seas, frozen fjords, and violent clans of carousing giants.

In these later sagas—which in any case had a well-developed taste for the fantastic and overtly supernatural—Greenland became the perfect stage for wild tales set in the icy wilderness. This tells us little about what was actually going on in Greenland in the later years of the Norse settlements, or after they collapsed. After all, when Hans Egede sailed to Greenland in the 1720s, it's unlikely that a red-bearded pagan god appeared to him and threatened to wreck the ship, or that miniskirt-clad troll-women tried to proposition him when he came ashore. But these sagas provide hints of how the Icelanders came to perceive Greenland, and the place that the country came to occupy in their cultural imagination.

How much information the Icelanders had about what was happening in Greenland isn't clear. Perhaps they knew even less than we do today, as the lines of communication were gradually cut. Perhaps they knew much more, from the few sailors who were still willing to make the journey out there, or young couples who had immigrated to Iceland. But one way or another, over time, reports of ice-clogged shipping routes, ever-fiercer storms, diminishing resources, and trouble in the settlements must have worked their way back east. With fewer and fewer ships travelling to and from Greenland, the country's perceived position in the Norse diaspora shifted, becoming increasingly remote, until it had little or no tangible connection to the world back east. With the desolate glacial wilderness having replaced the Norse settlements as its theatrical backdrop, the Greenlandic saga stage was set for a new act, ready for a host of supernatural creatures to stride on from the wings and menace any unlucky human who crossed them.

Helluland reborn

What of the lands west of Greenland? What of Helluland, Markland, and Vinland, which featured so prominently in the Vinland sagas? Other than in this famous pair of sagas, the countries drop out of the saga record almost entirely. That is, apart from one exception: rocky, sterile Helluland. This is intriguing, because in the Vinland sagas this land is the least significant of all, in comparison to wooded Markland and bountiful Vinland. When Leif and his men reach Helluland in the *Saga of the Greenlanders*, 'it seemed to them that the land was barren'.[43] Likewise, according to the *Saga of Erik the Red*, the only living creatures that call Helluland home are arctic foxes. But Helluland takes on a new life in the later sagas, as an abode of monstrous creatures and a place of evil deeds. It also becomes geographically unanchored: bobbing around the ocean like an iceberg, steadily working its way north.

In the *Saga of Arrow-Odd* (the third of the *Hrafnista sagas* that we encountered earlier), Helluland is the hideout of Ogmund, the hero's terrible nemesis. Ogmund—and his Helluland hideout—only gains a prominent role in the later version of the saga, which survives in a fifteenth-century manuscript. It has been suggested that he symbolizes death itself, a theme that 'seems to have been a preoccupation widespread throughout Europe, after the great plagues had stimulated obsession with death'.[44] Like a deranged Bond villain, Ogmund hides out 'in the wastelands of Helluland', sending sea-monsters out into the Greenland Sea to kill his enemies.[45] The geographical location of Helluland is basically correct: in order to battle Ogmund, the hero (Odd) and his son (Vignir) must skirt the bottom of Greenland and continue west across the sea. But unlike the Vinland sagas, there is no real sense of place or navigational accuracy. The only topographical references are to the rocks and cliffs that the name 'Helluland'—'Stone Slab Land'—implies. This is where the final struggle between Ogmund and Vignir takes place, out on the clifftops above the sea:

Then they began to wrestle, so ferociously and inhumanly that they tore up earth and stones like loose snow.... Ogmund shoved Vignir so that he fell over, and immediately bent over him and ripped his throat apart.... Then Ogmund darted quickly away, hurled himself from the cliff, and dived head-first into the sea, so that white foam sprayed up.[46]

In the *Saga of Halfdan Brana's Foster Son* (*Hálfdanar saga Brönufóstra*), written around the beginning of the fourteenth century, Helluland is the abode of creatures every bit as dangerous and unpleasant as the murderous Ogmund. Its glacial fjords are riddled with ogresses, led by a grotesque creature with three invisible heads. Washed up on the shores of Helluland after a storm, the human hero sneaks up to the mouth of a cave, where he finds a pair of trolls sitting by the fire:

...and they had a cooking-pot between them. In it was both horse and man flesh. The male troll had a hook in his nose, and the female troll had a ring. This was their game: he hooked the hook into the ring, and they ended up in various positions. When the hook slipped out of the ring, the troll-woman fell backwards. Then she said: 'I don't want to play this game, my dear Jarnnef!'[47]

Jarnnef, meaning 'Iron Nose', is an appropriate name for a troll with a hook in his nose. The Helluland he calls home is given an implied—if vague—northern location far to the east of where the landmass should be: Halfdan is sailing to Bjarmaland (inhabited by the same Bjarmians that we met in the north, whose northern territory was near the White Sea in Russia) when sea storms and mists descend, blowing him off course and driving his ship onto the rocky cliffs of Helluland.

A monstrous northern Helluland also features in the same *Saga of Bard* that described young Helga drifting across the sea to Greenland on an ice floe. In this case, Helluland is haunted by the dead pagan king Raknar, a ghost in need of some industrial-strength deodorant. He appears at the Norwegian king's court one Yule, 'huge and hideous, dark-faced and twitchy-eyed, black-bearded and long-nosed'.[48] In a scene that bears more than a passing resemblance to the Middle English poem *Sir Gawain and the Green Knight*, Raknar challenges King Olaf Tryggvason to find a hero brave enough to make the journey to Helluland and take treasure from his burial mound. When he departs, leaving a pungent cloud of fusty foulness in the air, his identity is revealed:

He rules over Helluland and many other lands. And when he had ruled the lands for a long time, he buried himself alive with five hundred men in his ship *Slodinn*. He murdered his father and mother and many other people; it seems to me that his burial mound might be in the northern wastelands of Helluland, as other men say.[49]

As far as this saga is concerned, Helluland's location is decidedly northern: further north than even Ohthere and the whale hunters got. In order to reach it, the voyagers sail north from Norway up to the Arctic Ocean, past Halogaland and Finnmark. This is a north of magical deceptions and dangerous paganism, where the one-eyed pagan god Odin materializes on the shore, preaching heathen lore and urging men to conduct pagan sacrifices. From there, they come to the wintry wastes of Greenland, a shifting landscape of devilish illusions where pagan sorcerers are swallowed up by the earth itself. The party travels overland across Greenland, navigating a nightmarish, fantastical terrain of glaciers and burnt lava-fields (a very Icelandic topography, for there are no lava-fields in Greenland). Finally they reach Helluland, but the route they take bears no resemblance to the hyper-accurate navigational details described in the Vinland sagas. In reality, Helluland lay many dangerous days' sailing from Greenland, across the Davis Strait. But here, Helluland is just off Greenland's coast, connected by a causeway at low tide:

When they had struggled through the lava, they came to the sea. There was a big island off the coast, and leading out to the island was a long, narrow reef. It was dry at low tide, and so it was when they arrived. They walked out to the island, and they saw a large burial mound standing there. Some men say that this island lay off Helluland, but wherever it was, there were no settlements nearby then.[50]

That night, the hero of the expedition breaks into the mound while the priest keeps watch outside, plagued by trolls, monsters, fiends, and other magical creatures. But it's much worse inside the mound, where the hero comes face to face with Raknar's five-hundred-strong zombie army. Having dispatched them all by cutting off their heads, he finds Raknar sitting on his burial chair, down in the stinking, cold pit of the earth. Eventually the zombie king is vanquished, but as the party scramble off Helluland, the landscape itself is in turmoil: the waves are so enormous that they almost swamp the whole island,

and the earth trembles violently beneath them. Only the priest is able to save them, parting the waves with his crucifix so they can walk to land.

This Helluland is a long way from the Helluland of the Vinland sagas, discovered by intrepid explorers such as Leif the Lucky and Karlsefni. Suddenly the arrow-shooting uniped that featured in the *Saga of Erik the Red* seems positively mundane by comparison. But the clue to Helluland's reincarnation as a glacial abode of murderous man–ogre crossbreeds, exhibitionist trolls, and pagan zombie kings may well lie in its northerly location. For as we have already seen in earlier chapters, the far north of the sagas was imagined as the habitat of precisely such supernatural inhabitants.

Of course, Baffin Island (aka Helluland) does have a very northerly location, but the idea of reaching Greenland and then Helluland by sailing past northern Norway and into the Arctic Ocean—as in the *Saga of Bard*—is not consistent with reality, nor with what the Vinland sagas reported. But while this may seem geographically implausible (which it is), that wasn't necessarily the case according to how the medieval Icelanders came to think of this part of the world. Several medieval Icelandic manuscripts include geographical descriptions that mention a land bridge stretching across the Arctic Ocean from Norway to Greenland. This is illustrated by a rather odd story about a man called Hall and his pet goat, which appears in two medieval Icelandic manuscripts:

There is a story found in Icelandic books that a man walked from Greenland to Norway, over all the glacial wastelands and wildernesses, which was thought to be big news. He brought a goat with him, and fed on her milk. Because of this he was called Goat-Hall.[51]

There isn't—and never was—any such land bridge stretching from Norway to Greenland. But such an imaginative and geographical shift from the west to the north might explain the presence of so many strange and supernatural creatures in Helluland. This was simply a continuation of their territory, across the frozen wastelands of the Arctic. If a man and his goat could manage it, then a troll or giant certainly could. In fact, we see this depicted visually on the so-called Skálholt Map, made in sixteenth-century Iceland. This is the earliest attempt to combine cartographic knowledge with the geographical information provided by the sagas. To the left of the map, 'Helleland', 'Markland', Skrælinge Land', and 'Winlandia' are all labelled. Over on the right are countries such as 'Britannia', 'Irland', 'Norvegia', 'Biarmaland', and 'Island'. In some ways, this is a work of scientific precision. As a matter of fact, it was this map, which labelled the northern tip of Newfoundland as 'Winelandia', that encouraged archaeologists to concentrate on this part of the coastline in their search for Vinland.[52] But in other ways, this is a work of fiction and fantasy. Right up at the top of the map, in the far north, is a strip of land stretching across from east to west. This land bridge is inscribed with its own labels: 'Iotun-heimar' and 'Riseland': in other words, the two Giantlands that we encountered in the north.

In the imaginative world of the sagas, then, it was giants, trolls, and other monsters who were the last denizens of the lands west of Iceland. If we are to believe what the records tell us, there would be no more Nordic inhabitants of Greenland until Hans Egede's missionary ship appeared on the horizon centuries later, inadvertently carrying salvation to the Inuit Greenlanders. Egede, too, would experience the intense difficulties of surviving and settling a marginal territory thousands of miles from home. Not for nothing was the largest

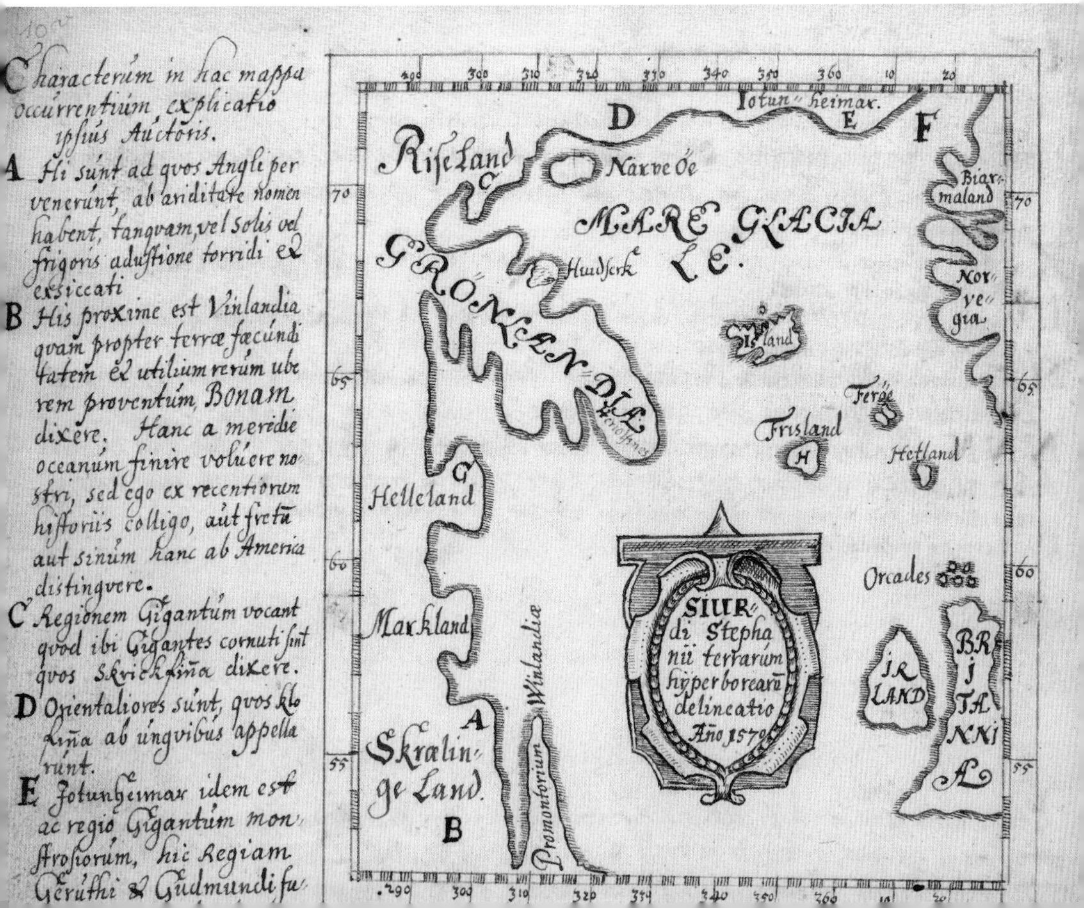

FIGURE 8.3 The Skálholt Map, featuring Helluland, Markland, and Vinland in the west, Riseland and Jotunheimar in the north, and Britain in the east (1690, copied from a lost original made in 1570)

of his ships that departed from Bergen in 1721 called *Håpet* ('The Hope'). Scurvy would strike down many of the colonists over the first winter. Smallpox followed a few years later, ravaging the local Inuit population and killing Hans Egede's own wife, Gertrud. Under such extreme circumstances—harsh by any standards, and barely habitable from a European perspective—it is easy to see how an imaginative transformation of the country might have taken place, of the kind seen in the later sagas. The difference is that in the case of the eighteenth-century missionaries, the colony endured and contact was not broken.

Hans Egede and his fellow missionaries may not have encountered trolls and giants when they reached Greenland, but on one occasion at least they witnessed a creature that bordered on the monstrous. As Poul Egede, son of the above, later recorded:

On the 6th of July there appeared a very horrible sea-creature that rose itself so high over the water that its head reached above our big yardarm. It had a long pointed snout and spouted like a whale. It had broad big flippers and the body seemed to be covered with shells, and it was very wrinkled and rough on its skin; it was otherwise created below like a serpent and where it went under the water again threw itself backwards and raised thereafter the tail up from the water, a whole ship's length from the body.[53]

Many attempts have been made to identify this 'very horrible sea-creature', which was often thought to be some sort of giant sea squid. Intriguingly, researchers from the University of St Andrews have suggested that the creature was in fact a sexually aroused whale, which would explain the so-called serpent's tail (whale penises can reach a couple of metres in length when hard).*

Sometimes monstrous or unnatural beings are conjured up when extraordinary or inexplicable phenomena are witnessed, as in the case of Poul Egede's amorous-whale-cum-sea-serpent. At other times such creatures are born in the absence of information, shaped in the imaginative space beyond knowledge and experience. In the case of the trolls and giants of the later sagas—both in the west and stretching north into Arctic Scandinavia—it could be said that they were conjured out of thin air.

---

* The same Charles Paxton who put forward the theory of the whale penis was also the co-winner of the 2002 Ig Noble Biology Prize for his work on 'Courtship Behaviour of Ostriches towards Humans under Farming Conditions in Britain'. During his acceptance speech, he was amorously assailed from behind with an ostrich-feather duster.

· East ·

Memorial stones rarely stand by the road, unless they
are raised by one kinsman to another.

Sayings of the High One (Hávamál)

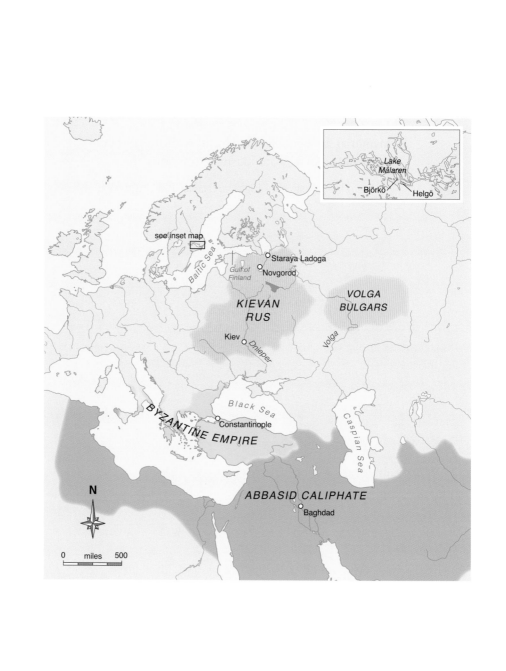

CHAPTER 9

Eastern Promise

Steppe by steppe

It was midsummer in the year AD 921 when the Caliph's ambassadors set off from Baghdad. As they turned north and travelled further into the desert, the great city grew smaller behind them, blistering and cracking under the fierce sun. Baghdad, known to locals as the 'City of Peace', was the capital of the Abbasid Caliphate. Under this mighty empire the Islamic Golden Age had flourished, an unparalleled era of international political influence and intellectual advancement in every conceivable field, not least mathematics, astronomy, literature, and engineering. But these cultured, sophisticated Arab diplomats were in for a shock. They were heading towards the wild and dangerous Russian steppes, on a mission to visit the Bulgars, a powerful, semi-nomadic tribe that lived by the river Volga. The Bulgars had recently adopted Islam as their religion, and the diplomats were tasked with strengthening their ties to the faith. It would be a year before they reached their destination, and thousands of miles and perilous adventures lay before them.[1]

Out on the steppes, and reliant on unknown barbarian tribes for hospitality and protection, the Arabs were about to embark on a steep anthropological learning curve. Accustomed to a high-status Baghdadi diet—fresh figs, dates, melons, char-grilled lamb, bread, coffee—the Arabs' attitude towards the native cuisine was one of polite horror. Without a drop of olive or sesame oil for hundreds of miles, they were disgusted to discover that the locals used fish oil in their cooking, which made everything smell and taste revolting. Worse, they soon found themselves enduring a winter so diabolically cold that their cheeks froze to their pillows while they slept and their beards turned to blocks of ice that had to be thawed out in front of the fire. On the other hand, there were certainly compensations for the physical hardships and disgusting food they had to endure, and they witnessed many marvels that they had never seen back home. One night the northern lights appeared above them as fiery red mists in the black winter sky, terrifying the Arabs who were unaccustomed to such sights.

The tribes that lived on the steppes could be as tricky and unpredictable to deal with as the food and climate. During their stay with one such group, the Arabs were perturbed enough to see that the women left their heads uncovered, unlike the modest women back home. But this paled into insignificance when they met the wife of one of their hosts, who gaily thrust aside her skirts in front of them to give her privates a good scratch. Their host guffawed heartily when he saw how horror-struck his pious guests were: 'better than covering them up and letting you get at them!' he chortled. Still riding their white-knuckle anthropological learning curve, the astonished diplomats met another even zanier lot who cut off each other's heads apparently without provocation, ate lice from their clothes, and worshipped penises. The sophistication and comfort of Baghdad must have seemed a world away.

After a year's dangerous travelling, the delegation reached the land of the Bulgars and met the king, a canny, quick-witted, good-tempered man, built 'like a great barrel speaking'.[2] It was there, on the banks of the river Volga, that the Arabs encountered a group of rough river-men who had arrived from the north to trade: perfect specimens of heavily tattooed, axe-wielding manhood who were ruddily fair-skinned and tall as palm trees. At the same time, their standards of personal hygiene were utterly abhorrent to the scrupulously clean Arab travellers. These tattooed hunks were 'the filthiest of God's creatures', not bothering to wash after sex, toilet breaks, or meals.[3] Their morning ablutions were even nastier: each man in turn would wash his hair and face in a basin of water, spit, blow snot, and do 'every filthy thing imaginable' in it, then pass it on to the next man.[4]

These men were not to be messed with. They were tough, uncouth traders who dealt in furs and slaves, fornicated with their slave girls in public, and prayed to their gods for meek merchants who wouldn't haggle over their prices. Much more disturbingly, they also practised human sacrifice at their funerals. Down by the Volga, the visitors witnessed the brutal, bloody killing of a slave girl, chosen to follow her dead master to paradise. The final funeral rituals took place on the dead man's ship, presided over by an old woman called the Angel of Death: 'a witch, thick-bodied and sinister'.[5] As seen from the point of view of the Arabs, the description of the slave girl's final moments is horrific. The Angel of Death seized the girl's head and pushed her into the pavilion where she was to die. The men began to bang their shields in order to drown out her screams. Six men entered the pavilion and had sex with her, before she was laid beside her master and a cord wrapped around her neck. Two of the men seized her feet, two more seized her hands, and the other two grasped each end of the cord. The Angel of Death approached with a dagger, and as the men began to pull on the cord she plunged the blade again and again between the young girl's ribs until she was dead.

Once the girl was on the funeral pyre, the dead man's closest relative set fire to the ship, stark naked, carrying a torch in one hand and covering his anus with the other hand. As the wind fanned the flames, smoke rose into the sky and the ship began to crumble. When the ship, its dead owner, and the slave girl were no more than cold ashes and dust, an earthen mound was raised on the banks of the river.

If, despite the outlandish and exotic location, some faint bells of recognition are ringing—tall, fair, axe-wielding sailors, burning ship, earthen burial mound—then there's a good reason for that. Almost certainly, these rough, tough traders were Norsemen, or at least of Norse descent. All cardinal directions are relative: as far as the Arab diplomats were concerned, they had come from the south to the north. But from a Nordic perspective this was the east, literally, for they called the route to and through Russia the *Austvegr*, or 'Eastern Way'.[6]

Another history

We're familiar with images of the Norse sailing chilly northern seas under slate-grey skies, exploring wide, open waters, foreign countries, and empty lands. We read thundering missives penned by fire-and-brimstone holy men in the churches and royal courts of Western Europe, conjuring up images of fleeing monks and bloodstained altars. We can picture them bartering with cautious natives for furs and skins, offering butter, cloth, and bloody cold steel in return. But the story of the Norse who went in the opposite direction is rather different. These east-facing Scandinavians were another breed. When we think of the words 'Norseman' or 'viking', the first image that pops into our heads is unlikely to be a Norse trader bartering with the nomadic tribes of the Slavic steppes. We are probably not thinking of Norse mercenaries fighting Russian civil wars for foreign kings. And, almost certainly, these words don't immediately conjure up a picture of Norse merchants sitting astride flea-bitten, stinky camels, jolting and bumping their queasy way to the markets of Baghdad.

Even so, all these images are just as true as the ones we're more familiar with. They are recorded in texts written in Arabic, Greek, and Cyrillic scripts, telling of brutal raiders, canny traders, hard-working mercenaries, and fearless adventurers who came from the north and enthusiastically launched themselves into some of the greatest civilizations the world has ever seen. These images are also reflected—albeit through a glass, darkly—in saga stories of far-travelling heroes who journey east for the courts of great princes and kings, or battle man-eating giants and gold-guarding dragons out on the Russian rivers.

Scandinavian activities in the east began even before the first ominous sails were spotted from the shores of Lindisfarne. Travellers from the medieval Nordic world came in many guises: traders, raiders, explorers, settlers, rulers, mercenaries, and political exiles. Just as in Western Europe, they were masters of the water. They navigated vast, dangerous waterways that ran for thousands of miles down the length of Russia, from northern forests and wide steppe plains to the balmy shores of the Black and Caspian Seas.

In Western Europe, as we have already seen, Nordic visitors were known by a name that reflected their activities: Vikings. Alternatively, they were named after the cardinal direction they came from: Northmen. To those living further east, they were named for different activities. They were the *Rus*.[7] The etymology of this word is debatable, but it is likely that *Rus* comes from the Old Swedish word *Roþz*, meaning 'band of rowers'. This was adopted into Finnish, where it became *Ruotsi*. Eventually, this word was carried down the Russian rivers towards Byzantium and beyond.[8] To Arab geographers and diplomats from the Abbasid Caliphate in the east, these people became known as *al-Rus*. To the Byzantines further west, they were the *Rhos*. If the word in its various manifestations looks familiar, it is because eventually it was the Rus who gave their name to the land whose waterways they navigated. This was 'the land of the Rus', or in Latin, *Russia*.

Small islands

Put a map in front of someone, and ask them to find the quickest route between two points. Most likely, they will try to find the easiest way overland.

Today, the default travel mode tends to be by land rather than by sea, on roads rather than over water. But if you want to start thinking like a medieval Norse traveller, look at the water first. Water was often easier than land to navigate at this time, more of a bridge than a barrier. With this shift in perspective, seemingly impassable channels of water suddenly become highways, and isolated islands become major stopping-off points.

In the early stages at least, Nordic travellers to the east came predominantly from eastern Scandinavia. Sweden's eastern seaboard was the springboard into Russia, particularly Lake Mälaren, which drains east into the Baltic Sea. In turn, this leads to the Gulf of Finland and the vast network of Russian rivers that snake their way down the land.

Lake Mälaren is a vast body of water just west of Stockholm, surrounded by deep forests and dotted with rocky, wooded islands. Today, a main road loops in a circle around the lake, and the quickest way to get from north to south is to take one of the two smaller roads that pass across it, bridging the water where the land runs out. The many islands scattered across Lake Mälaren are secluded havens away from the bustle of Stockholm city life. ABBA's Agnetha Fältskog famously retreated to one of them (Ekerö) after the band stopped performing. But seen from the point of view of medieval sailors and traders, these islands were at the centre of life, not at the peripheries. This explains why two of them in particular, Helgö and Björkö, are home to two of the most important archaeological sites from medieval Scandinavia, both of which serve as important windows on Norse activities out east.

The rocky, wooded island of Helgö looks just like any number of picturesque little islands in Lake Mälaren. But in the centuries leading up to the Viking Age, it was a bustling international trade centre that led to the sea. The extraordinary finds that have been uncovered are evidence of the international culture of trade and travel that existed there during the Middle Ages, and of the extensive links between East and West. For over one thousand years, Helgö was home to a far traveller who had been carried a very long way from where he had been made: a little Buddha statue. Tinged green with age, this bronze figure sits on a lotus flower, deep in serene meditation. Now his eyes are dull and empty, but once they sparkled with blue crystals. Above them, a silver caste mark protrudes from his forehead, symbolizing his third eye. When the Buddha was uncovered during excavations on Helgö in 1956, an expert was sent for. His immediate impressions were not encouraging. As he later wrote: 'I have to admit that my first reaction was that the figure was

FIGURE 9.1a Coptic christening scoop from Egypt found on Helgö

merely a tourist souvenir, a miniature of the colossal Buddha at Kamakura, brought home from Japan by a sailor, and not very long ago.'⁹ Soon enough, however, the Buddha's true age and origin became apparent. It had been made in the sixth century AD, in the borderlands between what is now northern India and Pakistan. Perhaps the expert was right and the statue had been brought home by a sailor as a tourist souvenir, only from nowhere near Japan and many centuries earlier than he imagined.

Today the little Buddha sits in serene majesty in a glass case in Stockholm's Historical Museum, in the company of two other former residents of the Helgö soil. One is an eighth-century bishop's crozier from Ireland, perhaps stolen during a viking raid. It is a beautiful piece of work, made from bronze and studded with coloured-glass beads. Around the top curves a snouty, dragon-like creature encircling what looks like a rather disgruntled man's head. It has been suggested that this scene is connected to the story of Jonah and the Whale, a symbol of resurrection and a popular motif on croziers from this period. The other item

FIGURE 9.1b Bishop's crozier from Ireland found on Helgö

is a large bronze baptismal scoop, the size of a porridge bowl. Like the Buddha, it dates from the sixth century, and likely comes all the way from Egypt.[10]

The international trade and manufacturing site on Helgö was already flourishing by the third century AD, but by around 750 the nearby island of Björkö had taken centre-stage. Today, boatloads of summer tourists make their way to Björkö from Stockholm, to visit the archaeological site of Birka. They can tour the lumpy bumpy fields with guides dressed in viking attire, peruse the reconstructed houses, and stock up in the museum shop for essentials such as bags of 'Odin's nuts' and packets of liquorice fashioned into the shape of disconcertingly phallic Thor's hammers.

The ashy, black earth of Birka is thick with remnants of the past. Ice-skates, ice-picks, children's toys, glass beads, and pagan amulets are only the tip of the archaeological iceberg. Several hoards have also been found, chock-full of Arab silver. The first of these was discovered in 1872, where amongst the silver arm-rings, bracelets, and pins were several hundred Arab coins. The ages of these coins span three centuries and several empires. The oldest was minted before 718 and the youngest in the 960s, only a few decades after the aforementioned Arab diplomats found themselves on the Volga.[11] To understand how the coins got to Birka, we literally have to follow the money: back out from Sweden, east into Russia and beyond.

Raiders and traders

Striking out from the islands and waterways of eastern Scandinavia, medieval travellers headed east, crossed the Baltic Sea, and sailed into the Gulf of Finland. From the mid-eighth century onwards, Scandinavian tendrils began to spread as traders, raiders, and tribute-collectors started to navigate the waterways of Russia. This complex network of rivers ended in two of the most important civilizations of the medieval world. The river Dnieper rises from the swampy bogs of north-west Russia. Eventually, via a series of twisting rivers, broad lakes, and dangerous rapids, it drains into the Black Sea. During the Middle Ages, on the far side of the Black Sea lay Constantinople, the capital of Byzantium. (The history of the Norse in—and saga accounts of—Constantinople is extensive, and we will return to it later in chapters on the

FIGURE 9.1C Buddha statue from northern India found on Helgö south.) Further east is the river Volga, which ends in the Caspian Sea and, during the Middle Ages, the Abbasid Caliphate.

As traders and raiders from Sweden began to make their way along these routes, they established outposts where they could mend their boats, barter with other traders, and extract tribute from—or just plain rob—the local tribes. Nordic traders in Russia were part of a vast network that ran the length and breadth of the continent. Writing at the end of the tenth century, an Arab geographer called Al-Muqaddasi drew up a list of goods exported along the river Volga:

Sable, Grey squirrel, Ermine, Mink, Fox, Marten, Beaver, Spotted hare, Goatskins, Wax, Arrows, Birch wood, Tall fur caps, Fish glue, Fish teeth, Castoreum oil, Amber, Tanned horse hides, Honey, Hazelnuts, Falcons, Swords, Armour, Maple wood, Saqa-lib slaves, Sheep, Cattle.[12]

Some of these items may be familiar from the earlier chapters on the north; the list includes Scandinavian specialities such as furs, slaves, amber, and 'fish teeth', better known as walrus ivory.* Often Rus traders were happy to 'go native' when necessary, adopting local forms of transport, assuming different religious identities, and even paying taxes. The lengths they would go to are detailed by a geographer and bureaucrat called Ibn Khordadbeh, who worked as the Caliph's spymaster and postmaster-general in what is now Iran. His ninth-century account of the peoples and provinces of the Abbasid Caliphate—called the *Book of Roads and Kingdoms*—describes what the Rus got up to south of the Caspian Sea: 'Sometimes they transport their merchandise on camel back from the city of Jurjan to Baghdad. There, Slavic-speaking eunuchs interpret for them. They pretend to be Christians and, like them, pay the poll tax.'[13] Other Rus visitors to the region were not so well behaved. Another Arab writer, called Al-Mas'udi, described an attack on the Caspian in 913. The account is eerily reminiscent of some of the earlier attacks on the British Isles: 'The Rus spilled rivers of blood, seized women and children and property, raided and everywhere destroyed and burned. The people who lived on these shores were in turmoil, for they had never been attacked by an enemy from the sea.'[14]

---

* Incidentally, castoreum oil is extracted from beavers' bottoms (or more specifically sacs located next to their anal glands). In the past it was used by everyone from doctors to beekeepers, and is still used today in flavourings and perfumes. There is even a Swedish schnapps called Bäverhojt ('Beaver Shout'), which is produced by steeping beaver glands in vodka.

Whether behaving themselves on camelback or causing havoc in their boats, the Rus in these descriptions are faceless and fleeting. Even in Arab writings the Rus are simply bit-players: canny traders and fierce raiders (sometimes with questionable personal hygiene), who exit the texts as swiftly as they enter them. But further north the Rus were busy creating their own, enduring legacy. These visitors from the north founded a powerful dynasty that came to control vast swathes of the East Slavic lands. The state they created became the cultural foundation of today's Russia, Ukraine, and Belarus.

Cold wars

Most nations have a founding myth. The Romans had Romulus and Remus. The Anglo-Saxons had Hengest and Horsa. And the Kievan Rus had a Scandinavian prince called Rurik (a variant of the Old Norse name *Hrœrekr*). Rurik is said to have established himself in Novgorod in 862, an event that is often taken to be the major starting-point in Russian history. His dynasty was called the Rurikid, and they remained powerful for many centuries. Hundreds of years later, the brilliant but brutal Ivan the Terrible (r. 1533–47) was also of the Rurikid line.

Like most founding myths, this one rests on shaky historical foundations. The main source for this information is the *Russian Primary Chronicle*, a history of Kievan Rus originally recorded in around 1113 in Kiev. Like any other medieval chronicle, the text is a tricky customer: a part-annalistic, part-anecdotal, part-literary text, with religious and political agendas and a gap of several centuries separating the time of composition from the earliest events described. As might be expected, the chronology of the early period is particularly dubious. On the other hand, there are good reasons to believe that Scandinavians were involved in the establishment and growth of Kievan Rus, as we will see.

Novgorod, where Rurik is said to have set up his power-base, was situated in a strategically significant location. Going north, it was connected via the river Volkhov to the prosperous town of Staraya Ladoga, a multicultural trading port. The oldest cultural layers of the settlement show evidence of a strong Scandinavian presence, with artefacts such as a bronze handle with a man's head, which sports some sort of horned headdress and looks rather like a novelty bottle-opener.[15]

South of Novgorod, the rivers flowed towards Kiev and beyond. Novgorod itself was a damp and soggy place to live, at least according to the Arab writer Ibn

FIGURE 9.2 Bronze handle found in the earliest occupation layers of Staraya Ladoga

Rusteh. Writing at the start of the tenth century—a decade or so before the diplomatic corps set off north from Baghdad—he described how certain Rus lived on an island on a lake, which was so 'pestilential and the soil so damp that when a man steps on it, it quivers underfoot'.[16] These squelchy surroundings may be reflected in the Norse name for Novgorod—*Holmgarðr*—meaning 'Island Enclosure' or 'Island Fortification'. Two decades later, the centre of power shifted south to Kiev, which in 882 was seized by Rurik's successor Oleg (derived from the Old Norse name *Helgi*). From Kiev, the Rus consolidated their position as traders and tribute-collectors, with Novgorod as a secondary power-base in the north. As a result of this shift, historians now refer to this state as Kievan Rus. In the Old Norse sagas it is called *Garðaríki*—'Kingdom of Fortifications'—probably because of the various strongholds and settlements that were located along the river.

History is rarely straightforward, but even by normal standards the early history of Russia is a prickly issue. The difficulty centres on who the founders of Kievan Rus actually were, and where they came from. This is part of a steely debate cast in the fires of nineteenth-century nationalism and tempered in the chilly political climate of the Soviet Era. As the split between East and West widened, the Russians became keen to play down the role of European Scandinavians in the founding of their nation, emphasizing the part played by the Slavs instead. In this growing atmosphere of political mistrust, archaeological collaborations began to suffer. In the 1920s and 1930s joint investigations by Soviet and European archaeologists faltered in the drive to bring Russian intellectual life into line with the new government's Marxist ideology. Soviet researchers were forbidden from working with foreign collaborators. In 1938 the Finnish archaeologist Aarne Michaël Tallgren wrote: 'I am no longer able personally to keep in touch with archaeological research in the Soviet Union. I receive no more books, letters remain unanswered. I do not intend to do any more work in this sphere that is so dear to me.'[17] On the Soviet side of the fence, certain topics remained off-limits. Tallgren's opposite number, the Soviet archaeologist Artemij Artsikhovsky, found himself in a very delicate position when investigating Novgorod's earliest occupation layers. The merest hint of Scandinavian occupation was enough to make him twitchy. As the historian Fjodor Androshchuk has noted: 'Even simple interlacing decoration on some ancient items made him irritated. Only in private conversation was he able to say: "Nevertheless, there is something Scandinavian in this interlacing."'[18]

The Second World War only exacerbated the issue, and Adolf Hitler himself had plenty to say on the subject. Records of his dinnertime conversations show that Hitler had a habit of directing his post-prandial vitriol east to Russia. 'In the eyes of the Russian,' he told his dining companions one summer's evening in 1941, 'the principal support of civilisation is vodka.' It was only due to the 'drop of Aryan blood in his veins' that the Russian had been able to create anything resembling an organized state.[19] At another dinner he expanded his view: 'Unless other peoples, beginning with the Vikings, had imported some rudiments of organisation into Russian humanity, the Russians would still be living like rabbits.'[20]

Today, this painful political past still casts a long shadow over the debate, but as is so often the case, the truth lies somewhere in the middle. There is plenty of evidence—textual and archaeological—to support the notion of a strong Nordic component amongst the Rus, particularly early on. But as with the Normans in northern France, the Scandinavians who made their way east were masters of cultural adaptation and assimilation. Theirs was a multicultural world in the truest sense of the word. Even in Novgorod and Kiev they were never in the majority, and the further down the waterways they travelled, the more they became a tiny minority in a landscape dominated by Slavic tribes. Just as the Normans adopted the local language, married local women, and took on local customs in a couple of generations until their origins were only hinted at by the word 'Norman' itself, so it was with the Rus. In any case, ethnicity is hard to define. There would have certainly been Rus who were of Scandinavian extraction, but at the same time there were probably plenty of non-Scandinavians in the mix. How they thought of themselves is even harder to work out, but one clue is the names they chose for their children.

We can see a possible shift from Norse to Slav identity taking place over two generations of Kievan Rus rulers. From 912 to 945 the ruler was a fearsome individual called Igor, who was married to the equally formidable Olga.* The names 'Igor' and 'Olga' may seem to be as typically Russian as possible, but they are actually Scandinavian in origin: Igor comes from the Norse name *Yngvarr/Ívarr* and Olga from the Norse name *Helga*. In naming their son, Igor and Olga broke with tradition, and gave him the decidedly Slavic moniker Svyatoslav. Once he came to power, Svyatoslav styled himself as a true Slavic king. He worshipped the Slavic gods Perun—god of thunder and lightning—and Volos—god of flocks—and refused to convert to Christianity in case his men laughed at him.[21] The manner of Syvatoslav's death also befitted a Slavic prince of the Russian steppes. In the spring of 972 Svyatoslav was ambushed and killed by the Pechenegs (described by one contemporary writer as 'a very numerous nomadic people, who eat lice').[22] The *Russian Primary Chronicle* reports that: 'The nomads took his head, and made a cup out of his skull, overlaying it with gold, and they drank from it.'[23]

Kings of the east

The saga writers have little interest in or information about these rulers and their doings. It was not *their* history in any real sense. But they have far more to

---

* During Igor's rule, the number of tribes forced to pay tribute to Kievan Rus expanded dramatically. He was finally killed in 945, attempting to extract one tribute too many. Following Igor's death, his wife Olga exacted the sort of bloody revenge typical of the heroines of Old Norse literature. According to the *Russian Primary Chronicle*, when the Drevlians sent twenty of their best men to bargain with Olga, she had them buried alive. When the next batch arrived, she roasted them alive in a bathhouse. Finally, she commanded her soldiers to massacre a further 5,000 of them during a funeral feast for her dead husband.

say about Svyatoslav's son and grandson, who were both rulers of Kievan Rus after him. In saga narratives the east occupies a very different position to that of the north and west. In the case of the north and west, to some extent, the saga writers were on home turf. Many of the saga protagonists who travelled west set off from Iceland itself. Those who travelled to the far north usually began their journeys in Norway, the ancestral home of the Icelanders. By contrast, saga protagonists travelling to the east were operating decidedly beyond the Icelanders' own cultural sphere. Twice-outlawed killers such as Erik the Red wouldn't have ended up in saga tales of the east; they belonged in the borderlands of the wild west. Likewise, the far north was home to the kings' enemies, who wielded power and collaborated with tribes out on the margins of Norse society. But in the sagas, Norse visitors to Russia are significant, high-status figures in their own right: kings, princes, and chieftains. The east, with its exotic, powerful kingdoms, is a suitable travel location for kings themselves, operating on an elevated level of royal connections and family ties.[24]

In the two generations of rulers after Svyatoslav, Kievan Rus reached its zenith. Svyatoslav's eventual successor—after a typically ungainly and bloody tussle for power—was his son Vladimir, who ruled from 980 to 1015. Vladimir was one for the high life, and the German chronicler Thietmar of Merseburg was not his biggest fan. Writing a few decades after Vladimir's reign, his opinion of the king was not flattering: 'Now I shall continue my criticism and condemnation of the wicked deeds of the king of the Russians, Vladimir....He was an unrestrained fornicator and cruelly assailed the feckless Greeks with acts of violence.'[25] This might sound like juicy material for a saga in its own right, but Vladimir is a far more majestic—and far less randy—figure in the sagas. His royal court is a place of safety for a youthful Olaf Tryggvason, the Norwegian king whom we last met in the north, torturing recalcitrant pagan chieftains with snakes and burning coals. Little Olaf had a bumpy start to life. According to the sagas, when his father was murdered, his pregnant mother fled east from Norway, was captured by pirates, and sold into slavery. Eventually, Olaf was rescued from the Estonian slave markets by his uncle, a powerful tribute-collector for King Vladimir, and taken to the royal court in Novgorod.

According to the version of his saga in *Heimskringla*, Olaf was a great favourite of Vladimir and his wife. Out in Russia he cut his teeth as a young warrior, commanding Vladimir's troops, winning many battles, and becoming very popular in the process. But not everything went Olaf's way: 'It happened—as often happens when foreign men acquire power or great fame surpassing that held by the men of the country—that many bore a grudge against him because of how dear he was to the king and no less the queen.'²⁶ As might be expected, the focus of the narrative is firmly on Olaf, rather than the Russian ruler. Vladimir functions as the young prince's mirror, reflecting Olaf's military prowess, popularity, and future promise at the very highest level. We learn very little about Vladimir himself. Elsewhere, the spiritual significance of Olaf's arrival in the east is magnified. In the *Longest Saga of Olaf Tryggvason* (*Óláfs saga Tryggvasonar en mesta*, a fat beast of a saga written in around 1300), Russian seers foresee the coming of a 'glorious and auspicious' foreigner whose light will spread throughout the region: 'They didn't know who he was or where he came from, but they affirmed with many words that the bright light that shone over him stretched out over the whole of Russia, far and wide across the eastern part of the world.'²⁷ The light, of course, was the light of Christianity. In the medieval Icelandic tradition, Olaf Tryggvason was the great Christianizing king of the Nordic world, who brought about the conversion of Iceland in particular. Little wonder, then, that in an Icelandic saga such as this, Olaf's future greatness—both as a king and as the converter of nations—is signalled in this prophecy. In his adulthood, according to the same saga, Olaf returned to Russia to convert Vladimir and his family, lecturing them sternly on the dangers of worshipping idols.

Vladimir did convert to Christianity, although he wasn't the first member of his family to do so. His grandmother, the formidable Olga, had been baptized, but as we already know Vladimir's father Svyatoslav worshipped the old Slavic gods and worried that his men would make fun of him if he converted. The claim that Olaf played a role in Vladimir's conversion seems to be nothing more than wishful thinking on the Icelanders' part: an invention spun by the saga and draped around Olaf to enhance his holy credentials.²⁸ In reality, as far as we can tell from limited sources, Vladimir shopped around before deciding which religion would be best—and most politically expedient—for him to adopt. According to the *Russian Primary Chronicle*, Vladimir sent envoys to meet with representatives of several religions, including the Muslim Volga Bulgars (who had been visited by the Islamic diplomats of the Abbasid Caliphate only a few decades earlier). While he rather liked that each Muslim man would be given seventy women in the afterlife ('for he was fond of women and indulgence'), he was unimpressed by the fact that he would have to be circumcised and give up pork and booze ('drinking is the joy of the

Russes!' he spluttered, prefiguring the snide dinner comments that Hitler would make a millennium later).[29] He was even less keen when his representatives visited the Bulgars and reported back that there was 'no happiness among them, but instead only sorrow and a dreadful stench'.[30] Orthodox Christianity seemed like a far more attractive prospect (at least as far as the *Chronicle* was concerned, but since it was written by monks this is hardly surprising).

Even more attractive to Vladimir was the idea of a strong political and military alliance between Kievan Rus and Byzantium. He had promised troops to the Byzantine emperor Basil II, to help put down a rebellion. In doing so, Vladimir was hitching his wagon to a very bright star: Basil II was one of the greatest leaders that would ever rule the Byzantine empire. In exchange for his loyalty, Vladimir was given the emperor's sister to marry: a prize certainly worth converting for. (Vladimir was already married to several other wives at the time, which may have fuelled his reputation as a bit of a ladies' man.) Saga descriptions of Olaf's pious preaching against heathen idols ring rather hollow compared to the complex political machinations and international diplomacy actually involved in the conversion of Vladimir and Kievan Rus. Out in the east, Olaf was merely a bit-player in another nation's history. Even so, the sagas manage to manoeuvre him out of the peripheries and into the centre of the action.

A clash of kings

In keeping with his reputation as a *fornicator immensus* (as Thietmar of Merseburg delicately puts it), Vladimir had rather a lot of wives, even more concubines, and very many children.[31] After his death, several of his sons continued the great Kievan Rus family tradition of brawling and scrapping until one of them triumphed. Eventually, the man on the top of the bloody pile was Yaroslav, who ruled from 1019 to 1054. Extraordinarily, the civil war between Yaroslav and his brothers also made its way into the sagas. It is the subject of the *Tale of Eymund Hring's Son* (*Eymundar þáttr Hringssonar*), where it is told from the point of view of the Scandinavian mercenaries who came to the aid of the warring would-be kings. Eymund, the chief protagonist of the tale, is introduced as the son of a minor Norwegian king. He travels to Russia with his men and offers Yaroslav military service in exchange for silver, beaver pelts, and sable furs. Unfortunately, Yaroslav proves tight-fisted when it comes to matters of payment:

When payday came, King Eymund went to find King Yaroslav and said: 'We have stayed here in your kingdom for a while, lord. You must decide now whether our bargain is to continue any longer, or whether you now want us to part company so that we can go look for another ruler. The pay has been slow in coming.' The king answered: 'I don't think I need as much support from your troops as I did before. We'd lose a lot of money if we gave you as much pay as you're asking for.'[32]

Fed up with the miserly Yaroslav not paying his dues, the mercenaries switch sides, and it is left to Yaroslav's wife to arbitrate. Yaroslav is given Novgorod, his surviving brother is given Kiev, and Eymund himself is given the rest of the kingdom and all its revenue, to persuade him to stay in the country.

As before, in this Norse version of events a Scandinavian bit-player has been coaxed out from the wings and propelled centre-stage. There is no suggestion from any other sources that a Scandinavian mercenary ended up in charge of a third of the kingdom following the civil war. Even so, the bare bones of the story are based on historical fact. There was certainly a civil war between Yaroslav and his brothers, and Yaroslav did employ Scandinavian mercenaries on a number of occasions. In the *Tale of Eymund*, names have been altered, events simplified, and new characters introduced, but in essence the events are strikingly similar to what we know from non-Norse sources.[33]

Even if the sagas exaggerate the importance of Norse contributions to Russian politics, during this period Kievan Rus maintained strong links to Scandinavia. Both Vladimir and Yaroslav had relied on Scandinavian support in their claims for the throne; Vladimir had fled to Norway on the death of his father, and mustered an army with the help of the Norwegian ruler Jarl Hakon in order to seize the kingdom from his brothers. There were also several high-status marriages made between Russian and Scandinavian royals; Vladimir may have had a Norse wife (amongst several others) while Yaroslav's own wife was Ingigerd, daughter of the king of Sweden. In reality, we know very little about Ingigerd as a historical person. But in the sagas she becomes the object of men's desires, not least the dashing young King Olaf Haraldsson, who ruled Norway from 1015 to 1028 (nicknamed 'the Holy' and, less flatteringly, 'the Fat'). *Morkinskinna*—the aforementioned 'mouldy parchment' containing one of the earliest compilations of Kings' Sagas from around 1220—opens with domestic violence at the Russian court between Yaroslav and Ingigerd. The cause of the argument is her old boyfriend Olaf:

We begin the story when King Yaroslav and Queen Ingigerd, daughter of King Olaf of Sweden, ruled Russia....Then the queen came into the hall with a fair following of ladies, and the king stood up to meet her and welcomed her warmly, saying, 'Where have you seen such a sumptuous hall, or one so equally well adorned, not only with such a retinue of men as those assembled here, but also with decorations of such splendour?' The queen answered, 'Lord, this hall is beautifully decorated, and there can be few instances of such pomp and expense gathered together under one roof, or so many excellent leaders and valiant men. Even so, the hall in which King Olaf Haraldsson sits is still better, even if it only stands on posts.' The king was furious with her, and answered, 'Such words are disgraceful, and reveal your love of King Olaf'— and he struck her on the face.[34]

Despite the fact that his wife spends her time mooning after this other man (whose inferior royal hall only stands on stumpy little posts), Yaroslav nevertheless remains loyal to his Norwegian counterpart, according to *Morkinskinna*. When Olaf Haraldsson is toppled from power by his Norwegian enemies, he flees east and takes refuge at Yaroslav's court. Following his death in battle (at the hands of the magical-reindeer-skin-clad Thorir the Hound), Olaf's young son is also taken to Russia for his own safety. Yaroslav's court then becomes a neutral stage upon which complex political negotiations are played out: the medieval northern equivalent of The Hague (except that, according to the sagas, Yaroslav was so furious about the death of Olaf that he imposed a decidedly non-neutral trade embargo on the Norwegians). The twelve most distinguished men in Norway then arrive to decide the succession: 'They stayed in the east over the summer engaged in negotiations, and when they left the east they took the king's son Magnus with them.'[35]

Tangled threads

High-status political links between Russia and Scandinavia continued into the next generation, with the marriage of Yaroslav and Ingigerd's daughter

Elizabeth—or Ellisif, as she is called in the sagas—to Olaf Haraldsson's half-brother. This is a man better known to generations of British schoolchildren as Harald Hardrada, or, to give him his proper nickname, *harðráði*, meaning 'hard ruler'. To most, Harald is a rather vague character, remembered as the warm-up act to the main events of 1066. At best, we might remember him as a viking who landed in northern England with a shaky claim to the English throne. We may also remember that he was killed at the Battle of Stamford Bridge near York, fighting against Harold Godwinson and his army. This meant that by the time the Anglo-Saxons arrived on the south coast to meet the Normans at Hastings, they were already worn out, which perhaps contributed to their defeat.

Harald Hardrada may be little more than a footnote in early English history, but he was a big deal in the medieval Nordic world. At the time of his death in 1066, he was king of Norway. He had also led an adventurous and colourful life in his youth, travelling as far afield as Russia, Constantinople, and Africa. Naturally, his deeds are commemorated in Norse sagas and poems. The Icelanders were particularly fond of him (he was remembered for helping them out during a particularly unpleasant famine), and present him in a favourable light. As this verse from *Morkinskinna* demonstrates, Harald is no shrinking violet but a great 'peace diminisher' (a kenning for a warrior), cutting down men in battle for the battlefield scavengers to feed on:

> Generous one, you wiped the sword's mouth
> when battle was over;
> you filled the raven with raw flesh;
> the wolf howled on the ridge.
> And, formidable warrior,
> the following years you were east
> in Russia, I never heard of a better
> peace-diminisher than you.[36]

Harald also had a reputation as a poet, and verses apparently composed by him are quoted in *Morkinskinna*. These are very different in tone, and all end with a refrain about Harald's love for the Russian princess Ellisif. True to the courtly conventions of medieval romance, she remains aloof and scorns Harald's love (or so the verse claims), right up to the moment when he returns from his adventures laden with vast amounts of gold and treasure. At this point he becomes a far more tempting marriage prospect. Yet despite such courtly sentiments, this is a very Norse love poem. Ellisif is styled as 'Gerd of the gold ring'; a kenning for 'woman' that refers to Gerd, the giantess wife of the pagan god Frey:

> Lady, we bailed sixteen at a time
> on four rowing benches,
> when the surf blustered and the dusky sea
> broke on the ship's heavy hull.
> I don't think a sluggish man
> would ever feel inclined to travel there.
> But back in Russia,
> the Gerd of the gold ring scorns me.[37]

Very little else is known about Ellisif, other than what is said about her in the sagas, and here her main role is as Harald's object of desire. But a faint image of Ellisif still survives on an eleventh-century fresco in the cathedral of St Sophia in Kiev, apparently painted before her marriage to the dashing Harald. The young girl stands staring steadily out from the wall, dressed in a brown tunic still faintly patterned with geometric designs. She is flanked by her Swedish mother Ingigerd and her sisters, a row of figures made ghostly by the accumulated centuries.

This was a history that must have seemed very far off and foreign to the Icelanders, writing their sagas thousands of miles away from Russia and centuries after the events themselves. Most likely, it feels far off and foreign to most of us today too: an alternative, lesser-known history of Norsemen who sailed to Russia and mingled with foreign kings. But if we start to unknot the tangled threads of international royal marriages and follow some of the strands back to their sources, we end up much closer to home than we might expect. The following passage comes from the *Saga of Knut's Descendants* (*Knýtlinga saga*), a collection of Kings' Sagas about Danish kings written in the thirteenth century. According to the text, it wasn't just the Scandinavian and Russian royal lines that were connected through marriage, but also those of Anglo-Saxon England, through King Harold Godwinson himself:

These were the children of Godwin and Gyda: King Harold of England, Earl Tostig who was nicknamed 'Tree-spear', Earl Morcar, Earl Waltheof and Earl Sweyn. Descended from them are many great men from England, Denmark, and Sweden, and east in Russia.[38]

FIGURE 9.3 Fresco in the cathedral St Sophia in Kiev, depicting Yaroslav's wife and three daughters

The saga goes on to tell us that Harold Godwinson's daughter Gyda married Vladimir, the eldest son of Yaroslav and Ingigerd (this information is repeated in other Norse texts). If this is indeed true, then the consequences get rather interesting a couple of centuries down the line. Gyda and Vladimir's son was Mstislav, the last ruler of a united Kievan Rus. One of *his* daughters, Euphrosyne, became the wife of King Geza II of Hungary. *Their* son was King Bela III of Hungary. *His* son was King Andrew II of Hungary. *His* daughter was Queen Yolanda, who became Queen consort of Aragon. *Her* daughter was Queen Isabella of France. *Her* son was King Philip IV of France. *His* daughter was Isabella, nicknamed the She-Wolf of France.

This may seem like rather a long and unnecessary list of names and countries. Except that Isabella the She-Wolf of France married King Edward II of England. Despite her husband's reputation for 'favourites' amongst the men at court (and anyone wanting to remind themselves how he is rumoured to have met his death should turn to Christopher Marlowe's play *Edward II*), Isabella gave birth to several children, including a son who became King Edward III.

This means that 261 years after Harold Godwinson was killed at Hastings, his great-great-great-great-great-great-great-great-grandson via the Kievan Rus dynasty ascended the same throne that he had fought for and lost. Through the tangle of English, Scandinavian, and Russian royal lines—not to mention Hungarian, French, and a whole host of other nationalities—Harold's descendants returned to England. If this is true, then it means that even today, the well-travelled Anglo-Saxon blood of Harold Godwinson still runs through the veins of the British royal family.

During Yaroslav's reign, Kievan Rus was at the height of its power. After his death, bitter power-struggles began to tear the state apart. With the coming of the crusades, the trade-routes that had sustained Kievan Rus began to fragment. Finally, in the 1220s, the Mongols invaded from the east. By 1240 Kievan Rus had crumbled and submitted to the Golden Horde. Yet, far from the smoke and ashes of Mongol desolation, the Icelandic sagas were just beginning to be written down, preserving a version of the Kievan Rus past that may or may not have been recognizable to the medieval Russians themselves.

CHAPTER 10

Set in Stone

Immortal memory

If you ever find yourself passing through Arlanda, Stockholm's international airport, make your way to Terminal 2. Bypass the bustling hordes of far travellers—lone businessmen in crumpled suits, sticky children astride miniature ladybird suitcases—resist the siren song of the frozen yogurt café, and look for the sign for the ladies' loo.

To the left of the sign, in front of long windows stretching from ceiling to floor, lurks a lump of stone taller than a man. Picked out in red paint are the fading outlines of two carved snakes, arching around the edge of the stone and looping back on themselves. At two points they appear to be bound together, as if to prevent them wriggling from the stone and slipping away silently to wreak havoc on the baggage belt. The bodies of these snakes are adorned with runes, running their whole lengths from curved tails to pointed heads. These runes translate as:

Gunnar and Bjorn and Thorgrim raised this stone in memory of their brother Thorstein, who died in the east with Ingvar, and made this bridge.[1]

Between the rune-riddled snakes is a Christian cross. This is no pagan stone from far back in the mists of time: it was erected after Christianity had reached the north, probably around the middle of the eleventh century. Originally it stood by a road and the bridge mentioned in the inscription, where it could be noted and admired by travellers passing along the busy route. Commissioning

FIGURE 10.1 Ingvar runestone in the grounds of Gripsholm castle

such a stone, not to mention the bridge, was an expensive undertaking. Through it, the three men sought to imprint their brother's name, and their own, on the landscape itself. This was not only an act of memorialization, but also immortalization.

In 1990 the stone—now broken into pieces and furry with lichen—was rediscovered during the construction of a new motorway to the airport. It was polished up, glued back together, and installed in Terminal 2. A millennium after they were carved, the silent runes remain, placid amid the noise and haste. Hordes of purposeful passengers hurry past every day in a fug of jet-lagged yawns, forgotten gate numbers, and last-boarding-calls. Even if a passing traveller bothered to pause by the runes, the story they tell has almost faded into oblivion. Almost, but not quite.

West of the airport lies Lake Mälaren, the vast body of water that contains the islands of Helgö and Björkö. On the shores of the lake, in the surrounding fields, by clumps of woodland, perched next to pagan barrows and cairns, are more runestones. Many commemorate men—fathers, sons, brothers—who, like Thorstein, went on the same eastern voyage and never returned. On each stone, the same mysterious name is repeated: *Ingvar*.

On the northern side of the lake, next to the main road, is a tall earthen mound raised high on the headland, overlooking water on both sides. On top of it stands a slender stone only a little wider than a man, looming over three metres high. The carvings are weathered and the surface is rough, but the runes loop around the edges of the stone, set into serpentine bodies. This stone was raised by five children to commemorate their father, who had been killed out east:

Andvett and Karr and Kiti and Blesi and Djarf raised this stone in memory of their father Gunnleif. He was killed in the east with Ingvar. May God help their souls. I, Alrik, carved the runes. He knew well how to steer a cargo-ship.[2]

On the southern shore of the lake stands the sixteenth-century castle of Gripsholm. On the grassy verge of the driveway is another runestone, raised by a mother for her son:

Tola had this stone raised in memory of her son Harald, Ingvar's brother. Bravely they travelled far for gold and in the east gave food to the eagle. They died in the south in Serkland.[3]

The stone at Gripsholm didn't always stand on the driveway. It was discovered in the cellar by the castle caretaker in the 1820s, where it had been used as a threshold stone. Other Ingvar runestones met a similar fate over the centuries, taken from their original locations and used as building materials. Two Ingvar runestones were built into the walls of the medieval cathedral in Strängnäs, just up the road from Gripsholm. Another chunk of stone pokes out of the grassy verge by the cathedral, like a stubby, rotten tooth. Fragments of fanged dragons peer out from the brickwork and grass, encircled by red runes. The inscriptions are incomplete, but the words and phrases that can be picked out are variations on the same theme:

Eimund's son—Ulf's brother—to the East—with Ingvar—south in Serkland…

FIGURE 10.2 Ingvar runestone set into the wall of Strängnäs cathedral

Altogether, there are nearly thirty Swedish runestones commemorating men who went to the east with Ingvar and never returned. Most are dotted close to Lake Mälaren, although others are further afield. Each is a public testament to private family loss, grief, and pride. For almost one thousand years they have stood, as centuries of midsummer roses tangle at the edges of fields and autumn mists hang low in the trees. Waters and woods echo silently with the names of almost-forgotten men:

Thorstein—Gunnleif—Harald—Saebjorn—Baggi—Gunnvid—Ulf—Gauti—Belgir—Hrodgeir—Tosti—Hugi—Thorbjorn—Skarf—Skardi—Bjorstein—Osni-kin—Orm—Onund…

These are only nineteen names amongst many more that have now vanished without a trace, all united in life and death through Ingvar and their adventure in the east.

Far travellers

No stone to Ingvar himself has ever been found. But the runes speak of Ingvar's voyage to the east rather like we might speak of an expedition led by Scott or Shackleton during the golden age of polar exploration. No further explanation is necessary. A name—*Ingvar*—and a cardinal direction—*East*—is sufficient.

Sufficient, that is, for the community who put up the runestones, and the generations that followed them. But completely insufficient, of course, for anyone who comes across one of these stones today. The whole event would have remained shrouded in mystery, were it not for an extraordinary text written down over a thousand miles west of Lake Mälaren, hundreds of years later. Incredibly, Ingvar is the star of his very own Icelandic saga, the *Saga of Yngvar the Far Traveller* (*Yngvars saga víðfǫrla*). His name is spelt 'Yngvar' in the saga rather than 'Ingvar' as it appears on the runestones, but undoubtedly this is the same man.

Yngvar is not the only far traveller in the sagas. Today, international airports such as Arlanda bustle with them. Their journeys take them all over the globe; north, south, east, and west. But in the sagas, those given the nickname 'far traveller' (*víðfǫrli*) tend to travel east.[4] The treacherous waters of Greenland, the balmy shores of Vinland, and the frozen wastes of the Arctic north may technically be as far away in terms of miles covered, but 'far' is a frame of mind. 'Far' also means 'unfamiliar', which, as we will see, becomes a problem for Icelandic saga writers describing a part of the world greatly removed from their own experience and knowledge.

The *Saga of Yngvar the Far Traveller* represents a unique and truly remarkable connection across time and space, but, as with all sagas, it is no straightforward historical document. In fact, even by saga standards it is pretty outlandish; one scholar has described it as 'one of the wildest and woolliest of all the sagas'.[5] This is a story in which a man might die fighting in foreign battles, or succumb to sickness. Equally, he might drop dead in sheer horror at the sight of a furious dragon deprived of its gold, whistling and whirling in the air. If this saga is a window onto any sort of historical past, it is a particularly murky, distorted window.

As we have already seen, the narrative effect of some sagas is akin to a Greek Chorus, with many faint, indistinguishable voices speaking to us from across time and space. In the case of Yngvar's story, this effect is magnified not only by the existence of the Swedish runestones, but also by the strong presence of one—quite possibly two—chorus leaders, the saga writers, who are keen to show us exactly how they directed the performance by identifying some of the other voices. Sometimes these are named sources, while at other times they are the anonymous voices of hearsay and tall tales, identified simply as 'some people', or 'wise men'. As we have already seen, if you try too hard to reconstruct historical reality through the sagas, you can easily end up tripping over your own feet. But sometimes it is possible to trace the changing shape of a story through the centuries, however indistinct the outline.

According to the saga, Yngvar comes from a powerful family descended from Swedish royalty. He is not the first of his family to go east to Russia; his father also spends his youth out east, fighting battles for King Yaroslav.[6] When Yngvar grows up, he leaves Sweden with enough men to fill thirty ships and sails east to Novgorod, where he is welcomed warmly by Yaroslav. Yngvar stays at the royal court for three years and learns to speak many languages. While there, he hears about a river worthy of a proper adventure: 'He heard talk of three rivers that flowed east through Russia, and the middle one was the biggest. So Yngvar travelled widely throughout the east and asked whether anyone knew where that river came from, but no one could tell him.'[7]

Yngvar sets off with his men, determined to find the source of the great river. Wild adventures await them in these unknown lands. They find a golden mound of sleeping dragons, glittering like the moon and protected by an enormous, angry über-dragon. They battle with a man-eating giant with corpses hanging from his belt. They enter a heathen city called Citopolis, ruled over by the beautiful, brainy Queen Silkisif. On the river itself they meet King Jolf, ruler of another exotic city called Heliopolis. When they finally reach the source of the river, they find it inhabited by a monstrous, gold-guarding dragon. No sooner have they escaped this creature than they find themselves in a city haunted by disgruntled demons. On the journey back, they return to Heliopolis, where they fight battles for King Jolf and suffer the indignity of being propositioned by sex-mad heathen floozies. Finally, just when things are looking up, sickness strikes, killing half the men including Yngvar. The saga is extremely precise, almost annalistic, on this point. In fact, the same information also appears in Icelandic annals:[8] 'When Yngvar died it was 1041 winters since the birth of Jesus Christ. He was 25 years old.'[9] Despite the apparent precision of this statement, the surrounding story is typically jazzed up: as Yngvar lies dying, he hints darkly at witchcraft and curses being responsible for the sickness, and predicts that they will end when he himself is dead.

In the reality attested to by the runestones, we don't know what actually killed Yngvar and his men, and the inscriptions are formulaic enough that they don't give us many clues. The stone now in Arlanda airport says that the man to whom it was raised was killed out east, possibly suggesting violence, while one raised to Harald says that they 'gave food to the eagle'; a stereotypical formulation for battle. But this same runestone simply says that Harald died south in Serkland, without specifying how. Most of the others are similarly vague: 'he met his end in the east'—'he died in the east'—'he met his end with Yngvar'—'he died in Yngvar's retinue'.

The second part of the saga describes the adventures of Yngvar's son, Svein, who does not appear on any runestones (and in any case would have had to be pretty young if Yngvar was 25 when he died). According to the saga he also travels east into Russia and sails along the same river, raiding pagan tribes and carrying off furs, clothes, and silver. He meets even odder inhabitants of the waterways: an enormous tribe of people known as 'Cyclopes', an apple-throwing man sporting a bird-beak, and a mysterious beast with a tower strapped on its back. Svein and his men have even more trouble with the heathen tribes of the region, and end up battling with a gruesome pagan army. Returning to Citopolis, Svein marries Queen Silkisif, but is eventually lost on the river, never to be heard of again.

A river runs through it

This is a very different sort of expedition compared to the great voyages west across the Atlantic, but it is no less dangerous. All the time in the saga, the great river churns and rumbles on in the background. (See Map 3.) Navigating these waters is distinctly tricky, and some stretches are completely unnavigable: 'Yngvar followed the course of the river until he came to a huge waterfall and a narrow rocky ravine. The cliffs were so high that they had to drag up their ships with ropes. Afterwards they dragged them back onto the river.'[10] Later on in the journey the boats are forced ashore once again by a mighty waterfall, and the sailors spend months digging a channel for their ships to pass through. The saga writer points out that according to some people, Yngvar and his men had to use candles for two weeks if they wanted to see anything, because the cliffs closed over the river so that it was like rowing through a cave. The author himself remains sceptical on this point, noting that 'wise men think that this can't be true' and 'although it might be possible, it's not very likely'.[11]

As the saga suggests, navigating Russian rivers was no easy task, even if the saga author himself suspects that tales of Yngvar's struggles have grown taller in the telling. The fearsome rapids of the river Dnieper are described in a tenth-century text *On the Governance of the Empire* (*De Administrando Imperio*), written by the Byzantine emperor Constantine VII as a kingcraft manual for his young son. In a lengthy passage he conjures up images of wild, untameable waters capable of swamping men and sinking ships. At times, boats must be dragged up onto dry land, not unlike the description in the saga:

And first they come to the first barrage, called Essoupi, which means in Russian and Slavonic 'Do not sleep!'; the barrage itself is as narrow as the width of the Polo-ground;* in the middle of it are rooted high rocks, which stand out like islands. Against these, then, comes the water and wells up and dashes down over the other side, with a mighty and terrific din. Therefore the Russians do not venture to pass between them, but put in to the bank hard by, disembarking the men on to dry land...When they have passed this barrage, they re-embark the others from the dry land and sail away, and come down to the second barrage, called in Russian Oulvorsi, and in Slavonic Ostrovouniprach, which means 'the Island of the Barrage'. This one is like the first, awkward and not to be passed through.[12]

---

* Byzantine emperors were very fond of polo, and it is said that Emperor Theodosius II (r. 408–50) had a polo field built in the grounds of the Great Palace.

The so-called 'Russian' names that Constantine gives for each of the rapids appear to be Scandinavian in origin, strengthening the idea of a strong Scandinavian *and* Slavic presence in the region. The proposed meanings of the original Norse names echo the tumult of the tempestuous, perilous waters: Essupi (from *ei sofi*, 'do not sleep!'), Gelandri (from *gjallandi*, 'yelling'), *aifor* (from *eiforr*, 'ever-fierce'), Leanti (from *hlæjandi*, 'laughing', or *leandi*, 'seething').[13] It would be unwise to make a direct connection between the rapids described by Constantine VII and those in the *Saga of Yngvar*, not least because, as we are about to see, Yngvar and his men probably sailed down the Volga rather than the Dnieper. Even so, tales of the dangerous rapids on the Russian rivers seem to have reached Iceland where their embellishment continued, at least if we are to believe the sceptical saga author.

The language of water-borne travel is also reflected in several of the Yngvar runestones, though in a less theatrical way. One stone was raised to a man called Saebjorn, who 'steered a ship east with Ingvar'; another is dedicated to Baggi, who 'alone owned his ship and steered to the east in Ingvar's company'; and we have already met Gunnlief, who 'knew well how to steer a cargo-ship'. It is also the runestones that reveal which river Yngvar must have sailed down, and more to the point where he was heading. Many of them simply say that the man commemorated went 'east with Ingvar'. Others—such as the stone raised outside Gripsholm Castle or one of the stubby fragments from Sträng-näs cathedral—say that the men died 'south in Serkland'. *Serkland* was the fairly loose Norse term for countries occupied by Muslims, particularly the lands that formed the Abbasid Caliphate.[14] If this is true, then Yngvar and his men would have been sailing down the Volga—the river where the Arab diplomats met the Rus traders—to the Caspian Sea. If Yngvar did indeed die in 1041 as the saga and annals tell us, then the voyage took place relatively late in terms of Norse activities in the east. It has been suggested that the real reason for the expedition was to reopen the north–south trading route stretching down through Russia to the Abbasid Caliphate.[15]

There are no references to Serkland in the *Saga of Yngvar*, nor is the name of the river specified. The text gives no indication of any motivation for the voyage other than to discover the source of the great river. In geographical terms, the saga's grasp of the Russian river system is rather vague and inaccurate, a long way from the more precise navigational details embedded in the Vinland sagas. The source of the river itself is said to be a spring, called Lindibelti:

From there another spring flows to the Red Sea, where there is a huge whirlpool called Gapi. Between the sea and the river is a peninsula known as Siggeum. The river flows for a short distance before it pours over the cliffs into the Red Sea, and there is the end of the world.[16]

Even leaving aside the whole 'end of the world' bit, this description is far from geographically accurate. The Red Sea is a considerable distance further south, bordered today by countries such as Egypt, Sudan, Saudi Arabia, and Yemen. The saga author may have confused the Red Sea with the Caspian Sea, but even if that were the case, we are still left with a vast whirlpool and waters pouring over the cliffs at the end of the world. The trouble with sagas of far travellers is that their protagonists travel to far-off, unfamiliar lands, where geographical knowledge begins to blur and tangle in the Icelandic saga writers' minds.

The cities named in the saga have also been displaced from their actual geographical locations. Citopolis might be equated with an ancient city on the river Jordan, which was called Scythopolis by the Greeks. Today it is part of Israel, and called Beit She'an. There are two possible candidates for Heliopolis, one in Lebanon, and the other an ancient Egyptian city that stood at the northern edge of what is now Cairo. It was here that the sun-god Ra was said to preside, and so the Greeks renamed it *Heliopolis*, meaning 'City of the Sun'. Siggeum—the spit of land that according to the saga lies at the edge of the world—is the Roman name for the ancient Turkish city of Sigeion. Just as the saga says, this city did sit on a promontory, but one jutting out into the Aegean Sea rather than the Red or Caspian Sea.[17]

While the saga geography is jumbled up and confused, it certainly isn't fantastical. The saga author visualizes the river—and Yngvar's expedition—moving south, but has incorporated the Red Sea and the lands of the Middle East into this geographical framework. This also affects the types of creatures that the men encounter on the river—as we will see in the next chapter.

Lost in translation

According to the *Saga of Yngvar*, the east is a realm of many languages. Historically, we have already seen how multicultural this part of the world was, where waterways were the highways for international traders, towns and ports were cultural melting-pots, and even the ferocious river rapids evolved multiple names in response to the different ethnic groups navigating them. A few Norse loanwords did make their way into Slavic languages, such as *jabednik* ('official'). A few more came the other way, including *torg* ('marketplace') and *græns* ('border'), and, perhaps most significantly of all, *tolk* ('interpreter').[18] Consciously or unconsciously, this multicultural environment is reflected in the *Saga of Yngvar*, where both Yngvar and his son stay at the Russian court for three years learning the languages that they might need on the waterways before striking out for more exotic climes. On the river itself, both men meet a number of talented and sophisticated polyglots. When the beautiful Queen Silkisif greets Yngvar, he stays quiet so he can find out how many languages she can speak:

She asked who they were and where they were heading, but Yngvar didn't answer, because he wanted to find out if she knew how to speak more languages. It turned out that she could speak Latin, German, Norse, Greek, and many other languages used in the east.[19]

Likewise when Yngvar meets King Jolf on the river, the impression is of a multicultural world where the locals are used to interacting with travellers from distant lands. As before, Yngvar's tactic is silence. By not engaging in dialogue, he is able to ascertain the full capabilities of these internationally savvy foreigners: 'The man was dressed like a king and spoke many languages. When Yngvar kept quiet, he tried a few words in Greek.'[20]

It is only out on the waterways, where the landscape is wilder and the demographic more mixed, that the practicalities of international communication need to be addressed. The heathens that the Norsemen encounter have no foreign-language proficiencies, and as with the Skraelings of North America, the travellers can only communicate through sign language, which allows them to trade. But once again things go horribly wrong, and it's not long before a heathen is lying dead on the ground in a pool of his own blood. At this point, readers coming to this text with the Vinland sagas fresh in their minds might experience a distinct sense of déjà vu.

By contrast, in the Kings' Sagas that featured in the last chapter, Norse princes and kings travelling east to the Russian court seem able to communicate without learning foreign languages. In two cases (Olaf Tryggvason and Magnus Olafsson), this can be explained by the fact that they were brought up at these courts as children and so language-learning might be assumed; even so, it is never mentioned. On the other hand, both Olaf Haraldsson and his half-brother Harald Hardrada only travel to Russia as adults, but even so there is no sense of any language barrier. Royalty, it seems, is a *lingua franca* in its own right.

Telling tales

As is so often the case in the sagas, past a certain point there is little to be gained from trying to distil hard fact from fiction. Facts, such as they are, dissolve into the melting-pot of the story and become legends. Even so, the saga itself provides some clues as to how news of Yngvar's expedition might have travelled all the way from the balmy Caspian Sea to the chilly shores of an island out in the middle of the North Atlantic. Credit is given to one of Yngvar's travelling companions, an Icelander called Ketil, who is said to have had the best memory of all (a talent prized by the story-telling Icelanders). His nickname is Garda-Ketil or 'Ketil the Russian' (after the Norse word for this part of the world, *Garðaríki)*. If there really was an Icelander on Yngvar's expedition, named Ketil or otherwise, this might explain how the story got back to Iceland. After Yngvar's death, it is he who is said to have brought news of the expedition north, first to Sweden and then back home, for 'Ketil travelled to Iceland to see his relatives and settle down, and he was the first to tell of these events.'[21]

We will probably never know whether a man called Garda-Ketil was actually with Yngvar on his expedition. During the voyage down the river Ketil has his own little adventure, when he narrowly escapes being pulverized by an angry giant, so we can safely assume that if Ketil was a real person the part he played on the expedition grew in the telling. But the saga author offers additional clues to the further transmission of the story, claiming that several oral versions of it were doing the rounds amongst priests, merchants, and even Swedish nobility. A monk called Odd, we are told, heard the story from several sources, and adopted a pick-'n'-mix approach: 'from each of these stories he took whatever seemed most remarkable to him.'[22] The saga author goes on to claim that the monk was responsible for an earlier written account of Yngvar's adventures, upon which his own saga was based:

We have heard this saga told, but in writing it we have followed a book written by the wise monk Odd, according to the information provided by knowledgeable men, whom he himself mentioned in the letter he sent to Jon Loftsson and Gizur Hallson.[23]

It's hard to know whether this is true or not, because if Odd did write a version of Yngvar's life, then no trace of it survives today. Likewise, there is no sign of any letter written to Jon Loftsson and Gizur Hallson, who were two of the most politically and intellectually influential men in twelfth-century Iceland. All we have are two fifteenth-century defective manuscripts with versions of the Old Norse saga, and several later paper copies. Still, in light of the information provided in the saga, some scholars have suggested that there was an earlier version of Yngvar's life, written in Latin by the monk Odd Snorrason in around 1200.[24]

This might also explain other more unusual features of the saga narrative. The Swedish runestones commemorating men who fell with Yngvar may have featured the occasional cross (which is reasonable, given the Christian cultural milieu in which they were made), but there's no sense that religion played an important role in their voyage. The saga, by comparison, has been likened to a conversion narrative with Yngvar framed as an unconventional conversion hero. It has even been described as a christianized Legendary Saga 'which comes perilously near to becoming a saint's life'.[25] Most likely, the overtly religious dimension to the saga came later, when the story was committed to writing in a monastic environment, perhaps through the monkish Odd who may have written the first Latin version of the saga.

The heathen tribes that both Yngvar and Svein encounter out on the river represent not only a clash of cultures, but also a clash of religions. When the heathens see the Norse making the sign of the cross, they work themselves up into a frenzy and attack. Battle commences, and while Svein's men bear a crucifix before them, the heathens carry something far more gruesome: 'they raised a bloody man before the troop as a battle banner.'[26] During the battle—as the priests accompanying Svein pray on the sidelines like managers at a football match—the heathens are struck blind and flee into the forests.

Nor is heathenism confined to the wilds of the waterways. In the sophisticated cities of Heliopolis and Citopolis, another type of heathen 'otherness' manifests itself in the form of lustful and ungodly women. The first time it happens, Yngvar's reaction is brutal, if practical:

Yngvar prepared a hall for his men and locked it carefully, because there were signs of heathen worship everywhere. Yngvar told them to be careful about mixing with heathen men, and banned all women from entering his hall apart from the queen. Some of his men paid little heed to what he said, so he had them killed.[27]

Later on, a troop of wanton women—likened, with typical medieval misogyny, to 'the most poisonous snakes'—march into the Norse camp, and the highest-ranking one strolls up to Yngvar, determined to sleep with him.[28] His angry response leaves no room for misinterpretation: 'He became furious, pulled out a knife, and stabbed her in her genitals.'[29]

Perhaps such diabolically horny women were the only type that a sheltered, bookish monk such as Odd could imagine, other than maybe nuns and the Virgin Mary herself. Certainly, this is an unusual stance for a saga to adopt: heathens are rarely so censured, or female sexuality so reviled (remember the *Saga of Burnt-Njal* where a woman divorces her husband because he is unable to satisfy her in the bedroom—in the forward-thinking sagas, women are entitled to sexual gratification).

If Odd did write an earlier Latin version of Yngvar's story, then this tells us much about the ferment of oral and written sources from which such a saga could be created: learned, literary, and religious material mixing with tales circulating amongst travellers and in royal circles. Today things are very different: a writer will usually publish a single version of a book and be credited as the author. By contrast, whoever put the *Saga of Yngvar* together wasn't territorial. He makes no claim to it being the final, authoritative version of the story. In fact, he invites further embellishment from others who might have other material to add, declaring: 'but those who think they know more details about this story must add to it, wherever it now seems lacking' (though this could also be interpreted as a challenge to critics who think they could do a better job).[30] There was a very good reason why the Norse phrase for the act of saga composition was *setja saman*, 'bring together'.

Although we have reached the end of the chapter, we're not finished with Yngvar quite yet. His saga also contains echoes of many fainter, even older voices, as well as a menagerie of far-voyaging creatures whose journey to medieval Iceland—through time and space—was far longer and far more complicated than even Yngvar's. Who these creatures are and where they come from is the subject of the next chapter. But travellers be warned, for here be dragons.

CHAPTER 11

Far-Travelling Beasts

Beauty and the bestiary

Not all saga far travellers are human. We already know about the raiders, traders, royals, and adventurers—both historical and literary—who sailed east from Scandinavia into distant and unknown lands, down the Russian rivers and beyond. But the east of the medieval Icelanders' imagination was also populated by a different breed of far traveller: outlandish literary voyagers who came north to Iceland over the course of a millennium or more, pressed between stiff parchment pages in written form. These are beasts, monsters, and marvellous races that started life in writings from the Classical world, such as Pliny the Elder's *Natural History* (*Naturalis historia*) written in the first century AD. They then graduated into medieval encyclopedic manuscripts via influential texts such as Isidore of Seville's *Etymologies* (*Etymologiae*), a twenty-volume encyclopedia of universal history written around the beginning of the seventh century. As we will see, some of them got all the way up to Iceland before making the leap into the unpredictable world of the Icelandic sagas (though this career change didn't always pay off: such creatures have a tendency to be murdered by saga heroes in a variety of cruel and unusual ways).

In addition to the bloodthirsty pagan tribes, inhabitants of exotic kingdoms, and over-sexed heathen women that we met in the last chapter, the *Saga of Yngvar* populates the east with a veritable menagerie of the bizarre, including some animals with very ancient origins. Such creatures haven't simply been plucked from the saga writer's imagination and dumped into the saga for the sake of a good story, or to fill in unknown parts of the world. Remember that an earlier version of Yngvar's life may well have been written in Latin by Odd, the 'learned monk', as the surviving Norse saga describes him. This same saga also tells us that Odd not only used oral informants to gather information about Yngvar's travels, but also written sources (for instance, it mentions an unidentified Latin text called the *Gesta Saxonum* or 'History of the Saxons'). If this is the case, then it's hardly surprising that the saga features some particularly well-educated, well-travelled monstrosities.

As the Norse explorers travel further into Russia and find themselves in *terra incognita*, it isn't just the landscapes that become strange and unfamiliar, but the wildlife as well: 'the animals' colours and habits were changing, from which they could see that they were getting further away from their homelands.'[1] Some of these beasts are very bizarre indeed, while others are at the more realistic end of the natural-history spectrum (at least from the modern reader's point of view). The unfortunate creature that Yngvar's son Svein encounters towards the end of the saga may or may not be recognizable from this description:

One day they saw ten men leading some sort of creature behind them. It seemed rather extraordinary to them, because they saw that the animal had a tall wooden tower on its back.... But when the men who were leading it saw the ship's crew, they abandoned it and fled. Svein's men went up to the animal and wanted to lead it away, but it put its head down and wouldn't move from the spot, even though they tried to tug on the ropes that hung from its head.... because they didn't know what sort of animal it was, or what food it needed to eat, they attacked it with spears until it fell down dead.[2]

From the 'tall wooden tower' strapped on this creature's back, we can deduce that Svein and his men have met (and, I regret to say, murdered) an elephant. The tower—a *howdah*—is one of the defining features of elephants as they appear in medieval bestiaries from across medieval Europe. Bestiaries were manuscripts detailing the essential characteristics of animals, such as how they were born, where they lived, and what they looked like. Each entry was usually accompanied by an illustration of the animal, and often a moralizing story or allegory linked to the creature itself (so the asp illustrates the dangers of worldly wealth, the phoenix is an allegory for Christ's death and resurrection, while the devilish wolf preys on the sheepfold like Satan preys on mankind). Many bestiary animals we would definitely recognize today: wild boars, hedgehogs, ants, badgers, moles, crocodiles, weasels, tigers, bats, and so on. Others would give us one heck of a shock if we bumped into them in real life: griffins, centaurs, manticores, dragons, unicorns, and basilisks, to name but a

FIGURE 11.1 Illustration of the Cremona elephant from Matthew Paris' *Chronica Majora*

few. The best and most famous bestiaries are multicoloured, magnificently illustrated works of art, such as the twelfth-century Aberdeen Bestiary, with its vivid illustrations against gold-leafed backdrops: animals such as a posse of hedgehogs capering at the foot of a tree with grapes spiked on their bristles; a gangly hyena ripping at man's corpse with its sharp fangs; and a mournful little black owl, strutting across the page with beak downturned.

Not all animals are instantly recognizable from their bestiary portraits, particularly exotic creatures from far-off countries that the artists had never seen. Bestiary drawings of elephants are a mixed bag in terms of their resemblance to the animal itself. Usually they are identifiable by their *howdah*, the fact that they are being attacked by dragons (their mortal enemies), and their trunks. Occasionally these trunks challenge the talents and credulity of the bestiary artists: one unfortunate-looking specimen from a fourteenth-century German manuscript has a trunk protruding from its forehead like a giant hose, and bears a striking resemblance to a donkey. As a result it looks extremely distressed, and may well be in the throes of an existential crisis.[3] It

FIGURE 11.2 Elephant from the Icelandic *Physiologus* (c.1190–1210)

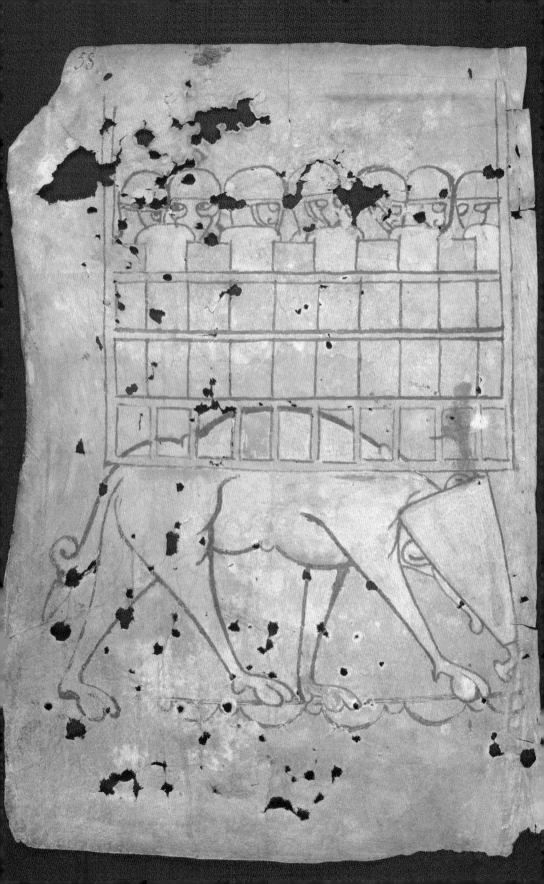

was only in the thirteenth century that occasional elephants began to put in an appearance in medieval Europe, as diplomatic gifts presented to rulers. In 1255 one took up brief residence at the Tower of London, a gift from the king of France to King Henry III. The king issued a writ to the sheriffs of London, commanding that, 'without delay you have made at our Tower of London one house 40 feet long and 20 feet wide, for our elephant'.[4] The beast was part of a royal menagerie that also included three leopards and the aforementioned polar bear that caught fish in the Thames for its dinner. Famously, the monk and chronicler Matthew Paris went to see it and produced a beautifully realistic drawing of the animal. This was not the only elephant living in thirteenth-century Europe: Matthew also made a drawing of the so-called Cremona elephant that was given to the Holy Roman Emperor Frederick II by the Sultan of Egypt in 1229. This drawing features an elephant that looks like a heffalump from Winnie-the-Pooh—an enormous *howdah* is strapped to the poor creature's back, filled with excited men blowing trumpets, banging drums, and ringing bells. To add insult to injury, the man at the back is pricking the elephant's bottom with a big pointy stick to keep it moving.

Images of elephants occasionally crop up in the medieval Nordic world as well. The Norwegian cathedral of Nidaros in Trondheim is home to a pair of stone elephants, dated to around the first half of the thirteenth century. The elephants are fairly recognizable with their long trunks and tusks, and one seems to be having a sneaky nibble on a piece of fruit that looks like a pineapple. The enigmatic sculpture is usually called 'Christ on Elephant Throne', because the poor elephants are being sat on by a figure in a flowing tunic (possibly, but not definitely, Christ).

Closer to home, a picture of an elephant also appears in one of two surviving fragments of the medieval Icelandic *Physiologus* (the other features the pole-vaulting uniped we met in the west).[5] In the illustration, the head of this noble, if rather odd, beast is covered in battle armour, with only a little snouty pipe of a trunk sticking out at the end. It is dwarfed by an enormous castle-like box perched on its back, filled with seven suspicious-looking warriors ready for battle. The text is fragmentary, but what can be seen reads:

The animal that is called *elephans* in Latin is called *fíll* in our language. It is used during battles in foreign lands. It is so strong and mighty that more [...] ten men and [...] with all the war weapons and the fortress, which is made from wood like a castle, which they use when they fight battles, as is written in the Book of Maccabees.[6]

It is worth noting that the Old Norse word for elephant—*fíll*—bears no resemblance to its more recognizable Latin equivalent. This is because it is borrowed from the Persian word—*fíl*—once again highlighting the strong ties of trade and communication that stretched from the Nordic world via Russia down to the Middle East.

It may or may not be significant that the fragments of this Icelandic *Physiologus* date to around 1200, the same time that the hypothetical Latin version of Yngvar's life may have been written by the monk Odd Snorrason. We don't know whether Odd had access to either copies of the *Physiologus* or other similar texts, but this was certainly a possibility. Odd was based at the monastery of Þingeyrar in north-west Iceland, while the *Physiologus* fragments were discovered close by, in the Westfjords. Maybe one or more copies of the Icelandic *Physiologus* were written at Odd's monastery, either by Odd himself or by his monkish mate on a nearby bench in the scriptorium.

Here be dragons

A battle elephant wouldn't be the first animal that springs to mind when we consider the flora and fauna of Russia. On the other hand, at the point at which the elephant appears in the saga, the explorers have already travelled a long way south, and are clearly—as the saga author envisages them—somewhere fairly close to the elephant's natural habitat. Other creatures that the Norse adventurers encounter in the saga are even further removed from any sense of realistic natural history. As the Norsemen make their way into *terra incognita*, here be dragons—literally.*

There are few mythological beasts more Nordic than a good old-fashioned dragon. Think of Fafnir, the treasure-loving serpent of Norse myth and legend who was dispatched by Sigurd the Dragon-Slayer (and who subsequently enjoyed a long and fruitful afterlife as Fafner in Wagner's *Ring* Cycle and as the

---

* Actually, the phrase 'here be dragons' (or in its Latin original, *hic sunt dracones*) only appears twice in medieval depictions of the world. Once is on the Hunt–Lenox Globe from the first decade of the sixteenth century, now housed in the New York Public Library. This was thought to be the only use of the term, until an even older globe was discovered engraved on an ostrich egg and dated to 1504. Off the coast of south-east Asia are the words *hic sunt dracones*. Elsewhere, other creatures perform similar functions, such as on the Cotton Tiberius map from Anglo-Saxon England (*c.*1025–50), which places a lion in south-east Asia together with the words: *hic abundant leones* ('here lions abound').

inspiration for Tolkien's gold-hoarding Smaug in *The Hobbit*). In the *Saga of Yngvar*, at the source of the river itself, something truly monstrous lurks: an enormous dragon worthy of any Bilbo Baggins adventure, parked on a fat pile of gold that is 'as hot as if it had just been forged'.[7] Yngvar and his men hack off a piece of the treasure, and the dragon rises up on its tail, whirling and whistling in the air like a spinning-top. The men who witness this terrifying sight run back to report what they have seen and immediately drop dead from shock.

Another dragon that the Norsemen encounter on their journey is no native of the northern imagination, but an immigrant from the hot desert sands of Africa. They catch sight of what seems to be a golden half-moon, rising up ahead of them. Upon closer inspection, one of Yngvar's men realizes what is on the ground:

It was carpeted with dragons. Because they were asleep, he stretched out his spear-shaft towards a particular gold ring, and pulled it towards himself. At once, one of the little dragons woke up and stirred the others close to him, until the jaculus was awake.[8]

This jaculus, the biggest dragon of them all, swoops over the river, full of rage at being woken up, and wipes out a ship and its terrified crew by spewing venom down onto them. The clue to the identity of the jaculus lies in its name, which is no Norse invention. In fact it appears as early as the first century AD, in Pliny the Elder's *Natural History*: 'As concerning serpents, it is generally stated…that the javelin-snake (*iaculus*) hurls itself from the branches of trees, and that serpents are not only formidable to the feet but fly like a missile from a catapult.'[9] This snakelike species also features in the epic poem the *Civil War* (*Bellum civile*), also from the first century AD. It was written by the Roman poet Lucan, describing the civil war between Julius Caesar and Pompey. According to this poem, the jaculus is said to live in the burning African desert with its venomous reptilian friends, bringing horrible deaths to the soldiers marching across the scorching sands. The jaculus does not kill with poison, but by puncturing the victim's skull:

Look—from afar a savage serpent, called by Africa
the jaculus, twists round the trunk of a barren oak and hurls itself
and pierces through the head of Paulus and his temples and escapes.
Poison played no part this time: death came with the wound and took him.[10]

It may well be via Lucan that the jaculus reached medieval Iceland and made its way into the *Saga of Yngvar*. Passages from Lucan's work were paraphrased in Old Norse and combined with translated material from the Roman historian Sallust. The resulting text is called the *Saga of the Romans* (*Rómverja saga*). Here too the jaculus pops up in a descriptive list of all the horrible snakes that live in Africa, 'so fierce that no other snakes dare to go near him'.[11]

There are further complexities regarding the evolution of the jaculus through time and space. Eagle-eyed readers may have noticed that, in Pliny and Lucan's writings, the jaculus was a decidedly snake-like creature that launched itself from trees and hurled itself through the skulls of wretched men. By the time it reaches the *Saga of Yngvar*, though, the jaculus has become an enormous flying dragon sitting on a pile of gold. This is a small part of the creature's broader transformation from Classical desert snake to medieval flying dragon. It made its way into the bestiaries of the Middle Ages via encyclopedic texts such as Isidore of Seville's *Etymologies*:

The *iaculus* is a flying snake. Concerning it Lucan says (*Civil War* 9.720): 'And the flying *iaculi*.' For they spring up into trees, and whenever some animal happens by they throw (*iactare*) themselves on it and kill it, whence they are called *iaculus*.[12]

Building on these traditions, later medieval bestiaries also include the jaculus in their catalogue of marvellous beasts. In the sumptuous gold-leafed Aberdeen Bestiary the jaculus is barely more than a muddy brown stick. It is a singularly unimpressive creature—one can only imagine that it injures its victims by tripping them up—and entirely overshadowed by the image of a coiled boa above, spiralling around itself in an amazing display of boneless gymnastics.[13]

Other specimens of jaculushood are rather cuter; one in a thirteenth-century bestiary from northern France resembles a nervous, well-meaning dog, hovering above the next line of text on his neat little wings.[14] Meanwhile, another bestiary from thirteenth-century England shows a jaculus having just launched itself from a nearby tree to sink its teeth into the neck of a naked man. As in Lucan's poem, the man is crawling through the desert, and his grey, naked body shows that he is in a bad way already. The expression on his face suggests that things have just got a whole lot worse for him.

In most illustrations from medieval bestiaries the jaculus is no longer a darting serpent that launches itself from trees. It has wings and can fly, and looks more like what we would think of as a dragon from a children's cartoon. In the Peterborough Bestiary (*c*.1300–10) now housed in the library at Corpus Christi College in Cambridge, a dog-like, hairy-faced jaculus with wings sits in a tree, staring hungrily at three cheery and oblivious sheep. On the opposite

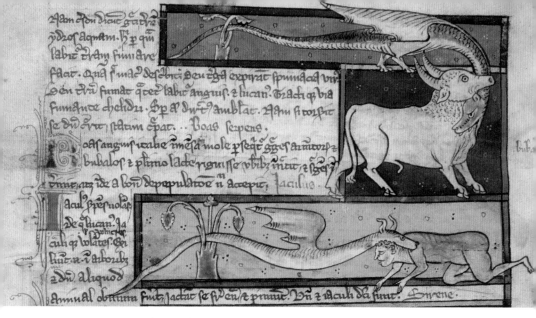

FIGURE 11.3 Jaculus attacking a man in the desert (English bestiary, late 13th century)

FIGURE 11.4 Jaculus perched in a tree eying up dinner, Peterborough Bestiary (c.1300)

side of the page stands a hairy beast of a dragon with an extra head on his tail; the two heads appear to have had an argument, and are no longer speaking. At the bottom of the page is what can only be described as a proto-Gruffalo, lying flat on his back and in the middle of devouring some poor unfortunate winged beast.* Finally, a drawing of the jaculus from a mid-fifteenth-century French bestiary is basically a cartoon version of a dragon, with green, lizard-like skin, a scaly tail, wings, and a stubby snout. He is no longer in the desert and does not even have a tree to perch in; instead, his clawed feet pad over a grassy mound as the stars twinkle in the sky above.

In the *Saga of Yngvar* the jaculus is clearly some kind of dragon rather than a snake; in fact it is also described as a *dreki*, the Norse word for dragon. It does not launch itself from trees, nor does it live in the desert. Instead, it soars over the river on its wings, spewing out enough venom to obliterate shiploads of men. True to Darwinian principles of evolution, the jaculus has evolved over the millennium, from Pliny and Lucan in the Mediterranean to the saga compiler in Iceland.

Marvels and monsters

The jaculus and his posse of teeny tiny dragonlets are not the only monstrous and marvellous inhabitants of the waterways with such learned origins. Yngvar's son Svein comes across a tribe called the 'Cyclopes', who are said to be 'as strong as the fierce animal' (i.e. the lion) and 'as tall as a house or forest'.[15] The name of this race would seem to have some connection to the one-eyed cyclops of Classical mythology: in Book IX of Homer's *Odyssey* Odysseus meets the cyclops Polyphemus, who lives far away with others of his race. The cyclops made its way into European geographical texts of the Middle Ages via Isidore of Seville's *Etymologies*, listed alongside giants and dog-headed men. It also features in two Old Norse encyclopedic manuscripts, in lists of the world's marvellous races. One of these is *Hauksbók*, where the defining feature is his single eye: 'those men known as "Cyclopes" have one eye in the middle of their head.'[16] But in the *Saga of Yngvar* there is no mention of a single eye and no suggestion that the members of this tribe are anything other than very strong,

---

* Upon closer inspection, I managed to ascertain that he does indeed have knobbly knees and turned-out toes, although as yet I have not been able to identify a poisonous wart at the end of his nose.

very tall, and very aggressive. This is mildly confusing, not least because the one thing that everyone knows about the Cyclopes is that they only have a single eye, though clearly this was not the case in medieval Iceland.

Another creature that the Norse meet in this saga is even more confusing: an unknown, unnamed race that blurs the boundaries between the animal and the human, the possible and the impossible. Svein and his men have come ashore to hunt pigs when this happens:

Next they saw a great host coming down to the ships, with one man walking in front holding three apples. He threw one of them up into the air, and it landed right at Svein's feet, followed immediately by another one that landed in the same place. Svein said he didn't want to wait for the third apple: 'There's some sort of devilish power and potent heathenism in this.' He put an arrow to his bow and shot at the man. The arrow struck his nose with a sound like a horn breaking apart, and when he jerked back his head they saw that he had a beak like a bird. Then he screamed loudly and ran back to his men.[17]

No explanation is offered for this bizarre episode; a Norse version of the William Tell story apparently dreamt up by a saga writer high on the medieval equivalent of acid. The actions of these people have moved beyond rational comprehension. As with Norse–Skraeling interactions in Vinland, the geographical logic of the world has started to unravel at the edges.

Or has it? As with the cyclops and the jaculus, it might just be possible to trace this creature back to some sort of Classical model, although to do so requires a great deal of speculation and circular thinking. The saga doesn't give this strange beaky man or his tribe a name, but there is a possible parallel, and it lurks on the upper left-hand corner of the Hereford *mappa mundi*. In north-east Asia a mysterious creature stands by the bank of a river, with the body of a man and the head of some sort of long-beaked bird. He is identified with the words *cicone gentes*, which makes him one of the 'stork people' (*ciconia* is Latin for 'stork').[18] The *Cicones* also appear in the *Iliad* and the *Odyssey*, but with absolutely no sense that they are human–animal hybrids or related to storks in any way. Instead, they are a race that comes from Thrace, in what is now modern Greece. In the *Iliad*, they join the war and ally themselves with the Trojans. In the *Odyssey*, Odysseus and his men slaughter the men of that tribe and take the women captive. Perhaps the name, if not the identity, of this people made it into the Middle Ages, where a false etymological association was created with the Latin word for 'stork'.

There is one more—extremely tenuous—geographical link to be made. On the Hereford *mappa mundi*, this strange stork-man is shown standing by the river Oxus, which flows into the Caspian Sea. Today the Oxus is called the Amu Darya, a major river in Central Asia. Its course has changed over the centuries, but between the thirteenth and sixteenth centuries it did indeed empty into the Caspian Sea, as does the Volga. Perhaps by chance or perhaps by design, if we are to link this member of the *cicone gentes* with the creature described in the *Saga of Yngvar*, the saga author has placed it in roughly the same location. This may well be nothing more than a fluke: two similar sets of beaked-heads-on-human-bodies pulled from a lucky-bag of 'build your own marvellous and monstrous races' and plonked down in roughly the same part of the world. Then again, perhaps it isn't.

So if you ever find yourself passing through Arlanda, take a detour to Terminal 2 on behalf of the far travellers who journeyed east from there a millennium ago. When this runestone—and many others like it—was erected by the dead man's relatives, they had no idea how extraordinary the afterlife of this story would be. Their attempt to preserve their brother's memory and his part in this famous voyage succeeded, at least for a little while. But over the following centuries, as the stone started to crumble and crack under a tangle of bushes and lichen, the story of the expedition was travelling, growing, and evolving.

Stories, wherever they come from and whatever facts lie behind them, are moulded by each new storyteller's mouth, writer's pen, or artist's tool that takes possession of them. But even by normal saga standards, the story of Yngvar's expedition to the east is extraordinarily polyphonic, a tangled chorus of voices resonating faintly across the centuries: the measured voices of the survivors, who returned from the east to tell of their adventures; the grieving voices of relatives who raised runestones to remember lost fathers, husbands, and sons; the theatrical voices of far-travelling seafarers, Swedish nobles, and Icelandic farmers, entertaining companions with dramatic tales of dead heroes; the learned voices of monks and other writers, weaving together strands of oral tales, Christian faith, and bookish learning into sagas—even the bemused voices of modern saga scholars, trying to make sense of the whole messy business. And at the heart of everything, an extraordinary man whose voice we will never hear and whose story we will never really know: Yngvar himself.

· South ·

He had a broad knowledge of southern lands
and wrote a book about them.

Saga of the Sturlungs (Sturlunga saga)

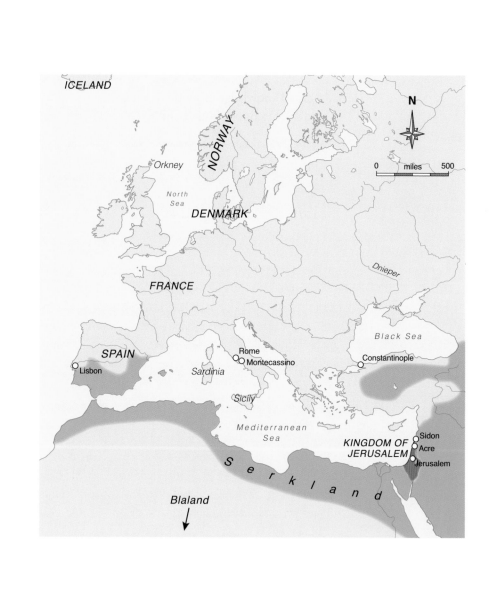

CHAPTER 12

Journey to the Centre of the Earth

From the frozen edge

Imagine medieval Norse travellers bound for Jerusalem, sweating in the heat of an unfamiliar southern sun. Dirty red desert sand gathering in the folds of their clothes. Pious Christian prayers on their lips. Sharpened swords by their sides. The Church of the Holy Sepulchre on the horizon.

Now imagine the many miles that lay behind them, the weeks and months they had travelled to get to this point. Retrace their path back across choppy seas and jagged mountain ranges, through thick forests, rolling fields, and boggy moors, all the way to the cold north where their long journey began. Not in Scandinavia or Iceland, but craggy, wind-blasted Orkney off the northern coast of Scotland, shivering in the black depths of a northern winter. Snow and hail clinging to their hoods. Ungodly curses muttered through frozen lips. Axes strapped to their backs. The dark hump of an ancient barrow looming on the horizon: a perfect shelter from the wet wild night. Grunts and puffs mingling with the whistling wind. The thud of metal on turf. Hands scrabbling through soil and grit. The scraping of stone on stone. A midnight break-in.

Inside the blackness, the mound visitors stoop blindly down the low, narrow passageway. The howling wind outside is muffled, then silenced. Finally, they find that they can straighten up in the darkness. Torches are lit, revealing the high, dry, stone-lined chamber that lies in the middle of the mound. Warm fires are kindled. Booze and food emerge from travelling-bags. As the group

221

FIGURE 12.1 Maeshowe in the snow, Orkney

settles down to wait out the storm, the dusty heat and fierce sunlight of Jerusalem seem vague and far away: an abstract unreality.

The chambered cairn that was hastily transformed into a temporary shelter by the Norse has had many names in the 5,000 years since it was built. We will never know what its Neolithic builders called their sacred burial site, built so the sun shines down the passageway at midwinter and floods the central chamber with light. Today it is known as Maeshowe. To the medieval Norse, it was simply the *Orkhaugr*: 'Orkney Mound.'

We know Norse travellers to Jerusalem found themselves in this unlikeliest of holy places, because they carved runes into the stone walls of the cairn. At the bottom of one of the stone slabs holding up the central chamber, a series of runes reveal that: 'Jerusalem-men broke this mound.'[1] On the other side of the wall, a second inscription—this time written by a woman—tells us that: 'Jerusalem-travellers broke into Orkhaugr. Hlif, the Jarl's housekeeper, carved.'[2] Another member of the party, his mind on his sacred destination, scratched a cross on the rock and signed his name: 'Benedikt made this cross.'[3]

Over the years, other Norse visitors made use of Maeshowe and left runes revealing their names and—occasionally X-rated—deeds. Some are boastful:

FIGURE 12.2 Norse runes inside Maeshowe, which can be translated as: 'Ingibjorg the fair widow. Many a woman has gone stooping in here. A great show-off, Erling.'

'The man who is most skilled in runes west of the ocean carved these runes.' Others tell of hidden hoards spirited away in the dead of night—'Treasure was carried away three nights before they broke this mound'—or hint at more wealth still to be found: 'In the north-west great treasure is hidden.' There are also runes carved by those with a more rugby-team-on-a-night-out mentality: 'Ingibjorg the fair widow—many a woman has gone stooping in here' and 'Thorni fucked, Helgi carved'. Even so, if we believe what the runes tell us, it was the Jerusalem travellers who first broke into the mound, thousands of years after it fell out of first use and memory.* But all the runes tell us is a handful of names. To find out who these travellers were, we have to turn to the sagas.

---

* It's impossible to know when all these runes were carved. They could have been done on one single occasion, but more likely, Maeshowe served different functions for different visitors over the years. A warm, dry place to shelter from a bitter Orcadian winter's night. A foreboding barrow, possibly inhabited by malevolent forces, against which young men could test their courage and hunt for treasure. A 'behind-the-bikesheds' for young couples—looking at you, Thorni and Helgi—wanting a bit of privacy.

The clue to the identity of these Jerusalem travellers is in the second inscription, by Hlif the housekeeper, and the unnamed jarl who was her employer.* Most likely, he was Jarl Rognvald: poet, adventurer, and ruler of Orkney in the mid-twelfth century. We know that Rognvald made a journey to the Holy Land in around 1150, and we have a saga to thank for the information: the *Saga of the Orkney Islanders* (*Orkneyinga saga*). The saga was brought together in the mid-thirteenth century from a patchwork of historical sources only a few decades after the latest events it describes took place. It recounts many generations of Norse men and women who lived in Orkney, which was a Norse colony until the fifteenth century. It includes political wrangles, love affairs, murders, martyrdoms, and outlandish tales such as a cursed battle banner that brings death to the one who carries it.

Jarl Rognvald is a major player in the saga, and several chapters describe his adventures in the Holy Land. Starting with no more than an allusion to a nameless jarl scratched onto the walls of a Neolithic burial mound, we can flesh out a man who fell in love, travelled the world, and composed poetry (including one verse boasting of his many skills: chess, reading, runes, skiing, shooting, rowing, harp-playing, and poetry).†

Rognvald's was a long and dangerous journey south. This was an epic voyage that would take him and his fellow travellers from carving runes in the

---

* A jarl is a Norse nobleman or chieftain; the word is often translated as 'earl'. Or, according to www.urbandictionary.com, 'the flyest guy in a crew, usually the strongest or fittest, and knows how to walk the walk and talk the talk. A downright gangsta.' (Note that this slang definition doesn't convey the hereditary nature of Norse jarldom.)

† The *Saga of the Orkney Islanders* isn't considerate enough to include an episode in which Rognvald and his party break into Maeshowe and have a big rune-carving knees-up before going off to Jerusalem. So admittedly, the picture painted at the start of this chapter takes a little bit of artistic licence. We don't actually know the circumstances under which they entered the mound, although it may well have been stormy, icy weather. In fact, the saga tells us that Rognvald set off for the Holy Land during the winter, but the weather was so treacherous that his ships were driven back to Orkney again and again. It isn't even certain whether they broke into Maeshowe before or after they went to Jerusalem. But rather remarkably, the *Saga of the Orkney Islanders* actually describes a night when men were forced to shelter in Maeshowe during a terrible blizzard, led by another Orcadian jarl. This happened when Rognvald was still abroad in the south, and the saga doesn't say that this other party had to break into the mound (which may or may not suggest that Rognvald had already done the job for them). According to the saga, Jarl Harald sailed to Orkney over Christmas with 100 men. During a snowstorm they sheltered in Maeshowe, and two of them went mad. Anyone who has visited Maeshowe will know that it would have been one hell of a squeeze to fit that many bodies into the burial mound. If Jarl Harald really did get 100 of his men in there, the biggest surprise is that only two of them went mad.

belly of a prehistoric Orcadian barrow to what was, in the minds of medieval Christians, the very centre of the world. They had this information directly from the Bible, for according to the Book of Ezekiel: 'Thus says the Lord God: This is Jerusalem. I have set her in the centre of the nations, with countries all around her.'[4] Jerusalem's centrality is shown in many of the world maps from the Middle Ages, specifically those known as T–O maps. Such maps depict the world as a circle with the three continents inside. The T and the O are the world's waters: the O is the ocean that encircles the world, and the T inside it represents the Mediterranean, the Nile, and the river Don, dividing the three continents. These maps were literally 'oriented', with the east—Asia—in the top half of the map. The west—Europe—was in the bottom-left quarter, while the south—Africa—was in the bottom-right quarter. Jerusalem was often depicted as being in the middle of the world. For instance, in the thirteenth-century Hereford *mappa mundi*, itself a T–O map, the holy city sits splendidly at the centre with its round city walls and towers: a series of circles within circles. Scans of the parchment have even revealed a pinprick under the ink, where a pair of compasses was used to set out Jerusalem in the middle of all things.[5] The same idea was also current in medieval Iceland. In the four-teenth-century manuscript *Stjórn* ('Guidance'), a series of translations from the bible, it is said that Jerusalem is 'the centre and best part of all the lands'.[6] Elsewhere in the fourteenth-century manuscript *Hauksbók*, a map of Jerusa-lem is set out as a cross within the circular city walls, a ground-plan of the city's most famous buildings.

Yet many other things lie at the centre, the eye of the storm not least. Jerusa-lem was—and still is—a hotbed of political unrest, endlessly fought over by different religions and tribes who felt they had a claim to this holiest of cities. Back in 1095, Pope Urban II had made an infamous speech at the Council of Clermont, ordering men from across the Christian world to take up arms and head south to retake what he claimed were Christian lands overrun by the Muslim infidel. His description of what that 'accursed and foreign race' had done to Christians was especially gory:

They desecrate and overthrow the altars. They circumcise the Christians and pour the blood from the circumcision on the altars or in the baptismal fonts. Some they kill in a horrible way by cutting open the abdomen, taking out a part of the entrails and tying them to a stake; they then beat them and compel them to walk until all their entrails are drawn out and they fall to the ground. Some they use as targets for their arrows.

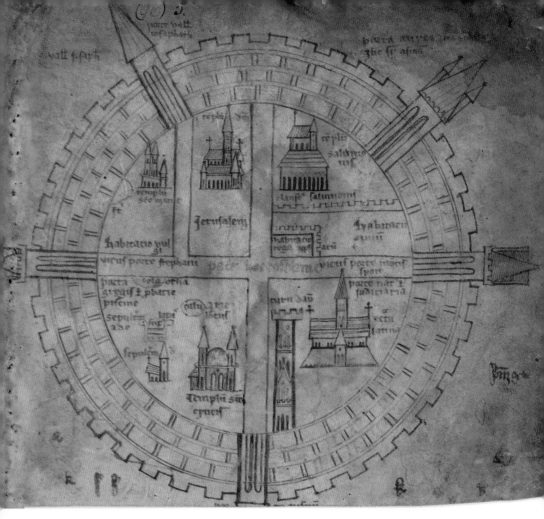

FIGURE 12.3 Map of Jerusalem from the Icelandic manuscript *Hauksbók* (c.1290–1360)

They compel some to stretch out their necks, and then they try to see whether they can cut off their heads with one stroke of the sword. It is better to say nothing of their horrible treatment of the women.[7]

According to accounts of the speech, the assembled crowd shouted in response, *Deus vult!*—'God wills it!'—which became the rallying cry of the (un)holy army as they set off. Tens of thousands marched south, in what is known today as the First Crusade. Initially, their aim was to help the Byzantines, who were being attacked by the Muslim Turks. But their ultimate goal was to recapture Jerusalem, a royal city 'held captive by her enemies, and made pagan by those who know not God', according to Urban II. In 1099—after many battles, sieges, and attacks on ethnic minorities as the disorderly rabble swept through Europe and into the Middle East—Jerusalem was captured by the crusaders. Soon afterwards the Kingdom of Jerusalem was established, ruled by King Baldwin, one of the French leaders of the crusade.

All this was history to Rognvald too. By the time he reached Jerusalem, in the early 1150s, the crusader states had reached their zenith. It was only in the following decades that the neighbouring Muslims began to reclaim territory from the Christian invaders, and not until 1187 that Jerusalem itself would fall to Saladin. The whole messy business was still rumbling on by the time the sagas started to be written down in the mid-thirteenth century, by which time what little Scandinavian involvement there had been was a very distant memory. Even so, the sagas offer us a unique window onto this bloody medieval phenomenon from the perspective of the northernmost lands to participate, albeit from their usual chronological distance. Here, war and peace are bound together inextricably, and it soon becomes clear that the veins of the Christian Norsemen still run with the blood of their pagan viking forebears.

War and peace

Today we tend to distinguish between pious pilgrims and combative crusaders. But as far as the crusaders themselves were concerned, they were merely armed pilgrims, as Pope Urban II's speech implies. The word 'crusade' wasn't used at all until several centuries later. Of course, there were plenty of pilgrims who simply wanted to go on straightforward pilgrimages, either to Rome or the Holy Land, and we will come back to them later on. But armed pilgrims saw no moral difficulty in combining religiously sanctioned war with an excursion to the lands where Jesus himself once walked.* In any case, crusades tended to turn into a bloody free-for-all when the chips were down and the masses started to run out of food. As the crusade historian Christopher Tyerman explains: 'Pilgrimage and crusade were fused together. *Crucesignati* ['cross bearers' or 'those marked with a cross'] bore the staff and satchel of the pilgrim: pilgrims bore crosses and carried arms.'[8]

---

* These blurred semantics continue beyond the Middle Ages. Shakespeare created a Henry IV obsessed by the idea of going on pilgrimage to the Holy Land to atone for the death of Richard II. But Henry's imagined pilgrimage is filled with crusading fire. He plans 'To chase those pagans in those holy fields / Over whose acres walk'd those blessed feet / Which fourteen hundred years ago were nail'd / For our advantage on the bitter cross' (*The First Part of King Henry the Fourth*, I. i. 22–5).

Pope Urban made his notorious speech in 1095, by which time the inhabitants of the Nordic lands—once the scourge of monasteries across Western Europe—had been brought into the Christian fold. Even so, what many Norsemen got up to on their journeys to the south was little more than religiously sanctioned viking-style looting and murder. It was simply that the tables had turned, and it was now the heathens who were fair game rather than Christians: 'Saracens, whom we call Mohammed's heretics', as the *Saga of the Orkney Islanders* describes them.[9] This is made abundantly clear in saga accounts of expeditions to the Holy Land, where the distinction between pilgrimage and crusade fades to a bloody blur.

Today, visitors to Kirkwall, the city in Orkney, can hardly miss St Magnus Cathedral: an elegant Romanesque creation of red sandstone that stretches up into the wide, open sky. This is a Norse cathedral, which came to be built through a combination of bloody murder and spiritual piety. According to the *Saga of the Orkney Islanders*, it was Rognvald himself who had the cathedral built in 1137 in honour of his martyred uncle Magnus, but his motivations were more politically savvy than devout. Jarl Magnus of Orkney had been executed on the Orcadian island of Egilsay in around 1116. According to the saga, Rognvald was advised to build a magnificent cathedral and dedicate it to his uncle, to curry favour with the islanders. He duly became Jarl of Orkney and today his bones lie in the cathedral, as much a testament to his political ruthlessness as to his Christian devotion.

Likewise, spiritual piety isn't high on Rognvald's list of motivations when he decides to go to Jerusalem. In the saga, it is mooted as a way for the jarl to bump himself up the hierarchical ladder, for his friend tells him:

It seems strange to me, jarl, that you don't want to go to the Holy Land and have more than tales of what is told of there. It is the most fitting place for men of ability like you, and you'll be highly respected if you mix with high-born men.[10]

What follows reads rather like a gap year for wealthy students, featuring holiday romances, sightseeing, foreign tummy-bugs, and charitable acts on behalf of the locals. There are also plenty of rowdy, booze-filled nights out, which

FIGURE 12.4 Stained-glass window depicting Rognvald the Crusader in Lerwick Town Hall, Shetland (19th century)

probably irritated those living in the area just as much as today. In Greece, one man comes a cropper after a heavy night on the town. As the saga puts it, 'Erling slipped off the quay and down into the mud below, and his men had to jump after him, drag him back up, and take all his clothes off.'[11]

Other parts of the journey are darker and more violent, and the men who once mucked around in a dark burial mound on Orkney become armed killers with a dangerous god on their side. The fiercest Muslim–Christian clash is a brutal sea battle off the coast of Sardinia. As a ship materializes through the sea mist, the Norse plan their response with the sort of shaky theological reasoning and half-baked generosity that justifies any amount of ethnic cleansing. If the ship is carrying Christian merchants, then everyone will go on their way peacefully, but if they're heathen, 'then almighty God in his mercy will grant us victory over them, and whatever booty we pick up there, we'll give a fiftieth of the money to the poor!'[12] The poetry that intersperses the prose description of the battle is couched in the language of warmongering crusaders, not peaceful pilgrims:

> There we reddened our weapons
> —eternal God willed it—
> with the blood of the people:
> black corpses fell on the deck.[13]

Having butchered the sailors, identified as ethnically other by their black skin (translated as 'black', but in the original *blá*, that same strange blue-black colour), the Norse set fire to the ship and leave it to sink into the sea in flames and smoke. From there they sail on towards the centre of the world, their keels churning up a salty, bloody, bawdy wake behind them. *Deus vult.*

Battle-happy kings

Rognvald wasn't the first Norseman to journey south to the Holy Land, and when he set off he may well have had the specific example of a famous figure in mind. His name was Sigurd Magnusson, nicknamed 'Jerusalem-Farer' and king of Norway from 1103 to 1130. If Rognvald needed a swashbuckling hero to imitate as he journeyed south, then this was the man. Sigurd arrived in Jerusalem in 1110, a decade after the Kingdom of Jerusalem had been established, in the aftermath of one of the most dramatic, politically inflammatory moments in the country's perpetually dramatic, politically inflamed history. Sigurd appears in an account called *A History of the Expedition to Jerusalem* (*Historia Hierosolymitana*), written by King Baldwin's personal chaplain Fulcher of Chartres. He was only 19 when he arrived, but according to Fulcher's description he was no spotty, awkward teenager, despite his tender years. Rather, he was a natural-born leader: 'a very handsome youth', with a fleet of fifty-five ships.[14]

Sigurd's life, including his journey to the Holy Land, is described in several Kings' Sagas, including versions in *Morkinskinna* and *Heimskringla*. Once again, Christian piety and mass genocide are surprisingly easy bedfellows, and the king and his men cut a bloody swathe through every town and city they visit. Sigurd is a 'battle-happy king', as one verse describes him, with a gruesome litany of casual homicide and wholesale looting that begins in northern Spain.[15] When their hosts run out of food to give them over the winter, Sigurd and his men march on the castle, seize food and booty, and sail away. Things only get worse when they reach parts of the country occupied by Muslims, where they battle pirates, besiege castles, and butcher so many people that whole towns are left deserted. If the inhabitants agree to convert to Christianity, they are usually spared. If they refuse then they are slaughtered, wiped out in a worthy Christian cause.

Sigurd seems far more concerned with gaining 'great fame and fortune' than saving souls, as he repeatedly reminds his men.[16] Poetry intersperses descriptions of the carnage, said to have been composed by court poets to immortalize the king's glorious achievements. In these verses the extent of the bloodshed emerges; these are viking wolves in Christian sheep's clothing. The hungry 'corpse-gull'—a poetic term for a raven or other carrion bird—flies down to pick at the newly made wounds of fallen men, typical of the 'beasts of battle' imagery that runs throughout so much Germanic heroic literature:

> You dared redden the sword's edge
> east of the Straits of Gibraltar
> —God helped you—
> the corpse-gull flew to fresh wounds.[17]

As he moves towards the holy centre of the world, the king cleanses the lands of heathen evil, whilst, conveniently, accumulating a vast amount of loot on the way. Over the course of a couple of pages of the saga Sigurd makes five booty calls—Norse style—culminating in the Jerusalem-farers picking up 'the most booty that they had taken anywhere on their journey'.[18] As with Rognvald, status and material goods are far worthier prizes for Sigurd than any amount of spiritual wealth, although in Jerusalem itself he manages to combine the two, receiving many holy relics from King Baldwin, including a piece of the True Cross. Later, he uses his expedition to taunt his brother as they argue, any semblance of piety forgotten as he brags:

I travelled to the river Jordan via Apulia, and I didn't see you there. I won eight battles, and you fought in none of them. I travelled to the Lord's sepulchre, and I didn't see you there. I entered the river just as our Lord did and swam across it, but I didn't see you there. I tied a knot for you, and it's still there waiting for you. I captured the town of Sidon with the king of Jerusalem, and we didn't have your help or advice.[19]

In contrast to the journey south, Jerusalem, the eye of the storm itself, is portrayed in the sagas as a place of peaceful pilgrimage, where the visiting Norsemen swim in the river Jordan, cleanse themselves of sin, and pick up a few holy relics to bring home as souvenirs. But not all is as it seems. Sigurd has dirty work to do in the aftermath of the crusade, riding by the side of King Baldwin to capture and loot the Muslim city of Sidon. Sigurd may be a Christian king, but as before the verses that sing his praises are thick with traditional Norse poetic images. Sigurd brings subjugation and bloody death, making fresh corpses for the scavenging she-wolf—the 'bitch of wounds'—to pick at. The same verse also implies that he surpassed or even supplanted Baldwin through his battle prowess, before magnanimously allowing him to rule again:

> Feeder of the bitch of wounds,
> you captured the heathen city with force
> but graciously gave it away again;
> you fought each battle with bravery.[20]

When Rognvald arrives in the Holy Land a few decades later, he too takes a dip in the river Jordan, like Sigurd before him. Here the saga seems to be looking back to Sigurd, the original Jerusalem-farer, as a model of behaviour for Rognvald to follow. But Rognvald goes one better than Sigurd and uses the opportunity to compose poetry as he swims, in which images of peaceful pilgrimage abound:

> A cross hangs on this poet's breast,
> a palm between his shoulders,

> anger shall be laid aside,
> travellers press forward up the slopes.[21]

Yet once again, peace and war go hand in hand. Another of his verses hints at darker, bloodier deeds:

> I think that it will seem
> a long way to travel
> to all stay-at-homes;
> warm blood fell on the wide plain.[22]

Whose warm blood this is or how it came to be spilled is not expanded on in the prose. Perhaps it was shed during recent holy wars. Alternatively, this could be a less politically loaded reference to Christ's passion. Either way, as these far-travelling Norsemen bathe peacefully in the Jordan, bloody undercurrents flow beneath.

Sigurd and Rognvald are the sort of action-hero travellers who might star in whatever epic historical/fantasy TV series happened to be flavour of the month. But not all southbound saga travellers had their sights set on religious war. Take Erik the Good, king of Denmark from 1095 to 1103, whose life is described in the *Saga of Knut's Descendants*. According to the saga, Erik was well nicknamed, certainly compared to some of the more unsavoury Danish kings (who had suitably colourful nicknames such as 'Forkbeard', 'Hunger', and 'Scorcher'). His is the most genuinely pious—or at any rate, least blood-thirsty—of all royal journeys to Jerusalem, but even so the saga includes a verse that describes him in traditionally warlike terms. He is the 'army-bold king', the 'troubler of chieftains', setting out from the north and journeying south to heal his soul's wounds. These seem to be simply conventional sentiments typical of a royal pilgrim (or at least there is no elaboration on what dastardly deeds he might be atoning for):

> It shall be illuminated,
> how the army-bold king was eager
> to heal his innermost wounds.
> The troubler-of-chieftains travelled from the north
> with a hard host to heal his soul.
> The ruler prepared himself for a higher world.
> He travelled out to explore the city of Jerusalem,
> secured with peace; the king wished to win an illustrious life.[23]

It's probably just as well that Erik was already so holy, because he never made it as far as Jerusalem, dying on the way. Before that, the saga takes pains to note that he was honoured everywhere he went: priests put on holy processions for him and the emperor of Byzantium showered him with gold, clothes, and warships. However holy Erik might have been, he was still a king, and for kings, pilgrimage was always an exercise in prestige as well as piety.

Due south

As the journeys made by Sigurd, Rognvald, and Erik show, the voyage to the Holy Land was long, dangerous, and expensive, and so mainly undertaken by those with very heavy wallets. Even then, they had to loot and accept gifts as they made their way towards their final destination. So in purely economic terms, it makes sense that in the sagas there are many more pilgrimages to Rome than to distant Jerusalem, not 'armed pilgrimages' but straightforward pilgrimages during which travellers visit holy places and cleanse their souls. Historically, there is a good deal of evidence for Nordic pilgrimages. In a fraternity book listing the many thousands of pilgrims who stopped off at the south German monastery of Reichenau in the eleventh and twelfth centuries, there are approximately 600 Scandinavian names. Right at the end, squashed into the margin, are the names of a handful of Icelandic travellers, both men and women, who visited on their pilgrimage.[24]

In Norse texts, a pilgrimage to Rome was specifically called a *suðrferð*—literally, a 'journey south'—and there are plenty of these in the sagas. But quantity doesn't mean quality. Most of the accounts of pilgrimages to Rome are perfunctory at best, with little sense of space or place. Rather than follow the pilgrims to Rome and describe what they got up to, the saga narratives simply state that they went there and came back (or not, as the case may be). Sometimes it's a case of tying up loose ends as the character reaches the end of their story and their life. Several female saga characters go on pilgrimage to Rome in this way, such as in the *Saga of the Greenlanders*, where 'Gudrid travelled abroad, made a pilgrimage south, and came back afterwards to her son Snorri's farm'.[25] In the *Saga of Gisli Sursson* (*Gísla saga Súrssonar*), a tale of tragic outlawry and divided family loyalties, the womenfolk up sticks from Iceland after the men have butchered each other in a protracted and complicated feud.

The saga notes that the women 'travelled to Hedeby in Denmark, converted to Christianity, and went south on pilgrimage'. Quite reasonably, given the angst and bloodshed the women had to put up with, the saga concludes pointedly: 'they never came back.'[26]

Elsewhere, the descriptions are still brief, with little sense of place but various goals: penance, prestige, and personal transformation. At the end of the gory feud-fest that is the *Saga of Burnt-Njal* (*Brennu-Njáls saga*), two of the chief protagonists make pilgrimages to Rome in order to atone for bloody sins committed under dark northern skies. Of one, we are simply told:

From there, Flosi travelled south over the sea and then began his pilgrimage. He didn't stop going south until he came to Rome. There he received such great honour that he was given absolution from the Pope himself, and he donated lots of money for that.[27]

His former enemy's pilgrimage is even briefer: all we are told is that he starts off in Normandy, walks south, receives absolution, and returns home. In the *Saga of the Orkney Islanders*, several of the Orcadian jarls go on pilgrimage to Rome: a handy 'get out of jail free' card that enables them to murder their rivals on their way up the greasy political pole and atone for their sins afterwards.

Even longer pilgrimage narratives involving kings are sparing with information. King Knut—the same man who ruled England from 1016 to 1035— also sets out to go 'south to Rome', as described in the *Saga of Knut's Descendants*.[28] The account focuses on his hefty expenses bill as a way of highlighting his Christian piety:

King Knut set out on his journey abroad and travelled south to Rome, and his expenses on that journey were so enormous that no man could calculate the cost in marks and scarcely in pounds either.... While Knut was on the way to Rome, no man needed to beg for food if they met him, because he gave them all plenty of money to live on.[29]

The city of Rome itself is not even a sketchy outline in this pilgrimage account, and as soon as King Knut returns to England he dies, thus bringing his life to a suitably pious conclusion. Later in the same saga we read about King Erik the Good's pilgrimage to Rome (which he actually manages to complete, unlike his later trip to Jerusalem). There is no sense of Rome as a place; all we are given is the information that Erik made friends in high places and gave lots of money to monasteries. There is also a touch of high politics, when he meets the Pope and persuades him to create an archbishopric in Denmark, but these facts are conveyed without any sense of immediacy, drama, or physical place. The chapter

ends with the information that 'he became very famous because of this journey', once again emphasizing that this is as much about prestige as religion.[30]

Rough guide to Rome

For a medieval Nordic pilgrim arriving all the way from the chilly north,
Rome must have been intimidatingly impressive: a hot, sprawling warren of
dirty, busy streets bustling with people, elegant stone churches stuffed with
art, treasures, and relics, and the towering, crumbling ruins of a former world
superpower around every corner. But medieval Rome was not the global
heavyweight that ancient Rome had been. The Western Roman Empire had
crumbled centuries earlier, and the Renaissance was still a long way off. Rome's
population had been dwindling for some time, along with its importance on
the international stage. No longer the political, economic, or cultural centre of
action, it had become a city of faded glories, with its power largely dissipated to
important international trade centres such as Venice and Ravenna. Still, what
Rome had in spades was religion, and this became a chief commodity.

Since the sagas don't paint a vibrant picture of Rome for us, we need to turn
our attention elsewhere if we want to imagine the places that these northern
pilgrims visited and the sights they saw. Luckily, throughout the Middle Ages
many pilgrimage guides to Rome and Jerusalem were written all over Europe.
A tiny number were even written in Iceland, although not all survive today.
Sometimes a saga reference is all we have to go on. The *Saga of the Sturlungs*
(*Sturlunga saga*) is our main source for twelfth- and thirteenth-century Icelandic political history, mostly charting a series of powerful, ruthless families
intent on wiping each other out and burning down each other's farmhouses.
According to part of this saga, Gizur Hallsson (d. 1206), a scholar, historian,
and head of one of these powerful families, composed such a guide to Rome,
with a Latin title that means 'The Flower of Pilgrimage':*

He often travelled abroad and was better received in Rome than any other Icelander
before him because of his education and prowess. He had a broad knowledge of southern lands and wrote a book about them, which is called *Flos peregrinationis*.[31]

---

* Incidentally, this is the same Gizur who is mentioned in the *Saga of Yngvar the Far Traveller* as
one of the men that the monk Odd wrote to about his sources for the saga. Sometimes it's a very
small world, particularly in medieval Iceland.

Unfortunately, Gizur's text has been lost in the mists of time, but another itinerary from medieval Iceland survives, called *Itinerary and List of Cities* (*Leiðarvísir ok Borgarskipan*). This is a double pilgrimage route that covers both Rome and Jerusalem, taking us from Iceland to Denmark, and then through Germany and Switzerland, across the Alps, and down Italy to Rome. Having explored the holy sites and main tourist attractions of the Eternal City, the itinerary continues through southern Italy, Sicily, and Greece, before reaching Acre and the Holy Land.[32]

This itinerary is rather like the medieval equivalent of a travel guide: a sort of *Rough Guide to Pilgrimages* with details of travel practicalities, places to stay, and local colour apparently supplied by a traveller who had made the pilgrimage himself. The traveller in question is usually thought to be a twelfth-century Icelander called Abbot Nikulas. Three Icelandic annals record that he returned from abroad in 1154; this may have been the pilgrimage that formed the basis of his itinerary, although we don't know for certain. The only complete version of his itinerary that survives is in a manuscript from 1387 (AM 194 8vo), written more than two centuries after Nikulas' death. In the intervening years, extra details seem to have been added to the itinerary, including information that Nikulas couldn't have possibly known because it only happened later.[33] Just like modern *Rough Guides* or *Lonely Planets*, which are updated in subsequent editions, new information seems to have been added to this Icelandic itinerary over the years, perhaps supplied by later pilgrims or new written sources as they became available in Iceland.

This is a northerner's impression of the south, not only including place-names, holy sites, and distances but also references to Germanic legends (such as the place where Sigurd apparently slew the dragon Fafnir) and Norse heroes (such as the town in Switzerland claimed to have been destroyed by the sons of Ragnar Hairy-Breeches). The author is interested in natural history, and compares Sicily's volcanic fire and boiling water to the sort found in Iceland. He also has an opinion on where the prettiest ladies can be found (Siena, if you're curious).

Unlike the meagre saga accounts of pilgrimages to Rome, this guide allows us to travel in our minds as medieval northern pilgrims would have done, to stately patriarchal churches, dank early Christian catacombs, and crumbling Roman bath-houses. Walking around Rome today is a rather different experience—frenetic mopeds try to take you out every time you step onto a zebra-crossing, car horns blare the millisecond the traffic lights turn from red to green—but almost everything described in the *Itinerary* still stands, in one form or another. Modern pilgrims can still trace the routes described, using the guide just as it was intended.

Cosmetically at least, many of the major churches of Rome that Nikulas visited look rather different today, altered and added to over the centuries as fires, earthquakes, papal whims, and other suitably apocalyptic events dictated. But it doesn't take much rooting around before a modern visitor spots features that Nikulas and other medieval pilgrims of his time would have seen. Take the Basilica di Santa Maria Maggiore, where, according to the *Itinerary*, the pope had to sing mass on both Christmas Day and on Easter Sunday. Today this basilica stands in a piazza a few blocks behind Roma Termini, Rome's central and most chaotic railway station. Between the station and Santa Maria, a modern pilgrim will encounter chestnut-sellers, gaudy bag shops, stalls full of tourist tat, and commuters running for trains. But hurry up the front steps—dodge the man hawking extendable camera sticks and umbrellas—and dive through the front door, into a well of silence and the lingering musty sweetness of incense. The church remains largely as it would have been for medieval pilgrims, its open, almost cavernous nave supported by Athenian marble columns carved in the first centuries AD. In the triumphal arch and nave are fifth-century mosaics depicting scenes from the Old and New Testaments, almost impossibly detailed and vivid, as fresh as though they had been made last week rather than 1,600 years ago: the Annunciation, with Mary enthroned like a royal princess as the angel Gabriel soars across a multicoloured sunset; a worried-looking Joseph having a diplomatic chat with an angel sent to give him the lowdown; the Magi in their high hats and pointy yellow shoes, clothed in tunics of blue, green, and amber, toned calf-muscles rippling, bejewelled from head to toe like the pearly kings of London's East End; a crowd of women with wild, tangled hair, clutching their babies close to their breasts as anxious guards approach on Herod's orders; the walled city of Jerusalem studded with sapphires, emeralds, and pearls like a medieval reliquary, with a herd of confused, solemn sheep in the foreground. Medieval pilgrims all the way from Iceland would have seen nothing like it before in their lives.

Other churches mentioned in the *Itinerary* still hide treasures that medieval pilgrims would have gazed upon. The Basilica di Santi Giovanni e Paolo, looking down the hill towards the Colosseum, hasn't had much luck over the centuries. First it was damaged when Alaric I, king of the Visigoths, sacked Rome

FIGURE 12.5 Mosaics from Santa Maria Maggiore, Rome

in 410. The Normans arrived to have another go at it in 1084. After the second sacking a bell tower was added, the same high, rectangular belfry that can still be seen looming above the church. Today large, decorative coloured discs run the whole height of the bell tower, painted in purples and greens. But around the time when Nikulas and his fellow pilgrims were in Rome, glossy, brightly coloured pottery basins and plates would have been mounted on the belfry façades, most from the Islamic world and a few from Byzantium. The museum round the side of the church has rows and rows of these bowls on display, some decorated in metallic lustre typical of Iraqi ceramics, hardly cracked or discoloured despite the passing centuries. They are painted in turquoises, violets, and blues shimmering under green copper glazing, some with floral swirls, others with etchings of birds, and others with Arabic writing looping around the rim. The sentiments are of the type that might be found on a cheap, last-minute souvenir: cheery messages such as *al-yumn*, 'good luck!' and *as-salàma*, 'good health!'

Having taken in several more churches and basilicas and a spot of Roman sightseeing at the Diocletian Baths, we leave Rome bound for the Holy Land. The *Itinerary* takes us through southern Italy via the great monastery at Montecassino and down to the Mediterranean. We pass a pilgrimage hostel endowed by King Erik the Good so that every Norse traveller who came this way could drink free wine. In the Holy Land itself we get a whistle-stop tour of the must-see sites: Nazareth, where the angel Gabriel visited Mary; Jerusalem, with its miraculous signs of Christ's passion; the Church of the Holy Sepulchre; and Bethlehem where Christ was born.

All this is fairly standard stuff. But right at the end of the section on the Holy Land, just before we turn for home, Nikulas pauses to tell us: 'Out by the Jordan, if a man lies on his back on flat ground and bends his knee up with his clenched fist on top, then raises his thumb from his fist, then the pole star can be seen above it there, exactly that high but no higher.'[34] This is a touchingly personal detail with no known parallel in any other medieval text. Sagas may have reported that King Sigurd and Jarl Rognvald swam in the Jordan, but this is very different. Finally, we have a sense of actually *being* there. From a distance of nearly 900 years, suddenly we are lying by the river Jordan with a medieval Norse pilgrim in a far-off southern land, gazing up at the night sky, raising his arm and giving his northern homeland the thumbs up.

Despite the religious and historical weight of Rome and the Holy Land, prospects for travellers were limited. Jerusalem was an intermittent battleground, and Rome was, relatively speaking, down on its luck. For those looking for exciting commerce, employment, and travel opportunities there was a far more lucrative, bustling city to the east. Far travellers from Nordic lands were never ones to turn down opportunities for adventures and moneymaking. Perhaps this is why, then, in the sagas, Rome is something of a dowdy neighbour to another city that fizzes with energy and sparkles with political intrigue. The Norse called it *Miklagarðr*—the Big City.

CHAPTER 13

Sailing to Byzantium

What is past

The Norse took a practical approach to naming the world. Up north, *Finnmǫrk* was home to the *Finnar* or Sámi. Out west, vines grew in *Vínland*. In the Russian east, *Garðaríki*—the Kingdom of Cities—was a series of towns and trade outposts along the rivers. So when the Norse called somewhere *Miklagarðr*—the Big City—you can be pretty sure it was big, in all senses of the word.

For the Norse, this Big City was Constantinople. Today we know it as Istanbul, a bustling, international hub of trade, communication, and politics, strategically positioned between East and West. In this cultural melting-pot, a five-minute car or metro ride across the Bosphorus takes you from Europe to Asia. From the minarets of the city's thousands of mosques, calls to prayers ring out across the rooftops. From the skyscrapers of the financial district, electronic billions churn out across the world. Spanning the continents, home to more people than any other city in Europe or the Middle East, the importance of this great urban centre can hardly be underestimated. It's hard to believe that in the past it was even more powerful. In fact, for many centuries it was the capital of one of the greatest civilizations on earth.

Constantinople began life as a Greek colony called Byzantium, founded in the seventh century BC. Several hundred years later in AD 330, the Roman emperor Constantine moved his capital east from Rome and renamed the city after himself, and so it became 'Constantinople'. Today we think of Constantinople as the capital of the Byzantine Empire, and that term will also be used here, but at the time it was simply considered to be the continuation of the Roman Empire in the east, with Constantinople the heir to Rome.*

During the fifth century, the foundations of the Western Roman Empire trembled and cracked under the force of bloody political struggles, barbarian invasions, and local revolts. Meanwhile, as Rome crumbled, Constantinople prospered. For most of the Middle Ages, the Byzantine Empire was an international force to be reckoned with, influencing and even dominating Europe politically, militarily, economically, and culturally.

All major civilizations experience periods of acute crisis, and Byzantium was no exception. Constantinople's geographical position was one of its great strengths, but it also meant that it was sandwiched between potential enemies in both the East and the West. In 1071, at the Battle of Manzikert, the Turks trounced the Byzantine army and captured the emperor. Byzantine authority was weakened in Anatolia and Armenia as the Turks gained a foothold in the region, and it took several decades for stability to be restored. But there was worse to come, for in 1204 the crusaders paid Constantinople a visit. They brutally sacked the city, ripped it apart, carried off its treasures, and assumed political control. For several decades the city limped on, economically broken, its population diminished and its buildings decaying. In 1261 it was retaken by Emperor Michael VIII, but the rot had already set in. By the time the sagas came to be written down they were operating on their usual time-lag, looking back to a past that no longer existed. The golden age of Constantinople was over.

Yet while it prospered, medieval Constantinople was the place to be for ambitious go-getters from all corners of the world. It was a dazzling metropolis packed with mercenaries, travellers, and traders, all looking for opportunities for adventure, employment, and money-making. Few things were more embedded in the Norse DNA than the desire for adventure, excitement, and a tidy profit. Over the centuries many Norse travellers made their way to the Big City, first to raid, then to trade, and then to work as mercenaries for the emperor himself.

This is the Constantinople immortalized in the sagas, an idealized, sumptuous city of wealth, power, religion, and learning, visited by Norse kings and adventuring heroes. These include many of the names encountered in previous chapters: King Sigurd the Jerusalem-Farer, King Erik the Good, Jarl Rognvald of Orkney, and King Harald Hardrada. Some of them simply passed through and

---

* Even when the Turks captured much of its territory in the eleventh century, they referred to the new state as the Sultanate of Rum (i.e. Romans).

witnessed its splendour. Others built illustrious careers and lives far from their northern homelands. If the sagas depict Rome as a sober, almost invisible location where individuals travel for the health of their souls, and Jerusalem as the blood-tinged centre of Christendom, then Constantinople is a glossy Hollywood film-set, built to a larger-than-life scale and painted in bright, bold colours. The Big City is the imaginative heart of the world, an international hub of excitement and adventure, glittering with gold and swathed in silks.

God's holy fire

From Greek settlers to Roman emperors to Ottoman Turks to republican revolutionaries, everyone has always wanted a piece of this great city. The Norse were no exception. Their connections to Constantinople went back a long way, overland through Russia and the vast waterways of the east. Just as the Rus sailed down the Volga and attacked the rich Muslim lands around the Caspian Sea, so they navigated the wild rapids of the Dnieper, which flowed from the Russian steppes into the Black Sea. On the far side of the Black Sea lay Constantinople, a prize too juicy and too tempting to ignore.

Predictably, relations between the sophisticated southerners and the rough, tough northerners didn't get off to the best of starts. In June 860 the Rus attacked Constantinople for the first time, drawn to its wealth like hairy, bloodthirsty flies to honey. According to the *Russian Primary Chronicle*—though we can't be certain whether this is true or not—they were led by Askold and Dir, or to give them their Norse names, *Hǫskuldr* and *Dyri*. Their timing was perfect. The city was unprepared and undefended, with the emperor and his army away on a campaign. Without warning, the Bosphorus was suddenly thick with ships and boats from across the sea, around 200 vessels in all, capable of carrying many thousands of men. As the Rus besieged the city walls, Patriarch Photius delivered a sermon in the great basilica of Hagia Sophia, bewailing the city's terrible fate:

What is this? What is this grievous and heavy blow and wrath? Why has this dreadful bolt fallen on us out of the farthest north? What clouds compacted of woes and condemnation have violently collided to force out this irresistible lightning upon us? Why has this thick, sudden hail-storm of barbarians burst forth?[1]

Photius' sermon has echoes of the letters written in the aftermath of the raids on Lindisfarne and north-east England, shock and horror mingling with a sneaking fear that the raiders from the north were God's punishment for sinful deeds:

For this reason the Lord hath opened his treasury and brought forth the weapons of his anger. For this reason a people has crept down from the north, as if it were attacking another Jerusalem, and nations have been stirred up from the end of earth, holding bow and spear; the people is fierce and has no mercy; its voice is as the roaring sea.[2]

This time the inhabitants of Constantinople were lucky. After a couple of months the ships departed. But further attacks were to come. As the tenth century dawned, another army of Rus invaders—together with a whole host of other pagan peoples from the region—descended on Constantinople and ran riot, slaughtering its inhabitants and burning its palaces and churches.

The Byzantine response was remarkably diplomatic and politically astute. They made favourable trade-pacts with their attackers, offering legitimate Rus merchants a six-month supply of bread, meat, fish, fruit, and baths whenever they needed them (perhaps the last of these was a strong hint rather than a kindly offer, given the communal gobbing-and-spitting washing-bowl that had so horrified the Arab diplomats). They were also given supplies for the return journey, presumably in case they were tempted to outstay their welcome. A copy of this treaty is included in the *Russian Primary Chronicle*, with the extremely Norse names of Rus representatives who were present: 'Karl, Ingjald, Farulf, Vermund, Hrollaf, Gunnar, Harold, Karni, Frithleif, Hroarr, Angantyr, Throand, Laithulf, Fast, Steinvith.'[3]

No country for old men

Over time, links between the sophisticated Byzantines and their northern neighbours grew stronger. Eventually the Norsemen would come to form the core of the formidable fighting unit that served as the Byzantine emperors' personal bodyguard. This elite troop was known as the Varangian Guard. Along with 'Rus', the word 'Varangian' was used by Greek- and Arabic-speakers to describe Scandinavians operating in the region. Like 'Rus', the word 'Varangian' also had probable Norse origins, from *vár*, meaning 'pledge' or 'oath'. Initially, it likely referred to Norse traders and adventurers who came together on the waterways and swore allegiance to each other.

Not all members of the Varangian Guard were Norsemen, but contemporary descriptions depict these men as distinctly northern, axe-wielding barbarians. A tenth-century Syrian writer called Harun ibn Yahya described an imperial procession marching through Constantinople, on streets strewn with aromatic plants and green leaves.* Between the 10,000 boys in green brocade and the 5,000 eunuchs in white silk and holding golden crosses were '10,000 servants wearing clothes of brocade of the colour of the blue sky; in their hands they [held] axes covered in gold'.[4]

Axes and similar weapons are also the defining feature of the Varangian Guard in a mid-twelfth-century text called the *Alexiad*, a history of the Byzantine Empire and a biography of Emperor Alexius I (r. 1081–1118). The author of this account had a unique fly-on-the-wall perspective of life in the imperial palace, because she was Anna Comnena, the emperor's daughter. Anna mentions the Varangian Guard on several occasions, describing them as: 'the Varangians from Thule (by these I mean the axe-bearing barbarians)'.[5]

Images of axe-wielding Varangian Guardsmen also feature in the twelfth-century Skylitzes manuscript, a Byzantine historical text packed with hundreds of illustrations. One of these depicts the death of Emperor Leo V, who was assassinated in 820. Even though there was in fact no Varangian Guard at the time of Leo V's death, the picture nevertheless shows a dozen or so Varangian Guardsmen, heavily armoured in gold chainmail and helmets, holding scarlet shields and brandishing lethal axes, peeping over the rooftops of the palace and conferring anxiously as the emperor's body is carried away.

From Byzantine sources we see the Varangians at work as foreign professionals in a tough, often violent world. But from Scandinavian sources we see them as brothers, fathers, and sons, each one leaving a family behind to seek adventure and employment in a far-off foreign land. One Swedish woman called Fastve must have been a particularly proud mother. Her son scaled the dizzy heights of promotion out in Constantinople and ended up as the captain of the Varangian Guard. When she died he raised a runestone to her, which now stands in a wood north of Stockholm: a beast of a block with a circumference of 18 metres. One set of runes commemorates Fastve herself, while another reminds everyone what a great man her son was: 'Ragnvald had the runes carved. He was in Greece, was

---

* Harun ibn Yahya found his life plans unexpectedly turned upside-down when he was captured by Byzantines and brought to Constantinople. Once released, he went on a big road trip around Europe—the medieval equivalent of interrailing—and wrote a description of Constantinople, including this account of what appears to be the Varangian Guard.

FIGURE 13.1 Axe-wielding Varangians in the Skylitzes manuscript

commander of the retinue.'[6] 'Greece' in this case doesn't refer to the country itself, but rather to Byzantium. Despite being a Roman state, Constantinople was historically oriented towards Greek rather than Latin culture. If Latin was the *lingua franca* of the western part of the Roman Empire, then Greek was its equivalent in the east. In fact, while we think of Latin as the language of the Roman Empire, there probably hadn't been an emperor with Latin as his mother tongue since Justinian I (r. 527–65). Consequently, Norse runestones and literary texts refer to *Grikkland* ('Greece') and the *Grikkjar* ('Greeks') when they actually mean the area we call Byzantium, and Constantinople especially.*

* There are around thirty runestones that refer to Greece and the Greeks. Many still stand in the Swedish woods and fields where they were erected, but one has found its way to the basement of the Ashmolean Museum in Oxford, and now stands close to the museum café. Set within a knot of curling, whirling snakes, the runes commemorate the raiser's brother and father, who were 'out in Greece'. Whether they were there as traders or mercenaries is unclear. Incidentally, intrepid would-be rune-hunters should definitely check out this runestone, partly because of its historical significance and partly because they can then amble over to the café counter and reward themselves for their efforts with a slice of cake and a cup of tea. Research can be very hard work but its rewards come in many forms.

Ragnvald's runestone has been dated to the mid-eleventh century. Nothing more is known about Ragnvald or what he got up to in Constantinople, although he probably had a wild tale or two to tell when he got back. However, there is another mid-eleventh-century member of the Varangian Guard about whom we know much more. Perhaps he even knew Ragnvald, or served under him as a junior guardsman. We already met him, briefly in the chapters on the East: Harald Hardrada.

Lords and ladies

Harald may be a footnote in British history books, but he lived an extraordinary and dramatic life. We have already seen how he escaped from Norway in 1030 after his half-brother Olaf was killed in battle, and made his way to the Russian court of King Yaroslav. In around 1034 he travelled to Constantinople and joined the Varangian Guard. Several versions of his life-story—including his time in Constantinople—survive in various compilations of Kings' Sagas. As is often the case with Kings' Sagas, the different versions are all rather incestuous, and draw on each other heavily.[7] One of the earliest, most detailed accounts of his life comes from *Morkinskinna* (the 'mouldy parchment' that opens with domestic violence at the Russian court). It's likely that the saga itself was composed originally in around 1220, meaning that there was a gap of nearly 200 years between Harald's time in Constantinople and the period when sagas about him began to be recorded. That leaves lots of scope for embellishment, as we will see.

Morkinskinna's account of Harald's career in Constantinople reads like a collection of adrenaline-fuelled thrills and spills, some more plausible than others. Like a Norse action hero, Harald makes things exciting from the start by going undercover and calling himself Nordbrikt—'North-Bright'—a very appropriate pseudonym for a northern prince. From there, he acquires a suitably badass nemesis (the leader of the Byzantine army), has a love affair with a noblewoman, vanquishes a magical serpent who keeps on transforming himself into a man and sneaking into a woman's bed, and leads his plucky band of Varangians on many audacious campaigns further south.

Harald arrives in Constantinople flanked by warships and accompanied by a great retinue. The saga quotes a verse by a court poet, emphasizing both

Harald's magnificence and the city's remarkable appearance. Truly, this is the Big City, an almost futuristic place where the roofs seem to be thatched with metal:

> The cool rain shower fiercely urged forward
> the black prow of the warship
> along the coast, and armoured ships
> proudly bore their rigging.
> The honoured prince saw
> metal-thatched Constantinople beyond the prow;
> many fair-rimmed ships glided
> towards the city's high rampart.[8]

Metal roofing may not seem quite as impressive to a modern audience as, say, gold or silver, but before the invention of blast furnaces in the later Middle Ages, metals such as iron were much more expensive commodities than we might think today. The image of a city with metal-thatched roofing is a powerful one, underlining the opulence and wealth of the Big City.

The stories of Harald's time in the Varangian Guard take on highly dramatized, almost folkloric dimensions. When on their campaigns further afield, Harald and his fellow Varangians dig tunnels beneath a besieged city and burst through the floor to surprise their enemies. On another occasion they launch flaming birds into the sky to set a town on fire. Harald even fakes his own death so he can be carried into an enemy city, Trojan-horse style, and launch an attack. When we get to Constantinople, *Morkinskinna* introduces an element of sexual tension between the dashing Norwegian and the empress of Byzantium herself, Zoe. At their first, rather risqué encounter, Zoe marches up to Harald and demands: 'You, Northman. Give me a lock of your hair!' His response wouldn't win chat-up line of the year, but it seems to be effective: 'Majesty,' he says, 'let's make this a fair swap. Give me one of your pubic hairs.'[9] (Incidentally, if you've ever wanted to know the Old Norse for 'pubic hair', it's *magaskegg*, which literally means 'belly-beard'. You never know when this sort of information might come in useful.)

The idea of a relationship between Zoe and Harald seems to be little more than a Norse conceit; there is nothing to suggest that this was the case other than in the sagas. However, contemporary Byzantine sources do tell us that Zoe developed a chequered love-life in her mature years, racking up an impressive list of husbands, and even, in her seventh decade, a ménage-à-trois. At the age of 50 she married her first husband, the urban prefect Romanos,

FIGURE 13.2 Mosaic from Hagia Sophia in Istanbul featuring Constantine IX, Christ, and Empress Zoe

before cheating on him with her toyboy lover Michael, thirty-two years her junior. Suspiciously, Romanos was found dead in his bath one morning, and that afternoon Zoe married Michael. Both husbands ruled alongside Zoe as emperors in their turn, as Romanos III Argyros and Michael IV. After a rather unpleasant uprising under Michael V (more about him shortly) and the establishment of joint rule with her much-loathed sister Theodora, there was one more husband to come, Constantine IX Monomachos.

On the walls of the upper gallery in Hagia Sophia is a gloriously opulent mosaic, dripping in gold tesserae, depicting Christ flanked on one side by Zoe and on the other by Constantine. Gazing at Zoe with a slightly hangdog expression, her third husband sports a neat beard, rosy cheeks, and a dark blue tunic with a geometric pattern of blue-and-green squares and pink circles. In his hands is a fat money-pouch, symbolizing the donations he has made to the church. The only problem is that those are not his hands, nor is that his tunic. The clue lies in the brown patches around his head, and in the Greek inscription above him. Now, it reads: 'Constantine, pious emperor in Christ the God, king of the Romans, Monomachos.' But the two identifying words—Constantine and Monomachos—are all squished up and in a different style to the rest of the mosaic inscription. It seems that Constantine was not the first of Zoe's husbands who sat gazing at Christ. Originally the hands, tunic, and inscription probably belonged to Romanos III Argyros, one of his predecessors in the marital bed, now literally taken out of the picture.*

One more person is missing from this picture of marital bliss, and it isn't Harald Hardrada. As Zoe was well aware, there were three people in her final marriage: Zoe, Constantine, and his long-term mistress Maria Skleraina. Zoe doesn't seem to have been too bothered about this arrangement, quite the reverse, setting her up as a 'junior empress' and establishing a series of interconnected palace apartments for them all to live in. In her final years she handed over power to her husband and drifted around the palace trying out new creams to keep her wrinkles at bay.[10]

So, despite her reputation for having a colourful personal life, there is no evidence to suggest that Zoe actually carried a candle for Harald. But *Morkinskinna* doesn't let a little thing like truth get in the way of a good bit of gossip. Whenever Harald gets in trouble with Zoe—first for seducing a noblewoman, then for misappropriating funds that belonged to the crown—the saga hints that she may have had other reasons for getting cross with him, 'because people who were in Constantinople within memory of the Varangians say that Zoe wanted him for herself'.[11] Eventually, whether because Harald is far too sexy for his own good or because of rumoured funds that are 'just resting in his account', Harald is thrown into prison, together with two of his men. It is at this point that things get seriously peculiar, because it turns out that their cellmate is an enormous venomous serpent that lives by the stream running alongside the prison. Being tough, stoic Norsemen, the trio don't seem particularly fazed by their predicament, and respond with the sort of grim Nordic humour typical of the sagas:

The snake lived on the corpses of men who had come up against the emperor or his nobles and been thrown down there. They waded through the mud, where lay the

---

* Perhaps Romanos' face was in turn replaced by that of Zoe's second husband, Michael IV, before being replaced for a final time by Constantine IX. But it is hard to tell, and there is plenty more that is mysterious about the mosaic, such as the fact that Zoe and Christ also appear to have had face transplants.

rotting corpses of men who had been given as scraps to the snake. Then they sat down at the edge. Halldor Snorrason said, 'It's not a great lodging, but things can always get worse.'[12]

Having escaped from the prison cave, *Morkinskinna* tells us, Harald summons the Varangians and storms the palace to avenge himself on the emperor by gouging out his eyes. (We'll come back to this improbable-sounding episode later.) Having carried out this grisly task, Harald and his men escape secretly over the Bosphorus and flee back to the court of King Yaroslav in Kiev to pick up the vast amounts of treasure he has been sending there for safe keeping. From Kiev he sails to Norway in warships weighed down with gold. *Dreki* is both the Norse word for a dragon and for a dragonhead-ship, and in this verse quoted in the saga the poet transforms the vessel into an actual dragon as it sails over the ocean, with golden fire smouldering in its belly:

> It was like looking into the middle
> of a dragon's mouth,
> like fire was burning,
> as you steered your ships from the south.
> The warship bore its red snout,
> it glowed from pure gold;
> the dragon sailed a long day's journey,
> the wave broke beneath the hull.[13]

A drowsy emperor

Harald seems to have become something of a romantic, swashbuckling folk hero in medieval Icelandic storytelling tradition, certainly judging from this account in *Morkinskinna*. But despite the more outlandish aspects of his life story—not least the corpse-devouring dungeon serpent and the sexually available empress—the saga accounts of Harald's life are not devoid of historical facts. It is simply that many of them have got rather mangled and embellished in the telling. Perhaps some of these exaggerations came from Harald himself: as Harald flees Norway and makes his way east, *Morkinskinna* states that, 'from this point onwards the tale of Harald's travels comes from what Harald himself said, and those men who followed him'.[14]

As we might expect from an international jetsetter such as Harald, he occasionally crops up in non-Norse texts written in languages such as Greek and English. These have problems of their own—there is no such thing as a straightforward historical source—but they can help us to build a more complete picture of Harald and his life, looking past the imaginative flesh of the saga stories to the historical bones beneath.

Harald features in a Byzantine text called *Strategikon*, an all-purpose manual written in the 1070s, which dishes out advice on all sorts of things from warfare to government to domestic life. Whoever wrote it was a military man and seems to have known Harald personally. One passage describes how 'Aráltes', as he is known here, came to Constantinople with 500 men and joined the Varangian Guard to serve Michael IV:

Aráltes was then with the Emperor's expedition and performed great deeds of valour against the enemy, as was fitting for one of his noble race and personal ability. When the Emperor had reduced the Bulgarians to submission he returned [to Constantinople]; I was there myself, and fought for the Emperor as best I could. So, when we came to Mosynupolis, the Emperor rewarded him for his valour and gave him the title of *Spatharokandidatos*.[15]

Spatharokandidatos was one of the middling ranks of the Byzantine royal court; certainly an achievement, but hardly on a par with the glorious accomplishments detailed in the saga. Likewise, although the sagas make Harald the leader of the Varangians, this isn't necessarily the case (although if he arrived with 500 men, he must have had some considerable clout). In fact, it has been suggested that Harald himself had quite some part to play in the immortalization of his exploits and achievements, described as 'the chief patron of his own legend'.[16]

Even so, this doesn't mean that everything described in the saga is the conceit of a puffed-up king looking to inflate his ego still further. For instance, the passage in the *Strategikon* goes on to describe how, when Michael IV died, Harald wanted to go back home but was refused permission, so he escaped secretly. Even though the sagas may have come up with a more exciting reason for the escape, it seems that Harald did indeed have to sneak out of Constantinople against imperial wishes.

According to the accounts of Harald's life in *Morkinskinna* and other compilations of Kings' Sagas, Harald's swift and dramatic flight from Constantinople was because he had blinded an emperor. In fact, according to the version of his saga in *Heimskringla*, Harald himself was the witness for this story, together with his men. But the facts need unpicking, because some of them are patently wrong: for a start, *Morkinskinna* says that the emperor was Constantine IX Monomachos, who was actually Zoe's third husband and certainly wasn't blinded. The clue to what happened is in the saga itself, or more specifically two verses quoted in the saga said to be originally composed by Norse court poets. According to one:

> The prince obtained still more
> embers of the hands;
> the emperor of Greece became stone blind
> from the violent injury.[17]

'Embers of the hands' is a kenning for gold, which is often likened to fire in Old Norse poetry. Given Harald's reputation for acquiring enormous quantities of treasure in Constantinople, it seems likely that he is the prince of the poem. But if we separate out the verses from the surrounding prose, we can see that all the court poets actually say is that an emperor was blinded and that a wealthy royal became even wealthier. To understand the events that actually led up to this moment, we have to delve into the murky, cut-throat world of mid-eleventh-century Byzantine politics, with its many mysterious and convenient deaths, poisonous sibling rivalries, sexual intrigues, and political coups. As a prominent member of the imperial bodyguard, Harald would not only have had a ringside seat for the whole dastardly soap opera, but also perhaps a walk-on part. If he really did blind an emperor, then he wasn't exacting a terrible personal vengeance, as the saga suggests. Rather, he was simply doing his job.

These were the facts, as far as we can tell. Michael IV, Harald's employer and Zoe's toyboy husband, was a sickly man who suffered from epilepsy. Before he died in December 1041 he had persuaded Zoe to appoint his nephew, also called Michael, as her next co-ruler, with the understanding that Zoe was still in charge. But the newly crowned Michael V didn't want to play ball, and over Easter 1042 things turned nasty. Michael deposed Zoe, bundling her onto an imperial galley and shipping her off to a nunnery with her head shaved. But the good people of Constantinople were having none of it. A mob rose up against the rebel emperor, ably assisted by the Varangian Guard, and Zoe was returned to the capital, a little balder and a little chillier perhaps, but otherwise unharmed.

Michael V's punishment was terrible. The emperor was meant to be a perfect physical specimen, and if he was physically deformed he wasn't allowed to rule (as Justinian II, nicknamed 'Slit-Nosed', learned to his cost in 695, when he was deposed and de-nosed).* In order to make sure that Michael never tried another trick like that, his eyes were gouged out. The Byzantine monk and historian Michael Psellus was an eyewitness to the whole sorry debacle, and described how Michael clung to the altar of the church in which he had sought sanctuary, until the mob had to prise him away from the pillars and chase him out the door. When the time came for the gouging, he bellowed and squealed and thrashed about so violently that he had to be restrained: 'When the executioner saw him flinch away and lower himself to base entreaty, he bound him securely. He held him down with considerable force, to stop the violent twitching when he was undergoing his punishment.'[18] Perhaps, then, Harald was the one who blinded, or was involved in the blinding, of Michael V. These are probably the true events that lie behind the sagas.[19] Sometimes truth is stranger than fiction.

Monuments of magnificence

Everywhere in Istanbul there are echoes of the city's ancient Byzantine past. The Constantinople that Harald and his fellow Norsemen would have experienced isn't as far away as we might think, and in some places it's still possible to see where they left their mark. Up high in the southern gallery of Hagia Sophia, overlooking the cavernous centre below, a naughty Norseman—perhaps a bored Varangian guardsman, unimpressed by the pomp, splendour, and overly long mass—passed the time by carving his name in runes into the marble parapet. We know that his name was Halfdan, because that's the only bit of the inscription still visible, although the rest must have been something along the lines of 'Halfdan woz here'.

This is far from the only bit of graffiti defacing the marble of Hagia Sophia. In fact, this whole section of the gallery is crawling with graffiti written in all sorts of languages and alphabets—not only runes but also Latin, Greek, Cyrillic, Armenian—a reminder of just how multicultural Constantinople was, but

---

* A glutton for punishment, Justinian later returned to seize the crown for a second time, now wearing a glorious golden nose as a replacement.

also how badly behaved and irreverent its inhabitants and visitors could be. Further along the gallery are a series of Norse ships scratched into the stone. One even has a dragonhead prow, complete with pointy ears, snout, and a hairy goatee sprouting from its chin.[20]

It isn't really surprising that most of the graffiti occurs on the upper galleries of the cathedral. They were traditionally used by those who hadn't yet been baptized, although it has been pointed out that in reality they were used 'for just about every imaginable purpose, legitimate or not, including even temporary lodgings and sexual dalliance'.[21] With their conveniently thick pillars to hide behind and dark nooks and crannies, it is possible to see exactly why the upper floors would have been suitable for those wishing to conduct sneaky and nefarious activities of all kinds.

A short walk from Hagia Sophia are the ruins of the Great Palace, once inhabited by imperial rulers such as Empress Zoe. Little remains except for some of the palace's breathtakingly beautiful mosaics, protected from the elements by the museum buildings that have been constructed around them. On the floor and walls of what was once the palace, tessellated muscles and sinews bulge and ripple on the bodies of humans and animals alike, ready to pounce or flee—silent forms frozen in eternity. Some, age has not withered: perfect images of a downtrodden slave leading two pompous little boys on the back of a horse, a monkey dressed in a waistcoat gathering coconuts, a donkey kicking its master, a lapdog petrified in horror as it comes face to face with a snarling monster. Time has been less kind to others: it is just about possible to make out a band of baby bears snuffling for apples with their mother. In another corner of the palace almost all the tesserae have been lost, but just enough survives to show a man being mauled to death by an animal. As a member of the imperial bodyguard, Harald would have probably walked over these intricate, delicate tesserae many times, a world away from the rougher, draughtier royal halls of his homeland that he would one day inhabit as king of Norway.

Just over two decades later, Harald would be lying dead on a muddy, blood-soaked battlefield outside York. But his death had far-reaching consequences that he could have never foreseen, particularly for the Varangian Guard itself. When the Normans took over England there were suddenly rather a lot of landless Anglo-Saxon noblemen who found they had to exit the country quickly. They needed a destination that was suitably far away, and a change of career. For many of them, the answer was Constantinople and service in the

Varangian Guard. Quite possibly, they would have felt at home with their new comrades, despite their apparently different backgrounds. England had had more than its share of Scandinavian settlers, first under the Danelaw and later when the Danes—led by King Knut, whom we left in the last chapter dying after his pilgrimage to Rome—conquered England. It could be that these were exactly the sort of 'Anglo-Saxons' who decided to make the journey to Constantinople, perhaps because Cousin Magnus from Jutland or Uncle Olaf from Bergen was already over there. This exodus is described by the English monk and chronicler Orderic Vitalis, writing some decades after the event. Here we see the continuing close links between England and Scandinavia:

And so the English groaned aloud for their lost liberty and plotted ceaselessly to find some way of shaking off a yoke that was so intolerable and unaccustomed. Some sent to Svein, king of Denmark, and urged him to lay claim to the kingdom of England which his ancestors Svein and Cnut had won by the sword.... Some of them who were still in the flower of youth travelled into remote lands and bravely offered their arms to Alexius, emperor of Constantinople, a man of great wisdom and nobility.[22]

Thanks in part to Harald Hardrada—albeit indirectly—the ranks of the imperial bodyguard were soon swelled with men whose old lives had been wiped out almost overnight, and the barracks filled with voices telling tales from a different northern homeland.

Hammered gold

Harald may have been the most famous member of the Varangian Guard, but he was not the only one to make it into the sagas. From time to time in the stories, Icelanders who served as Varangians return home from Constantinople: strong, silent types, dripping with gold, swathed in expensive fabrics, and weighed down by top-of-the-range weaponry. The most extensive description of a blinged-up Varangian returning home is Bolli Bollason, born around the turn of the millennium and a character in the *Saga of the People of Laxardal* (*Laxdœla saga*). When he reaches Iceland, he is weighed down with so much finery that it's a wonder he doesn't fall off his horse. In fact, the saga description of him is so concerned with his armour and weapons that we hardly see Bolli at all:

Bolli was such a show-off when he came back from this journey that he wouldn't wear any clothes except those made of scarlet and fur, and all his weapons were ornamented with gold. He was called Bolli the Magnificent.... Bolli rode from his ship with twelve men; his followers were all dressed in scarlet and rode on gilded saddles. They were all elegant, but Bolli was the best of the lot. He wore furs that the emperor had given him and a scarlet cape over the top; his sword Leg-Biter hung at his side with its gilded hilt and its grip made of woven gold. He had a gilded helmet on his head and a red shield at his side, painted with a golden knight. He had a dagger in his hand, as is the custom in foreign lands, and wherever they took lodgings for the night, the women paid attention to nothing other than Bolli, his finery and his friends.[23]

Other ex-Varangians are not such shameless exhibitionists. Set around the start of the tenth century and probably written down in the thirteenth century, the *Saga of Hrafnkel* (*Hrafnkels saga*) features a former Varangian who comes to the aid of a man fighting for justice against a bent chieftain. He is introduced as a mysterious outsider with a touch of glamour, in the mould of one of the rangers from *The Lord of the Rings*: 'He was a tall, lean man in a leaf-green tunic and he had an ornamented sword in his hand. He had regular features, a ruddy complexion, and an imposing demeanour.'[24]

Unfortunately, not all Varangians are so respected when they return home. Set at around the same time, the *Saga of Hallfred the Troublesome Poet* (*Hallfreðar saga vandræðaskálds*) features an ex-Varangian named Gris, who is cuckolded by the troublesome poet of the saga title. Gris is introduced as a well-travelled, popular man who has won great honour out in Constantinople. When he meets up with his friends, they leave their spears propped up outside the farm where they are staying. Gris' spear stands out from the rest because it is inlaid with gold: a twinkle of Byzantine fire amidst the grey slivers of northern iron. Unfortunately for Gris, he is now past his prime, described as 'rather short-sighted and bleary-eyed', a figure of fun rather than respect.[25] Not content with bedding the former Varangian's wife, Hallfred the Troublesome Poet lives up to his nickname by composing scurrilous verses about the poor man and his sweaty ineptitude in the bedroom. Another of Hallfred's poems describes the poor ex-Varangian as the 'diminisher of the fjord fire', a kenning for a wealthy man ('fjord fire' is gold, its 'diminisher' is someone who gives it away to his followers).[26] But all the gold in Byzantium can't prevent the indignity of Hallfred's crass poetic insults, as he conjures images of the ex-Varangian trudging to the marital bed to hump and sweat over his pretty young wife.

Not only would-be Varangians visit Constantinople. For the high-status pilgrims-cum-crusaders whom we met in the previous chapter, Constantinople is the gateway to the south. King Sigurd the Jerusalem-Farer, King Erik the Good, and Jarl Rognvald of Orkney pass through Constantinople, either on their way to Jerusalem or on their way back home. They meet with Emperor Alexius I—called 'Kirialax'* in the sagas—and the reception they are given demonstrates the imaginative place that this city and its ruler occupied in the minds of the saga writers.

In the *Saga of Knut's Descendants*, Emperor Alexius lays on a magnificent banquet for Erik, and offers him a choice of gifts. Either he can have half a ton of gold, or a chance to witness the magnificent games held at the hippodrome. Erik chooses the gold, because he is still on his way to Jerusalem and racking up a vast expenses bill. The benevolent emperor adds fourteen ships and some of his own clothes to King Erik's goodie-bag.

The account of King Sigurd's time in Byzantium, particularly in the *Morkinskinna* version of his story, tops Erik's visit by far. In this extensive account of Sigurd's life, as the Old Norse scholar Ármann Jakobsson has argued, Sigurd's journey to the Holy Land is presented as a performance of feigned magnificence, in which this king from a peripheral northern country sets himself up as equal to the great kings and emperors of Europe.[27] According to *Morkinskinna*, when the emperor of Byzantium hears that Sigurd is on his way, he has precious fabrics scattered on the streets from the Golden Gate (his personal entrance to the city) all the way to his grandest palace. The gates are opened, and the Norwegian monarch swaggers in with his men. Whatever the Old Norse equivalent of 'fake it to make it' would have been, that's what Sigurd does. He instructs his men to play it cool as they strut through the streets, paying no attention to the song and dance that is (literally) going on around them. He even pimps his ride with the Norse equivalent of chrome plating, gold hubcaps, and a spoiler: 'It's said that King Sigurd had his horse shod with gold hooves before he and his men rode into the city.'[28]

---

* 'Kirialax' is the Norse name for Alexius I—specifically a contraction of the Greek version of his name, 'Kurios Alexios', *kurios* meaning 'lord' or 'master'—who ruled from 1081 to 1118 and welcomed kings Erik and Sigurd to Constantinople. He was also the star of the *Alexiad*, the inside scoop on palace life written by his daughter. In several sagas 'Kirialax' is used as a generic name for 'emperor of Byzantium' regardless of the actual identity of the emperor (the medieval equivalent of the hoover, sellotape, and thermos flask, all of which started off as specific brand names but eventually became generic terms).

Once installed in the royal hall, Sigurd continues with his inflated royal posturing, in an elaborate game of one-upmanship that verges on the farcical. The emperor's servants first bring him bags of gold and silver, then tubs of gold, and finally barrels of the reddest gold with a couple of gold rings garnishing the top. On the first two occasions Sigurd hardly deigns to look at the gifts, but divides them amongst his men. The baffled emperor concludes: 'This king is one of two things: either he is mightier and richer than other kings, or he is not as wise as a king should be.'[29] Like King Erik before him, Sigurd is offered the choice of gold or games at the hippodrome, and chooses the latter. (The *Saga of Knut's Descendants* also alludes to this, but is at pains to tell us that King Sigurd was on his way home and so didn't have as many expenses as Erik. It then adds, perhaps a little defensively: 'People are still divided about which choice was more kingly.'[30]) As Sigurd's over-the-top peacocking suggests, saga depictions of the splendour of Constantinople and the generosity of the emperor are as much—or more—about the largesse that was bestowed upon these kings as about Constantinople itself. As the kings from the north sally forth with the firm friendship of an emperor and tokens of his blessing, the take-home message is that these northern rulers are heavyweight players on the international stage, worthy of the honours bestowed on them.

Unageing monuments

It takes a bit of imagination to return us to the sights that Norse visitors to Constantinople might have seen all those centuries ago. Even today, with only a few battered fragments and one section of the wall still standing, the hippodrome is an impressive sight. In the shadow of the Blue Mosque, the outline of the racing-track is still visible, though often lost in the hustle and bustle of snap-happy tourists, eagle-eyed touts, and white-robed holy men hurrying to prayers. At one end, the Walled Obelisk still stands 32 metres high, like a giant grey-stoned Jenga tower about to totter. If King Sigurd really did enjoy games at the hippodrome, he would have seen it as a gleaming tower of bronze plaques, decorated with the war triumphs of Emperor Basil I. Marauding crusaders carried off the bronze in 1204, leaving nothing but pockmarked, crumbling stones. The same crusaders also stole four beautiful, bronze statues of racing-horses, forelocks raised and ears pricked as though mid-race, covered in a coppery sheen as if frozen in the very act of panting and sweating. Today the horses stand inside Venice's Basilica San Marco, although they were briefly pilfered in turn by Napoleon to go on top of his new Arc de Triomphe. (The horses that now top the Arc bear a striking resemblance to the Byzantine originals, although they have turned a rather psychedelic verdigris-blue.)

The Byzantines themselves had also done a fair amount of thieving in order to adorn their hippodrome. Modern tourists may not be particularly impressed by a stumpy bronze column, twisted like a candy cane, which stands in what was once the arena. But appearances can be deceptive; this little stub is around 2,500 years old and is part of a sacrificial tripod from Delphi in Greece. During the Byzantine era it would have been 8 metres high, topped with three bronze snakeheads, which in turn had a golden bowl balanced on top. Emperor Constantine decided it would look better in Constantinople than in Greece, so he 'liberated' it. In turn, the crusaders of 1204 decided to 'liberate' the golden bowl for themselves, at which point it disappeared from history. Prior to then, King Sigurd and any other Norse visitors to Constantinople would have been able to see this spectacular artefact, as the horses' hooves and chariot wheels thundered round the track and the crowd roared.

Clearly, whoever wrote the account in *Morkinskinna* had never seen such sights. In order to transport his readers in their imaginations to the high-octane drama and exoticism of the hippodrome in Constantinople, the writer had to fall back on a rather less exhilarating, more Icelandic frame of reference. The hippodrome is described in a way that would have made sense to a Norse readership, but the result has an artificially northern flavour:

Those who have been in Constantinople say that the hippodrome is built in such a way that a high wall runs around a field, which is like a circular home field, with steps all around the stone walls for men to sit on while the games are being played on the field. They are decorated with all kinds of ancient tales: the Aesir and Volsungs and Gjukungs, fashioned in copper and ore with such great skill that they appear to be alive and it seems to people that they might be participants in the games. The amusements are set up with such great ingenuity and artifice that people seem to ride in the air, and there is also Greek fire and some magical effects. Additionally, there are all sorts of musical instruments: psalteries, organs, harps, fiddles, violins, and all kinds of stringed instruments.[31]

The hippodrome—450 metres long and capable of holding 100,000 spectators, home to eight-chariot races, political riots, and state-sanctioned massacres—is here compared to the inner field surrounding a squat, wind-battered Icelandic farmstead. The effect is like comparing the glorious Hagia Sophia to an Icelandic cattle byre. Likewise, the 'ancient events' that decorate the walls include characters from Norse myths and legends: gods such as Odin and Thor and legendary heroes such as Sigurd the Dragon-Slayer. This description reveals the true disconnect that could develop between historical reality and literary re-creation in the sagas. Once upon a time, Icelandic travellers—perhaps members of the Varangian Guard—must have returned home from Constantinople and described the hippodrome to their friends and family. But by the time that this account was written down only the most basic elements remained: the outer wall (huge), the size of the arena (enormous), the decoration (realistic), the games (ingenious), and the musical instruments (all sorts).

Sensual music

Even so, for the most part the Constantinople of the Kings' Sagas and Sagas of Icelanders is rooted in the historical reality of Norse activities in Byzantium, even if the result is a typical saga tapestry of historical threads woven together with fictions and fantasies, strands of oral tales and literary influences, past events and present realities. But there is another Constantinople: the Constantinople of the Chivalric Sagas. These are sagas that were either translated and adapted from Continental romances, or newly created by Icelandic writers from the same generic pool of material. This Constantinople is based less in the historical past and more on learned and literary ideas. Their heroes who visit the Big City are not real-life kings and members of the Varangian Guard. Instead, the stories are drawn from the world of romance and chivalry, and the learned traditions of the medieval encyclopedia.

The Constantinople that features in sagas of this type is a fabulously wealthy city populated by the wise, the noble, the powerful, and the beautiful. If kings such as Erik and Sigurd got a good reception when they reached Constantinople, this is nothing compared to what the heroes of the Chivalric Sagas receive when they arrive. In the real, post-1204 world, Constantinople may have been a shadow of its former self. In the Chivalric Sagas its glory lived on, distilled into pure literary form. To take just one example, in the *Saga of Kirialax* (*Kirialax saga*), so great is the wealth and splendour of the city that it has become an overblown parody of itself. This saga was probably written in the fourteenth century, though it only survives in manuscripts from the fifteenth to eighteenth centuries. Yet rather than fading away, the themes that characterized Constantinople in more realistic sagas are here insanely embellished. Constantinople is so bling that nothing on earth can possibly compete:

Many hundreds of ships were launched from the city every day, loaded with all sorts of expensive aromatic herbs and spices, and all kinds of herb-flavoured drinks. Many halls were decorated with tapestries, and the great hall, which was prepared for the king, glittered from within with gold, and the upper and lower thrones blazed with fire-red gold.... After that, the patriarch came out with the bishops and other eminent priests, all singing sweetly and carrying long torches with exquisite ceremony. It seemed as though all the air flamed above the people when the golden fire-pan glittered in the sunshine.[32]

The superlatives don't stop there. The church is the most beautiful in Europe, the maidens are so gorgeous that everyone immediately falls in love with them, and the banquet platters, piled high with every imaginable delicacy, are made of pure gold. We are deep into the world of medieval romance, with a courtly Constantinople populated by jousting knights and fair damsels to be won. Other Chivalric Sagas feature even more extravagant processions, worthy of any West End or Broadway musical. The city towers themselves resound with song, there are processions featuring every musical instrument on earth, a band of castrated monks to sing hymns, and even a mythical phoenix soaring in the skies above.[33]

By the time the sagas came to be written down, Constantinople's glory days were over and its power was fading. The city was very different to the one once visited by crusading, pilgrimaging Norse kings and nobles. But out in Iceland the saga writers don't seem to have got the memo. The past casts a long shadow, and collective cultural memories operate on a much longer timescale than historical events. In the Kings' Sagas, Constantinople was the city where northern kings could take their rightful place on the international stage as rulers worthy of an emperor's praise and favour. In the Sagas of Icelanders, Constantinople was the city where warriors could prosper through their military prowess before returning home, battle-hardened and fabulously wealthy. In the Chivalric Sagas, with their most tenuous of grips on historical reality, Constantinople became bigger and better. It was a golden, glittering, literary fossil of a city filled with all-knowing emperors, strutting warriors, and beautiful women; the very stuff of medieval romance itself. In the imaginations of the medieval Icelanders, Byzantium would not diminish, and Constantinople would forever remain the Big City.

CHAPTER 14

World's End

Filling in the gaps

A modern map of the world has no blank spaces to fill in. There are no mysterious, hidden corners populated by men with faces in their chests, or one eye in their foreheads, or a single enormous foot to shelter themselves from the sun. There are no cannibals who eat their parents when they grow old, or mouthless, hairy little creatures who live on the scent of fruit, or conflicted polyglots who lure travellers to their deaths by pretending to know their relatives then mourn over their severed heads after dinner.[1] There are no suicidal flaming phoenixes, enormous gold-guarding ants, lynxes that piss precious stones, or bull–horse hybrids that fart fiery poo.

All in all, modern maps are disappointingly tame: a series of precise scientific measurements, lines of latitude and longitude, place-names and borders. We may think that this is an accurate, objective depiction of the world, but that isn't necessarily true. There is no such thing as objectivity when it comes to maps: all maps are highly selective in what aspects of the world they choose to include. The world is always open to interpretation, categorization, and explication. Everything is relative.

In our age of globalization and technology, the world is literally at our fingertips. We can talk face-to-face with someone on another continent or use virtual maps to touch down in the streets of Bhutan or Buenos Aires. The limits of our geographical knowledge have expanded. If we want to test those limits, we would probably have to look beyond the confines of the earth and explore the possibility of other worlds beyond our own, extraterrestrial life, or entire new universes on the other side of a black hole's unfathomable depths. In such cases, scientific knowledge can only take us so far. Most of us have to take on trust what we're told by astronomers, physicists, mathematicians, and so on, because we are not experts ourselves. We fill in the rest of the picture with our imaginations: little green men, flying saucers, government cover-ups in New Mexico, *Star Wars*, *Star Trek*, and *ET*.

In the Middle Ages the geographical limits of the known world were closer to home. Take, for example, the Hereford *mappa mundi*, a map that contains many layers of geographical meaning in the broadest possible sense. It doesn't just show continents, countries, cities, and rivers, but also legends and myths, the spiritual world, biblical stories, beasts both real and imaginary, and a whole host of weird and wonderful races. Time trickles down the map like sand through an hourglass. At the top is Judgement Day, with Christ in the centre showing his crucifixion scars, holy men and women rising from their graves, and other less fortunate souls being dragged off to hell. Below, Adam and Eve stand in Eden, naked and vulnerable in the midst of their snaky temptation.

As we already know, Jerusalem is positioned at the centre of this map. But there are other sorts of centres and peripheries to consider. Take a closer look, and it becomes clear that the real centre of the world is actually squashed into the bottom left-hand corner: southern England, where the map was made. Home is where the centre is, and the closer we get to home, the sharper the lens and the more precise the geographical focus. Cities, towns, castles, and cathedrals cluster thickly along the rivers, even the new castles at Conway and Caernarvon (built by Edward I only a few years before the map was made). The text accompanying each of them is minimal—only names—and there is no need to rely on learned geographical texts for this information. Western Europe is similarly detailed. Paris, that great hub of medieval learning, is also prominent, depicted as a great building with towering steeples and spires. But familiarity can also breed contempt: at some point in the map's history poor Paris was angrily scratched out with something sharp. We don't know why: perhaps it was during one of the wars between England and France, perhaps it was done by a jilted lover whose beloved had run off with a Frenchman.

As we move away from Europe, geographical precision fades and the lens starts to blur. Named cities, towns, and rivers become fewer and further between. Long explanatory passages start to appear by illustrations of foreign settlements and alien creatures, and learned sources are cited more frequently.

FIGURE 14.1 Marvellous and monstrous races on the Hereford *mappa mundi* (c.1290)

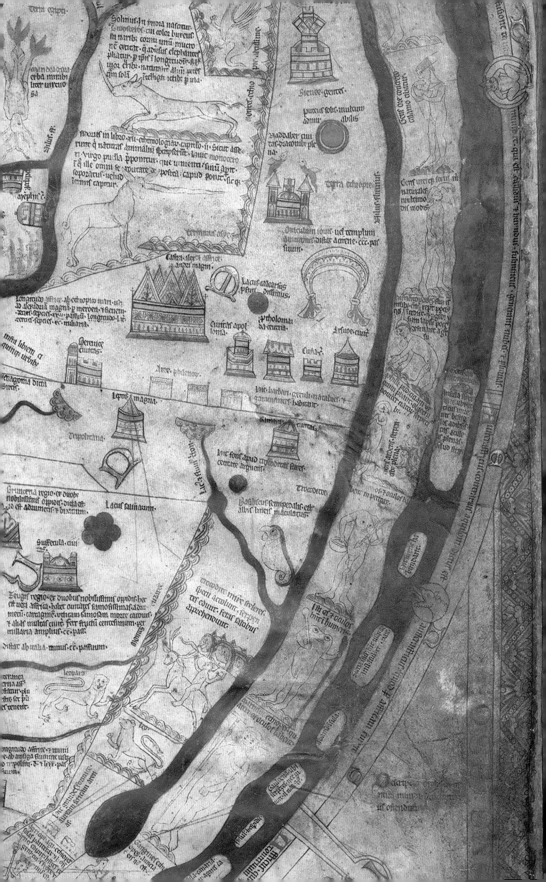

In the biblical lands the compilers have the Old and New Testaments for guidance. In wilder parts of Asia and Africa they rely on Classical and Late-Antique sources such as Pliny the Elder. In the blank spaces and at the edges of the world marvellous and monstrous races abound, and the limits of geographical knowledge become the limits of humanity itself. Close to the southern rim of the world the Nile curves downwards like a strip of blue ribbon. Beyond it, at Africa's outermost edge, are a series of cartoonish creatures, including a smiling figure with his head in his chest, another peeping out of the map with four eyes instead of two, and another studiously sucking his dinner out of a bowl with a straw.

The Hereford *mappa mundi* is one of the best-known, most-reproduced geographical artefacts of the Middle Ages, but it is a one-off: the glossy, photogenic supermodel of the medieval map world. Other maps are less glamorous. Tucked into the stiff brown pages of the manuscript GKS 1812 4to, medieval Iceland's largest *mappa mundi* isn't nearly so impressive. It is smaller than an A4 piece of paper, a paltry size in comparison to the Herford *mappa mundi's* more than 2 square metres. It's also fairly boring to look at, because there are no pictures on this map, only words. Even so, both maps share many geographical traits in terms of the way they depict and understand the world. Once again, the mapmaker's geographical knowledge of Europe is greater, and so here the focus is sharper. All the countries are placed in relation to each other, so that from the northern edge of the world the names of countries follow a line down from Thule to Iceland to Norway to Sweden to Denmark. Lined up across the Mediterranean Sea are the names of countries, regions, and cities: Greece, Thrace, Constantinople, Apulia, Italy, Rome, Langobardia, Germania, and Francia.

Crossing the Mediterranean and heading south into Africa, we get the same sense of geographical unfamiliarity and blurring as on the Hereford *mappa mundi*. The world suddenly becomes a series of rows and columns, with no sense of relative location at all. The compiler seems to have collected whatever he could find about this region and inserted the information here, perhaps as an attempt to impose some sort of order on it. The columns include statements such as: 'Libya is a province in Africa' and 'in the region of Pentapolis there are five cities'. At the bottom of the final column, information peters out entirely: 'in this place there are impenetrable wastelands and a desert.'[2]

Other sorts of geographical knowledge are hidden in these columns, not as obviously as on the Hereford *mappa mundi*, but still there. The first is a snippet of information about the exotic stones that can be found in Africa, seemingly lifted

FIGURE 14.2 Europe on a medieval Icelandic *mappa mundi* (c.1182–1400)

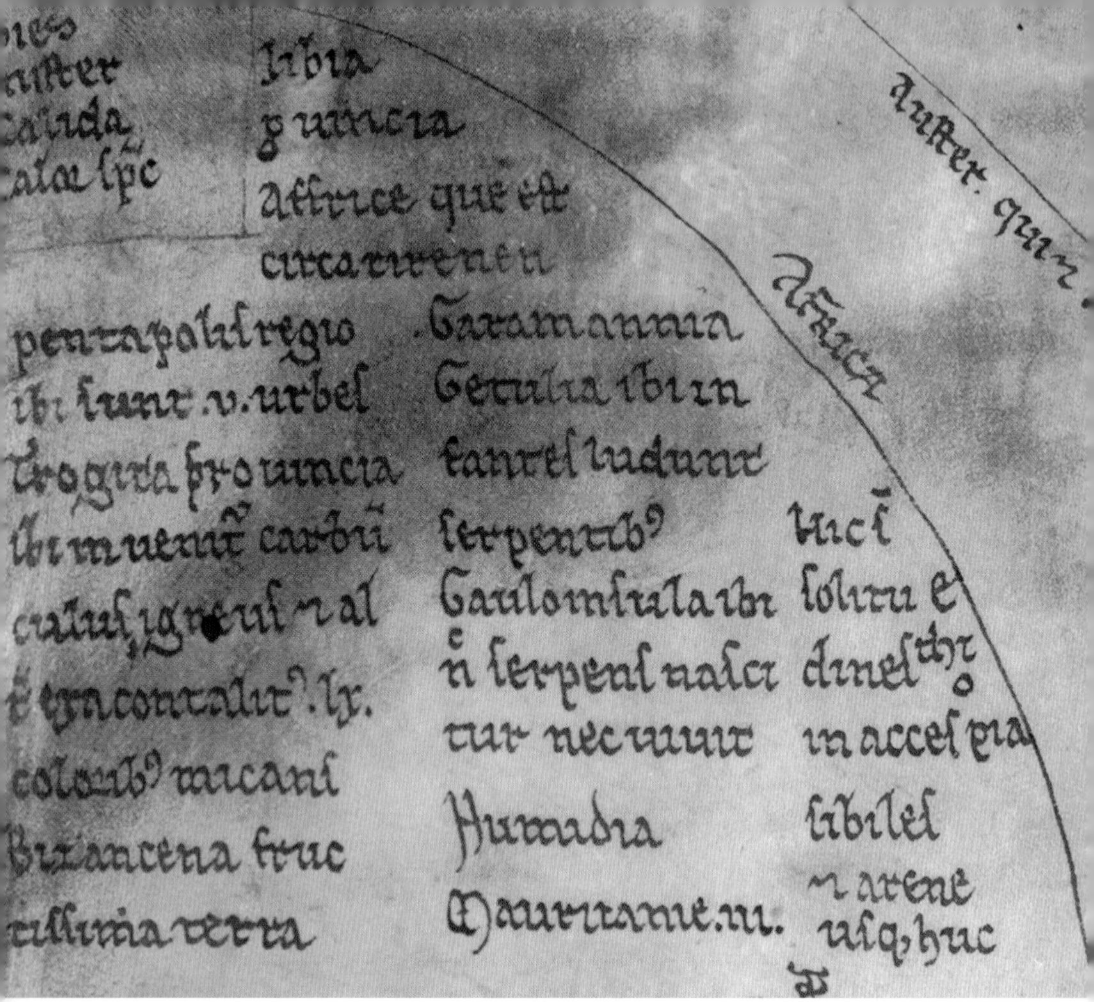

nes
ritter
cauda
aia lpc

libia
puincia
affrice que et
circarirenti

pentapolil regio · baramannu
ibi lunt ·v· urbel Getulia ibi in
trogita prouincia fanrel ludunt
ibi inuenit carbii lerpentib?
cuiul igneul 7 al Gaulomlula ibi hici
é ep contalit? ·lx· n lerpenl nalci lolitu é
colonb? maicani tur nec uiuit dinel tbr
Bizancena truc Humadia in accel pia
culuria rerra Mauritanie·m· libilel
7 arene
ulq; huc

FIGURE 14.3 Africa on a medieval Icelandic *mappa mundi* (c.1182–1400)

from the sort of lists of precious stones (called lapidaries) that appear in medieval encyclopedias: 'In Trogita province is found a fiery little coal, and another one, exacontalitus, glitters with sixty colours.'[3] There is even a marvellous race lurking amid the list of countries, a legend that reads: 'In Getulia children play with serpents.'[4] Getulia is a region bordering the Sahara, but the assertion that the children of Getulia play with serpents seems to be a fudged reference to two separate marvellous and monstrous races. One of these is the Getuli, who were said to expose their children to snakes to test whether they were legitimate. The same race appears on the Hereford *mappa mundi*, beyond the Nile at the southern rim of the world. The other race is mentioned in a list of marvellous and monstrous races in the medieval Icelandic manuscript *Hauksbók*. Here, the extensive description of strange beings at the edge of the world includes some interesting African races:

In Africa there is a race that is immune to snake venom, and the children play in their cradles with snakes. There are also those that are headless, with both their mouths and eyes on their chests. Some of the headless ones have their mouths below on their bellies but their eyes on their shoulders, and are hairy like animals.[5]

As we reach the geographical limits of the world, learning and imagination trump experience. The same thing happens in the Old Norse sagas. We have already seen this to some extent in the west, north, and east: the bow-and-arrow-wielding uniped of Vinland, or the beak-faced apple maniac of Russia. But just as on the maps, the further away the saga narratives move from the Norse geographical sphere, the fuzzier the narrative lens becomes and the more of these creatures stride, lollop, and bounce their way into the pages of the story. This is most extreme in the far south, where few Norse—indeed, few Europeans—ever ventured. Practical experience, cultural memory, and oral traditions fade away, to be replaced by the bizarre beasts, outlandish lands, and other monstrosities of Classical and medieval learning.

The colourful, exotic lands of the far south feature most often in the Chivalric Sagas. In fact, it has been pointed out that this type of saga could be easily renamed the Legendary Sagas of Southern Lands (*fornaldarsögur suðrlanda*), because the Chivalric Sagas are particularly interested in distant travel and exotic locations far beyond the Norse sphere.[6] The scholar Geraldine Barnes— appropriately based at the University of Sydney, further south than most Chivalric Saga authors could ever dream of—has described the authors of these sagas as 'armchair travelling author narrators'.[7]

The Chivalric Sagas are learned works, often drawing deeply on the body of European scholarship that was circulating in medieval Iceland. Foreign settings and learning are coded in the DNA of both translated and original Chivalric Sagas. This means that the heroes can end up in some very exotic locations, far beyond the practical experience of the medieval Icelanders and their forebears. The protagonists of these sagas are medieval avatars, who can explore the wide world as though they had been deposited into a virtual encyclopedia.

Far-south-facing sagas are interested in the limits of geographical experience and humanity itself. The saga writers are not drawing on the traditions, knowledge, and history of their own culture. They are filling in the unknown gaps of the world with book-based learning: the saga equivalent of the rows and columns that fill Africa in the Icelandic *mappa mundi*. Historical time breaks down, space becomes amorphous, and everything collapses into a fog of borrowed fantasies and inherited ideas. We are in the badlands of the medieval encyclopedia, where nothing is quite as it seems.

Monstrous regiments

Sometimes encyclopedic information is dumped into the saga as a straightforward cut-and-paste job. For instance, the *Saga of Dinus the Haughty* (*Dínus saga dramblátá*) is a fourteenth-century saga starring the snooty Prince Dinus of Egypt and Princess Philotemia of Blaland. The saga explains what this country is like and what lives there:

> The greatest of the kingdoms in Africa, called *Blaland the Great*, extends west along the outer ocean and south all the way to the Mediterranean Sea, where the ocean boils because of the sun's heat. Many places there are singed and burnt from the hot sun, and various giants and cursed *blamenn* and all kinds of monstrous beings are born there.[8]

But where is Blaland and who are the blamenn? Just as the location of Serkland is not fixed to a specific country and refers to any of the regions where Muslims live, so Blaland is a rather vague geographical region with its southerly location as its main defining feature. *Bláland*, to give the word in its original Old Norse form, is often translated as 'Black Land', while its inhabitants, the *blámenn*, are 'black men'. But things aren't quite that simple. The Old Norse word for 'black' is *svartr*, while *blá* technically means 'blue'. As we have already seen, the various contexts in which this word is used suggest that the Norse took it to mean something more along the lines of 'blue-black' or 'very dark blue'. *Blá* is a semantically loaded word: the colour of swollen corpses that crawl from their graves and cloaks worn by murderers when they set out to commit dark deeds. Similarly, while some blamenn simply have black skin and come from Africa, others are supernatural, malevolent creatures, more animal than human, and not necessarily linked to southern lands.[9] In this saga's depiction of 'Blaland the Great', geographical extremities, racial stereotyping, monstrosity, and even Christian morality blend together. At the physical, barely habitable limits of the world, where the earth itself is singed and burned by the heat, only inhuman, cursed creatures can survive: 'blamenn and terrifying giants and other monsters with hideous faces. There are many elephants in the army, captive, hooded, and with castles on their back, and after them hastens the host, speeding as fast as they can.'[10]

Nor is this the only occasion where marvellous races march to war from the far south, a monstrous regiment of nightmarish creatures. The *Saga of Sigurd the Silent* (*Sigurðar saga þögla*) was clearly popular in late medieval Iceland, and versions of it survive in over sixty manuscripts. In this tale, the prince of Blaland commands an even more terrifying army, made up not only of Blaland natives but also terrible creatures from Norse tradition such as berserkers, dwarves, giants, and trolls. The ranks are further swelled by monstrous and marvellous races transplanted straight from the pages of medieval encyclopedias:

…blamenn and berserkers, dwarves and giants and trolls. He has creatures from India that are called cynocephali, which bark like dogs and have dog heads. He also has men with one eye in the middle of their foreheads, and some that are headless and have their mouth and eyes on their chest. There are also some that have eyes on their shoulder blades. They are all as big as giants and the colour of pitch.[11]

This is clearly a theme that more than one saga author chooses to play on. In the *Saga of Kirialax*, one of the far-travelling prince's first tasks is to defeat the 'overwhelming army of all species and peoples', belonging to the African king Solldan of Babylon:[12]

…blamenn and giants and grotesque creatures with terrifying faces, and some have their eyes on their breast and chest and are headless, some

FIGURE 14.4 Marvellous and monstrous races from the Icelandic *Physiologus* (*c*.1190–1210)

are headless and have their mouth and nose on their shoulder blades, some have such enormous ears that they can wrap themselves up in them, and some have dog heads and bark like dogs.[13]

Outlandish animals as well as strange races roam the lands of the far south. In this particular monstrous army there are also war elephants, which, like the circus elephants in the Disney film *Dumbo,* are terrified of mice. Kirialax orders his men to stuff mice into wooden boxes and throw them into the middle of the advancing elephants like furry rodent hand-grenades:

Because there is no living thing in the world that an elephant fears more than mice, for as Isidore the bishop says in Book Eleven of his *Etymologies,* an elephant even flees from its own offspring when it becomes aware of such a thing, and they also greatly fear the creaking of wheels.[14]

The bookish author of this saga is at pains to name his sources, citing Isidore of Seville's encyclopedic *Etymologies,* written in the seventh century and one of the most influential texts of the Middle Ages. But in fact this is incorrect referencing; there is nothing about elephants and mice in Isidore's work. Pliny the Elder, on the other hand, mentions elephants being scared of mice in his encyclopedic masterpiece *Natural History,* written in the first century AD and another cornerstone of learning in the Middle Ages. Yet through one channel or another the tradition about musophobic pachyderms obviously reached Iceland, and for the saga writer, it was important that he showed himself to be drawing consciously on well-known sources of Continental learning, even if he got his referencing muddled up.[15]

To the ends of the earth

The monstrous southern armies of Blaland and Babylon may come from Africa, but another Chivalric Saga, called the *Saga of Vilhjalm of Sjod* (*Vilhjálms saga sjóðs*), takes us even further afield to what, in the saga author's mind, is the southernmost end of the earth. The tale is a tour-de-force of southern adventures and exploration, and the author sets out his stall from the opening sentence:

This saga begins in England, then travels to Saxony and Greece, and next west into Africa all the way out to where the sun sets. From there, it travels to the great city of Nineveh in the southern part of the world, and finally to the vast Caucasus Mountains at the world's end.[16]

In reality, the Caucasus Mountains stretch from the shores of the Black Sea all the way to the Caspian Sea; hardly the southernmost edge of the world for northern travellers such as Yngvar, or the Norse traders who visited Baghdad on camelback. But in Chivalric Sagas such as this, historical reality has been uncoupled from the story. Here, the rulers of these southernmost lands command a monstrous band of uglies, but if the armies already mentioned seem bizarre enough, then this one is even worse; it contains one-hundred thousand giants and evil creatures, and all sorts of grisly wild animals. One of the standard-bearers has eyes that are three-and-a-half handspans apart, while another has four legs and two hooves at the back for kicking like a horse. Whoever put this saga together seems to be riffing off the motif of marvellous southern armies, but drawing more on their imagination than on encyclopedic lists. Rather than enumerate all the races as the other sagas do, the narrator states laconically: 'parchment and energy would both be exhausted before the appearances of all those hideously shaped creatures could be described.'[17] In this instance, readers may start to suspect that they are not meant to take this saga very seriously.

Other encyclopedic beings await Vilhjalm as he roams across Africa with his pet lion, on a quest to reach the southernmost part of the world and collect the names of ninety trolls (a very Norse take on the theme of the chivalric quest). Descriptions of the topography are detailed, as the saga writer gives free rein to his imagination. There are boggy swamps, desolate forests that take forty days to get through, high mountains that take three days to cross, vicious wild animals, and no humans to be seen anywhere. The further south Vilhjalm travels, the more peculiar the creatures he encounters. The elephant, usually the gentle, plant-eating giant of the African plains, is cast as a ferocious howling beast with a taste for man-flesh, 'so enormous that its head was the same height as the trees'.[18]

Even stranger beings await in the furthest reaches of the south, but once again, whoever created the saga seems to be enjoying himself. Vilhjalm and his lion hear a loud roar and feel the ground shake beneath them, and suddenly two bizarre creatures jump out at them, perhaps the distant cousins of the Vinland uniped with a touch of cyclops in their ancestry:

They were weirdly shaped, with one eye in the middle of their forehead and a single leg that was very long and looked like the base of a wooden vessel at the bottom, with toes all the way around the foot. They could hop a very long way with their poles, and anything that was in their way when they landed was crushed to death.[19]

The ultimate goal of Vilhjalm's quest is to reach the southernmost ends of the earth, where the sun goes down and trolls roam. Just as the far north was known to have extremes of light and dark, so it was with the far south. What the medieval Icelanders didn't realize is that such extremes of light and dark occur much further south than they could have imagined, and certainly not near the Caucasus, which is where this saga pinpoints the ends of the earth:

> It is located so close to where the sun goes down that even at midday it is never so bright that the stars can't be seen. When you reach the edges of that country you will see a fertile land with grass and fruit trees. Here the sun shines at midnight when other places in the world are in the shadow of the earth and the days are shortest.[20]

The inhabitants of this land are not the traditional marvellous and monstrous races of Classical and medieval tradition, but the native Norse equivalent: ninety trolls. In this Nordic version of Rumpelstiltskin, the saga hero must name them all in order to defeat them. When the ninetieth name is called out, the trolls leap up and rip each other apart like wolves and an earthquake starts to shake the land to pieces, scattering troll corpses into the rock fissures. Despite the saga's sense of far-off exoticism, it still fills the empty spaces at the end of the world with creatures and topographies that would be culturally recognizable to a northern readership: cave trolls, rocks, and earthquakes.

This side of paradise

Finally, there is another saga that takes a very different approach to filling in the geographical blanks at the end of the world, not with ninety trolls, but a dragon, an angel, and Paradise itself. The *Saga of Erik the Far Traveller* (*Eíriks saga víðfǫrla*) uses a different blend of material to depict the furthest reaches of the globe: imaginative and theological geography. The hero of this fourteenth-century saga is a young prince from Norway, who travels the world performing adventurous deeds of derring-do. The tone is distinctly religious; readers may think that they are reading a story about a hero travelling to exotic climes to fight heathen armies and dragons, when without warning they find themselves ambushed from behind and forcibly enlightened, both spiritually and intellectually.

The object of Erik's quest is the Earthly Paradise, which is said to lie 'east of outermost India', according to the emperor in Constantinople (who dispenses spiritual and intellectual guidance like an encyclopedia brought to life).[21] India, it is said, is 'the outermost land of the southernmost part of the world', and so Erik vows to go south through the world until he finds what he seeks.[22] First stopping off in Constantinople, Erik and his men then travel south through unnamed distant lands and then across India, until they reach its outermost limits. Only at this point does the landscape begin to take on a touch of the encyclopedic. As before, the stars can be seen by day as well as night, but in addition to this, lumps of knobbly gold are scattered on the ground, reminiscent of the fragment of information about precious stones that was in the southern columns of the Icelandic *mappa mundi*.

There are no marvellous races waiting for Erik and his men at the edge of the habitable world, but a dragon, guarding the river that flows from Paradise. According to the Book of Genesis, four rivers flowed here: the Tigris, the Euphrates, the Pishon, and the Gihon. Erik concludes that he has probably come to the Pishon—which we might equate with the Ganges given Erik's proximity to India—but he has little time to ponder matters of fluvial identification. Brandishing his sword, he takes a running jump and leaps into the mouth of the dragon. Rather than skewering himself on razor-sharp dragon fangs, Erik finds himself wading through nothing nastier than mist. He has reached the Earthly Paradise, a lush, bright land of sweet scents and light breezes. Before him is a tower suspended in the air, with a room at the top furnished with sumptuous satin and velvet and a table laden with sweet bread and wine. There are even beds spread with velvet and gold for Erik to sleep on. For this whole description, the saga writer transplants chunks of learned material from the Continent again, possibly from several sources.[23] But this is not a land filled with marvellous and monstrous races, nor trolls dwelling in rocky mountain caves. The only inhabitant that Erik encounters in the Earthly Paradise is his guardian angel, who informs him: 'This place that you see here is like a wasteland compared to Paradise, though it isn't far from here, and that's where the river that you saw flows from. No one alive can get there, but the souls of the righteous shall dwell there.'[24] And so Erik can go no further. He jumps back over the river, the dragon vomits him up—although the saga puts it a bit more poetically than that—and he starts the long journey home to the north.

For this saga at least, this is where the limits of the physical world meet the limits of the human: not with ninety trolls, nor with men with their faces in their chests, one-eyed, pole-vaulting unipeds, or bloodthirsty killer elephants, but at the edge of Paradise itself. At the physical limits of the world, theological and imaginative geography come together, and the human converges with the divine. Learning and imagination may enable saga writers to fill in the blank spaces at the edges of the map, but when a saga hero reaches the ends of the earth itself, he must turn around and journey back into the world.

Epilogue

Thanks to each person who listened to and was amused by this story,
and may those who were annoyed by it (and who don't enjoy
anything anyway) wallow in their misery!

Saga of Gongu-Hrolf

Another summer's day on Lindisfarne, under a deep blue sky scuffed with white scratches. Out across the deep swell of the North Sea, hidden beyond the horizon, are Denmark and Norway. Carried across the island on the wind, the tang of woodsmoke mingles with sharp sea-salt. With them, the faint clatter of metal hitting metal, raised voices, distant laughter.

The vikings are back. But this time everyone is pleased to see them. In fact, it's the most popular event of the year.

In the ruins of the medieval priory tents have been pitched, their raised awnings fluttering in the breeze. Men and women bustle about dressed in coloured tunics: sage green, burnt orange, blood red. A woman sits in the grass and leans against the remnants of a stone wall, legs stretched straight out, face raised smiling to the sun. Nearby, long wooden trestle tables creak with bowls of red apples and green leeks, round loaves of bread, yellow pats of butter, boiled brown eggs, barrels of weak ale. A charred black pot swings gently over a smoking fire, bubbling with vegetable stew. Tucked away in a sheltered corner, two sturdy women bend over a loom, nimble fingers weaving strips of purple ribbon. At their feet a dog nuzzles hopefully in the grass, on the hunt for an early dinner.

At the end of our exploring we have arrived where we started. This time, however, things are rather different. On the open grass between the tents stands a warrior dressed for battle, his face almost entirely obscured by polished helmet above and unruly beard below. In spite of the heavy axe and ornate round shield grasped in his hands, he is gradually being engulfed by a horde of tiny children in the grip of an ungodly battle-fury, all demonstrating their 'shield wall' skills. Under the beard, he is still smiling. Just. In the crowd, someone mutters that the incoming tide will start cutting off the causeway in an hour, and the re-enactors had better get on with their storming-the-priory set piece if they don't want everyone to be stranded on the island for the night. Just outside the priory walls other visitors are wandering around the museum and shop, with varying degrees of interest. The 'Viking Raider' grave-marker always draws a crowd, tourists peering through the glass at the seven chillingly expressionless faces carved into stone.

Back outside, and tucked away in a corner, is a smaller tent with two pieces of wood hanging wonkily from the front pole. They bear the words: 'Snorri's School For Vikings'. The eponymous Snorri himself sits outside the tent, a scattering of children at his feet, enthralled by his tales of far-travelling vikings. He tells them about vikings who landed on the shores of Lindisfarne itself, butchered the monks, and took off with their treasures. He tells them about vikings who sailed west to Iceland, Greenland, and even North America. He tells them about vikings who travelled east down the Russian riverways, sacrificing their slave girls and burning their boats. Occasionally the historical details become slightly mangled in the telling. But this is as it should be: stories are *meant* to change. If stories aren't told, they wither and die. In the very act of telling they are transformed: new details are added, others forgotten, the tone alters, the emphasis shifts, and characters metamorphose with a million tiny embellishments and exaggerations. A good story keeps evolving long after the event itself.

Of course, there's usually more than one side to a story: a monk on Lindisfarne in 793 would have had a very different tale to tell, compared to a Norse raider. But ironically, given that this was a 'School for Vikings', most of the stories Snorri told the children didn't come from the Norse themselves. As we have seen, much of what we know about the medieval Norse comes from outsiders looking in: gory calling-cards of blood-splattered islands and salt-marshes, unflattering chronicle entries, poems and sermons that describe seaborne 'slaughter wolves' haunting the coastlines, longboats dredged from bogs and graves by generations of archaeologists. This is what the world thought, and often still thinks, of the Norse. But to understand what the Norse thought of themselves and their place in world history, we must also try to see things through their eyes. By examining the remnants of the stories that the Norse themselves told throughout the centuries, we can look out across the world and back in time with them, hoping to understand how the world was experienced, imagined, and described by a unique, complex, far-travelling people from the northern fringes of medieval Europe.

In many ways, of course, this is an impossible task. For one thing, the Norse were not a homogenous group; words such as 'Norse' and 'Viking' are convenient shorthand for a culture spread over several countries and centuries. If we could go back in time and speak directly to a Norwegian trader up in the Arctic, jump several hundred years to meet Erik the Red as he settled Greenland, zip several thousand miles east to witness Yngvar and his men heading down the Russian rivers, take a detour to Rome to join northern pilgrims tending to their Christian souls, and finally fast-forward another couple of centuries to meet the individuals who eventually recorded the sagas over in Iceland, we would end up with several very different views of the world. And that's before we factor in the outlandish troupe of trolls, giants, unipeds, and dragons that caper in the shadows of the saga manuscripts, not to mention the thousands of ordinary people whose own little sagas never had a hope of being retold or written down, and whose worldview extended not much further than the next fjord. So we have to be content to glimpse the Norse world through the lenses that are available to us: some sagas written down years after the events they describe took place, others that are barely on nodding terms with reality, fragments of archaeology to correct or con-fuse the picture, and of course other texts from inside and outside the Norse world, written by those who encountered these northerners in their various incarnations.

With the passage of time, remarkable events can be transformed into extraordinary stories. Swedish runic inscriptions testify to a real-life expedi-tion into Russia that can never be more than a shadow, but the saga version of Yngvar's life is resplendent with a colourful array of dragons, raunchy pagan women, an unlucky war elephant, and a beak-faced man with a penchant for apples. At other times it is the stories themselves that lead us towards the facts: the essential truth of the epic voyages described in the Vinland sagas was con-firmed with the discovery of an overwintering site on the tip of Newfound-land in the 1960s. Sometimes we may detect a hint of self-mythologizing in the shaping of a story: who knows how much of a hand Harald Hardrada had in creating the myth of his own Byzantine brilliance (fighter of dungeon serpents, avenger of wronged royals, and devilishly sexy empress-magnet)? Meanwhile, other people's stories never made it into the sagas and only survive as accidental fragments: three hunters caught out in a Greenlandic winter north of the Arctic Circle, scratching runes, piling cairns, their fates never to be known.

The Norse haven't given up all their stories yet. There are tales still to be told. Some may be waiting to be discovered on the shelves of dusty libraries or buried in the cold soil. Others will remain forever lost. But after the adventures are over, after the people are gone, after the boats, buildings, and bones have started to crumble into the ground, only the stories remain. The rest is silence.

ENDNOTES

Icelandic names are predominantly patronymic (sometimes matronymic), incorporating the name of an individual's parent rather than a surname. Therefore Björk Guðmundsdóttir means 'Björk, daughter of Guðmundur', and Hafþór Björnsson means 'Hafþór, son of Björn'. However, in the bibliographical details below, Icelandic names have been referenced like other names in order to make life easier for those unfamiliar with this convention.

Chapter 1

1. 'Her wæron reðe forebecna cumene ofer Norðhymbra land, 7 þæt folc earmlic bregdon, þæt wæron ormete þodenas 7 ligrescas, 7 fyrenne dracan wæron gesewene on þam lifte fleo-gende. Þam tacnum sona fyligde mycel hunger, 7 litel æfter þam…earmlice hæþenra manna hergunc adilegode Godes cyrican in Lindisfarnaee þurh hreaflac 7 mansliht', G. P. Cubbin, ed., *The Anglo-Saxon Chronicle: A Collaborative Edition*, vol. 6, *MS D* (1996), 17.
2. D. Whitelock, ed., *English Historical Documents*, vol. 1, *c.* 500–1042 (1979), 247.
3. Whitelock, ed., *English Historical Documents*, 1.776.
4. Whitelock, ed., *English Historical Documents*, 1.194.
5. 'on his dagum comon ærest .iii. scypu Norðmanna of Hæreðalande, 7 þa sæ gerefa þærto rad, 7 hie wolde drifan to þæs cyninges tune, þe he nyste hwæt hi wæron, 7 hine man ofsloh þa. Ðæt wæron þa ærestan scipu Dæniscra manna þe on Engelcynnes land gesohton', Cubbin, ed., *The Anglo-Saxon Chronicle*, 16.
6. A. A. Somerville and R. A. McDonald, eds., *The Viking Age: A Reader* (2010), 245.
7. See E. A. Rowe, *Vikings in the West: The Legend of Ragnarr Loðbrók and his Sons* (2012), 74.
8. <http://cdn.yougov.com/cumulus_uploads/document/7epehk7y1d/YG-Archive-140311-Viking.pdf>.
9. G. R. Bowden et al., 'Excavating Past Population Structures by Surname-Based Sampling: The Genetic Legacy of the Vikings in Northwest England', *Molecular Biology and Evolution* 25:2 (2008), 301–9.
10. J. Jones, 4 Mar. 2014, <http://www.theguardian.com/artanddesign/2014/mar/04/vikings-british-museum-ship-story>.
11. C. Fell, 'Old English *Wicing*: A Question of Semantics', *Proceedings of the British Academy* 72 (1986), 295–316, at 298.
12. 'Her syndan mannslagan and mægslagan and mæsserbanan and mynsterhatan; and her syndan mansworan and morþorwyrhtan; and her syndan myltestran and bearnmyrðran and fule forlegene horingas manege; and her syndan wiccan and wælcyrian; and her syndan ryperas and reaferas and woroldstruderas; and, hrædest is to cweþenne, mana and misdæda ungerim ealra', E. Treharne, ed., 'Wulfstan's *Sermo Lupi ad Anglos*', in her *Old and Middle English: An Anthology* (2000), 230.
13. See J. Jesch, 'Vikings', in her *Ships and Men in the Late Viking Age: The Vocabulary of Runic Inscriptions and Skaldic Verse* (2001), 44–56.

14. R. Cleasby and G. Vigfússon, *An Icelandic–English Dictionary* (1874), s.v. *víkingr*.
15. A. Wawn, *The Vikings and the Victorians: Inventing the Old North in Nineteenth-Century Britain* (2000), 58–9.
16. Quoted by Wawn, *The Vikings and the Victorians*, 283.
17. J. N. Moore, *Edward Elgar: A Creative Life* (1984), 203.
18. Ceremonial horned helmets have been found in Scandinavia, but these pre-date the Viking Age. See R. Simek, 'Doepler, Karl Emil', in his *Dictionary of Northern Mythology* (1993), 62.
19. H. Carpenter, ed., *The Letters of J. R. R. Tolkien* (1981), 55.

Chapter 2

1. 'Þá váru hér menn kristnir, þeir es Norðmenn kalla papa, en þeir fóru síðan á braut, af því at þeir vildu eigi vesa hér við heiðna menn, ok létu eptir bœkr írskar ok bjǫllur ok bagla', J. Benediktsson, ed., *Íslendingabók. Landnámabók*, Íslenzk fornrit 1 (1968), 5.
2. This description is typical of the sea-travel imagery used by later Norse poets in their skaldic verses; for examples see J. Jesch, *Ships and Men in the Late Viking Age: The Vocabulary of Runic Inscriptions and Skaldic Verse* (2001), 176–7.
3. A. Helgason et al., 'Estimating Scandinavian and Gaelic Ancestry in the Male Settlers of Iceland', *American Journal of Human Genetics* 67:3 (2000), 697–717; A. Helgason et al., 'mtDNA and the Islands of the North Atlantic: Estimating the Proportions of Norse and Gaelic Ancestry', *American Journal of Human Genetics* 68:3 (2001), 723–37.
4. '...at ætlun ok tǫlu þeira Teits fóstra míns, þess manns es ek kunna spakastan, sonar Ísleifs byskups, ok Þorkels fǫðurbróður míns Gellissonar, es langt mundi fram, ok Þóríðar Snorradóttur goða, es bæði vas margspǫk ok óljúgfróð,—es Ívarr Ragnarssonr loðbrókar lét drepa Eadmund enn helga Englakonung; en þat vas sjau tegum [vetra] ens níunda hundraðs eptir burð Krists', Benediktsson, ed., *Íslendingabók. Landnámabók*, 4.
5. See K. P. Smith, 'Landnám: The Settlement of Iceland in Archaeological and Historical Perspective', *World Archaeology* 26:3 (1995), 319–47.
6. See K. Grönvold et al., 'Ash Layers from Iceland in the Greenland GRIP Ice Core Correlated with Oceanic and Land Sediments', *Earth and Planetary Science Letters* 135 (1995), 149–55.
7. Saxo Grammaticus, *Gesta Danorum: The History of the Danes*, vol. 1, ed. K. Friis-Jensen, trans. P. Fisher (2015), 6–7.
8. As Margaret Clunies Ross has noted, 'Saga geography extends from Iceland to the rest of Scandinavia, then west to the British Isles, the North Atlantic, Greenland and North America, and south and east to the Mediterranean world, Russia and the Middle East. These historical and geographical settings map onto specific sub-genres.' M. Clunies Ross, *The Cambridge Introduction to the Old Norse-Icelandic Saga* (2010), 72–3.
9. Other genres include the Sagas of Holy Men (*Heilagra manna sögur*), with subject-matter ranging from the lives of the apostles to the twelfth-century martyrdom of the English archbishop Thomas Becket. There are also Contemporary Sagas (*Samtíðarsögur*), which describe the bloody decades of civil war and political turmoil leading to Iceland's takeover by the Norwegian crown in the 1260s. Neither will feature much in this book.
10. C. Fell, 'Pedagogy and the Manuscript', in *Care and Conservation of Manuscripts 4: Proceedings of the Fourth International Seminar held at the University of Copenhagen 13th–14th October 1997* (1999), 21–33, at 21–2.
11. See S. G. Guðmundsdóttir and L. Guðnadóttir, 'Book Production in the Middle Ages', in *The Manuscripts of Iceland*, ed. G. Sigurðsson and V. Ólason (2004), 45–62, at 53.

12. See Guðmundsdóttir and Guðnadóttir, 'Book Production in the Middle Ages', 54–7.
13. S. Steingrímsson, 'Árni Magnússon', in Sigurðsson and Ólason, *The Manuscripts of Iceland*, 85–99, at 86.
14. 'Enn til mega heyra þeir menn til slikra sagna at eigi þicki uijst huort sannliga se saman settar þuiat sa sem okunnik er landa skipun ma vera at hann kalli þat j austur sem hann ætti j uestur enn þat [j] sudr sem j nordur stendr', A. Loth, ed., *Vilhjálms saga sjóðs*, in *Late Medieval Icelandic Romances*, vol. 4 (1964), 3–4.
15. This is also the structure used by John Shafer in his Ph.D thesis 'Saga Accounts of Norse Far Travellers' (unpubl. Ph.D, Durham University, 2010), in which he takes a predominantly literary approach to far travel in the sagas (available online).

Chapter 3

1. For instance, in the *Annals of St Bertin* the word *Nortmanni* appears 116 times, while the word *Dani* (Dane) is used only 36 times, *pyratae* (pirate) only 18 times, and *pagani* (pagan) only 9 times. See S. Coupland, 'The Rod of God's Wrath or the People of God's Wrath? The Carolingian Theology of the Viking Invasions', *Journal of Ecclesiastical History* 42:4 (1991), 535–54, esp. 541.
2. See E. R. Barraclough, D. M. Cudmore, and S. Donecker, eds., *Imagining the Supernatural North* (2016).
3. 'Ratramnus and the Dog-Headed Humans', in *Carolingian Civilization: A Reader*, ed. P. E. Dutton, 2nd edn. (2004), 452–5, at 452.
4. S. Allot, *Alcuin of York: His Life and Letters* (1974), 40. Alcuin's quotation is a mashup of Jeremiah 1:14 and Job 37:22.
5. F. Nansen, *In Northern Mists: Arctic Exploration in Early Times*, vol. 1, trans. A. G. Chater (1911), 124.
6. 'undur þau er hier eru nordur med oss', F. Jónsson, ed., *Konungs skuggsjá: Speculum Regale. Udgivet efter håndskrifterne af det kongelige Nordiske Oldskriftselskab* (Copenhagen, 1920), 29.
7. 'þa mun þeim þickia þat meiri vndur ef svo er fra sagt vm þa menn er þad kunnu at temia trie og fialir til þess at sa madur er hann er eigi fimare a fæti enn adrir menn. medan hann hefr ecki annat en i sko sijna eina a fotum. Enn iafnskiott sem hann bindur fialir undir fætur sier annathvort VIII. alna langar edur IX. þa sigrar hann fugl a flaug edur miohunda á rás þeir sem mest kunna at hlaupa edur rein er hleypur halfu meira en hiortur', *Konungs skuggsjá: Speculum Regale*, 31.
8. For more on the association of Iceland with Ultima Thule, see D. Kedwards, 'Iceland, Thule, and the Tilensian Precedent in Medieval Historiography', *Arkiv för nordisk filologi* 130 (2015), 57–78.
9. *Finnr* (sing.) or *Finnar* (plu.) is an imprecise term that can occasionally refer to northern peoples other than the Sámi. However, to make life easier I will refer to the *Finnar* as Sámi throughout these chapters, because broadly speaking this is who they were. For a discussion of the complexities of the term *Finnar* see E. Mundal, 'The Perception of the Saamis and their Religion in Old Norse Sources', in *Shamanism and Northern Ecology*, ed. J. Pentikäinen (1996), 97–116, at 98.
10. See T. Dubois, *Nordic Religions in the Viking Age* (1999), 14; and N. Price, *The Viking Way: Religion and War in Late Iron Age Scandinavia* (2002), 239.
11. C. Keller, 'Furs, Fish and Ivory—Medieval Norsemen at the Arctic Fringe', *Journal of the North Atlantic* 3:1 (2010), 1–23, at 1.
12. For information on the close relationship between the Norse and the Sámi and the archaeological evidence in particular see T. DuBois, 'Ethnomemory: Ethnographic and Culture-Centered Approaches to the Study of Memory', *Scandinavian Studies* 85:3 (2013), 306–31; B. Olsen, 'Belligerent Chieftains and Oppressed Hunters? Changing Conceptions of Interethnic Relationships in Northern Norway during the Iron Age and the Early Medieval Period',

in *Contact, Continuity, and Collapse: The Norse Colonization of the North Atlantic*, ed. J. H. Barrett (2003), 9–31; N. Price, 'Drum-time and Viking Age: Sámi–Norse Identities in Early Medieval Scandinavia', in M. Appelt, J. Berglund, and H. C. Gulløv, ed., *Identities and Cultural Contacts in the Arctic* (2000), 12–27; I. Zachrisson, 'The Sami and their Interaction with the Nordic Peoples', in *The Viking World*, ed. S. Brink and N. Price (2008), 32–9.

13. *A History of Norway and the Passion and Miracles of the Blessed Óláfr*, trans. D. Kunin, ed. C. Phelpstead (2001), 6.

14. *A History of Norway*, 6.

15. *A History of Norway*, 6–7.

16. *A History of Norway*, 7.

17. See N. Price, *The Viking Way: Religion and War in Late Iron Age Scandinavia* (2002), 266.

18. S. Mitchell, 'Magic as an Acquired Art and the Ethnographic Value of the Sagas', in *Old Norse Myths, Literature and Society*, ed. M. Clunies Ross (2003), 132–52.

19. Mitchell, 'Magic as an Acquired Art', 133.

20. See A. Jennings, 'The Finnfolk: Text of a public talk Dr Andrew Jennings gave at the Shetland Museum' <https://www.uhi.ac.uk/en/research-enterprise/cultural/centre-for-nordic-studies/conferences/the-finnfolk>.

21. C. von Maurer, *Isländische Volkssagen der Gegenwart. Vorwiegend nach mündlicher Überlieferung gesammelt und verdeutscht* (1860), 91.

22. Strandagaldur: Museum of Icelandic Sorcery and Witchcraft <http://www.galdrasyning.is/index.php?option=com_content&task=view&id=212&Itemid=60>.

23. There have been several other studies of the *Finnar*/Sámi in the sagas, focusing particularly on their uncanniness and magical abilities. See S. Aalto, 'Alienness in *Heimskringla*: Special Emphasis on the *Finnar*', in *Scandinavia and Christian Europe in the Middle Ages. Papers of the 12th International Saga Conference, Bonn/Germany, 28th July–2nd August 2003*, ed. R. Simek and J. Meurer (2005), 1–7; P. Cardew, '"Mannfögnuður er oss at smjöri þessu": Representation of the Finns within the Icelandic Sagas', in *Text and Nation: Essays on Post-Colonial Cultural Politics*, ed. A. Blake and J. Nyman (2001), 146–58; J. DeAngelo, 'The North and the Depiction of the *Finnar* in the Icelandic Sagas', *Scandinavian Studies* 82:3 (2010), 257–86; J. Lindow, 'Supernatural and Ethnic Others: A Millenium of World View', *Scandinavian Studies* 67:1 (1995), 8–31; V. Ólason, 'The Marvellous North and Authorial Presence in the Icelandic *fornaldarsaga*', in *Contexts of Pre-Novel Narrative: The European Tradition*, ed. R. Eriksen (1994), 101–34; H. Pálsson, 'The Sami People in Old Norse Literature', *Nordlit* 5 (1999), 29–53.

24. 'kómu norðan', E. Ó. Sveinsson, ed., *Vatnsdæla saga*, Íslenzk fornrit 8 (1939), 34.

25. 'vil ek gefa yðr smjǫr ok tin, en þér farið sendiferð mína til Íslands', Sveinsson, ed., *Vatnsdæla saga*, 34.

26. 'Semsveinum er erfitt, ok mikit starf hǫfu vér haft…mega mikit atkvæði Finnunnar, því at vér hǫfu lagt oss í mikla ánauð', Sveinsson, ed., *Vatnsdæla saga*, 35.

27. 'hann tók alt saman ok hǫnd hennar, ok þegar var sem eldshiti kvæmi í hǫrund hans ok vildi þegar hafa hana á þeiri nótt', B. Aðalbjarnarson, ed., *Haralds saga ins hárfagra*, in *Heimskringla I*, Íslenzk fornrit 26 (1941), 126.

28. 'Ok þegar er hon var hrœrð ór rekkjunni, þá slær ýldu ok óþefani ok hvers kyns illum fnyk af líkamanum. Var þá hvatat at báli, ok var hon brennd. Blánaði áðr allr líkaminn, ok ullu þar ór ormar ok eðlur, froskar ok pǫddur ok alls kyns illyrmi', Aðalbjarnarson, ed., *Haralds saga ins hárfagra*, 127.

29. S. Aalto, 'Alienness in *Heimskringla*: Special Emphasis on the *Finnar*', in *Scandinavia and Christian Europe in the Middle Ages. Papers of the 12th International Saga Conference, Bonn/Germany, 28th July–2nd August 2003*, ed. R. Simek and J. Meurer (2005), 1–7.

30. This overlap is discussed in Zachrisson, 'The Sami and their Interaction with the Nordic Peoples', 32–9.

31. Adam of Bremen, *History of the Archbishops of Hamburg-Bremen*, trans. F. J. Tschan (2002), 212.

32. 'báðir eru þeir svá vísir, at þeir rekja spor sem hundar bæði á þá ok á hjarni, en þeir kunnu svá vel á skíðum, at ekki má forðask þá, hvártki menn né dýr, en hvatki er þeir skjóta til, þá hœfa þeir. Svá hafa þeir fyrir komit hverjum manni, er hér hefir komit í nánd. Ok ef þeir verða reiðir, þá snýsk jǫrð um fyrir sjónum þeira, en ef nǫkkut kvikt verðr fyrir sjónum þeira, þá fellr dautt niðr', Aðalbjarnarson, ed., *Haralds saga ins hárfagra*, 12

33. The first episode comes from the *Saga of Egil Skallagrimsson* (*Egils saga Skallagrímssonar*) and the second is from the *Saga of Burnt Njal* (*Brennu-Njáls saga*).

34. V. Ólason, 'The Marvellous North and Authorial Presence in the Icelandic *Fornaldarsaga*', in *Contexts of Pre-Novel Narrative: The European Tradition*, ed. R. Eriksen (1994), 101–34, at 103.

35. 'Sonr Þorsteins ok Lopthœnu var Hrosskell, er átti Jóreiði Ǫlvisdóttur sonar Mǫttuls Finnakonungs', J. Benediktsson, ed., *Íslendingabók. Landnámabók*, Íslenzk fornrit 1 (1968), 82.

36. See G. Steinsland, 'Origin Myths and Rulership. From the Viking Age Ruler to the Ruler of Medieval Historiography: Continuity, Transformations and Innovations', in *Ideology and Power in the Viking and Middle Ages: Scandinavia, Iceland, Ireland, Orkney and the Faeroes*, ed. G. Steinsland et al. (2011), 15–67, at 47–8.

Chapter 4

1. Ohthere's ship may have been similar to the famous Gokstad ship from the late ninth century, discovered in a burial mound in Vestfold, Norway. For more information about the ship see A. E. Christensen, 'Ohthere's Vessel', in *Ohthere's Voyages: A Late-9th Century Account of Voyages along the Coasts of Norway and Denmark and its Cultural Context*, ed. J. Bately and A. Englert (2007), 112–16.

2. See A. Englert, 'Ohthere's Voyages seen from a Nautical Angle', in Bately and Englert, *Ohthere's Voyages*, 117–29.

3. S. Keynes and M. Lapidge, trans., *Alfred the Great: Asser's Life of King Alfred and Other Contemporary Sources* (1983), 101.

4. 'Ohthere sæde his hlaforde, Ælfrede cyninge, þæt he ealra Norðmonna norþmest bude. He cwæð þæt he bude on þæm lande norþweardum wiþ þa west sæ. He sæde þeah þæt [þæt] land sie swiþe lang norþ þonan, ac hit is eal weste, buton on feawum stowum styccemælum wiciað Finnas, on huntoðe on wintra 7 on sumera on fiscaþe be þære sæ. He sæde þæt he æt sumum cirre wolde fandian hu longe þæt land norþryhte læge, oþþe hwæðer ænig mon be norðan þæm westenne bude. Þa for he norþryhte be þæm lande', Old English from J. Bately, ed., 'Text and Translation', in Bately and Englert, *Ohthere's Voyages*, 44.

5. 'for unfriþe', Bately, 'Text and Translation', 45.

6. 'swa feor norþ swa þa hwælhuntan firrest faraþ', Bately, 'Text and Translation', 44.

7. 'micel ea', Bately, 'Text and Translation', 45.

8. 'Swiþost he for ðider, toeacan þæs landes sceawunge, for þæm horshwælum, for ðæm hie habbað swiþe æþele ban on hiora toþum—þa teð hie brohton sume þæm cyninge—7 hiora hyd bið swiðe god to scipraþum', Bately, 'Text and Translation', 45.

9. 'He hæfde þa gyt, ða he þone cyninge sohte, tamra deora unbebohtra syx hund', Bately, 'Text and Translation', 45.

10. 'Þa deor hi hataðhranas; þara wæron syx stælhranas, ða beoð swyðe dyre mid Finnum, for ðæm hy foð þa wildan hranas mid', Bately, 'Text and Translation', 45–6.

11. I. McDougall, 'Foreigners and Foreign Languages in Medieval Iceland', *Saga-Book of the Viking Society* 22 (1986–9), 180–233, at 217. The manuscript in question is AM 194 8vo.

12. 'Fela spella him sædon þa Beormas ægþer ge of hiera agnum lande ge of þæm landum þe ymb hie utan wæron, ac he nyste hwæt þæs soþes wæs, for þæm he hit self ne geseah. Þa Finnas, him þuhte, 7 þa Beormas spræcon neah an geþeode', Bately, 'Text and Translation', 45.

13. For more about the linguistic situation in England at this time, see M. Townend, *Language and History in Viking Age England: Linguistic Relations between Speakers of Old Norse and Old English* (2005), 102 and throughout ch. 4.

14. See T. Hofstra and K. Samplonius, 'Viking Expansion Northwards: Mediaeval Sources', *Arctic* 48:3 (1995), 235–47, at 243.

15. 'fór með þeim allt í makendum ok í vinskap, en sumt með hræzlugœði', S. Nordal, ed., *Egils saga Skalla-Grímssonar*, Íslenzk fornrit 2 (1933), 27.

16. 'Um várit lét hann gera langskip mikit ok á drekahǫfuð, lét þat búa sem bezt, hafði þat norðan með sér. Þórólfr sópask mjǫk um fǫng þau, er þá váru á Hálogalandi, hafði menn sína í síld-veri ok svá í skreiðfiski; selver váru ok gnóg ok eggver; lét hann þat allt at sér flytja. Hann hafði aldregi færa frelsingja heima en hundrað; hann var ǫrr maðr ok gjǫfull ok vingaðisk mjǫk við stórmenni, alla þá menn, er honum váru í nánd; hann gerðisk ríkr maðr ok lagði mikinn hug á um skipa búnað sinn ok vápna', Nordal, ed., *Egils saga Skalla-Grímssonar*, 28.

17. Famous royal ships with animal heads include Olaf Tryggvason's 'Long Serpent', Olaf Har-aldsson's 'Bison', and Harald Hardrada's 'Serpent'. For further information about the con-nection between dragons and ships in Norse texts see J. Jesch, *Ships and Men in the Late Viking Age: The Vocabulary of Runic Inscriptions and Skaldic Verse* (2001), 127–8.

18. 'lét þar á bera skreið ok húðir ok vǫru ljósa; þar lét hann ok fylgja grávǫru mikla ok aðra skinnavǫru, þá er hann hafði haft af fjalli, ok var þat fé stórmikit', Nordal, ed., *Egils saga Skalla-Grímssonar*, 41–2.

19. 'Hafði hann kaup ǫll; guldu Finnar honum skatt, en hann bazk í því, at sýslumenn yðrir skyldi ekki koma á mǫrkina. Ætlar hann at gerask konungr yfir norðr þar, bæði yfir mǫrkinni ok Hálogalandi', Nordal, ed., *Egils saga Skalla-Grímssonar*, 43.

20. G. Jones, *A History of the Vikings* (2001), 135.

21. See E. Heide, 'Holy Islands and the Otherworld: Places Beyond Water', in *Isolated Islands in Medieval Nature, Culture and Mind*, ed. G. Jaritz (2011), 57–80, at 73.

22. 'Hann var ríkr maðr. Fylgði honum mikill fjǫldi Finna, þegar er hann þurfti. Rauðr var blót-maðr mikill ok mjǫk fjǫlkunnigr', B. Aðalbjarnarson, ed., *Óláfs saga Tryggvasonar*, in *Heim-skringla I*, Íslenzk fornrit 26 (1941), 324.

23. 'Sigurðr biskup tók allan messuskrúða sinn ok gekk fram í stafn á konungsskipi, lét tendra kerti ok bar reykelsi, setti róðukross upp í stafninn, las þar guðspjall ok margar bœnir aðrar, støkkði vígðu vatni um allt skipit', Aðalbjarnarson, ed., *Óláfs saga Tryggvasonar*, 326.

24. 'ek má enga skírn fá. Ek em einn andi, kviknaðr í mannslíkam með fjǫlkynngi Finna, en faðir minn ok móðir féngu áðr ekki barn átt', Aðalbjarnarson, ed., *Óláfs saga Tryggvasonar*, 323.

25. 'með svá mikilli fjǫlkynngi, at ekki vápn festi á', B. Aðalbjarnarson, ed., *Óláfs saga helga*, in *Heimskringla II*, Íslenzk fornrit 27 (1945), 345.

26. 'Sverðit beit ekki, en svá sýndisk sem dyst ryki ór hreinbjálbanum', Aðalbjarnarson, ed., *Óláfs saga helga*, 383.

27. 'Mildr fann gǫrst, hvé galdrar, / gramr sjalfr, meginrammir / fjǫlkunnigra Finna / fullstórum barg Þóri, / þás hyrsendir Hundi / húna golli búnu / slætt réð sízt at bíta / sverði laust of herðar', Aðalbjarnarson, ed., *Óláfs saga helga*, 383–4.

Chapter 5

1. 'Mannfögnuðr er oss at smjöri þessu', G. Jónsson, ed., *Ketils saga hœngs*, in *Fornaldar sögur Norðurlanda*, vol. 2 (1954), 159.

2. 'Hví býðr þú trölli þessu hér at vera?', Jónsson, ed., *Ketils saga hœngs*, 165.

3. 'er þat illt, at þú vilt elska tröll þat', Jónsson, ed., *Ketils saga hœngs*, 165.

4. 'Hallbjörn, vinr minn', Jónsson, ed., *Ketils saga hœngs*, 156.

5. 'Hún var eigi hæri en sjau vetra gamlar stúlkur, en svá digr, at Grímr hugði, at hann mundi eigi geta feðmt um hana. Hún var langleit ok harðleit, bjúgnefjuð ok baröxluð, svartleit ok svipilkinnuð, fúlleit ok framsnoðin. Svört var hún bæði á hár ok á hörund. Hún var í skörpum skinnstakki. Hann tók eigi lengra en á þjóhnappa henni á bakit. Harðla ókyssilig þótti honum hún vera, því at hordingullinn hekk ofan fyrir hváftana á henni', G. Jónsson, ed., *Gríms saga loðinkinna*, in *Fornaldar sögur Norðurlanda*, vol. 2 (1954), 191.

6. 'er henni þótti hann óspakr í vöggunni, lagði hún hann í sæng hjá sér ok vafðist utan at honum, ok kom þá svá, at Oddr lék allt þat, er lysti; gerðist þá harðla vel með þeim', G. Jónsson, ed., *Örvar-Odds saga*, in *Fornaldar sögur Norðurlanda*, vol. 2 (1954), 274.

7. 'þat mætti ólíkligra þykkja, at þú værir til þeira hluta færr, svá lítill ok auvirðiligr sem þú ert at sjá. Er þar þó engi í tigi til nema þú at vera faðir at barni því', Jónsson, ed., *Örvar-Odds saga*, 275.

8. 'þeir fengu eina gýgi undan forsi stórum, galdra fulla ok gerninga, ok lögðu í sæng hjá Háreki konungi, ok við henni átti hann son; sá var vatni ausinn ok nafn gefit ok kallaðr Ögmundr. Flestum mennskum mönnum var hann ólíkr þegar á unga aldri, sem ván var sakir móðernis hans, en faðir hans var þó inn mesti blótmaðr. Þegar er Ögmundr var þrévetr var hann sendr á Finnmörk ok nam hann þar alls kyns galdra ok gerninga ok þá er hann var í því fullnuma fór hann heim til Bjarmalands. Hann var þá sjau vetra ok svá stórr sem fullrosknir menn rammr at afli ok illr viðskiptis. Ekki hafði hann batnat yfirlits hjá Finnunum, því at hann var þá bæði svartr ok blár en hárit sitt ok svart ok hekk flóki ofan fyrir augun þat er topprinn skyldi heita', Jónsson, ed., *Örvar-Odds saga*, 281.

9. 'Ekki þótti mönnum hann vera líkr um neitt inum fyrrum frændum sínum, sem var Ketill hængr ok aðrir Hrafnistumenn, nema á vöxt', G. Jónsson, ed., *Áns saga bogsveigis*, in *Fornaldar sögur Norðurlanda*, vol. 2 (1954), 368.

10. R. Simek, 'Elusive Elysia or Which Way to Glæsisvellir? On the Geography of the North in Icelandic Legendary Fiction', in *Sagnaskemmtun: Studies in Honour of Hermann Pálsson on his 65th Birthday, 26th May 1986*, ed. R. Simek, J. Kristjánsson, and H. Bekker-Nielsen (1986), 247–75, at 249.

11. Another geographical description of the far north occurs in the *Saga of Samson* (*Samsons saga*), where once again there are two 'Giantlands', *Jotunheimar* and *Risaland* (*jǫtunn* and *risi* both mean 'giant'). Likewise, on the sixteenth-century Icelandic Skalhólts map, both *Jotunheimar* and *Risaland* are labelled as being in the far north beyond Halogaland. This map will be returned to in later chapters on the west.

12. C. Tolkien, ed., *The Saga of King Heidrek the Wise* (1960).

13. 'Svá finnsk ritat í fornum bókum, at Jǫtunheimar váru kallaðir norðr um Gandvík, en Ymisland fyrir sunnan í millum Halogalands.…byggðu norðrhálfurnar risar ok sumt hálfrisar; gerðisk þá mikit sambland þjóðanna', (U-redaction), Tolkien, ed., *The Saga of King Heidrek the Wise*, 66.

14. From the *Hauksbók* version of the saga (known as the H-text), compiled in the early fourteenth century. See Tolkien, ed., *The Saga of King Heidrek the Wise*, 66, n. 2.

15. 'Guðmundr hét höfðingi í Jǫtunheimum; bœr hans hét á Grund, en heraðit Glasisvellir. Hann var ríkr maðr ok vitr, ok varð svá gamall ok allir hans menn, at þeir lifðu marga mannsaldra', Tolkien, ed., *The Saga of King Heidrek the Wise*, 66.

16. *The Tale of Thorstein Mansion-Might* (*Þorsteins þáttr bæjarmagns*).

17. *The Saga of Bosi and Herraud* (*Bósa saga ok Herrauðs*).

18. 'Ok þat hefi ek heyrt sagt af Guðmundi af Glæsisvöllum, at hann sé mjök fjölkunnigr ok illu megi helzt við hann skipta, ok eru þeir menn illa komnir, er undir hans valdi eru', G. Jónsson, ed., *Helga þáttr Þórissonar*, in *Fornaldar sögur Norðurlanda*, vol. 4 (1954), 351.

19. 'Þat var á einu sumri, at þeir bræðr höfðu kaupferð norðr til Finnmerkr ok höfðu smjör ok flesk til kaups við Finna', Jónsson, ed., *Helga þáttr Þórissonar*, 347.

20. 'en fyrir bænir yðrar lét hann mik lausan, svá at þér mættið vita, hvat er af mér væri orðit', Jónsson, ed., *Helga þáttr Þórissonar*, 352.

21. 'Hún þóttist eigi mega liggja hjá mér nema með meinlætum, ef hún kæmi við mik beran, ok því fór ek mest í brott', Jónsson, ed., *Helga þáttr Þórissonar*, 353.

22. 'ór trölla höndum', Jónsson, ed., *Helga þáttr Þórissonar*, 353.

23. '"Allgott," segir hann, "ok hvergi hefir mér betra þótt." Þá spurði konungr at um síðu Guð-mundar konungs ok at fjölmenni eða athöfn. En hann lét yfir öllu vel ok sagði, at hans var miklu fleiri en hann fengi talit', Jónsson, ed., *Helga þáttr Þórissonar*, 352.

24. 'Sótti mik nú svá mikil ergi, at ek þóttumst eigi mannlaus lifa mega', G. Jónsson, ed., *Egils saga einhenda ok Ásmundar berserkjabana*, in *Fornaldar sögur Norðurlanda*, vol. 3 (1954), 350.

25. 'Lá ek fyrst hjá Óðni, ok hljóp ek síðan yfir bálit, ok fekk ek skikkjuna, ok er ek síðan skinn-laus um allan kroppinn', Jónsson, ed., *Egils saga einhenda ok Ásmundar berserkjabana*, 352.

26. 'smjörtrog svá mikit sem hún gat lyft, ok sagði hún, at sá gripr mundi torgætr þykkja í Jötun-heimum', Jónsson, ed., *Egils saga einhenda ok Ásmundar berserkjabana*, 363.

27. Þótti kerlingu þessir gripir betri en þótt þeir hefði gefit henni byrði sína af gulli', Jónsson, ed., *Egils saga einhenda ok Ásmundar berserkjabana*, 363.

28. 'Segja skal þursi, ef hann sitr nøkkviðr við eld', S. Nordal and G. Jónsson, eds., *Heiðarvíga saga*, in *Borgfirðinga sǫgur*, Íslenzk fornrit 3 (1938), 258.

29. 'þú ert brúðr Svínfellsáss, sem sagt er, hverja ina níundu nótt ok geri hann þik at konu', E. Ó. Sveinsson, ed., *Brennu-Njáls saga*, Íslenzk fornrit 12 (1954), 314.

Chapter 6

1. 'þægar er orsœkir hinum mæsta haleic hafsens þa er sva mikell gnotr isa ihafino at ec vita æigi dœmi til þvilicra annar staðar íallum heiminom', F. Jónsson, ed., *Konungs skuggsjá: Specu-lum Regale. Udgivet efter håndskrifterne af det Kongelige Nordiske Oldskriftselskab* (Copenhagen, 1920), 67.

2. 'Oc sumer þeir er þar hafa í komit þa hafa tynnz en sumir hafa oc or komiz ok hofum ver noccora set af þeim oc heyrt þeira rœður oc frasagnir. En þat hafa aller til raðs tækit þær sæm iþæssa isa voc hafa komit at þeir hafa tækit smabata oc drægit áisa upp mæð ser oc hafa sva leitað lannzens en hafskip oc allr annnarr fiarlutr þa hæfir þar æpter dvalz oc tynz', *Konungs skuggsjá: Speculum Regale*, 67–8.

3. See N. Lynnerup, 'Life and Death in Norse Greenland', in *Vikings: The North Atlantic Saga*, ed. W. W. Fitzhugh and E. Ward (2000), 285–94, at 292.

4. See J. Mirsky, *To the Arctic! The Story of Northern Exploration from Earliest Times to the Present* (1970), 218.

5. However, as early as 1756 the words 'daily seal meat' had been replaced by 'our needs' (*pissat-sinnik*). See K. Langgård, 'The Ordination of Pastors and Bishops in the Evangelical-Lutheran Church of Greenland', in *Rites of Ordination and Commitment in the Churches of the Nordic Coun-tries: Theology and Terminology*, ed. H. R. Iversen (2006), 149–74, at 154.

6. J. Arneborg, 'Greenland and Europe', in Fitzhugh and Ward, *Vikings: The North Atlantic Saga*, 304–17, at 305–6.

7. C. Keller, 'Furs, Fish, and Ivory: Medieval Norsemen at the Arctic Fringe', *Journal of the North Atlantic* 3 (2010), 1–23, at 5–6.

8. N. Lynnerup, 'Life and Death in Norse Greenland', in Fitzhugh and Ward, *Vikings: The North Atlantic Saga*, 285–94, at 287.

9. The *Saga of Erik the Red* is preserved in *Hauksbók* (early 14th century) and *Skálholtsbók* (early 15th century). The *Saga of the Greenlanders* is preserved in *Flateyjarbók* (c.1387). For a summary

of the dating of the Vinland sagas and their relationship to each other see G. Sigurðsson, *The Medieval Icelandic Saga and Oral Tradition: A Discourse on Method*, trans. N. Jones (2004), 263–6.

10. A table of the conventional dates for sagas with Greenlandic episodes (and their earliest surviving manuscripts) is set out in J. Grove, 'The Place of Greenland in Medieval Icelandic Saga Narrative', in *Norse Greenland: Selected Papers from the Hvalsey Conference 2008. Journal of the North Atlantic*, special volume 2, ed. J. Arneborg, G. Nyegaard, and O. Vésteinsson (2009), 30–51, at 33.

11. 'fyrir víga sakar', E. Ó. Sveinsson and M. Þórðarson, eds., *Eiríks saga rauða*, in *Eyrbyggja saga*, Íslenzk fornrit 4 (1935), 197.

12. 'Hann var inn fyrsta vetr í Eiríksey, nær miðri inni eystri byggð. Um várit eptir fór hann til Eiríksfjarðar ok tók sér þar bústað. Hann fór þat sumar í ina vestri óbyggð ok gaf víða ørnefni', Sveinsson and Þórðarson, eds., *Eiríks saga rauða*, 201.

13. The *Saga of Erik the Red* tells us that Erik went 'all the way north to *Snæfell*'. *Snæfell* means 'Snow Mountain', a name often used for prominent snow-capped mountains. There are plenty of snow-capped mountains and glaciers in Greenland fit to bear that name. A *Snæfell* located in the vicinity of Greenland's northern hunting grounds is mentioned in a letter from 1266–7, written by a Greenlandic priest named Halldor. The letter described how the Greenlandic priests sent a ship to discover what the land was like further north than anyone had ever been. See J. R. Enterline, *Erikson, Eskimos, and Columbus: Medieval European Knowledge of America* (2002), 103–5.

14. 'því at hann kvað menn þat mjǫk mundu fýsa þangat, ef landit héti vel', Sveinsson and Þórðarson, eds., *Eiríks saga rauða*, 201.

15. This is discussed in Grove, 'The Place of Greenland in Medieval Icelandic Saga Narrative', 30–51.

16. A number of law-codes from medieval Scandinavia contain variations on the theme *með lǫg skall land byggjast*. See E. Haugen, *The Scandinavian Languages: An Introduction to Their History* (1976), 186.

17. See A. Sanmark, 'The Case of the Greenlandic Assembly Sites', *Norse Greenland: Selected Papers from the Hvalsey Conference 2008. Journal of the North Atlantic*, special volume 2, ed. J. Arneborg, G. Nyegaard, and O. Vésteinsson (2009), 178–92.

18. 'at grœnlenzkum lǫgum', E. Ó. Sveinsson and M. Þórðarson, eds., *Grœnlendinga þáttr*, in *Eyrbyggja saga*, 279.

19. 'viljum vér þau lǫg hafa, er hér ganga', Sveinsson and Þórðarson, eds., *Grœnlendinga þáttr*, 280.

20. See Grove, 'The Place of Greenland in Medieval Icelandic Saga Narrative', 30–51 and E. R. Barraclough, 'Sailing the Saga Seas: Narrative, Cultural, and Geographical Perspectives in the North Atlantic Voyages of the Íslendingasögur', *Journal of the North Atlantic* 7 (2012), 1–12.

21. 'landit var vatnat', Sveinsson and Þórðarson, eds., *Grœnlendinga saga*, in *Eyrbyggja saga*, 246.

22. 'lagði á norrœnur ok þokur, ok vissu þeir eigi, hvert at þeir fóru', Sveinsson and Þórðarson, eds., *Grœnlendinga saga*, 246.

23. 'Í þenna tíma var hallæri mikit á Grœnlandi; hǫfðu menn fengit lítit fang, þeir er í veiðiferðir hǫfðu farit, en sumir ekki aptr komnir', Sveinsson and Þórðarson, eds., *Eiríks saga rauða*, 206.

24. 'hon hafði yfir sér tuglamǫttul blán, ok var settr steinum allt í skaut ofan; hon hafði á hálsi sér glertǫlur, lambskinnskofra svartan á hǫfði ok við innan kattsskinn hvít; ok hon hafði staf í hendi, ok var á knappr; hann var búinn með messingu ok settr steinum ofan um knappinn; hon hafði um sik hnjóskulinda, ok var þar á skjóðupungr mikill, ok varðveitti hon þar í tǫfr sín, þau er hon þurfti til fróðleiks at hafa. Hon hafði á fótum kálfskinnsskúa loðna ok í þvengi langa, ok á tinknappar miklir á endunum. Hon hafði á hǫndum sér

kattskinnsglófa, ok váru hvítir innan ok loðnir', Sveinsson and Þórðarson, eds., *Eiríks saga rauða*, 206–7.

25. 'Heiðit var fólk á Grœnlandi í þann tíma', Sveinsson and Þórðarson, eds., *Grœnlendinga saga*, 245–6.

26. 'Þjóðhildr vildi ekki samræði við Eirík, síðan hon tók trú, en honum var þat mjǫk móti skapi', Sveinsson and Þórðarson, eds., *Eiríks saga rauða*, 212.

27. P. Nörlund and A. Roussel, 'Norse Ruins at Gardar, the Episcopal Seat of Mediaeval Greenland', *Meddelelser om Grønland* 76 (1929), 138. The question of when and how Greenland was converted, and how the Icelanders chose to interpret these events, has been discussed by R. Bonté, 'Conversion on the Margins: Greenland', in 'Conversion and Coercion: Cultural Memory and Narratives of Conversion in the Norse North Atlantic', unpubl. Ph.D thesis, University of Cambridge (2015), 155–200.

28. 'fásinni er mikit með mér at vera, því at tvau erum vit þar hjón, því at ek em einþykkr mjǫk', Sveinsson and Þórðarson, eds., *Grœnlendinga saga*, 258.

29. 'Eigi er fœrt at svá búnu; hér er nú liðit þat allt it dauða fyrir durunum, ok Þorsteinn, bóndi þinn, ok þar kenni ek mik; ok er slíkt hǫrmung at sjá', Sveinsson and Þórðarson, eds., *Eiríks saga rauða*, 215.

30. 'at þar væri varla kyrrt, ok húsfreyja vildi fœrast á fœtr ok vildi undir klæðin hjá honum', Sveinsson and Þórðarson, eds., *Eiríks saga rauða*, 215.

31. 'var þá búit til jólaveizlu, ok var hon in sœmiligsta, svá at menn þóttusk trautt þvílíka rausn sét hafa í fátœku landi', Sveinsson and Þórðarson, eds., *Eiríks saga rauða*, 220.

32. See J. P. Hart Hansen, 'The Mummies from Qilakitsoq—Paleopathological Aspects', *Meddelelser om Grønland/Man & Society* 12 (1989), 69–82. See also M. T. P. Gilbert et al., 'mtDNA from Hair and Nail Clarifies the Genetic Relationship of the 15th Century Qilakitsoq Inuit Mummies', *American Journal of Physical Anthropology* 133:4 (2007), 847–53.

33. See K. Seaver, *The Frozen Echo: Greenland and the Exploration of North America, ca.* A.D. 1000–1500 (1995), 37.

34. F. Nansen, *In Northern Mists: Arctic Exploration in Early Times*, vol. 1, trans. A. G. Chater (1911), 297.

35. F. Magnusen and C. C. Rafn, eds., *Grønlands Historiske Mindesmærker*, 3 vols. (1838–45), 2.656–7. The information about Lika-Lodinn comes from the so-called Greenland Annals (*Grœnlands annáll*), a collection of information about Greenland compiled in the seventeenth century by a man called Bjorn Jonsson.

36. 'Skip þeira kom í óbyggðir á Grœnlandi, ok týndust men allir. En þess varð svá víst, at fjórtán vetrum síðar fannst skip þeira, ok þá fundust sjau men í hellisskúta einum. Þar var Ingimundr prestr. Hann var heill ok ófúinn ok svá klæði hans, en sex manna bein váru þar hjá honum. Vax var ok þar hjá honum ok rúnar þær, er sǫgðu atburð um líflát þeira', J. Jóhannesson, M. Finnbogason, and K. Eldjárn, eds., *Prestssaga Guðmundar góða*, in *Sturlunga saga*, vol. 1 (1946), 138.

37. The two texts are the *Prose Edda* by Snorri Sturluson and the *Third Grammatical Treatise* by Snorri's nephew Óláfr Þórðarson *hvítaskáld* ('white poet').

38. 'Þá er élreifar ófu / Ægis dœtr ok teygðu / fǫls við frost of alnar / fjallgarðs rokur harðar', Snorri Sturluson, *Edda. Skáldskaparmál 1: Introduction, Text and Notes*, ed. A. Faulkes (1998), 37.

39. 'fingrgull ok vaðmálsmǫttul grœnlenzkan ok tannbelti', Sveinsson and Þórðarson, eds., *Eiríks saga rauða*, 210.

40. 'at heimta sik fram við hǫfðingja', Sveinsson and Þórðarson, eds., *Grœnlendinga þáttr*, 273–4.

41. 'Þat var hvítabjörn fulltíði ok vandr ágæta vel. Annar gripr var tanntafl ok gert með miklum hagleik. Þriðji gripr var rostungshaus með öllum tönnum sínum; hann var grafinn allr ok víða rennt í gulli', J. Halldórsson, ed., *Króka-Refs saga*, in *Kjalnesinga saga*, Íslenzk fornrit 14 (1959), 142.

42. For more on the importance of walrus in Norse Greenlanders see K. M. Frei et al., 'Was it for Walrus? Viking Age Settlement and Medieval Walrus Ivory Trade in Iceland and Greenland', *World Archaeology* 47:3 (2015), 439–66.

43. M. Ciklamini, '*Exempla* in an Old Norse Historiographic Mold', *Neophilologus* 81:1 (1997), 71–87, at 74.

44. 'gersimi mikla', B. K. Þórólfsson and G. Jónsson, eds., *Auðunar þáttr Vestfirzka*, in *Vestfirðinga sǫgur*, Íslenzk fornrit 6 (1943), 361.

45. 'máttu á þat líta, at dýrit mun deyja fyrir þér, þars it þurfuð vistir miklar, en fé sé farit, ok er búit við, at þú hafir þá ekki dýrsins', Þórólfsson and Jónsson, eds., *Auðunar þáttr Vestfirzka*, 363.

46. 'Rex Vicecomitibus Londoniæ salutem. Præcipimus vobis, quod custodi albi ursi nostri, qui nuper missus fuit nobis de Norwagia et est in Turri nostra Londoniæ, habere faciatis unum musellum et unam cathenam ferream, ad tenendum ursum illum extra aquam, et unam longam et fortem cordam ad tenendum eundem ursum piscantem in aqua Thamistæ', T. Maddox, *The history and antiquities of the Exchequer of the kings of England, in two periods: to wit, from the Norman conquest, to the end of the reign of K. John; and from the end of the reign of K. John, to the end of the reign of K. Edward II* (1769), 2.376.

Chapter 7

1. Doug Cabot, 3 July 2008 <http://www.dougcabot.com/live/journals/98_07_04/index.html>. See also W. Hodding Carter, *A Viking Voyage: In Which an Unlikely Crew of Adventurers Attempts an Epic Journey to the New World* (2000).

2. Hodding Carter, 14 Sept. 2008 <http://www.dougcabot.com/live/journals/98_09_15/index.html>.

3. Adam of Bremen, *History of the Archbishops of Hamburg-Bremen*, trans. F. J. Tschan (2002), 219.

4. 'hefir Karlsefni gørst sagt allra manna atburði um farar þessar allar, er nú er nǫkkut orði á komit', E. Ó. Sveinsson and M. Þórðarson, eds., *Grœnlendinga saga*, in *Eyrbyggja saga*, Íslenzk fornrit 4 (1935), 269.

5. Gísli Sigurðsson has written extensively on the 'mental maps' described in the Vinland sagas. See G. Sigurðsson, 'Part III: The Sagas and Truth', in his *The Medieval Icelandic Saga and Oral Tradition: A Discourse on Method*, trans. N. Jones (2004).

6. 'sigldu þeir tvau dœgr í suðr. Þá sá þeir land ok skutu báti ok kǫnnuðu landit, fundu þar hellur stórar, ok margar tólf álna víðar. Fjǫldi var þar melrakka. Þeir gáfu þar nafn ok kǫlluðu Helluland. Þaðan sigldu þeir tvau dœgr, ok brá til landsuðrs ór suðri, ok fundu land skógvaxit ok mǫrg dýr á. Ey lá þar undan í landsuðr; þar drápu þeir einn bjǫrn ok kǫlluðu þar síðan Bjarney, en landit Markland. Þaðan sigldu þeir suðr með landinu langa stund ok kómu at nesi einu; lá landit á stjórn; váru þar strandir langar ok sandar.... Þeir kǫlluðu ok strandirnar Furðustrandir, því at langt var með at sigla. Þá gerðist landit vágskorit. Þeir heldu skipunum í einn vág', E. Ó. Sveinsson and M. Þórðarson, eds., *Eiríks saga rauða*, in *Eyrbyggja saga*, Íslenzk fornrit 4 (1935), 222–3.

7. 'Þar var grunnsævi mikit at fjǫru sjávar, ok stóð þá uppi skip þeira; ok var þá langt til sjávar at sjá frá skipinu. En þeim var svá mikil forvitni á at fara til landsins, at þeir nenntu eigi þess at bíða, at sjór felli undir skip þeira, ok runnu til lands, þar er á ein fell ór vatni einu.... ok báru af skipi húðfǫt sín ok gerðu þar búðir; tóku þat ráð síðan, at búask þar um þann vetr, ok gerðu þar hús mikil', Sveinsson and Þórðarson, eds., *Grœnlendinga saga*, 250–1.

8. 'Hann talaði þá fyrst lengi á þýzku ok skaut marga vega augunum ok gretti sik, en þeir skilðu eigi, hvat er hann sagði. Hann mælti þá á norrœnu, er stund leið: "Ek var genginn eigi miklu

lengra en þit. Kann ek nǫkkur nýmæli at segja; ek fann vínvið ok vínber."' Sveinsson and Þórðarson, eds., *Grænlendinga saga*, 252.

9. For a summary of these debates see G. Sigurðsson, 'The Quest for Vinland in Saga Scholarship', in *Vikings: The North Atlantic Saga*, ed. W. W. Fitzhugh and E. Ward (2000), 232–7.

10. As the archaeologist Birgitta Linderoth Wallace has noted: 'The traces indicate the presence of a male work force performing tasks such as carpentry, iron manufacture, boat repair, and exploration.' B. Linderoth Wallace, 'Vikings at L'Anse aux Meadows', in Fitzhugh and Ward, *Vikings: The North Atlantic Saga*, 208–16, at 213. This is a fantastic summary of the archaeological site and its implications, and I draw much of my information here from her work.

11. This identification is strengthened by the presence of jasper strike-a-lights that came from Greenland and Iceland. See Kevin P. Smith, 'Who lived at L'Anse aux Meadows?', in Fitzhugh and Ward, *Vikings: The North Atlantic Saga*, 217.

12. 'Þa kom ok skip af Grænlandi minna at vexti enn sma Islandz fór.... Þat var akkeris laust. Þar voru á .xvij. menn ok hófðu farit til Marklandz enn siðan vordit hingat hafreka.' From the Skálholts Annals, in G. Storm, ed., *Islandske Annaler Indtil 1578* (1888), 213.

13. H. Pringle, 19 Oct. 2012, 'Evidence of Viking Outpost Found in Canada', <http://news.nationalgeographic.com/news/2012/10/121019-viking-outpost-second-new-canada-science-sutherland/>.

14. R. Blumenthal, 'View from Space Hints at a New Viking Site in North America', <http://www.nytimes.com/2016/04/01/science/vikings-archaeology-north-america-newfoundland.html>.

15. 'Þeir fundu þar á landi sjálfsána hveitiakra, þar sem lægðir váru, en vínvið allt þar sem holta vissi. Hverr lœkr var þar fullr af fiskum. Þeir gerðu grafar, þar sem mœttisk landit ok flóðit gekk ofast, ok þá er út fell sjórinn, váru helgir fiskar í grǫfunum. Þar var mikill fjǫldi dýra á skóginum, með ǫllu móti', Sveinsson and Þórðarson, eds., *Eiríks saga rauða*, 226–7.

16. 'þeir ætluðu at byggja landit, ef þeir mætti þat', Sveinsson and Þórðarson, eds., *Grænlendinga saga*, 261.

17. 'þá lýsir Karlsefni, at hann vill eigi þar vera lengr ok vill fara til Grœnlands. Nú búa þeir ferð sína ok hǫfðu þaðan mǫrg gœði í vínviði ok berjum ok skinnavǫru', Sveinsson and Þórðarson, eds., *Grænlendinga saga*, 264.

18. A. Roussell, 'Sandnes and the Neighbouring Farms', *Meddelelser om Grønland* 88:2 (1936), 107.

19. 'Skrælingar skutu á þá um stund, en flýja síðan burt sem ákafast, hverr sem mátti. Þá spurði Þorvaldr menn sína, ef þeir væri nǫkkut sárir; þeir kváðust eigi sárir vera. "Ek hefi fengit sár undir hendi," segir hann, "ok fló ǫr milli skipborðsins ok skjaldarins undir hǫnd mér, ok er hér ǫrin, en mik mun þetta til bana leiða."' Sveinsson and Þórðarson, eds., *Grænlendinga saga*, 256.

20. See S. L. Cox, 'A Norse Penny from Maine', in Fitzhugh and Ward, *Vikings: The North Atlantic Saga*, 206–7 and P. D. Sutherland, 'The Norse and Native Americans', in Fitzhugh and Ward, *Vikings: The North Atlantic Saga*, 238–47, at 241. For the Baffin Island site see H. Pringle, Nov. 2012, 'Vikings and Native Americans', <http://ngm.nationalgeographic.com/2012/11/vikings-and-indians/pringle-text>.

21. See D. Odess, S. Loring, and W. W. Fitzhugh, 'Skræling: First Peoples', in Fitzhugh and Ward, *Vikings: The North Atlantic Saga*, 193–205.

22. See K. Seaver, '"Pygmies" of the Far North', *Journal of World History* 19:1 (2008), 63–87, at 72.

23. 'Þeir váru svartir menn ok illiligir ok hǫfðu illt hár á hǫfði; þeir váru mjǫk eygðir ok breiðir í kinnum', Sveinsson and Þórðarson, eds., *Eiríks saga rauða*, 227.

24. 'Hvárigir skildu annars mál', Sveinsson and Þórðarson, eds., *Grænlendinga saga*, 262.

25. 'Ok einn morgin snimma, er þeir lituðusk um, sá þeir mikinn fjǫlða húðkeipa, ok var veift trjám á skipunum, ok lét því líkast sem í hálmþúst, ok var veift sólarsinnis. Þá mælti Karlsefni: "Hvat mun þetta hafa at teikna?" Snorri Þorbrandsson svaraði honum: "Vera kann, at þetta sé friðarmark, ok tǫkum skjǫld hvítan ok berum at móti."' Sveinsson and Þórðarson, eds., *Eiríks saga rauða*, 227.

26. 'Þeir Skrælingar tóku spannarlangt rautt skrúð fyrir ófǫlvan belg ok bundu um hǫfuð sér. Gekk svá kaupstefna þeira um hríð. Þá tók at fættask skrúðit með þeim Karlsefni, ok skáru þeir þá svá smátt í sundr, at eigi var breiðara en þvers fingrar, ok gáfu Skrælingar þó jafnmikit fyrir sem áðr eða meira', Sveinsson and Þórðarson, eds., *Eiríks saga rauða*, 228.

27. 'Þeir báru sinn varning í brott í mǫgum sínum, en Karlsefni ok fǫrunautar hans hǫfðu eptir bagga þeira ok skinnavǫru', Sveinsson and Þórðarson, eds., *Grœnlendinga saga*, 262.

28. P. D. Sutherland, 'The Norse and Native Americans', in Fitzhugh and Ward, *Vikings: The North Atlantic Saga*, 238–47, at 241. The relative value of trading goods is discussed by C. Larrington, '"Undruðusk þá, sem fyrir var": Wonder, Vínland, and Mediaeval Travel Narratives', *Mediaeval Scandinavia* 14 (2004), 91–114, at 106–7.

29. R. White, *The Middle Ground: Indians, Empires, and Republics in the Great Lakes Region, 1650–1815* (1991), 27.

30. Sutherland, 'The Norse and Native Americans', 238–47, at 247.

31. 'á stǫng knǫtt stundar mikinn, því nær til at jafna sem sauðarvǫmb, ok helzt blán at lit, ok fleygðu af stǫnginni upp á landit yfir lið þeira Karlsefnis, ok lét illiliga við, þar sem niðr kom', Sveinsson and Þórðarson, eds., *Eiríks saga rauða*, 228–9.

32. 'Ballista, or Demon's Head.—Algonkin tradition affirms that in ancient times, during the fierce wars which the Indians carried on, they constructed a very formidable instrument of attack, by sewing up a large round boulder in a new skin. To this a long handle was tied. When the skin dried, it became very tight around the stone, and, after being painted with devices, assumed the appearance and character of a solid globe upon a pole. This formidable instrument was borne by several warriors, who acted as ballisters. Plunged upon a boat or canoe, it was capable of sinking it. Brought down among a group of men on a sudden, it produced consternation and death.' H. R. Schoolcraft, *The Indian Tribes of the United States: Their History, Antiquities, Customs, Religion, Arts, Language, Traditions, Oral Legends, and Myths*, 2 vols. (1884), 1. 73.

33. 'Þá bar skugga í dyrrin, ok gekk þar inn kona í svǫrtum námkyrtli, heldr lág, ok hafði dregil um hǫfuð ok ljósjǫrp á hár, fǫlleit ok mjǫk eygð, svá at eigi hafði jafnmikil augu sét í einum mannshausi. Hon gekk þar at, er Guðríðr sat, ok mælti: "Hvat heitir þú?" segir hon. "Ek heiti Guðríðr; eða hvert er þitt heiti?" "Ek heiti Guðríðr," segir hon. Þá rétti Guðríðr húsfreyja hǫnd sína til hennar, at hon sæti hjá henni, en þat bar allt saman, at þá heyrði Guðríðr brest mikinn, ok var þá konan horfin, ok í því var ok veginn einn Skrælingr af einum húskarli Karlsefnis, því at hann hafði viljat taka vápn þeira. Ok fóru nú brott sem tíðast, en klæði þeira lágu þar eptir ok varningr. Engi maðr hafði konu þessa sét, útan Guðríðr ein', Sveinsson and Þórðarson, eds., *Grœnlendinga saga*, 262–3.

34. See B. Almqvist, 'My Name is Guðríðr', in *Approaches to Vinland: A Conference on the Written and Archaeological Sources for the Norse Settlements in the North-Atlantic Region and Exploration of America*, ed. A. Wawn and Þ. Sigurðardóttir (2001), 15–30.

35. 'svarri mikill', 'lítilmenni', Sveinsson and Þórðarson, eds., *Grœnlendinga saga*, 245.

36. 'Nú váru þar allir karlar drepnir, en konur váru eptir, ok vildi engi þær drepa. Þá mælti Freydís: "Fái mér øxi í hǫnd." Svá var gǫrt. Síðan vegr hon at konum þeim fimm, er þar váru, ok gekk af þeim dauðum', Sveinsson and Þórðarson, eds., *Grœnlendinga saga*, 266.

37. 'Þat var einn morgin, er þeir Karlsefni sá fyrir ofan rjóðrit flekk nǫkkurn, sem glitraði við þeim, ok œpðu þeir á þat. Þat hrœrðist, ok var þat einfœtingr ok skauzt ofan á þann árbakkann, sem þeir lágu við. Þorvaldr Eiríksson rauða sat við stýri, ok skaut einfœtingr ǫr í smáþarma honum. Þorvaldr dró út ǫrina ok mælti: "Feitt er um ístruna. Gott land hǫfu vér fengit kostum, en þó megu vér varla njóta." Þorvaldr dó af sári þessu litlu síðar', Sveinsson and Þórðarson, eds., *Eiríks saga rauða*, 231–2.

38. For a potted history of the uniped in medieval culture see Larrington, '"Undruðusk þá, sem fyrir var": Wonder, Vínland, and Mediaeval Travel Narratives', esp. 111–13.

39. 'Ein fœtingar hafa sua mikinn fot við iorð at þeír skykgia ser i suefní við solo. þeir ero sua skioter sem dyr oc laupa við stong', E. Jónsson and F. Jónsson, eds., *Hauksbók* (1892–96), 166. The other manuscript containing a description of a uniped is AM 194 8vo (*c.*1387).

Chapter 8

1. C. Brahic, 19 Sept. 2011, 'Times Atlas Grossly Exaggerates Greenland Ice Loss'. <http://www.newscientist.com/article/dn20939-times-atlas-grossly-exaggerates-greenland-ice-loss.html>.

2. 19 Sept. 2011, 'Scientists Raise Concerns Regarding Erroneous Reporting of Greenland Ice Cover'. <http://www.cam.ac.uk/research/news/scientists-raise-concerns-regarding-erroneous-reporting-of-greenland-ice-cover>. P. Christoffersen, 21 Sept. 2011, 'Times Atlas Ice Error was a Lesson in How Scientists Should Mobilise'. <http://www.guardian.co.uk/environment/2011/sep/21/times-atlas-error-scientists-mobilise>.

3. HarperCollins, 22 Sept. 2011, 'Clarification on the Times Comprehensive Atlas of the World—13th Edition'. <http://corporate.harpercollins.co.uk/uk/press-releases/103/clarification-on-the-times-comprehensive-atlas-of-the-world-13th-edition>.

4. N. C. Johnson, 'Political Landscapes', in *The Wiley-Blackwell Companion to Cultural Geography*, ed. N. C. Johnson, R. H. Schein, and J. Winders (2013), 173–85, at 174.

5. To read more about how the Little Ice Age affected Europe see B. M. Fagan, *The Little Ice Age: How Climate Made History 1300–1850* (2000) and D. Macdougall, *Frozen Earth: The Once and Future Story of Ice Ages* (2004), especially chapter 11, 'The Last Millennium'.

6. For an overview of how and when the changing climate affected the Eastern and Western Settlements respectively, see A. Kuijpers et al., 'Impact of Medieval Fjord Hydrography and Climate on the Western and Eastern Settlements in Norse Greenland', *Journal of the North Atlantic: In the Footsteps of Vebæk Vatnahverfi Studies 2005–2011*, special volume 6 (2014), 1–13.

7. 'Saa sigger vise Mend, som føde ehre udi Grönnland, och sist komne aff Grönnland, att norden aff Stad udi Norge er vij Dagge Seyling rett udi Vester thill Horns, som ligger østen paa Island. Item fraa Snefelsnes aff Island, som er stackist till Grönnland, 2 Dage och thou Netters Seyling, rett i Vester att zeylle, och der ligger Gunbjernerschier rett paa Mittveyen emellum Grönland och Island. Thette vaar gammell Sayelling; en nu er kommen Is udaff landnorden Botnen saa ner forschreffne Scher, att ingen kan uden Liffs Fare denn gamble Leed seyle', F. Magnusen and C. C. Rafn, eds., *Grønlands Historiske Mindesmærker*, vol. 3 (1838–42), 250.

8. F. C. C. Hansen, 'Anthropologia medico-historica Groenlandiæ antiquæ I. Herjolfsnes', *Meddelelser om Grønland* 67 (1924), 293–547, at 520.

9. N. Lynnerup, 'The Human Skeletons from Herjólfsnes', in *Norse Greenland: Selected Papers from the Hvalsey Conference 2008. Journal of the North Atlantic*, special volume 2, ed. J. Arneborg, G. Nyegaard, and O. Vésteinsson (2009), 23–7, at 26.

10. *A History of Norway and the Passion and Miracles of the Blessed Óláfr*, trans. D. Kunin, ed. C. Phelpstead (2001), 3.

11. 'Skrælíngjar herjuðu á Grænlendínga ok drápu af þeim XVIII menn, ok tóku tvo sveina ok þrælkuðu', Magnusen and Rafn, eds., *Grønlands Historiske Mindesmærker*, 3.32.

12. T. H. McGovern, 'The Demise of Norse Greenland', in *Vikings: The North Atlantic Saga*, ed. W. W. Fitzhugh and E. Ward (2000), 327–39, at 336.

13. There are some exceptions to this pattern, such as an almost toothless antler comb found at a farm in the Western Settlement that seems to be of Inuit origin. See H. C. Gulløv, 'Natives and Norse in Greenland', in Fitzhugh and Ward, *Vikings: The North Atlantic Saga*, 318–26, at 323.

14. H. Rink, *Tales and Traditions of the Eskimo: With a Sketch of their Habits, Religion, Language and Other Peculiarities*, ed. R. Brown (1875), 320.

15. See A. J. Dugmore et al., 'Norse Greenland Settlement and Limits to Adaptation', in *Adapting to Climate Change: Thresholds, Values, Governance*, ed. W. N. Adger, I. Lorenzoni, and K. L. O'Brien (2009), 96–113, at 106.

16. J. Vahtola, 'Population and Settlement', in *The Cambridge History of Scandinavia*, vol. 1: *Prehistory to 1520*, ed. K. Helle (2003), 567.

17. 'Þetta ár fóru þeir til Grænlands Þorsteinn Helmíngsson, Snorri Torfason ok Þorgrímr Sölfason á einu skipi; létu þeir út af Noregi ok ætlaðu til Íslands; voru þeir í Grænlandi IV vetur', Magnusen and Rafn, eds., *Grønlands Historiske Mindesmærker*, 3.40.

18. J. Diamond, *Collapse: How Societies Choose to Fail or Survive* (2005), 246–7.

19. See J. Arneborg et al., 'Change of Diet of the Greenland Vikings Determined from Stable Carbon Isotope Analysis and 14C Dating of their Bones', *Radiocarbon* 41:2 (1999), 157–68. See also T. H. McGovern, 'The Demise of Norse Greenland', in Fitzhugh and Ward, *Vikings: The North Atlantic Saga*, 327–40, at 333, and N. Lynnerup, 'Life and Death in Norse Greenland', in Fitzhugh and Ward, *Vikings: The North Atlantic Saga*, 285–94, at 292.

20. A. J. Dugmore et al., 'Cultural Adaptation, Compounding Vulnerabilities and Conjunctures in Norse Greenland', *Proceedings of the National Academy of Sciences of the United States of America*, 109:10 (2012), 3658–63. More fully, the argument is that 'the Norse Greenlanders created a flexible and successful subsistence system that responded effectively to major environmental challenges but probably fell victim to a combination of conjunctures of large-scale historic processes and vulnerabilities created by their successful prior response to climate change. Their failure was an inability to anticipate an unknowable future, an inability to broaden their traditional ecological knowledge base, and a case of being too specialized, too small, and too isolated to be able to capitalize on and compete in the new protoworld system extending into the North Atlantic in the early 15th century' (3658). See also Dugmore et al., 'Norse Greenland Settlement and Limits to Adaptation', 96–113.

21. D. Mathers, 'A Fourteenth-Century Description of Greenland', *Saga-Book of the Viking Society* 33 (2009), 67–94, at 75.

22. 'Nu haffuer Skrellinge all Vesterbygden ud; daa er der noch Heste, Geder, Nød, Faar, alt villdt och ingen Follch, christenn eller hedenn. Item dette alt, som forsagt er, sagde oss Iffver Bardsen Grönlænder, som var Forstander paa Bischobsgarden i Gardum paa Grönnland udi mange Aar, at hand haffde alt dette seett, och hand var en aff dennem, som var udneffender aff Lagmanden, at fare till Vesterbygden emod de Skrelinge, att uddriffve de Schrellinge udaff Vesterbygd; och da de komme didt, da funde de ingen Mand, endten christenn eller heden, uden noget villdt Fæ og Faaer, och bespissede sig aff det villtt Fæ, och toge saa meget som Schivene kunde berre, och zeylede saa der med hjemb, och forschreffne Iffver var der med', Magnusen and Rafn, eds., *Grønlands Historiske Mindesmærker*, 3.259.

23. L. K. Barlow et al., 'Interdisciplinary Investigations of the End of the Norse Western Settlement in Greenland', *The Holocene* 7:4 (1997), 489–99, at 491.

24. This is explored by J. Berglund, 'The Decline of the Norse Settlements in Greenland', *Arctic Anthropology* 23:1/2 (1986), 109–35.

25. 'Var brendr einn maðr í Grænlandi er Kolgrímr hét, fyrir þá sök at hann lá eina manns kvinnu er Steinunn hét, dóttur Hrafns lögmanns…Fékk Kolgrímr hennar vilja með svarta kvonstr; var hann síðan brendr eptir dómi; var kvinnan ok síðan aldrei með jafnri sinnu ok áðr, ok deyði þar litlu síðar', Magnusen and Rafn, eds., *Grønlands Historiske Mindesmærker*, 3.40.

26. E. Oster, 'Witchcraft, Weather and Economic Growth in Renaissance Europe', *Journal of Economic Perspectives* 18:1 (2004), 215–28.

27. 'Egh Semundur Odds son kennest með þessu mijnu brefe, ad egh var ner i Hualzey i Grenlande, sa egh og heyrðe uppá ad Sigrijd Biornzdotter frendkona mijn gifte sig Þorsteine Ólafssyne til eigenqvinnu, með mijnu ráde og samþycke', Magnusen and Rafn, eds., *Grønlands Historiske Mindesmærker*, 3.156. For the other two documents see 3.148 and 152.

28. G. Nyegaard, 'Restoration of the Hvalsey Fjord Church', *Norse Greenland: Selected Papers from the Hvalsey Conference 2008, Journal of the North Atlantic*, special volume 2, ed. J. Arneborg, G. Nyegaard, and O. Vésteinsson (2009), 7–18, at 11.

29. K. Seaver, *The Frozen Echo: Greenland and the Exploration of North America, ca. A.D. 1000–1500* (1995), 151.

30. Dating the sagas is a notoriously difficult and thankless task. Many of them existed as oral tales before being written down, the sagas continued to be copied once they had been recorded, and most of the manuscripts that survive today are probably not the oldest version of a particular saga. The dates I have given here are based on individual saga entries in P. Pulsiano and K. Wolf, eds., *Medieval Scandinavia: An Encyclopaedia* (1993), the table in J. Grove, 'The Place of Greenland in Medieval Icelandic Saga Narrative', in Arneborg, Nyegaard, and Vésteinsson, *Norse Greenland: Selected Papers from the Hvalsey Conference 2008*, 30–51, at 33, and V. Ólason's discussion of the dating and classification of sagas in his *Dialogues with the Viking Age* (2005), 114–16.

31. For an excellent survey of these themes and patterns see Grove, 'The Place of Greenland in Medieval Icelandic Saga Narrative', 30–51.

32. 'Þorgils bíðr nú byrjar ok dreymir, at maðr kæmi at honum, mikill ok rauðskeggjaðr, ok mælti: "Ferð hefir þú ætlat fyrir þér, ok mun hon erfið verða." Draummaðrinn sýndist honum heldr greppligr. "Illa mun yðr farast," segir hann, "nema þú hverfir aptr til míns átrúnaðar; mun ek þá enn til sjá með þér."…Síðan þótti honum Þórr leiða sik á hamra nökkura, þar sem sjóvarstraumr brast í björgum,—"í slíkum bylgjum skaltu vera ok aldri ór komast, utan þú hverfir til mín." "Nei," sagði Þorgils, "far á burt, inn leiði fjandi!"', Þ. Vilmundarson and B. Vilhjálmsson, eds., *Flóamanna saga*, in *Harðar saga*, Íslenzk fornrit 13 (1991), 278–9.

33. 'Váru nú allmiklar aptrgöngur ok sóttu mest Þorgils', Vilmundarson and Vilhjálmsson, eds., *Flóamanna saga*, 285.

34. 'Mjök var þar allt blóðugt….Burt var sópat öllum vistum', Vilmundarson and Vilhjálmsson, eds., *Flóamanna saga*, 288.

35. 'Einn morgun er Þorgils einn úti ok sér í vök rekald mikit ok þar hjá tröllkonur tvær, ok bundu byrðar miklar. Þorgils hleypr til þangat ok hafði sverðit Jarðhússnaut ok höggr til annarrar með sverðinu, í því er hon færist undir byrðina, ok rekr af henni höndina. Byrðrin fellr niðr, en hon hljóp í burt. Síðan taka þeir rekaldit, ok eru þá vistir nógar', Vilmundarson and Vilhjálmsson, eds., *Flóamanna saga*, 290.

36. 'rakki fagr ok mikill', Vilmundarson and Vilhjálmsson, eds., *Flóamanna saga*, 303.

37. 'Þá bjó í Brattahlíð Eiríkr rauði…Eiríkr átti Þjóðhildi…Þeira son var Leifr inn heppni. Þá hafði Eiríkr einum vetri áðr byggt Grænland. Helga þá hjá Eiríki vetrvist', Þ. Vilmundarson and B. Vilhjálmsson, eds., *Bárðar saga*, in *Harðar saga*, Íslenzk fornrit 13 (1991), 115.

38. 'Um vetrinn kómu tröll ok óvættir ofan í Eiríksfjörð ok gerðu mönnum it mesta mein, lömdu skip, en beinbrutu menn', Vilmundarson and Vilhjálmsson, eds., *Bárðar saga*, 116.

39. This pattern has been explored in other analyses. As Geraldine Barnes has noted: 'As drift ice encroached on Greenland from the late thirteenth century, travel west of Iceland became hazardous and infrequent. The vision of Eiríksfjǫrðr harried by trolls and monsters during the winter after Eiríkr's arrival there in *Bárðar saga Snæfellsás* suggests that, for the author of

this late-thirteenth- or early fourteenth-century saga, things did not bode well for the settlements.' G. Barnes, *Viking America: The First Millennium* (2001), 35. Likewise, as Jonathan Grove states: 'The tendency towards the adoption of a narrative mode concerned with superhuman feats in outlandish settings complies with the changing generic parameters of post-classical saga literature in the 14th century. It is nevertheless striking that the remaking of Greenland as a rendezvous for fabulous adventures…becomes most apparent at a time when regular communications with Greenland were diminishing', Grove, 'The Place of Greenland in Medieval Icelandic Saga Narrative', 37.

40. 'með miklum hríðum og frostum, svó sýldi hvern dropa, er inn kom', J. Halldórsson, ed., *Jökuls þáttr Búasonar*, in *Kjalnesinga saga*, Íslenzk fornrit 14 (1959), 47.

41. 'þær vóru næsta ófrýnligar, nefsíðar, og hekk vörrin ofan á bringu; skinnstökkum vóru þær klæddar, síðum í fyrir, svó þær stigu að mestu á þá, en bak til fylgdu þeir ofanverðum þjóhnöppum; þær skelldu á lærin og fóru mjög ókvenliga', Halldórsson, ed., *Kjalnesinga saga*, 9.

42. 'konungr er yfir öllum óbyggðum', Halldórsson, ed., *Kjalnesinga saga*, 54.

43. 'sýndisk þeim þat land vera gœðalaust', E. Ó. Sveinsson and M. Þórðarson, eds., *Grœnlendinga saga*, in *Eyrbyggja saga*, Íslenzk fornrit 4 (1935), 249.

44. T. Tulinius, *The Matter of the North: The Rise of Literary Fiction in Thirteenth-Century Iceland*, trans. R. C. Eldevik (2002), 164.

45. 'í Hellulands óbyggðum', G. Jónsson, ed., *Örvar-Odds saga*, in *Fornaldar sögur Norðurlanda*, vol. 2 (1954), 288.

46. 'Þá tóku þeir til ok glímdu með miklum atgangi ok ómannligum, því at þeir ruddu upp jörðu ok grjóti sem lausri mjöllu….Ok í því brá Ögmundr Vigni, svá at hann fell, ok þegar jafnskjótt greyfðist hann niðr at honum ok beit sundr í honum barkann….Ögmundr brá þá skjótt við ok steypti sér ofan fyrir hamrana í sjóinn at höfðinu, svá at hvítfyssti upp á móti.' Jónsson, ed., *Örvar-Odds saga*, 291–2.

47. 'ok höfðu soðketil í milli sín. Þar var í bæði hrossa slátr ok manna. Karl hafði krók í nefinu, en kerling hring. Þat var gaman þeira, at hann krækti króknum í hringinn, ok var þá upp á þeim ýmsir endarnir, en þá krókrinn slapp ór hringnum, fekk kerling bakfall. Hún mælti þá: "Eigi vil ek þetta gaman hafa, Járnnefr minn sæll."' G. Jónsson, ed., *Hálfdanar saga Brönufóstra*, in *Fornaldar sögur Norðurlanda*, vol. 4 (1954), 298.

48. 'mikill ok illiligr, skrámleitr ok skoteygr, svartskeggjaðr ok síðnefjaðr.' Vilmundarson and Vilhjálmsson, eds., *Bárðar saga*, 160.

49. 'hefir hann ráðit fyrir Hellulandi ok mörgum öðrum löndum. Ok er hann hafði lengi löndum ráðit, lét hann kviksetja sik með fimm hundruðum manna á Raknarsslóða; hann myrði föður sinn ok móður ok margt annat fólk; þykki mér ván, at haugr hans muni vera norðarliga í Hellulands óbyggðum at annarra manna frásögn', Vilmundarson and Vilhjálmsson, eds., *Bárðar saga*, 161.

50. 'En er hraunit þraut, kvámu þeir at sjó fram; þar var hólmr stórr fyrir landi; út til hólmsins lá eitt rif mjótt ok langt. Þar var þurrt um fjöru, ok svá var, þá er þeir kvámu at. Gengu þeir þá út í hólminn, ok þar sá þeir standa haug einn stóran. Segja sumir menn, at þessi hólmr hafi legit fyrir Hellulandi; en hvar sem þat hefir verit, þá hafa þar öngvar byggðir í nánd verit', Vilmundarson and Vilhjálmsson, eds., *Bárðar saga*, 165.

51. 'Sú fra saga finst í Íslenskum bókum ad enn madr komst úr Grænlande til Noregs fótgangande, yfir öll þau þræfe jökla & óbygder, hvad micel tídinde hafa þótt, hann leidde med Sjer geit eina, & fæddizt vid nyt hennar. því var hann þadan kalladr geitar hallr.' This version of the story comes from AM 779b, 4to (17th C), quoted in R. Simek, *Altnordische Kosmographie: Studien und Quellen zu Weltbild und Weltbeschreibung in Norwegen und Island vom 12. bis 14. Jahrhundert* (1990), 588. A land bridge is described in several other manuscripts, including AM 736 I 4to (*c.*1300) and AM 194 8vo (*c.*1387). For more about Helluland in the sagas see Barnes, *Viking*

America, 34, n. 97, and Grove, 'The Place of Greenland in Medieval Icelandic Saga Narrative', 30–51, at 45.

52. See B. Linderoth Wallace, 'An Archaeologist Interprets the *Vinland Sagas*', in Fitzhugh and Ward, *Vikings: The North Atlantic Saga*, 225–31, at 229.

53. Translation adapted from C. G. M. Paxton, E. Knatterud, and S. L. Hedley, 'Cetaceans, Sex and Sea Serpents: An Analysis of the Egede Accounts of a "most dreadful monster" Seen off the Coast of Greenland in 1734', *Archives of Natural History* 32:1 (2005), 1–9.

Chapter 9

1. We know all about these adventures because they were chronicled—with an extraordinary degree of intelligence, humour, and humanity—by a member of the diplomatic mission called Ahmad ibn Fadlan. See C. Stone and P. Lunde, trans., *Ibn Fadlan and the Land of Darkness: Arab Travellers in the Far North* (2011).

2. Stone and Lunde, *Ibn Fadlan and the Land of Darkness*, 29.

3. Stone and Lunde, *Ibn Fadlan and the Land of Darkness*, 46.

4. Stone and Lunde, *Ibn Fadlan and the Land of Darkness*, 47.

5. Stone and Lunde, *Ibn Fadlan and the Land of Darkness*, 51.

6. For further discussion of this term and what it designates in Old Norse sources see S. Jakobsson, 'On the Road to Paradise: "Austvegr" in the Icelandic Imagination', in *The Fantastic in Old Norse/Icelandic Literature—Sagas and the British Isles: Preprint Papers of the 13th International Saga Conference, Durham and York, 6th–12th August, 2006*, vol. 2, ed. J. McKinnell, D. Ashurst, and D. Kick (2006), 935–43.

7. For comprehensive studies of the Rus see H. R. Ellis Davidson, *The Viking Road to Byzantium* (1976); O. Pritsak, *The Origin of Rus'*, vol. 1: *Old Scandinavian Sources other than the Sagas* (1981); J. Shepard and S. Franklin, *The Emergence of Rus: 750–1200* (1996); and W. Duczko, *Viking Rus: Studies on the Presence of Scandinavians in Eastern Europe* (2004). For excellent introductions to the topic see J. Haywood, *The Penguin Historical Atlas of the Vikings* (1995), 100–9; T. S. Noonan, 'Scandinavians in European Russia', in *The Oxford Illustrated History of the Vikings*, ed. P. Sawyer (1999), 134–55; J. Shepard, 'The Viking Rus and Byzantium' and F. Androshchuk, 'The Vikings in the East', in *The Viking World*, ed. S. Brink and N. Price (2008), 496–516 and 517–42.

8. This theory, and other possibilities, are discussed by Þórir Jónsson Hraundal in 'Rus in Arabic Sources: Cultural Contacts and Identity', unpubl. Ph.D thesis, University of Bergen (2013), 25. For a summary see H. Stang, 'Russia, Norse in', in *Medieval Scandinavia: An Encyclopaedia*, ed. P. Pulsiano and K. Wolf (1993), 556–8.

9. B. Gyllensvärd, 'The Buddha found at Helgö', in *Excavations at Helgö XVI: Exotic and Sacral Finds*, ed. H. Clarke and K. Lamm (2004), 11–27, at 11. For details of the Helgö finds see W. Holmqvist, ed., *Excavations at Helgö I. Report for 1954–1956* (1961), esp. 112–14.

10. For a discussion about this interpretation see P. Harbison, 'The Helgö Crozier-Head', in *Excavations at Helgö XVI*, 29–34, esp. 30–2.

11. T. Zachrisson, 'Silver and Gold Hoards from the Black Earth', in *Investigations in the Black Earth. Birka Studies*, vol. 1, ed. B. Ambrosiani and H. Clarke (1992), 52–63, at 54.

12. Stone and Lunde, *Ibn Fadlan and the Land of Darkness*, 169–70.

13. Stone and Lunde, *Ibn Fadlan and the Land of Darkness*, 112. Jurjan, or Gorgan as it is called today, is now an Iranian city around 20 miles from the Caspian Sea.

14. Stone and Lunde, *Ibn Fadlan and the Land of Darkness*, 145.
15. Androshchuk, 'The Vikings in the East', 520.
16. Stone and Lunde, *Ibn Fadlan and the Land of Darkness*, 126.
17. M. Svedin, 'Archaeology in the Shadow of Political Changes: Archaeological Relations between Sweden and Eastern Europe 1846–2006', in *Cultural Interaction Between East and West: Archaeology, Artefacts and Human Contacts in Northern Europe*, ed. U. Fransson et al. (2007), 24–41, at 26.
18. Androshchuk, 'The Vikings in the East', 530.
19. 5 July 1941: N. Cameron and R. H. Stevens, trans., *Hitler's Table Talk 1941–1944: His Private Conversations* (2000), 3.
20. 17 Sept. 1941: *Hitler's Table Talk 1941–1944*, 34.
21. When Svyatoslav made peace with the Greeks, he swore an oath by Perun and Volos: 'may we become as yellow as gold, and be slain by our own weapons', S. H. Cross and O. P. Sherbowitz-Wetzor, trans. and eds., *The Russian Primary Chronicle: Laurentian Text* (1953), 176, for the year AD 971.
22. A. M. Talbot and D. F. Sullivan, eds., *The History of Leo the Deacon: Byzantine Military Expansion in the Tenth Century* (2005), 200.
23. Cross and Sherbowitz-Wetzor, *The Russian Primary Chronicle*, 177, for the year AD 972.
24. These connections are explored in J. Shafer's chapter on the 'East' in 'Saga Accounts of Norse Far Travellers', unpubl. Ph.D thesis, Durham University (2010).
25. D. A. Warner, trans., *Ottonian Germany: The Chronicon of Thietmar of Merseburg* (2001), 357–8.
26. 'En varð þat, sem optliga kann at verða, þar er útlendir menn hefjask til ríkis eða til svá mikillar frægðar, at þat verði um fram innlenzka menn, at margir ǫfunduðu þat, hversu kærr hann var konungi ok eigi síðr dróttningu', B. Aðalbjarnarson, ed., *Óláfs saga Tryggvasonar*, in *Heimskringla I*, Íslenzk fornrit 26 (1941), 251–2.
27. 'En eigi uissu þeir huerr eða huadan hann var. ok þo sonnuðu þeir þat með morgum ordum at þat hit biarta lios er yfir honum skinn. dreifiz vm alt Garda riki ok viða vm austr halfu heimsins', Ó. Halldórsson, ed., *Óláfs saga Tryggvasonar en mesta*, vol. 1 (1958), 105.
28. For more on this see T. N. Jackson, 'The Role of Óláfr Tryggvason in the Conversion of Russia', in *Three Studies on Vikings and Christianization*, ed. M. Rindal (1994), 7–25, at 17.
29. Cross and Sherbowitz-Wetzor, *The Russian Primary Chronicle*, 97, for the year AD 986.
30. Cross and Sherbowitz-Wetzor, *The Russian Primary Chronicle*, 111, for the year AD 987.
31. R. Holtzmann, *Die Chronik des Bischofs Thietmar von Merseburg und ihre Korveier Überarbeitung* (1935), 486.
32. 'Ok er eindagi kom málagjaldsins, þá gekk Eymundr konungr á fund Jarizleifs konungs ok mælti svá: "Hér höfum vér verit, herra, í yðru ríki um hríð. Kjósið nú, hvart kaup várt skal standa lengr, eðr viltu nú, at skili með oss várt félag ok leitum vér annars höfðingja, því at tregt hefir fét út greiðzt?" Konungr svarar: "Ek ætla nú eigi jafnmikla nauðsyn til bera sem fyrr til yðvars liðsinnis. Verðr oss þat mikil fjárauðn at gefa yðr svá mikinn mála sem þér kveðið á."' S. Nordal, ed., *Eymundar þáttr Hrings*, in *Flateyjarbók*, vol. 2 (1945), 206.
33. As Robert Cook has noted: 'One might wish for closer correspondences, but in fact these differences are only to be expected when a twelfth-century monkish chronicle written in Russia (and itself not wholly to be trusted) and fourteenth-century Icelandic secular history reflect the same eleventh-century events. The distances in time and place alone would account for the distortions, but there is in addition the fact that the Icelandic tale very deliberately…substituted a certain kind of story for history', R. Cook, 'Russian History, Icelandic Story, and Byzantine Strategy in *Eymundar þáttr Hringssonar*', *Viator* 17 (1986), 65–89, at 69.
34. 'Þar hefjum vér upp frásǫgn er Jarizleifr konungr ræðr Garðaríki ok Ingigerðr dróttning, dóttir Óláfs konungs ins sœnska….Síðan gekk dróttning í hǫllina með fagrligri kvenna sveit, ok stóð konungr upp í móti henna ok kvaddi hana vel ok mælti síðan: "Hvar sáttu jafn

dýrliga hǫll eða jafn vel búna, fyrst at sveitinni slíkra manna sem hérru saman komnir ok í annan stað búningr hallarinnar með miklum kostnaði?" Dróttning svaraði, "Herra," segir hon, "þessi hǫll er vel skipuð, ok fá dœmi munu til at slík prýði eða meiri ok fékostnaðr komi saman í eitt hús eða jafn margir góðir hǫfingjar ok vaskir menn. En betr er þó sú hǫll skipuð er Óláfr konungr Haraldsson sitr í, þó at hon standi á súlum einum." Konungr reiddisk henni ok mælti, "Svívirðing er í slíkum orðum," segir hann, "ok sýnir þú enn ást þína við Óláf konung,"—ok laust hana kinnhest', Á. Jakobsson and Þ. I. Guðjónsson, eds., *Morkinskinna I*, Íslenzk fornrit 23 (2011), 3–4.

35. 'Nú dveljask þeir þar austr um sumarit í þessum ráðagørðum, ok við þetta fara þeir austan ok hafa Magnús konungsson með sér', Jakobsson and Guðjónsson, eds., *Morkinskinna I*, 21.

36. 'Mildingr, straukt um mækis / munn es lézt af gunni; / holds vannt hrafn um fylldan / hrás; / þaut vargr í ási. / En, gramr—né ek frá fremra / folkherði þér verða— / austr vastu ár et næsta, / ǫrðiglyndr, í Gǫrðum', Jakobsson and Guðjónsson, eds., *Morkinskinna I*, 84.

37. 'Senn jósum vér, svanni, / sextán, þás brim fexti, / —dreif á hlaðna húfa / húm—í fjórum rúmum. / Vættik miðr at motti / myni enn þinig nenna. / Þó lætr Gerðr í Gǫrðum / gollhrings við mér skolla', Jakobsson and Guðjónsson, eds., *Morkinskinna I*, 115–16.

38. 'Váru synir þeira Guðina ok Gyðu: Haraldr Englakonungr ok Tósti jarl, er kallaðr var tréspjót, Mǫrukári jarl ok Valþjófr jarl ok Sveinn jarl. Þaðan er mart stórmenni komit í Englandi ok í Danmǫrku ok í Svíaríki ok austr í Garðaríki', B. Guðnason, ed., *Danakonunga sǫgur*, Íslenzk fornrit 35 (1982), 111.

Chapter 10

1. 'Gunnar ok Bjǫrn ok Þorgrímr re[istu s]tein þenna at Þors[tein] bróður sinn, er var austr dauðr m[eð Ingv]ari, ok gerð[u br]ú þessa' (U Fv 1992: 157). All inscriptions are taken from the website Skaldic Poetry of the Scandinavian Middle Ages <http://abdn.ac.uk/skaldic/db. php>.

2. 'A[ndv]éttr ok Kárr ok [kiti] ok [B]lesi ok Djarfr reistu stein þenna eptir Gunnleif, fǫður sinn. Er var austr með Ingvari drepinn. Guð hjalpi ǫnd þeira. Al[r]íkr reist-ek rúnar. En kunni vel knerri stýra' (U654).

3. 'Tóla lét reisa stein þenna at son sinn Harald, bróður Ingvars. Þeir fóru drengila fjarri at gulli ok austarla erni gáfu, dóu sunnarla á Serklandi' (Sö 179).

4. Several saga characters are given the nickname *víðfǫrli* or 'far traveller'. As Sverrir Jakobsson has noted: 'A common characteristic of the persons called by the byname *víðfǫrli* is that their journeys took them partly or exclusively to the East.' S. Jakobsson, 'On the Road to Paradise: "Austvegr" in the Icelandic Imagination', in *The Fantastic in Old Norse/Icelandic Literature—Sagas and the British Isles: Preprint Papers of the 13th International Saga Conference, Durham and York, 6th–12th August, 2006*, vol. 2, ed. J. McKinnell, D. Ashurst, and D. Kick (2006), 935–43, at 936.

5. T. M. Andersson, 'Exoticism in Early Iceland', in *International Scandinavian and Medieval Studies in Memory of Gerd Wolfgang Weber*, ed. M. Dallapiazza et al. (2000), 19–28, at 26.

6. In respect to this first part of the saga there are some literary and historical cross-currents with the *Tale of Eymund*, which featured in the last chapter. Yngvar's father is also called Eymund, and he goes to Russia to fight in Yaroslav's civil war. But while in the *Tale of Eymund* the eponymous Eymund comes from Norway and dies childless, the Swedish Eymund of the *Saga of Yngvar* is the father of Yngvar.

7. 'Hann heyrði umræðu á því, at þrjár ár fellu austan um Garðaríki ok var sú mest, sem í miðit var. Þá fór Yngvarr víða um Austrríki ok frétti, ef nokkurr maðr vissi, hvaðan sú á felli, en engi kunni þat at segja', G. Jónsson, ed., *Yngvars saga víðförla*, in *Fornaldar sögur Norðurlanda*, vol. 2 (1954), 434.

8. For the year 1041, two annals—*Konungsannáll* and *Lǫgmannsannáll*—record that 'Yngvar the Far Traveller died' ('O. Yngvarr hinn viðfǫrli', G. Storm, *Islandske Annaler Indtil 1578* (1888), 108, 250).

9. 'En þá er Yngvarr andaðist, var liðit frá burð Jesú Kristí MXL ok einn vetr. Þá var hann hálfþrítugr', Jónsson, ed., *Yngvars saga víðförla*, 447–8.

10. 'Yngvarr fór þar til eftir ánni, at hann kemr at fossi miklum ok þröngum gljúfrum. Þá váru hávir hamrar, svá at þeir drógu upp í festum skip sín. Síðan drógu þeir þau aftr á ána', Jónsson, ed., *Yngvars saga víðförla*, 438.

11. 'vitrum mönnum þykkir þat ekki sannligt vera mega'; 'þó at þetta megi vera, þá er þó eigi sannligt', Jónsson, ed., *Yngvars saga víðförla*, 459.

12. Constantine Porphyrogenitus, *De Administrando Imperio*, ed. G. Moravcsik, trans. R. J. H. Jenkins (revised edn. 1969), 59.

13. These are the translations suggested in H. R. Ellis Davidson, *The Viking Road to Byzantium* (1976), 86.

14. *Serkir* may be the Norse equivalent of 'Saracens'. Alternatively, the word *Serkland* may have come from the Latin word *sericum*—'silk'—referring to the lands that produced silk. See J. Shepard, 'Yngvarr's Expedition to the East and a Russian Inscribed Stone Cross', *Saga-Book of the Viking Society* 21 (1984–5), 222–92, at 235.

15. See Ellis Davidson, *The Viking Road to Byzantium*, 88, 168.

16. 'Þaðan fellr ok önnur til Rauðahafs, ok er þar mikili svelgr, sá er Gapi er kallaðr. Á milli sjóvar ok árinnar er nes þat, er Siggeum heitir. Áin fellr skammt, áðr hún fellr af bjargi í Rauðahaf, ok köllum vér þar enda heims', Jónsson, ed., *Yngvars saga víðförla*, 439.

17. This is discussed by H. Pálsson and P. Edwards, 'Introduction', *Vikings in Russia: Yngvar's saga and Eymund's saga* (1989), 7, and expanded by G. Glazyrina, 'On Heliopolis in *Yngvars saga víðfǫrla*', in *Scandinavia and Christian Europe in the Middle Ages. Papers of the 12th International Saga Conference, Bonn/Germany, 28th July–2nd August 2003*, ed. R. Simek and J. Meurer (2005), 175–8. As Glazyrina notes: 'The author of YS seems to have been convinced that all the geographical names that he mentioned belonged to the same geographical region, i.e. to the southern þriðjungr [third] of the known world' (176).

18. See H. Stang, 'Russia, Norse in', *Medieval Scandinavia: An Encyclopaedia*, ed. P. Pulsiano and K. Wolf (1993), 556–8, at 557.

19. 'Hún spurði, hverir þeir væri eða hvert þeir gerðist, en Yngvarr svarar engu, því at hann vildi freista, ef hún kynni fleiri tungur at tala; ok svá reyndist, at hún kunni at tala rómversku, þýversku, dönsku ok girsku ok margar aðrar, er gengu um Austrveg', Jónsson, ed., *Yngvars saga víðförla*, 437.

20. 'Sá var skrýddr konungs skrúða ok mælti margar tungur. Yngvarr þagði við. Þá mælti hann nokkur orð á girsku', Jónsson, ed., *Yngvars saga víðförla*, 438.

21. 'En Ketill fór til Íslands á fund frænda sinna ok staðfestist þar ok sagði fyrstr frá þessu', Jónsson, ed., *Yngvars saga víðförla*, 458.

22. 'Af þeira frásögn hafði hann þat, er honum þótti merkiligast', Jónsson ed., *Yngvars saga víðförla*, 459.

23. 'En þessa sögu höfum vér heyrt ok ritat eftir forsögn þeirar bækr, at Oddr munkr inn fróði hafði gera látit at forsögn fróðra manna, þeira er hann segir sjálfr í bréfi sínu, því er hann sendi Jóni Loftssyni ok Gizuri Hallssyni', Jónsson, ed., *Yngvars saga víðförla*, 459.

24. See D. Hofmann, 'Die *Yngvars saga víðförla* und Oddr munkr inn fróði', in *Speculum Norroenum: Norse Studies in Memory of Gabriel Turville-Petre*, ed. H. Becker-Nielsen et al. (1981), 188–222. See also G. Jensson, 'Were the Earliest *fornaldarsögur* Written in Latin?', in *Fornaldarsagaerne: Myter og virkelighed. Studier i de oldislandske* fornaldarsögur Norðurlanda, ed. A. Ney, Á. Jakobsson, and A. Lassen (2009), 79–91, at 82–4.

25. M. Cormack, 'Saint's Lives and Icelandic Literature in the Thirteenth and Fourteenth Centuries', in *Saints and Sagas: A Symposium*, ed. H. Bekker-Nielsen and B. Carlé (1994), 27–47, at 38.

26. 'þeir báru mann blóðgan fyrir liðinu ok höfðu hann fyrir merki', Jónsson ed., *Yngvars saga víðförla*, 453.

27. 'Yngvarr bjó eina höll öllu liði sínu ok lukti hana vandliga, því at fullt var af blótskap allt umhverfis. Yngvarr bað þá við varast allt samneyti heiðinna manna, ok öllum konum bannaði hann at koma í sína höll utan drottninguna. Nokkurir menn gáfu lítinn gaum at hans máli, ok lét hann þá drepa', Jónsson, ed., *Yngvars saga víðförla*, 437.

28. 'ina verstu eitrorma', Jónsson, ed., *Yngvars saga víðförla*, 445.

29. 'Þá reiddist hann ok tók tygilkníf ok lagði til hennar í kvensköpin', Jónsson, ed., *Yngvars saga víðförla*, 445.

30. 'En þeir, er vita þykkjast innvirðuligar, auki við, þar sem nú þykkir á skorta', Jónsson, ed., *Yngvars saga víðförla*, 459.

Chapter 11

1. 'þeir sáu annan sið ok lit á dýrum, ok af því skildu þeir, at þeir fjarlægðust sín heruð eða lönd', G. Jónsson, ed., *Yngvars saga víðförla*, in *Fornaldar sögur Norðurlanda*, vol. 2 (1954), 436.

2. 'þeir sáu um daginn, at tíu menn leiða eftir sér kvikendi nokkut. Þat þótti þeim nokkut undarligt, því at mikinn turn af viðum gervan sáu þeir standa á baki dýrinu…. En er þeir sáu skipaliðit, er dýrit leiddu, fálust þeir ok fyrirlétu dýrit. En Sveins menn gengu til dýrsins ok vildu leiða eftir sér, en þat drap höfðinu niðr, svá at þat gekk eigi ór stað, þó at þeir tæki allir at toga þær taugir, er á váru höfðinu dýrsins….En með því at þeir vissu eigi náttúru dýrsins ok hvat því þurfti til matar at ætla, þá lögðu þeir dýrit spjótum, til þess at þat fell dautt', Jónsson, ed., *Yngvars saga víðförla*, 452.

3. For a selection of bestiary elephants see <http://bestiary.ca/beasts/beastgallery77.htm#>.

4. 'sine dilatione construi faciatis apud Turrim nostrum Londoniæ, unum domum longitudinis xl pedum et latitudinis xx pedum, ad Elefantem nostrum', T. Maddox, *The history and antiquities of the Exchequer of the kings of England, in two periods: to wit, from the Norman conquest, to the end of the reign of K. John; and from the end of the reign of K. John, to the end of the reign of K. Edward II* (1769), 1.37.

5. The two fragments are known as AM 673 a I 4to (which contains the uniped amongst other marvellous and monstrous races) and AM 673 a II 4to (which features the elephant on its final page).

6. 'Elephans heitir dýr á látínu en á óra tungu fíll. Þat er haft í orrustum á útlöndum. Þat er svá sterkt ok máttugt, at þat heldr…tigum manna ok…með hervápnum ǫllum ok virki því, er gǫrt er úr trjám sem kastali sé, er þeir þurfa at hafa, þá er berjask í orrustum, svá sem skrifat er í Machabeorum bók', H. Hermannsson, ed., *The Icelandic Physiologus* (1938, repr. 1966), 21.

7. 'svá heitt sem nýrunnit í afli', Jónsson, ed., *Yngvars saga víðförla*, 442.

8. 'þar var allt þakit ormum. En fyrir því at þeir sváfu, þá rétti hann spjótskefti sitt þar til, sem einn gullhringr var, ok dró hann at sér. Þá vaknaði einn yrmlingr, ok vakti sá þegar aðra hjá sér, unz Jakúlus var vaktr', Jónsson, ed., *Yngvars saga víðförla*, 436.

9. *Pliny: Natural History* 8.35.85, ed. and trans. H. Rackham (repr. 2006), 62–3.

10. Lucan, *Civil War* 9.822–5, trans. S. M. Braund (1992), 199.

11. 'sua grimmr at engín ormr þorir sua nær honum at vera', Þ. Helgadóttir, ed., *Rómverja saga* (2010), cxv.

12. Isidore of Seville, *The Eymologies*, trans. S. A. Barney et al. (2006), 257.

13. For an image see <http://www.abdn.ac.uk/bestiary/comment/69r.hti>.

14. Bibliothèque Nationale de France, lat. 6838B, folio 33v; for more bestiary images of the jaculus see <http://bestiary.ca/beasts/beastgallery273.htm#>.

15. 'svá sterkir sem it óarga dýr ok hávir sem hús eða skógar', Jónsson, ed., *Yngvars saga víðförla*, 450.

16. 'Cikoplex heita menn er auga er eítt i hofðe. en þat er i miðiu enni', E. Jónsson and F. Jónsson, eds., *Hauksbók* (1892–6), 166. The Cyclops also appears in another encyclopedic manuscript, AM 194 8vo, with a similar description (for more information see R. Simek, *Altnordische Kosmographie: Studien und Quellen zu Weltbild und Weltbeschreibung in Norwegen und Island vom 12. bis 14. Jahrhundert* (1990), 470).

17. 'En því næst sáu þeir mikinn her fara af landi ofan til skipanna, ok fór einn maðr nokkut svá frá liðinu fram. Sá hafði þrjú epli ok varp einu í loft upp, ok kom þat niðr fyrir fætr Sveini, ok þegar öðru eftir; þat kom ok í sama stað. Þá kveðst Sveinn eigi mundu bíða ins þriðja eplisins: "Þessu fylgir nokkurr djöfulligr kraftr ok rammr átrúnaðr." Sveinn lagði ör á streng ok skaut at honum. Örin kom á nef honum. Þá var því líkast at heyra, sem þá horn brestr í sundr, ok vatt hann upp við höfðinu, ok sáu þeir, at hann hafði fugls nef. Síðan æpir hann hátt ok hljóp í mót liði sínu ok svá hverr á land upp, sem fara mátti, þá er þeir sáu síðast til', Jónsson, ed.,*Yngvars saga víðförla*, 451.

18. For a reproduction of this stork-man see the 'Section 1' map in S. D. Westrem, *The Hereford Map: A Transcription and Translation of the Legends with Commentary* (2001). For a discussion of this race and its origins see there p. 74. From time to time crane-headed men crop up in medieval texts; see J. B. Friedman, *The Monstrous Races in Medieval Art and Thought* (2nd edn., 2000), 94, 126.

Chapter 12

1. 'iorsalaminburtuhaukþ(æ)': M. Barnes, *The Runic Inscriptions of Maeshowe, Orkney* (1994), 114.

2. 'iorsalafararbrutuorkǫuh·lifmtsæiliaiarls ræist': Barnes, *The Runic Inscriptions of Maeshowe, Orkney*, 186.

3. 'binititk(i)rþikrosæ(n)a': Barnes, *The Runic Inscriptions of Maeshowe, Orkney*, 166.

4. Ezekiel 5:5 (English Standard Edition).

5. Not all medieval maps are T–O maps. For instance, there are zonal maps that divide the world vertically into five climatic zones (two frigid zones at the top and bottom, two habitable temperate zones, and the equatorial tropical zone). Likewise, not all medieval maps or written descriptions of the world placed Jerusalem in the middle of the world, but the holy city's positioning became increasingly important with the coming of the crusades, when Jerusalem's centrality became a tool of spiritual propaganda. See R. Simek, *Heaven and Earth in the Middle Ages* (1996), 73.

6. 'miðlutr & hinn bezti partr af ǫllu landinu', R. Simek, *Altnordische Kosmographie: Studien und Quellen zu Weltbild und Weltbeschreibung in Norwegen und Island vom 12. bis 14. Jahrhundert* (1990), 529.

7. Pope Urban II's speech as recorded by Robert the Monk, in *The Crusades: A Reader*, ed. S. J. Allen and E. Amt (2003), 41.

8. C. Tyerman, *The Invention of the Crusades* (1998), 20.

9. 'Saraceni, þat kǫllum vér Maúmets villumenn', F. Guðmundsson, ed., *Orkneyinga saga*, Íslenzk fornrit 34 (1965), 225.

10. 'Þat þykki mér undarligt, jarl, er þú vill eigi fara út í Jórsalaheim ok hafa eigi sagnir einar til þeira tíðenda, er þaðan eru at segja. Er slíkum mǫnnum bezt hent þar sakar yðvarra lista; muntu þar bezt virðr, sem þú kemr með tignum mǫnnum', Guðmundsson, ed., *Orkneyinga saga*, 194.

11. 'stǫkk Erlingr af bryggjunni ok ofan í leirinn, er undir var, ok hljópu menn hans til at draga hann upp ok urðu at fœra hann af hverju klæði', Guðmundsson, ed., *Orkneyinga saga*, 234.

12. 'þá mun almáttigr guð vilja veita oss þá miskunn, at vér munum vinna sigr á þeim. En af herfangi því, er vér fám þar, skulum vér fá fátœkum mǫnnum inn fimmtøganda penning', Guðmundsson, ed., *Orkneyinga saga*, 224.

13. 'Þar nǫðum vér þjóðar, / því hefr aldar guð valdit, / bolr fell blár á þiljur, / blóði vǫpn at rjóða', Guðmundsson, ed., *Orkneyinga saga*, 227.

14. Fulcher of Chartres, *A History of the Expedition to Jerusalem 1095–1127*, ed. H. S. Fink, trans. F. R. Ryan (1969), 199.

15. 'Gramr…ógnblíðr', Á. Jakobsson and Þ. I. Guðjónsson, eds., *Morkinskinna II*, Íslenzk fornrit 24 (2011), 89.

16. 'mikit fé ok svá frama', Jakobsson and Guðjónsson, eds., *Morkinskinna II*, 79.

17. 'Treystuzk egg fyr austan / —yðr tjóði Goð—rjóða, / náskári flaug nýra, / Nǫrvasund, til unda', Jakobsson and Guðjónsson, eds., *Morkinskinna II*, 81.

18. 'mest herfang í einum stað, þess er þeir tœki í ferðinni', Jakobsson and Guðjónsson, eds., *Morkinskinna II*, 82.

19. 'Fór ek til Jórdánar, ok kom ek við Púl, ok sá ek þik eigi þar. Vann ek átta orrostur, ok vartu í ǫngarri. Fór ek til grafnar Dróttins, ok sá ek þik eigi þar. Fór ek í ána, þá leið er Dróttinn fór, ok svam ek yfir, ok sá ek þik eigi þar. Ok knýtta ek þér knút, ok bíðr þín þar. Þá vann ek borgina Sídon með Jórsalakonungi, ok hǫfðum vér eigi þinn styrk eða ráð til', Jakobsson and Guðjónsson, eds., *Morkinskinna II*, 133.

20. 'Borg heiðna þátt, bræðir / benja tíkr, af ríki / —háðisk hver við prýði / hildr—en gaft af mildi', Jakobsson and Guðjónsson, eds., *Morkinskinna II*, 94.

21. 'Kross hangir þul þessum, / þjóst skyli lægt, fyr brjósti, / flykkisk fram á brekkur / ferð, en palmr meðal herða', Guðmundsson, ed., *Orkneyinga saga*, 233.

22. 'En hykk, at þó þykki / þangat langt at ganga, / blóð fellr varmt á víðan / vǫll, heimdrǫgum ǫllum', Guðmundsson, ed., *Orkneyinga saga*, 232.

23. 'Lýst skal hitt, es læknask fýstisk / liðhraustr konungr sǫr en iðri. / Norðan fór með helming harðan / hersa mœðir sǫl at grœða. / Harri bjósk til heims ens dýrra. / Hann gerði fǫr út at kanna, / buðlungr vildi bjart líf ǫðlask, / byggð Jórsala friði tryggða', B. Guðnason, ed., *Knýtlinga saga*, in *Danakonunga sǫgur*, Íslenzk fornrit 35 (1982), 235.

24. Þ. Helgadóttir, 'On the Sallust Translation of *Rómverja saga*', *Saga-Book of the Viking Society* 22 (1986–9), 263–77, at 270.

25. 'fór Guðríðr útan ok gekk suðr ok kom út aptr til bús Snorra, sonar síns', E. Ó. Sveinsson and M. Þórðarson, eds., *Grœnlendinga saga*, in *Eyrbyggja saga*, Íslenzk fornrit 4 (1935), 269.

26. 'fara til Danmerkr í Heiðabœ, tóku þær við trú ok gengu suðr ok kómu eigi aptr', B. K. Þórólfsson and G. Jónsson, eds., *Gísla saga Súrssonar*, in *Vestfirðinga sǫgur*, Íslenzk fornrit 6 (1943), 118.

27. 'Flósi fór þaðan suðr um sjá ok hóf þá upp gǫngu sína ok gekk suðr ok létti eigi, fyrr en hann kom til Rómaborgar. Þar fekk hann svá mikla sœmð, at hann tók lausn af páfanum sjálfum ok gaf þar til mikit fé', E. Ó. Sveinsson, ed., *Brennu-Njáls saga*, Íslenzk fornrit 12 (1954), 462.

28. 'suðr til Róms', Guðnason, ed., *Knýtlinga saga*, 123.

29. 'Knútr konungr byrjaði ferð sína af landi í brott, ok fór hann suðr til Róms, ok hafði hann í þeiri ferð svá mikinn fékostnað, at engi maðr kunni markatal um ok varla pundatal.... Meðan Knútr konungr var á Rómavegi, þá þyrfti engi maðr sér matar at biðja, sá er hans fundi mátti ná, svá gaf hann ǫllum nóga skotpenninga', Guðnason, ed., *Knýtlinga saga*, 123.
30. 'Varð hann allfrægr af ferð þessi', Guðnason, ed., *Knýtlinga saga*, 220.
31. 'Oft fór hann af landi brott ok var betr metinn í Róma en nökkurr íslenzkr maðr fyrr honum af mennt sinni ok framkvæmð. Honum varð víða kunnigt um suðrlöndin, ok þar af gerði hann bók þá, er heitir Flos peregrinationis', J. Jóhannesson, M. Finnbogason, and K. Eldjárn, eds., *Haukdæla þáttr*, in *Sturlunga saga* I (1946), 60.
32. For more on this pilgrimage account see F. P. Magoun, 'The Rome of Two Northern Pilgrims: Archbishop Sigeric of Canterbury and Abbot Nikolás of Munkathvera', *Harvard Theological Review* 33:4 (1940), 267–89; F. P. Magoun, 'The Pilgrim-Diary of Nikulas of Munkathvera: The Road to Rome', *Mediaeval Studies* 6 (1944), 314–54; and J. Hill, 'From Rome to Jerusalem: An Icelandic Itinerary of the Mid-Twelfth Century', *Harvard Theological Review* 76:2 (1983), 175–203. More recently, T. Marani has challenged some of the traditionally held views about the guide in 'Leiðarvísir: Its Genre and Sources, with Particular Reference to the Description of Rome', unpubl. Ph.D thesis, Durham University (2012).
33. For more on these inconsistencies see Marani, 'Leiðarvísir: Its Genre and Sources'.
34. 'Ut vid Iordan, ef madr liggr opinn á slettum velli ok setr kne sitt upp ok hnefa á ofan ok reisir þumal-fingr af hnefanum upp, þa er leiþarstiarna þar yfir ath sea iafn-ha en eigi héra', N. Beckman and K. Kålund, eds., *Alfræði Íslenzk: Islandsk Encyklopædisk Litteratur*, vol. 1 (1908), 23.

Chapter 13

1. 'The Rūs Attack Constantinople', in *The Viking Age: A Reader*, ed. A. A. Somerville and R. A. McDonald (2010), 305.
2. 'The Rūs Attack Constantinople', 305–6.
3. 'A Treaty with Byzantium, 911–912', in Somerville and McDonald, *The Viking Age: A Reader*, 312.
4. A. Vasiliev, 'Harun-Ibn-Yahya and his Description of Constantinople', *Seminarium Kondakovianum* 5 (1932), 149–63, at 158.
5. E. R. A. Sewter, trans., *The Alexiad of Anna Comnena* (1969), 95.
6. 'Rúnar rista lét Ragnvaldr. Var á Grikklandi, var liðs forungi' (U112).
7. Other sagas describing Harald Hardrada's life include a version in the manuscript *Fagrskinna* and Snorri Sturluson's *Heimskringla*, both of which date from the first half of the thirteenth century.
8. 'Hart knúði svǫl svartan / snekkju brand fyr landi / skúr, en skrautla bǫru / skeiðr brynjaðar reiði. / Mætr hilmir sá malma / Miklagarðs fyr barði; / mǫrg skriðu beit at borgar / barmfǫgr hǫum armi', Á. Jakobsson and Þ. I. Guðjónsson, eds., *Morkinskinna I*, Íslenzk fornrit 23 (2011), 87.
9. '"Þú, Norðmaðr, gef mér lokk ór hári þínu." "Dróttning," segir hann, "jafnmæli skal með okkr. Gef mér hár ór magaskeggi þínu"', Jakobsson and Guðjónsson, eds., *Morkinskinna I*, 89. For more about the representation of Zoe in the sagas, see L. Lönnroth, 'The Man-eating Mama of Miklagard: Empress Zoe in Old Norse Saga Tradition', in *Kairos: Studies in Art History and Literature in Honour of Professor Gunilla Åkerström-Hougen*, ed. E. Piltz and P. Åström (1998), 37–49.
10. In fact there were actually four interconnected apartments, belonging to Constantine, Maria, Zoe, and Zoe's co-empress, her sister Theodora. See L. Garland, *Byzantine Empresses: Women and Power in Byzantium AD 527–1204* (1999), 146–56.

11. 'Því at þat segja menn, þeir er verit hafa í Miklagarði, at Væringja minni svá frásagnar at Zóe sjálf vildi hafa hann', Jakobsson and Guðjónsson, eds., *Morkinskinna I*, 109.

12. 'Ormrinn hafði dauða menn til fœzlu ok þá er missáttir urðu við konung eða ríkismenn ok var þangat kastat. Þeir óðu þar í goglann, er menn lágu fúnaðir, því at jafnan hǫfðu orminum til leifa gefnir verit menn. Settusk síðan niðr á bakkana. Þá mælti Halldórr Snorrason: "Eigi er þetta góð vist, ok kann þó vera at heðan af versni"', Jakobsson and Guðjónsson, eds., *Morkinskinna I*, 110.

13. 'Inn vas í sem brynni / iðglíkt séa miðjan / eldr, þars yðrum helduð, / orms munn, skipum sunnan. / Skeið bar skolpt enn rauða, / skein af golli hreinu, / dreki fór dagleið mikla, / dúfu braut und húfi', Jakobsson and Guðjónsson, eds., *Morkinskinna I*, 124.

14. 'heðan frá er sú frásǫgn um farar Haralds er hann, Harald, sagði sjálfr, ok þeir menn er honum fylgðu', Jakobsson and Guðjónsson, eds., *Morkinskinna I*, 84.

15. Translation from S. Blöndal, *The Varangians of Byzantium: An Aspect of Byzantine Military History*, translated, revised, and rewritten by B. S. Benedikz (1978), 58.

16. T. M. Andersson and K. E. Gade, trans., *Morkinskinna: The Earliest Icelandic Chronicle of the Norwegian Kings (1030–1157)* (2000), 59. Harald as a source for his own saga is discussed in A. Finlay, 'History and Fiction in the Kings' Sagas: The Case of Haraldr Harðráði', *Saga-Book of the Viking Society* 39 (2015), 77–102.

17. 'Náði gørr enn glóðum, / Grikklands, jǫfurr handa, / stólþengill gekk strǫngu / steinblindr aðalmeini', Jakobsson and Guðjónsson, eds., *Morkinskinna I*, 112.

18. E. R. A. Sewter, trans., *Fourteen Byzantine Rulers: The Chronographia of Michael Psellus* (1966), 150.

19. This episode is discussed by H. R. Ellis Davidson, *The Viking Road to Byzantium* (1976), 225, and Blöndal, *The Varangians of Byzantium*, 93–4.

20. See T. Thomov, 'Four Scandinavian Ship Graffiti from Hagia Sophia', *Byzantine and Modern Greek Studies* 38:2 (2014), 168–84.

21. R. Taft, 'Women at Church in Byzantium: Where, When—and Why?', *Dumbarton Oaks Papers* 52 (1998), 27–87, at 59, and discussed by Thomov, 'Four Scandinavian Ship Graffiti from Hagia Sophia', 168–84.

22. M. Chibnall, ed. and trans., *The Ecclesiastical History of Orderic Vitalis*, vol. 2, *Books III and IV* (1969), 202–3.

23. 'Bolli var svá mikill skartsmaðr, er hann kom út ór fǫr þessi, at hann vildi engi klæði bera nema skarlatsklæði ok pellsklæði, ok ǫll vápn hafði hann gullbúin. Hann var kallaðr Bolli inn prúði....Bolli ríðr frá skipi við tólfta mann; þeir váru allir í skarlatsklæðum fylgðarmenn Bolla ok riðu í gyldum sǫðlum; allir váru þeir listuligir menn, en þó bar Bolli af. Hann var í pellsklæðum, er Garðskonungr hafði gefit honum; hann hafði ýzta skarlatskápu rauða; hann var gyrðr Fótbít, ok váru at honum hjǫlt gullbúin ok meðalkaflinn gulli vafiðr; hann hafði gyldan hjálm á hǫfði ok rauðan skjǫld á hlið, ok á dreginn riddari með gulli; hann hafði gladel í hendi, sem títt er í útlǫndum, ok hvar sem þeir tóku gistingar, þá gáðu konur engis annars en horfa á Bolla ok skart hans ok þeira félaga', E. Ó. Sveinsson, ed., *Laxdœla saga*, Íslenzk fornrit 5 (1934), 225.

24. 'Sá var hár maðr ok ekki þrekligr, er fyrstr gekk, í laufgrœnum kyrtli ok hafði búit sverð í hendi, réttleitr maðr ok rauðlitaðr ok vel í yfirbragði, ljósjarpr á hár ok mjǫk hærðr', J. Jóhannesson, ed., *Hrafnkels saga freysgoða*, in *Austfirðinga sǫgur*, Íslenzk fornrit 11 (1950), 111.

25. 'Heldr óskyggn ok súreygr', E. Ó. Sveinsson, ed., *Hallfreðar saga*, in *Vatnsdœla saga*, Íslenzk fornrit 8 (1939), 145.

26. 'fúrskerðandi fjarðar', Sveinsson, ed., *Hallfreðar saga*, 182.

27. Á. Jakobsson, 'Image is Everything: The *Morkinskinna* Account of King Sigurðr of Norway's Journey to the Holy Land', *Parergon* 30:1 (2013), 121–40. As Jakobsson puts it, 'The audience of

Morkinskinna is clearly expected to realize that Sigurðr's nonchalant attitude is nothing but a clever mask and that Norway is in fact not as rich, nor as splendid as these southern lands. However, the audience is also expected to side with the Norwegian king and his entourage, to approve of their deception, and feel that Norway's prestige is important; that it is admirable to make such an impression on foreign monarchs so that they are tricked into believing that Norway is a country more splendid than it actually is' (135).

28. 'Þat er sagt at Sigurðr konungr léti með gulli skúa hesta sína ok sinna manna áðr hann reið í borgina', Á. Jakobsson and Þ. I. Guðjónsson, eds., *Morkinskinna II*, Íslenzk fornrit 24 (2011), 96.

29. 'Tveim mun um skipta konung þenna: at hann mun vera yfir ǫðrum konungum at ríki ok fé eða hann mun vera eigi með jǫfnum vitrleik sem konungi sœmði', Jakobsson and Guðjónsson, eds., *Morkinskinna II*, 96.

30. 'Ok greinask menn at því, hvárt hǫfðingligar þótti kosit vera', B. Guðnason, ed., *Knýtlinga saga*, in *Danakonunga sǫgur*, Íslenzk fornrit 35 (1982), 237.

31. 'Þat segja þeir menn er verit hafa í Miklagarði at paðreimr sé á þá leið gǫrr at veggr hár er settr um einn vǫll, at jafna til víðs túns kringlótts, ok gráður umhverfis með steinveggnum, ok sitja menn þar á, en leikr er á vellinum. Eru þar skrifuð margs konar forn tíðendi, Æsir ok Vǫlsungar ok Gjúkungar, gǫrt af kopar ok málmi með svá miklum hagleik at þat þykkir kviktvera. Ok með þessi umbúð þykkir mǫnnum sem þeir sé í leiknum, ok er leikrinn settr með miklum brǫgðum ok velum; sýnisk sem menn ríði í lopti, ok við er ok skoteldr hafðr, ok sumt af forneskju. Þar við eru hǫfð alls konar sǫngfœri, *psalterium* ok organ, hǫrpur, gígjur ok fiðlur ok alls konar strengleikr', Jakobsson and Guðjónsson, eds., *Morkinskinna II*, 97–8.

32. 'Ok er fleytt at borginni mǫrg hundruð skipa á hvern dag, hlaðin af allra handa kostuligum jurtum ok kryddum, ok allra handa grasaðr drykkr; eru margar hallir tjaldaðar með guðvef. Og su micla holl, er kongunum var buinn, gloade oll innann með gull, ok hásætit hit efra ok neðra logandi ǫll af tandrauðu gulli…En eptir þat ferr út patriarchinn með biskupum ok ǫðrum kennimanna skara, allir sætt syngjandi, berandi stór lys, með fǫgrum prís; ok svó sýnisk nú, sem alt loptit logi yfir lýðnum, er gullig glóðar-ker glitra i sólskininu', K. Kålund, ed., *Kirialax Saga* (1917), 85–6.

33. Geraldine Barnes describes Constantinople's 'metamorphosis into virtual Camelot' in the *Saga of Kirialax*; see G. Barnes, *The Bookish Riddarasögur: Writing Romance in Late Mediaeval Iceland* (2014), 180. This book also includes a full and detailed analysis of Byzantium in the Chivalric Sagas.

Chapter 14

1. In order, these are: Blemmyae, Cyclopes, Sciapods, Anthropophagi, Astomi, and Donestre. These races worked their way from Classical works such as Pliny the Elder's *Natural History* (where the first comprehensive list of marvellous and monstrous races appears) into the medieval world through summaries and encyclopedic works by writers such as Gaius Julius Solinus (3rd century AD) and Isidore of Seville (6th/7th century AD).

2. 'Libia prouincia Affrice'; 'Pentapolis regio ibi sunt v urbes'; 'Hic sunt solitudines inaccessibiles et arene usque huc', N. Beckman and K. Kålund, eds., *Alfræði Íslenzk: Islandsk Encyklopædisk Litteratur*, vol. 3, (1917–18), 72.

3. 'Trogita prouincia ibi in uenitur carbunculus igneus et alter exacontalitus LX coloribus micans', Beckman and Kålund, eds., *Alfræði Íslenzk*, 72.

4. 'Getulia ibi infantes ludunt serpentibus', Beckman and Kålund, eds., *Alfræði Íslenzk*, 72.

5. 'Su þjoð er i Afrika er eigi sakar orma eítur oc born i voggu leíka með eitr ormum. þeir ero enn þar er hofuð lausir ero en a bringunní er beði munnr oc augu. sumír hofuð lausir þa er munnren ofan a bukenum. en augu a herðar bloðum. oc er har a sem a dyrum', E. Jónsson and F. Jónsson, eds., *Hauksbók* (1892–6), 166.

6. M. E. Kalinke, 'Riddarasögur, Fornaldarsögur, and the Problem of Genre', in *Les Sagas des Chevaliers (Riddarasögur), Actes de la Vme Conférence Internationale sur les Sagas*, ed. R. Boyer (1985), 77–91, at 77.

7. G. Barnes, *The Bookish Riddarasögur: Writing Romance in Late Medieval Iceland* (2014), 139.

8. 'eirninn mestur hlutur rijkis j Affrichä, er kallad er Bläland hid mikla, þad geingur vestur allt med vthaffinu, og sudur allt ad Midjardar siö, þar sem haffed vellur aff sölarhita, þar eru marger stader suidner og brunner, aff sölar hitanumm, þar fædast mieg jøtnar jmissliger og bläämenn bannsetter, og allskins skiesseligar skiepnur', J. Kristjánsson, ed., *Dínus saga dramblláta* (1960), 11.

9. See K. Wolf, 'The Color Blue in Old Norse-Icelandic Literature', *Scripta Islandica* 57 (2006), 55–78, and J. Lindow, 'Supernatural and Ethnic Others: A Millennium of World View', *Scandinavian Studies* 67:1 (1995), 8–31.

10. 'suarter blämenn, og hrædeliger risar, og ønnur skrimsl, med ögurlegumm äsiönumm. fijlar voru marger j hernumm og wlffalldar, og høfdu kastala ä bake, eptter þetta fluttu þeir herinn j veg, skunda sem mest meiga þeir', Kristjánsson, ed., *Dínus saga dramblláta*, 71–2.

11. 'blamenn og berserkj duerga og dularfolc risa og regintroll. hann hafdi folc af Jndia lande er Cenoefalj het. þeir gou sem hunndar og hófdu hunndz hófud. Hann hafdi og þæ menn er hofdu eitt auga j midiu enne. enn sumir uoru haufudlausir og hofdu munn og augu aa briostj. þeir uoru og þar er augu hofdu aa herdarblódum. þetta folc war stort sem risar en biartir sem bic', A. Loth, ed., *Sigurðar saga þogla*, in *Late Medieval Icelandic Romances*, vol. 2 (1963), 177.

12. Traditionally a distinction was made between two Babylons: Old Babylon in Asia and New Babylon in Egypt. This Babylon is the African Babylon; see A. Divjak, *Studies in the Traditions of Kirialax Saga* (2009), 144–6.

13. 'blamanna ok iotna, ok skringiligar skepnur med hrædiligum ásionum, ok hafa sumir augu á brioste ok bringu ok eru haufud-lauser, sumir eru en haufut-lauser ok hafa mun ok naser á herder blaudum, sumir hafa eyru svo micil, at þeir mega hylia sig i, sumir hafa hundz hofut ok geyia sem hundar', Kålund, ed., *Kirialax Saga*, 28.

14. 'þvi þat er ecki kvikendi i verollduni, at fillin ottezt svo sem musena, eptir þvi sem Ysidorus biskup segir i sinni xi. bok Ethimologiarum, at fillin flye iafnvel sinn burd, þar sem hann verdr vid þvilika hlute var, ok hiola nisting ottazt þeir ok miog', Kålund, ed., *Kirialax Saga*, 29–30.

15. This information is also mentioned in the *Saga of Alexander* (*Alexanders saga*), which is the Old Norse version of the life of Alexander the Great, and *Stjórn* ('Guidance'), the aforementioned fourteenth-century Old Norse translation of Old Testament material. See Divjak, *Studies in the Traditions of Kirialax Saga*, 158.

16. 'Saga þessi hefzt fyst j Englandi og fer sidan ut til Saxlandz og þa til Gricklandz og þui næst uestur j Affrika allt ut under solarsetrit og þadan j sudrhalfu heimsins til hinnar miklu borgar Ninive. og þadan ut at heims enda til hinna miklu fialla Kakausi', A. Loth, ed., *Vilhjálms saga sjóðs*, in *Late Medieval Icelandic Romances*, vol. 4 (1964), 3.

17. 'enn fyr þrytur bædi bokfellit og nenninginna enn vær getum sagt fra yferlitum allra þeirra sem þar uoru afskræmiliga skapader', Loth, ed., *Vilhjálms saga sjóðs*, 98.

18. 'suo mikil var hæd hans at hann bar jafnhatt skoginum', Loth, ed.,*Vilhjálms saga sjóðs*, 47.
19. 'þeir voru vndarliger j skópun, eitt hóffdu þeir auga og stod þat j midiu enne, eirn var foturenn og var hann här mióg og skaptur nedan sem kieralldz bótn, og voru tær wmmhuerffez fötenn, enn þa þeir stykludu med sinne stóng þa var þad langur vegur ad þeir skræmdust, enn huad sem vnder var þar sem þeir koma nidur fieck allt bana', Loth, ed.,*Vilhjálms saga sjóðs*, 57–8.
20. 'Þat er so komid nærre solarsetre ad þar verdur alldre biartara enn þar sier stiornur vm midiann dag, enn þa þu kemur a þad land utanvert sier þu blomligt land med grosum og alldentriam og vmm midnætte skyn þar sól þa annarstadar j heyminum er dagur sem styrstur, þvi þa er þessi hlutur heymz j skugga jardarinnar', Loth, ed.,*Vilhjálms saga sjóðs*, 52–3.
21. 'j austr er land fra Jnndia lande hinu yzsta', H. Jensen, ed., *Eiríks saga víðfǫrla* (1983), 46. In the saga, the Earthly Paradise (as it tends to be translated) is referred to variously as 'The Deathless Acre' (*Odáinsakr*), 'The Land of the Living' (*jörð lifandi manna*), or Paradise (*Paradisum*). Generally speaking, the location and definition of the 'Earthly Paradise' is rather vague, and depends very much on the text in question. In the Middle Ages a distinction was made between a paradise in heaven and a paradise on earth, which was sometimes—but not always—equated with the Garden of Eden.
22. 'yzst land j sudr halfu hæimsins', Jensen, ed., *Eiríks saga víðfǫrla*, 44.
23. For a discussion of the possible sources for this saga see R. Simek, 'Die Quellen der Eiríks saga víðförla', *Skandinavistik: Zeitschrift für Sprache, Literatur und Kultur der Nordischen Länder* 14:2 (1984), 109–14.
24. 'En sa stadr er þu ser her er sem eyde mork til at iafnna vid Paradisum. en skamt hedan er sa stadr ok fellr þadan aa su er þu sátt þangat skulu óngir lifs koma ok skulu þar byggia andir rettlatra manna', Jensen, ed., *Eiríks saga víðfǫrla*, 90–2.

SAGAS IN TRANSLATION

The saga translations in this book are my own. However, for anyone interested in reading any of the sagas in their entirety, this is a list of some available translations. The saga titles listed here are those used in the published translations, and are not always identical to the translations used in this book. For further translations of Old Norse texts see the Viking Society Web Publications < http://vsnrweb-publications.org.uk>.

T. M. Andersson and K. E. Gade, trans., *Morkinskinna: The Earliest Icelandic Chronicle of the Norwegian Kings (1030–1157)* (2000).

R. Cook, trans., *Njal's Saga* (2001).

A. Divjak, *Studies in the Traditions of Kirialax Saga* (2009) (including translation on pp. 297–352).

P. Edwards and H. Pálsson, trans., *Orkneyinga Saga: The History of the Earls of Norway* (1981).

P. Edwards and H. Pálsson, trans., *Seven Viking Romances* (1985) (containing *Arrow-Odd*; *Egil and Asmund*; *Helgi Thorisson*).

P. Edwards and H. Pálsson, trans., *Knytlinga Saga: The History of the Kings of Denmark* (1986).

P. Edwards and H. Pálsson, trans., *Vikings in Russia: Yngvar's Saga and Eymund's Saga* (1989).

A. Finlay and A. Faulkes, trans., *Heimskringla I: Beginnings to Óláfr Tryggvason* (2011).

A. Finlay and A. Faulkes, trans., *Heimskringla II: Óláfr Haraldsson (The Saint)* (2014).

A. Finlay and A. Faulkes, trans., *Heimskringla III: Magnús Óláfsson to Magnús Erlingsson* (2016).

J. H. McGrew and R. G. Thomas, trans., *Sturlunga saga*, 2 vols. (1970–4).

Ö. Thorsson et al., *The Complete Sagas of Icelanders Including 49 Tales*, 5 vols. (1997) (containing *Eirik the Red's Saga*; the *Saga of the Greenlanders*; *Egil's Saga*; the *Saga of Hallfred the Troublesome Poet*; the *Tale of Audun from the West Fjords*; *Gisli Sursson's Saga*; the *Saga of Grettir the Strong*; *Bard's Saga*; *Njal's Saga*; the *Saga of the People of Floi*; *Jokul Buason's Tale*; the *Saga of Ref the Sly*; the *Saga of the People of Vatnsdal*; the *Saga of the People of Laxardal*; the *Saga of Hrafnkel Frey's Godi*; the *Tale of the Greenlanders*).

Ö. Thorsson et al., *The Sagas of Icelanders: A Selection* (2000) (containing *Egil's Saga*; the *Saga of the People of Vatnsdal*; the *Saga of the Greenlanders* and *Eirik the Red's Saga*; the *Saga of Ref the Sly*; the *Tale of Audun from the West Fjords*; *Gisli Sursson's Saga*; the *Saga of Hrafnkel Frey's Godi*; the *Saga of the People of Laxardal*).

C. Tolkien, trans., *The Saga of King Heidrek the Wise* (1960).

B. Waggoner, trans., *The Hrafnista Sagas* (2012) (containing the *Saga of Ketil Trout*; the *Saga of Grim Shaggy-Cheek*; the *Saga of Arrow-Odd*; the *Saga of An Bow-Bender*).

PICTURE ACKNOWLEDGEMENTS

© akg-images/Album/Oronoz: **13.1**; © All Canada Photos/Alamy Stock Photo: **7.2**; © B.O'Kane/Alamy Stock Photo: **12.5**; © RIA Novosti/Alamy Stock Photo: **9.3**; © Robert Huberman/Alamy Stock Photo: **7.1**; © The Art Archive/Alamy Stock Photo: **1.4**; Astérix®-Obélix®/© 2016 Les Éditions Albert René/Goscinny-Uderzo: **3.1**; © Arnamagnæan Collection, Copenhagen. Photo: Suzanne Reitz: **4.3** (AM 45, f. 23v); **12.3** (AM 544 4to, f. 19r); © Árni Magnússon Institute, Reykjavík. Photo: Jóhanna Ólafsdóttir: **2.3** (AM 133, f. 59v); **2.4** (AM 350, f. 51r); **7.4**, **14.4** (AM 673a I 4to, 2v); **11.2** (AM 673a II 4to, 7v); **3.3**, **14.2**, **14.3** (GKS 1812 4to, 5v-6r); © The Author: **5.1**, **6.1**, **6.2**, **6.5**, **10.1**, **10.2**, **13.2**; © Reidar Bertelsen: **4.2**; Bibliothèque nationale de France: **11.3**; © Manchester Art Gallery, UK/Bridgeman Images: **1.5**; State Hermitage Museum, St Petersburg, Russia/Bridgeman Images: **9.2**; © James Brown: **2.1**, **2.2**; © John-Henry Clay: **1.1**, **1.2**; The Master and Fellows of Corpus Christi College, Cambridge: **11.1** (MS 16, folio 152v), **11.4** (MS 53 f. 206 R); © The Easton Foundation/VAGA, New York/DACS, London 2015. Photo: © The Author: **3.5**; illustration by Peter Firmin: **3.2**; © David Conniss/Getty Images: **1.3**; © Greenland National Museum and Archives: **6.3**, **8.1**; © Greenland National Museum and Archives. Photo: © Georg Nyegaard: **6.6**; Courtesy of the Dean and Chapter of Hereford Cathedral: **14.1**; © Lerwick Community Council: **12.4**; © Nasjonalmuseet, Oslo, Norway: **4.4**; © Georg Nyegaard: **6.4**, **8.2**; © Parks Canada/Dale Wilson: **7.3**; The Royal Library, Copenhagen (GKS 2881 4°, f. 10v: The Skálholt Map): **8.3**; © Runar Storeide/Lofotr Vikingmuseum: **4.1**; © Gabriel Hildebrand/ The Swedish History Museum: **9.1**; © Charles Tait: **12.1**, **12.2**; © The Viking Ship Museum, Denmark. Photo: Werner Karrasch: **2.5**; Wellcome Library, London: **3.4**.

INDEX